Boy Princess

Vol. 6

Seyoung Kim

Boy Princess Vol. 6

Story and Art by Seyoung Kim

English translation rights in USA, Canada, UK, NZ, Australia arranged by
Ecomix Media Company
395-21 Seogyo-dong, Mapo-gu, Seoul, Korea 121-840 info@ecomixmedia.com

- Produced by **Ecomix Media Company**
- Translator **Jeanne**
- Editor **Philip Daay**
- Managing Editor **Soyoung Jung**
- Graphic Designers **Hyekyoung Choi, Eunsook Lee**
- President & Publisher **Heewoon Chung**

P.O. Box 16484, Jersey City, NJ 07306
info@netcomics.com
www.NETCOMICS.com

ISBN: 978-1-60009-035-6

First printing: March 2007
10 9 8 7 6 5 4 3 2 1
Printed in Korea

Boy Princess

Vol. 6

Seyoung Kim

Story so far...

The kingdom buzzes with anticipation of a royal wedding aimed at maintaining peace with a powerful neighboring realm. However, when the intended bride Princess Elena elopes with her lover two days before the ceremony, the ruling family desperately dresses up their youngest son as a woman and sends him to get married in her place.

Nobody bats an eye at Prince Nicole's disguise as the new bride, with his pretty blue eyes, cascading blond hair, pretty pubescent form and strategically placed apples. But, how long can he keep up the charade? Soon, Princess Elena returns to free her little brother Nicole from playing her replacement in a political marriage of convenience between two kingdoms. However, in the short time they spent together, feelings of passion awoke between the two princes.

Bewildered, Nicole aches to discern his true feelings for Prince Jed, risky as they may be, and feels compelled to be close to him once again. Suspicious eyes and ears loom everywhere, especially those of the jealous Princess Reiny who constantly follows her brother Jed, waiting to influence his next move. Jed feels the political schemes aimed at his position in his kingdom. He knows that the lives of those he loves will constantly be in danger. He stands firm in his decision that when Princess Elena arrives, Nicole will go home.

Despite his tender pleading, Nicole returns without any acknowledgement from Jed. Their marriage is over and Jed must respect his official wife Elena. Back home, Nicole trains hard and burns with ambition to become a great man, hoping that he'll earn Jed's respect someday.

A stunning revelation shatters everyone's plans. Princess Elena is pregnant from her former lover. Jed knows her life is in immediate danger. Everyone assumes the child belongs to him and his enemies don't welcome a potential heir to the throne. This time the price he must pay–to save Elena and be near his heart's desire–will be facing the full wrath of his own royal court. Prince Derek and the Apothecary Shahi stand at the center of the deadly political games against Jed. But, what dark history binds them so closely together? How far will they go?

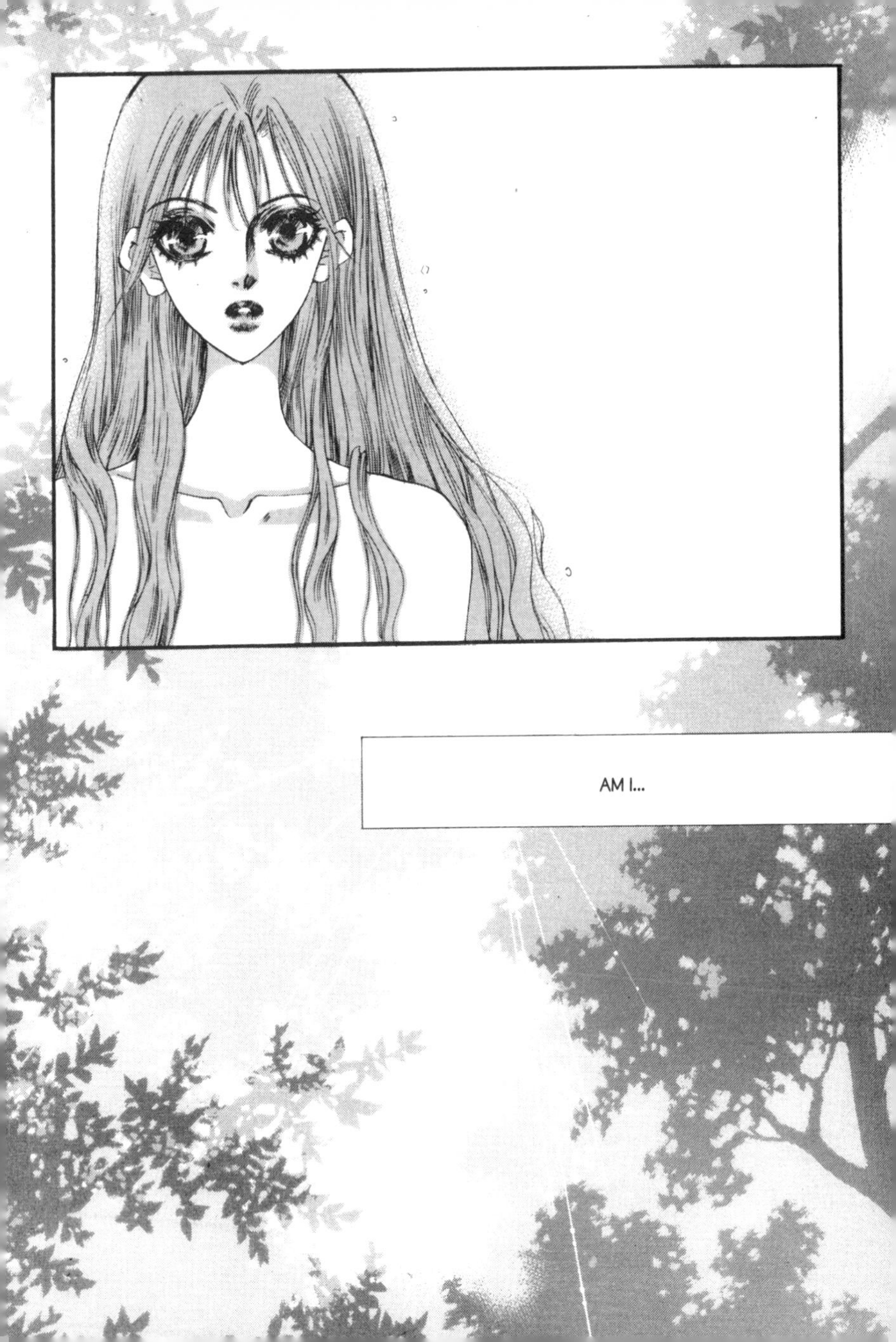
AM I...

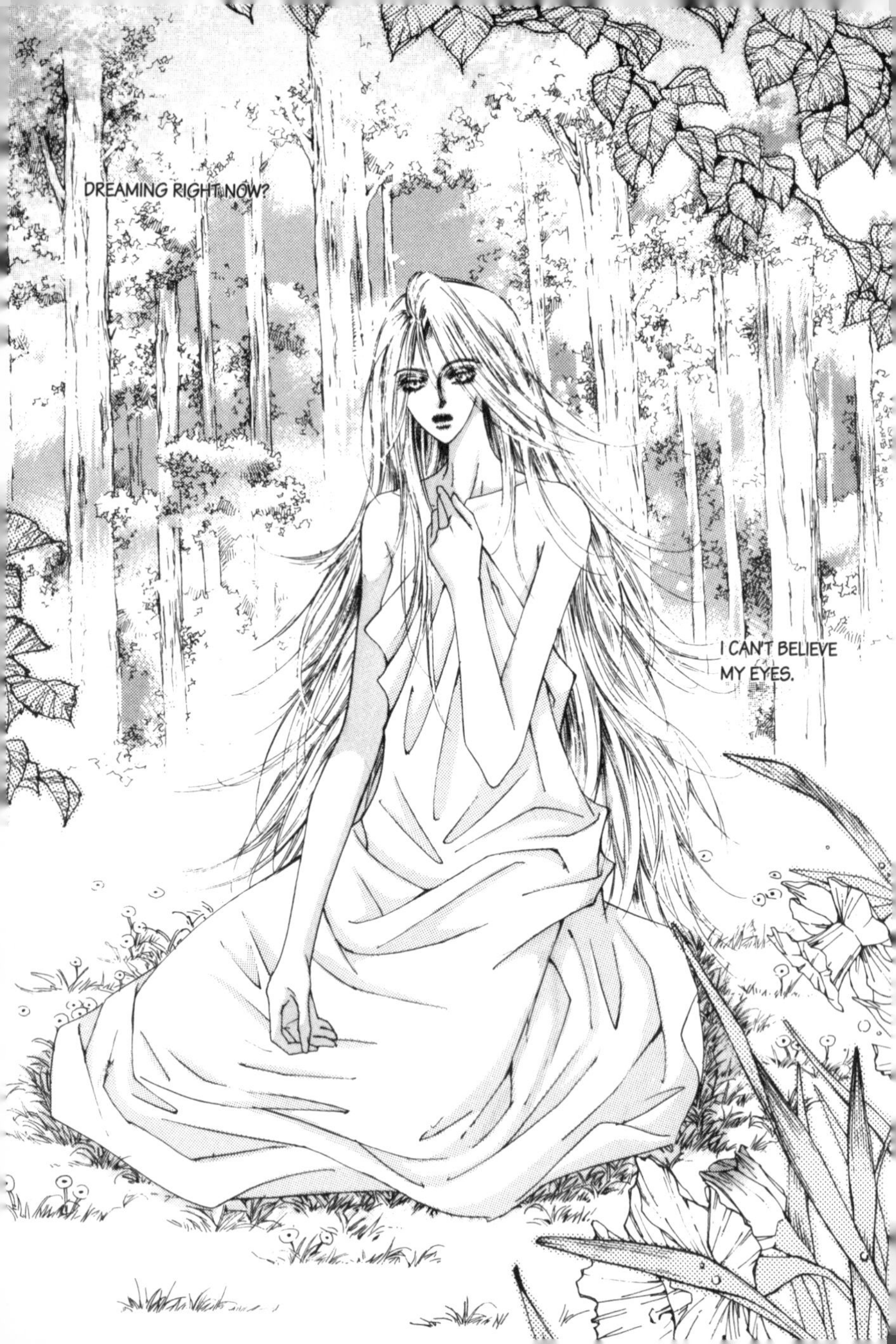
DREAMING RIGHT NOW?
I CAN'T BELIEVE MY EYES.

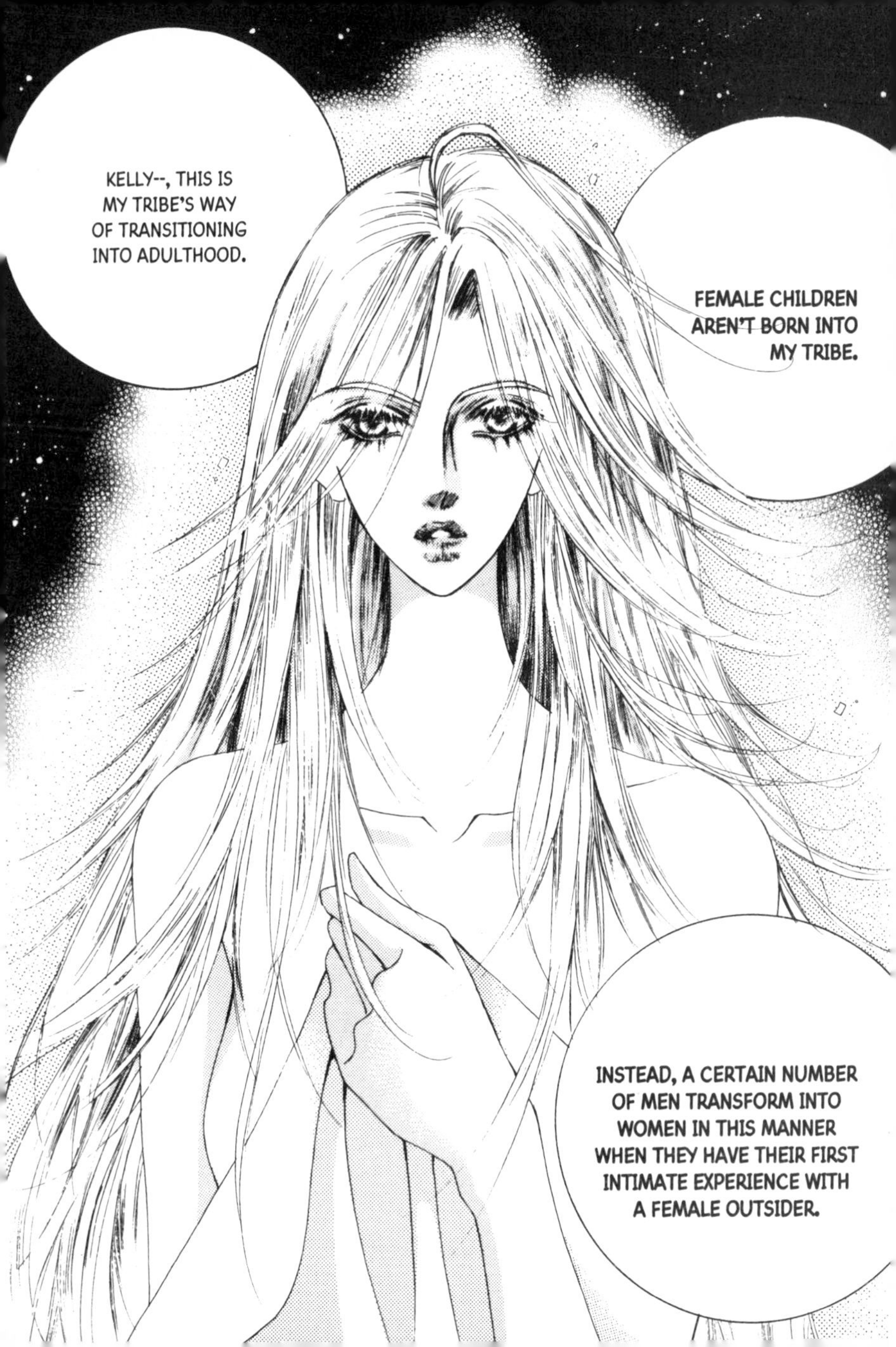
KELLY--, THIS IS MY TRIBE'S WAY OF TRANSITIONING INTO ADULTHOOD.
FEMALE CHILDREN AREN'T BORN INTO MY TRIBE.
INSTEAD, A CERTAIN NUMBER OF MEN TRANSFORM INTO WOMEN IN THIS MANNER WHEN THEY HAVE THEIR FIRST INTIMATE EXPERIENCE WITH A FEMALE OUTSIDER.

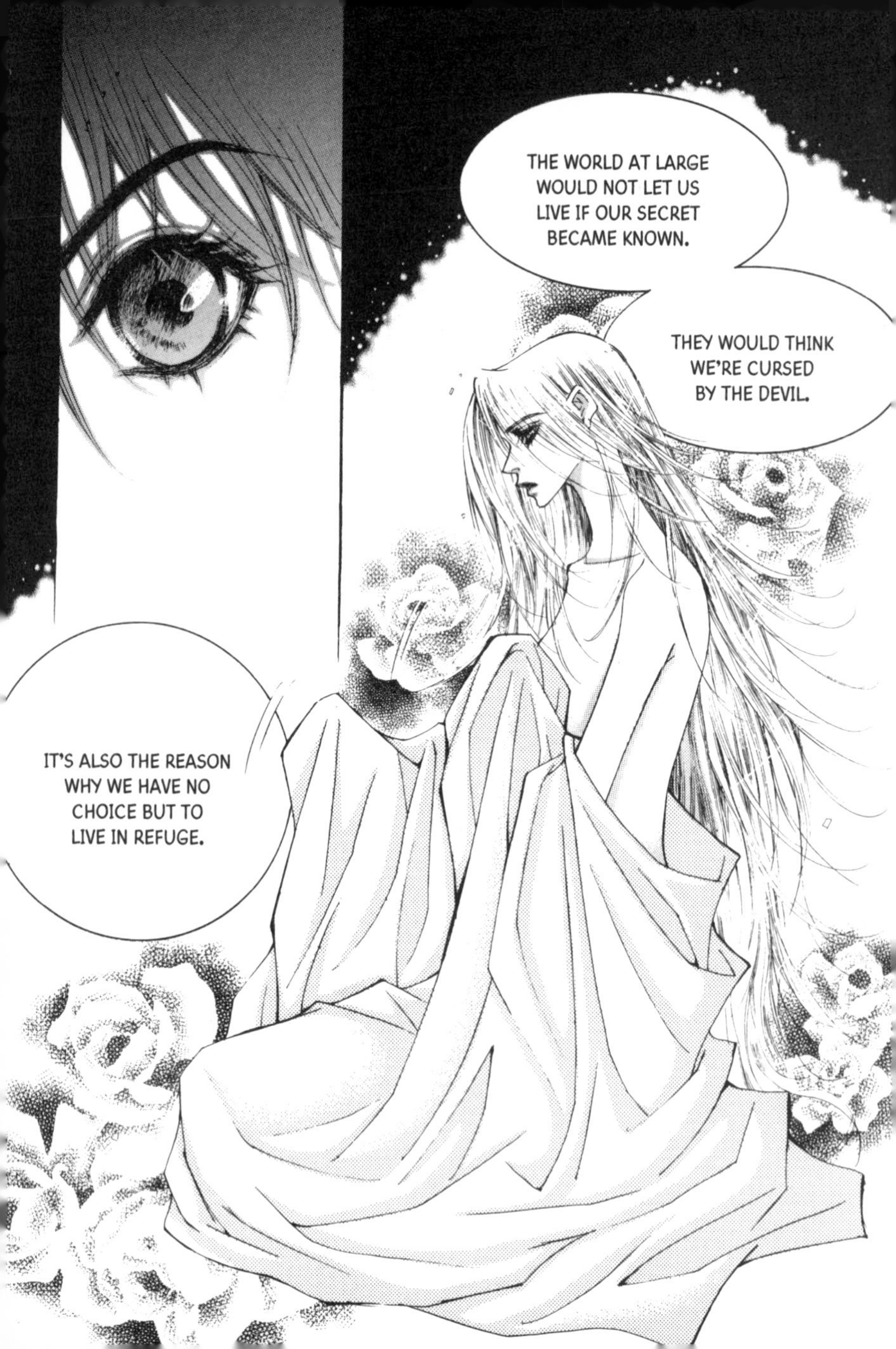
THE WORLD AT LARGE WOULD NOT LET US LIVE IF OUR SECRET BECAME KNOWN.
THEY WOULD THINK WE'RE CURSED BY THE DEVIL.
IT'S ALSO THE REASON WHY WE HAVE NO CHOICE BUT TO LIVE IN REFUGE.

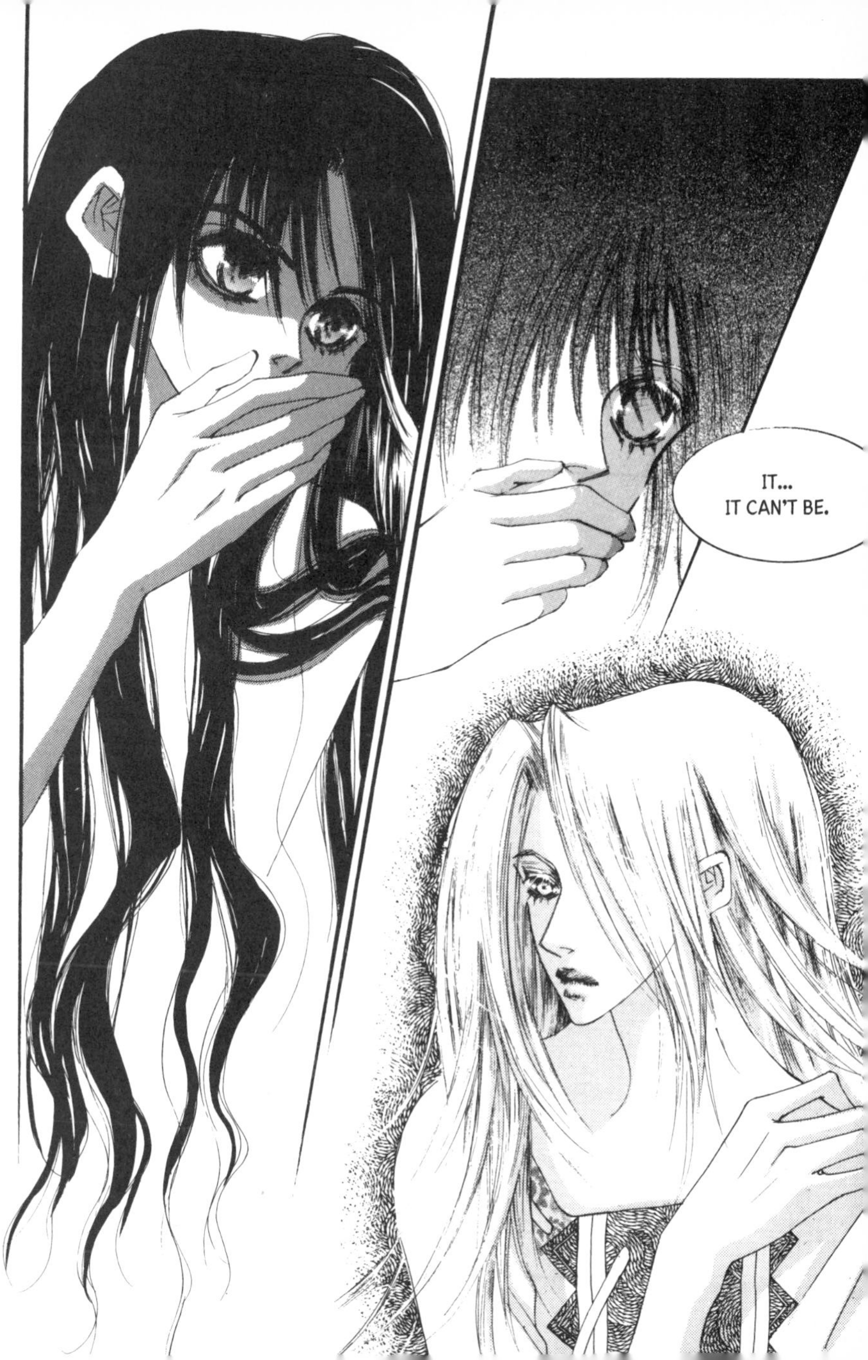
IT...
IT CAN'T BE.

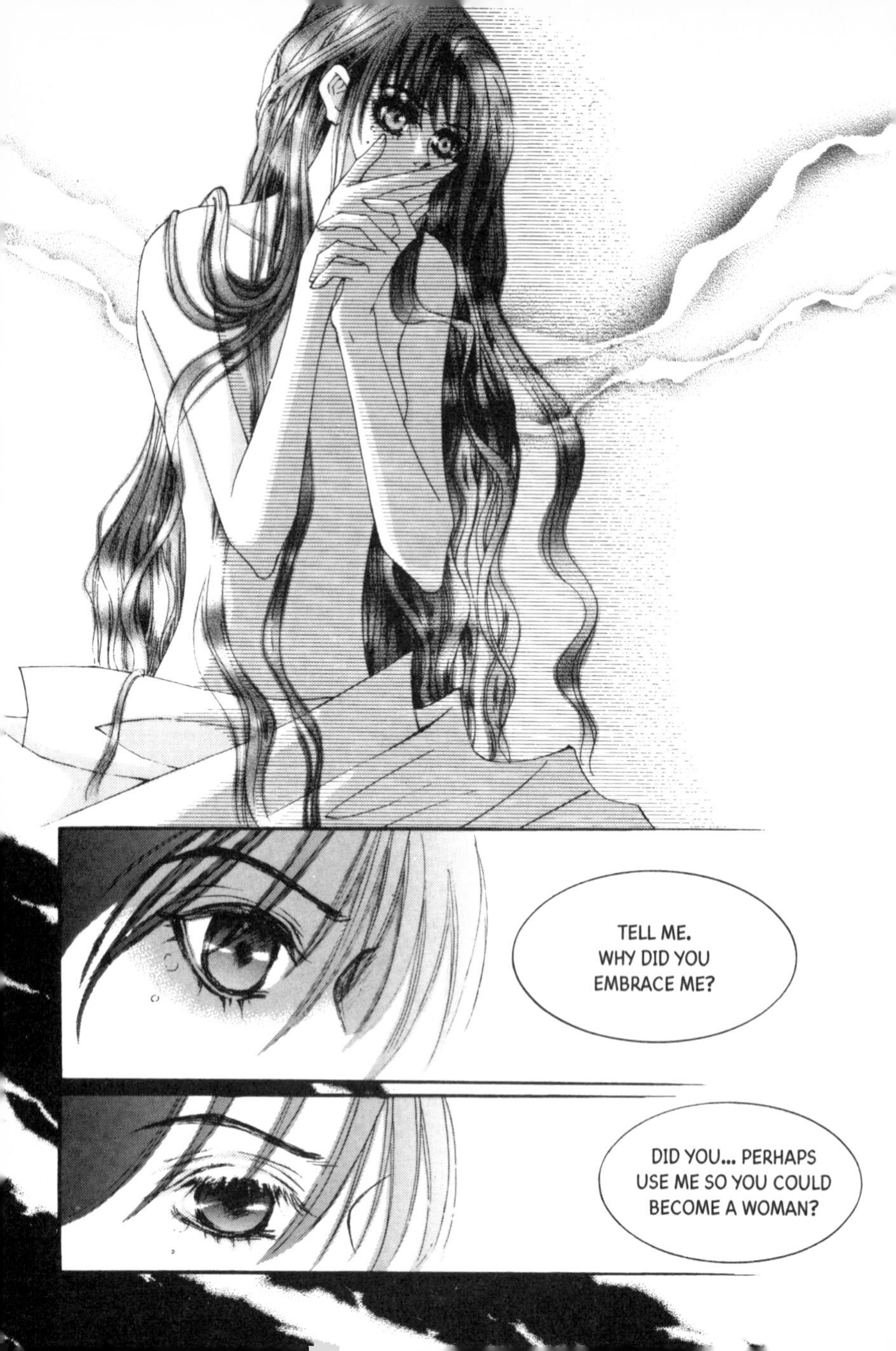
TELL ME. WHY DID YOU EMBRACE ME?
DID YOU... PERHAPS USE ME SO YOU COULD BECOME A WOMAN?

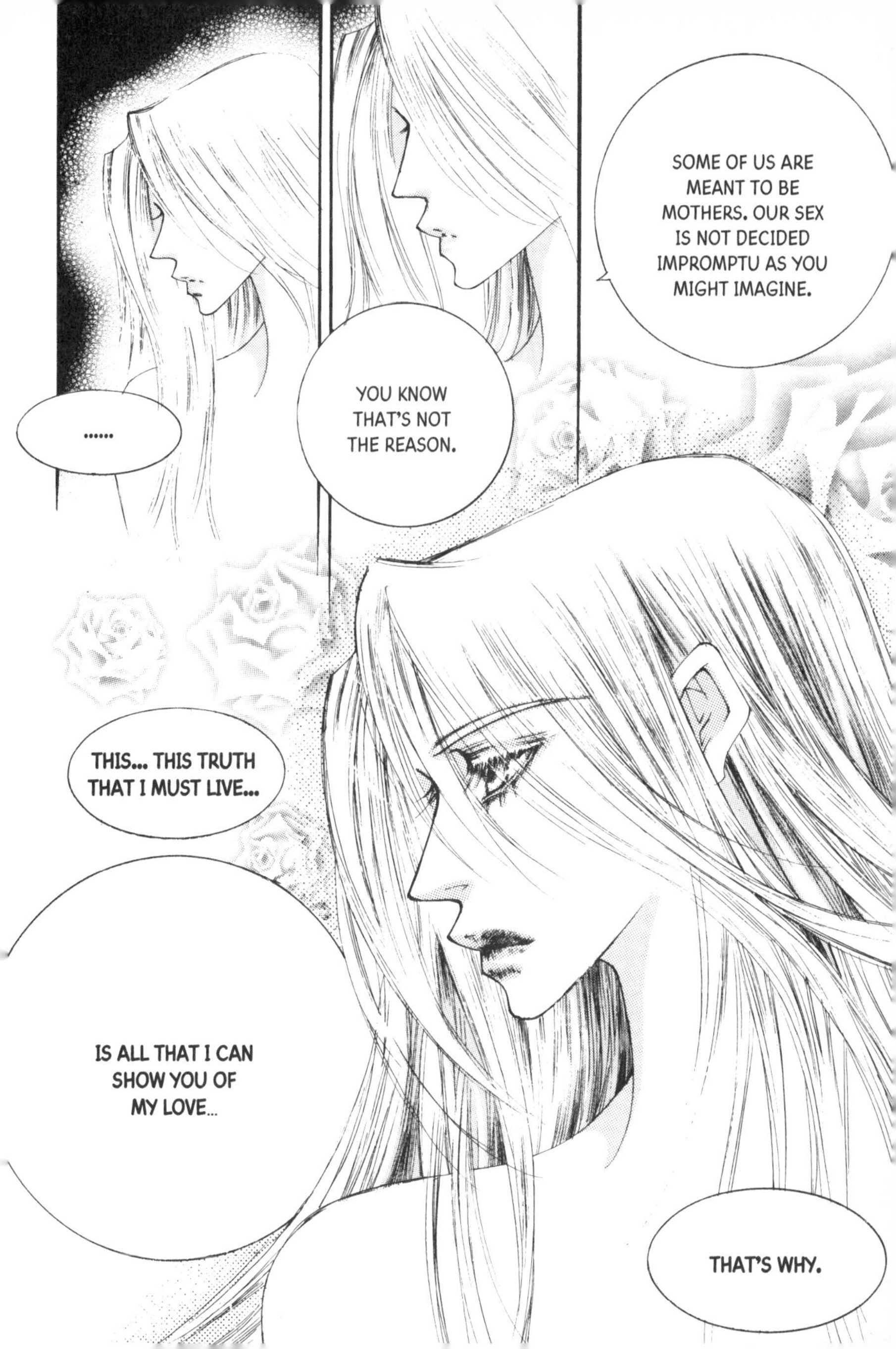
......
YOU KNOW THAT'S NOT THE REASON.
SOME OF US ARE MEANT TO BE MOTHERS. OUR SEX IS NOT DECIDED IMPROMPTU AS YOU MIGHT IMAGINE.
THIS... THIS TRUTH THAT I MUST LIVE...
IS ALL THAT I CAN SHOW YOU OF MY LOVE...
THAT'S WHY.

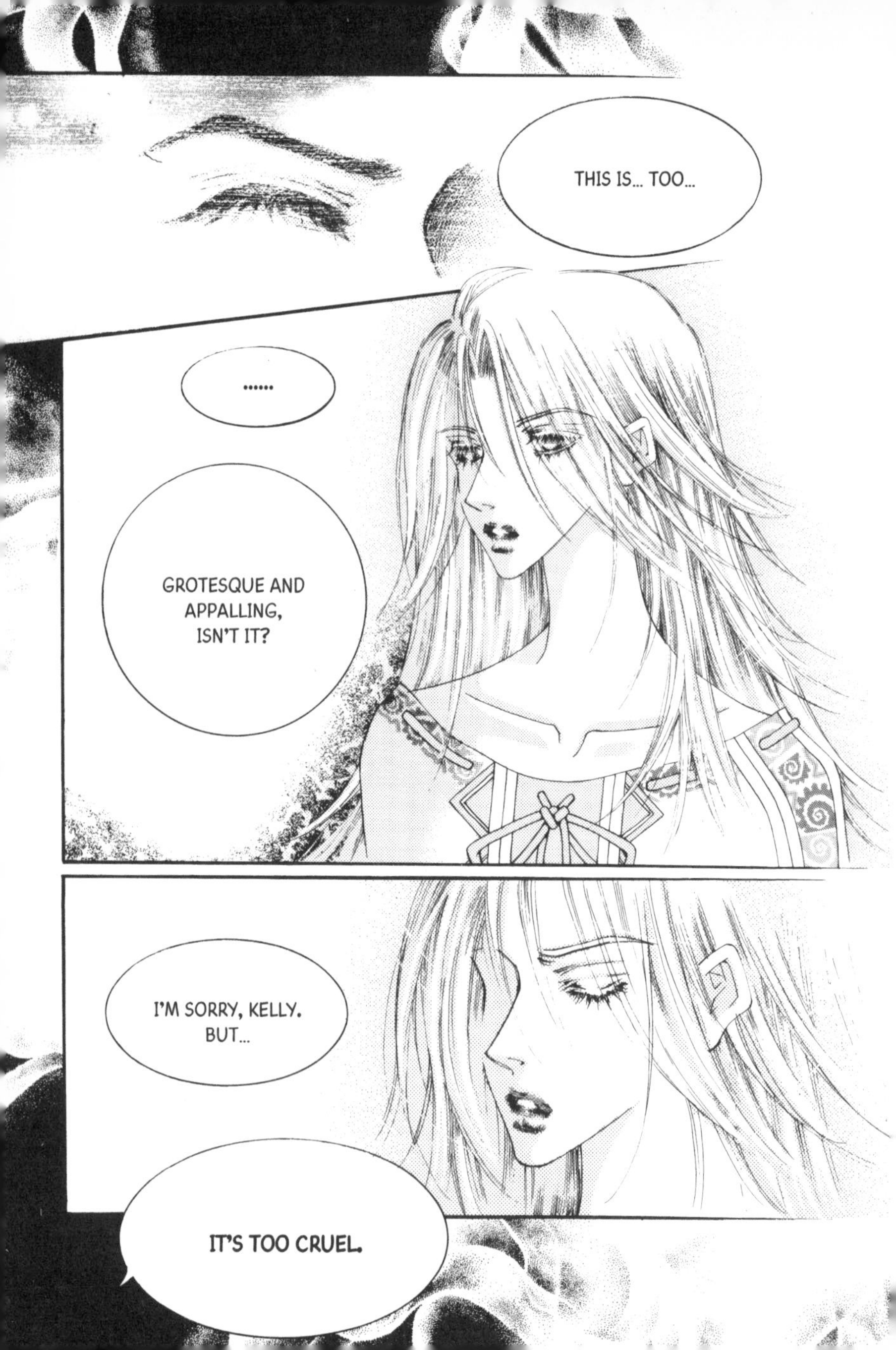
THIS IS... TOO...
......
GROTESQUE AND APPALLING, ISN'T IT?
I'M SORRY, KELLY. BUT...
IT'S TOO CRUEL.

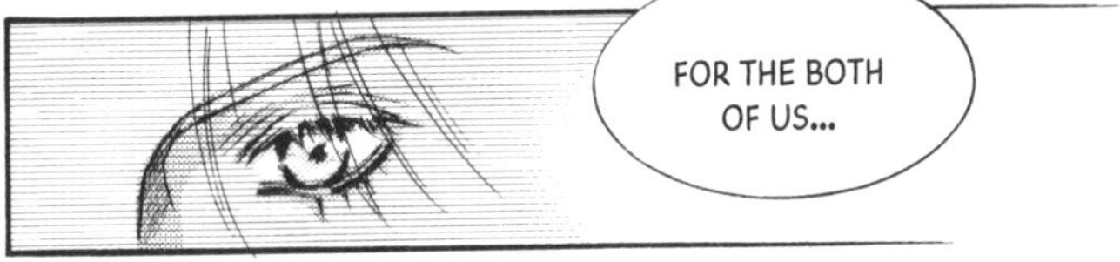
FOR THE BOTH OF US...

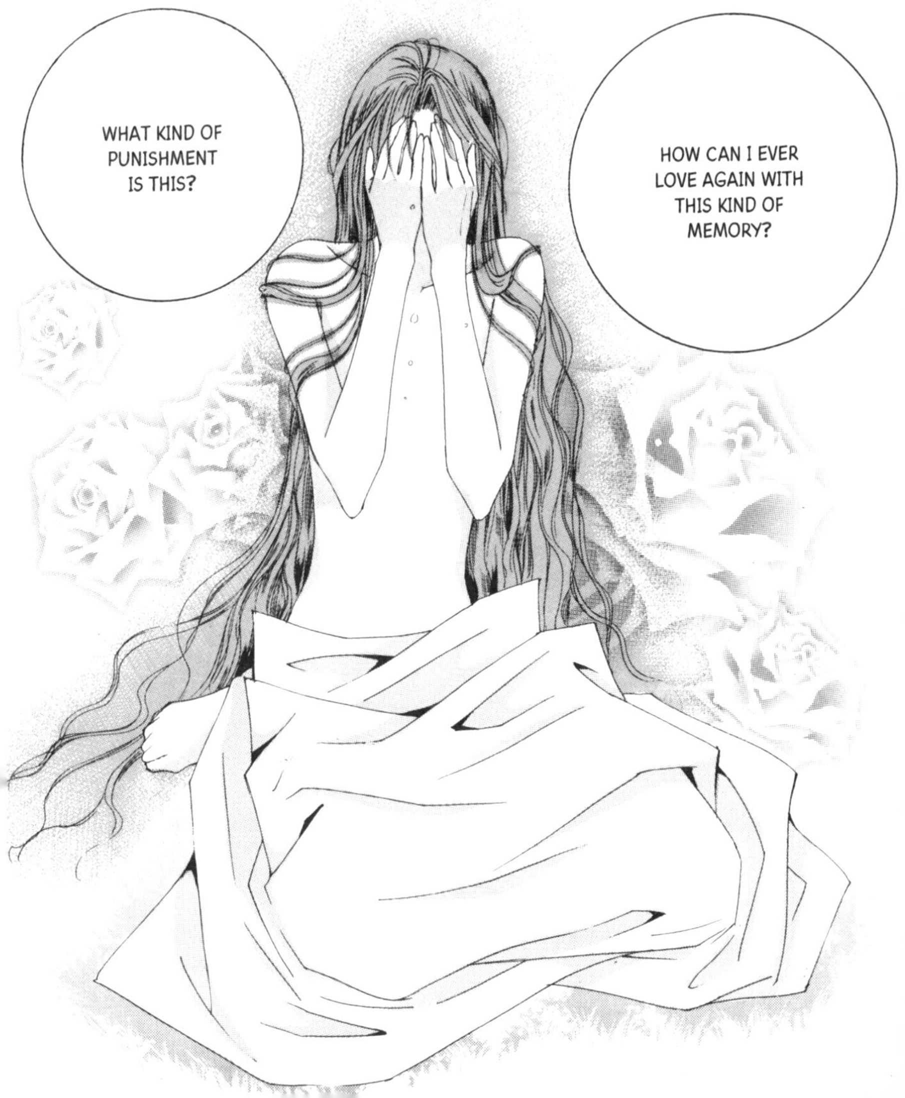
WHAT KIND OF PUNISHMENT IS THIS?
HOW CAN I EVER LOVE AGAIN WITH THIS KIND OF MEMORY?

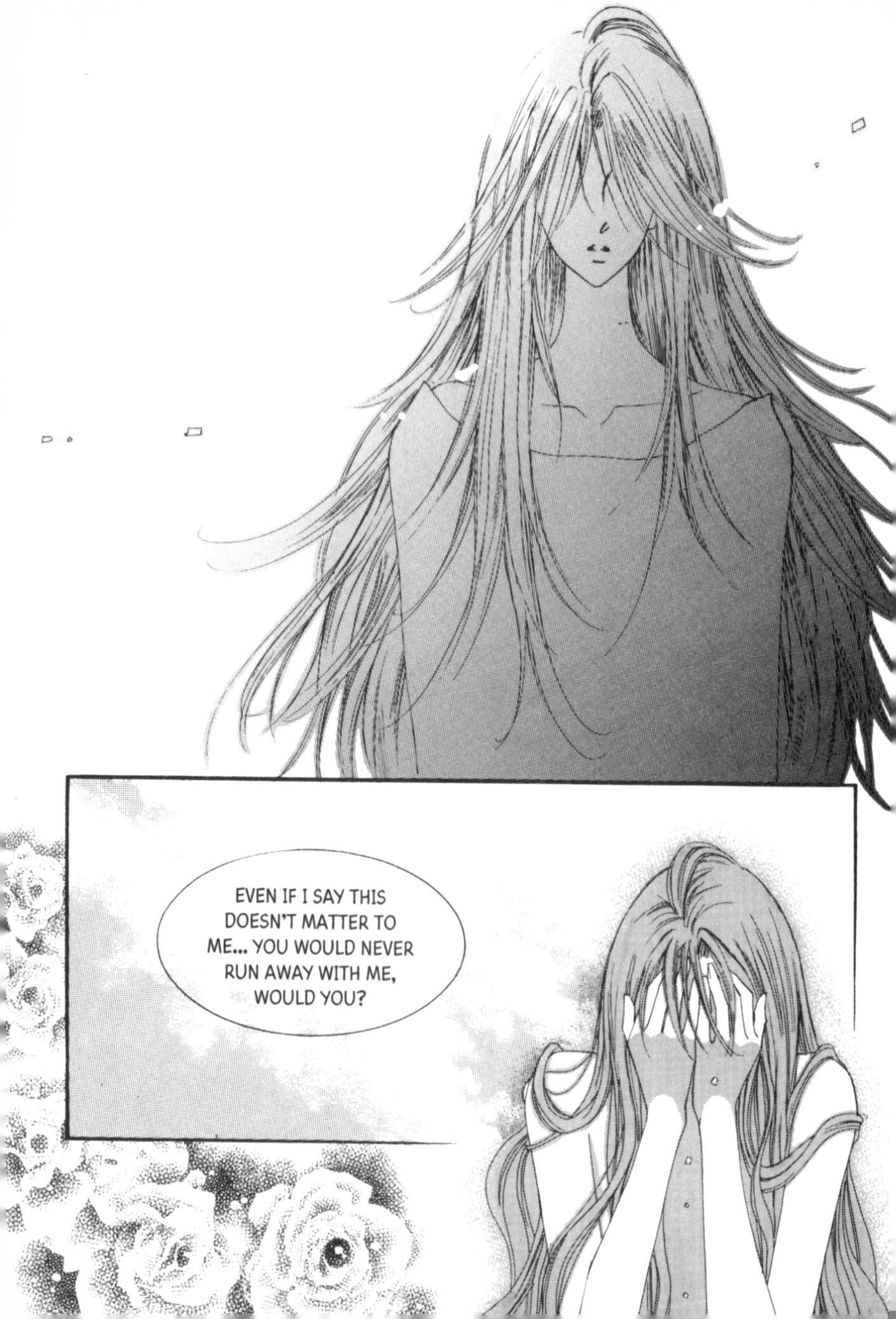
EVEN IF I SAY THIS DOESN'T MATTER TO ME... YOU WOULD NEVER RUN AWAY WITH ME, WOULD YOU?

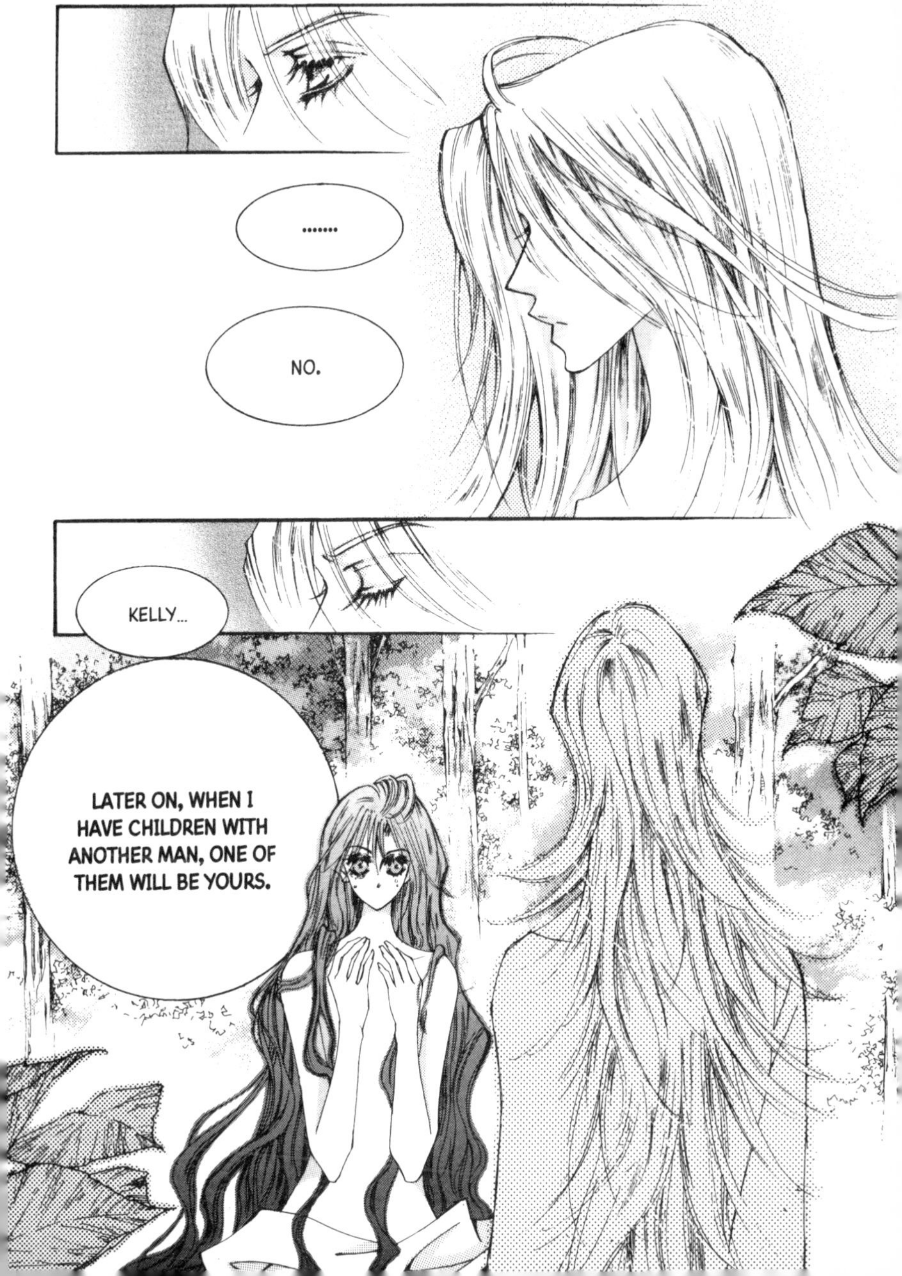
....
NO.
KELLY...
LATER ON, WHEN I HAVE CHILDREN WITH ANOTHER MAN, ONE OF THEM WILL BE YOURS.

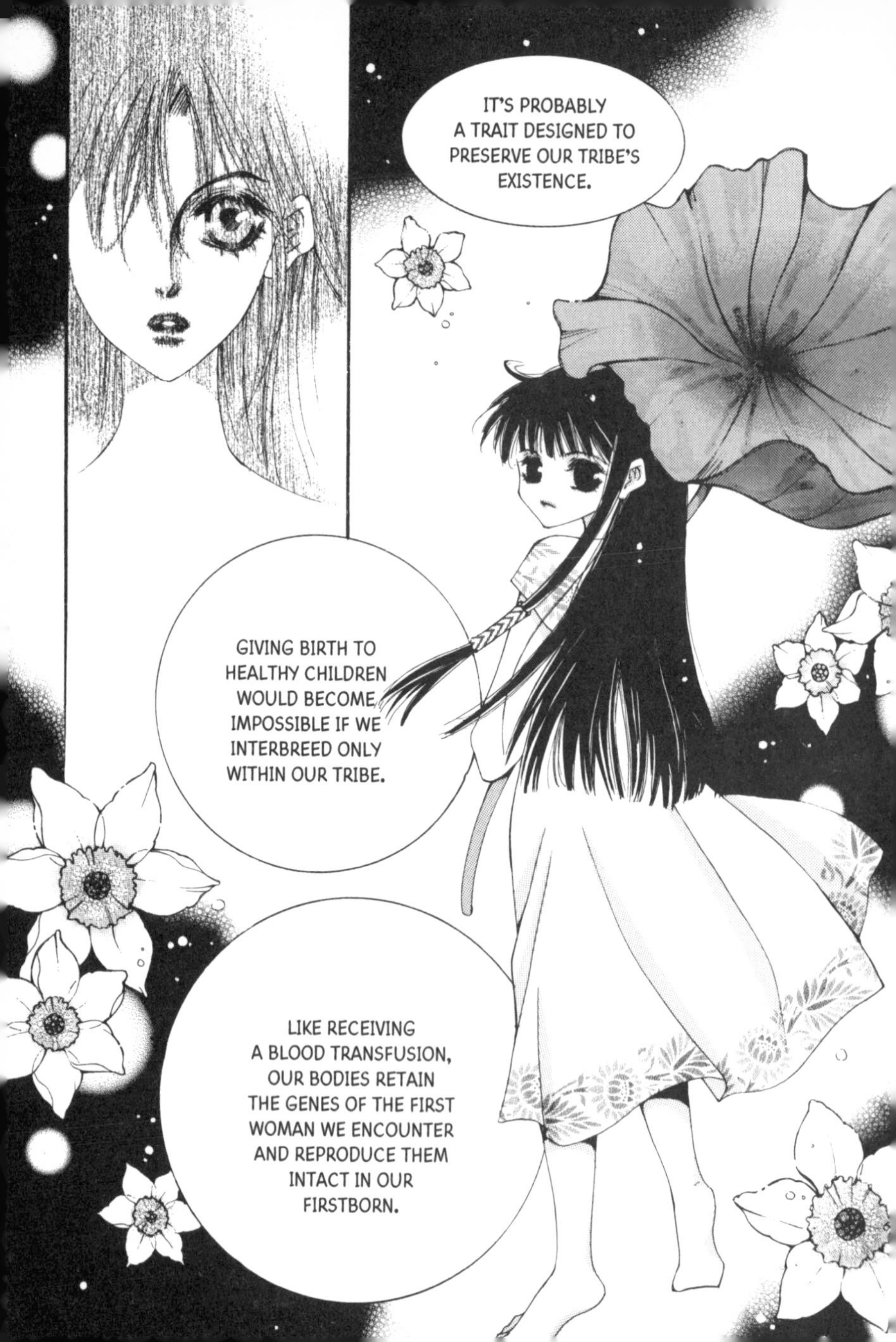
IT'S PROBABLY A TRAIT DESIGNED TO PRESERVE OUR TRIBE'S EXISTENCE.
GIVING BIRTH TO HEALTHY CHILDREN WOULD BECOME IMPOSSIBLE IF WE INTERBREED ONLY WITHIN OUR TRIBE.
LIKE RECEIVING A BLOOD TRANSFUSION, OUR BODIES RETAIN THE GENES OF THE FIRST WOMAN WE ENCOUNTER AND REPRODUCE THEM INTACT IN OUR FIRSTBORN.

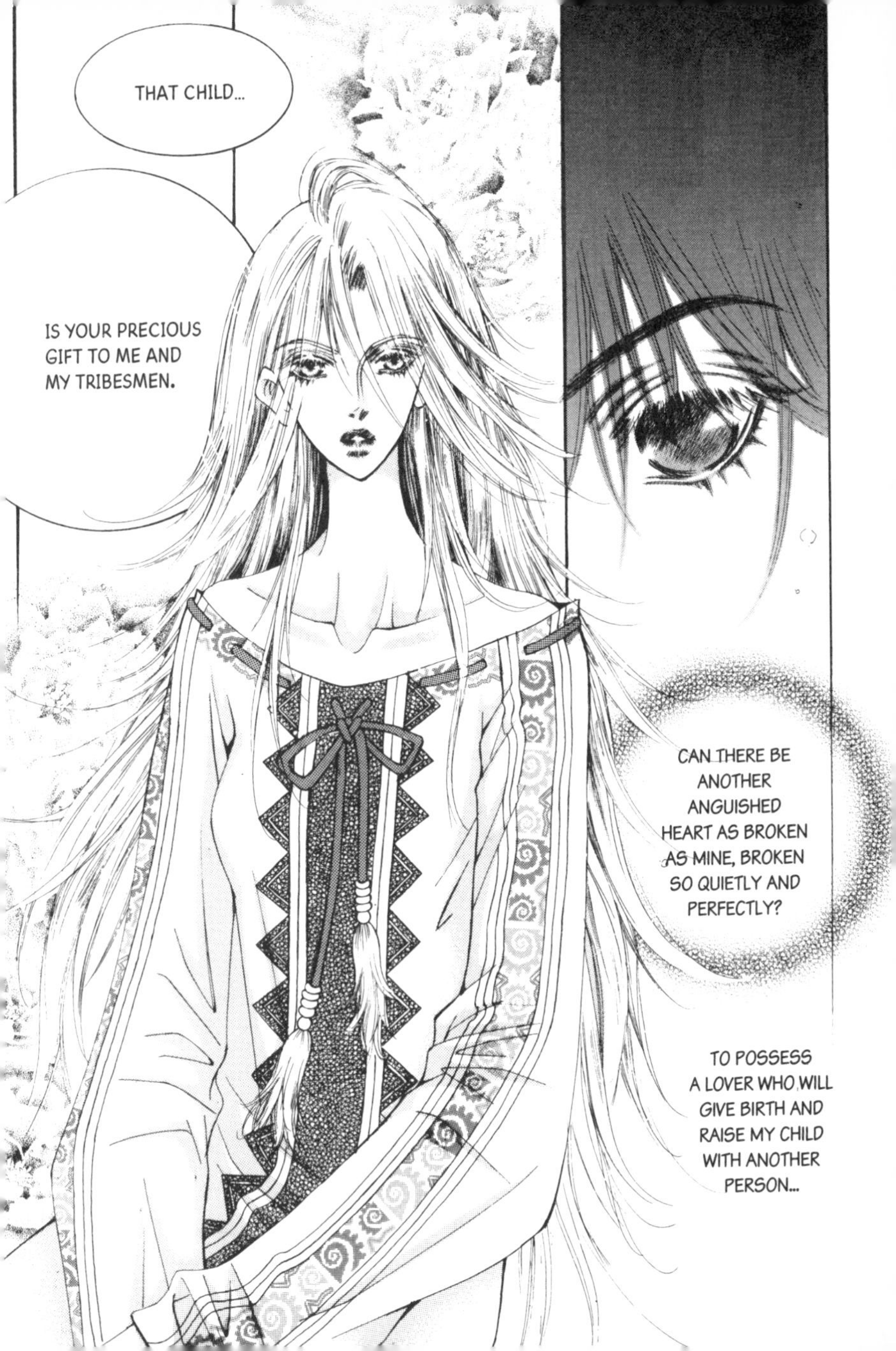
THAT CHILD...
IS YOUR PRECIOUS GIFT TO ME AND MY TRIBESMEN.
CAN THERE BE ANOTHER ANGUISHED HEART AS BROKEN AS MINE, BROKEN SO QUIETLY AND PERFECTLY?
TO POSSESS A LOVER WHO WILL GIVE BIRTH AND RAISE MY CHILD WITH ANOTHER PERSON...

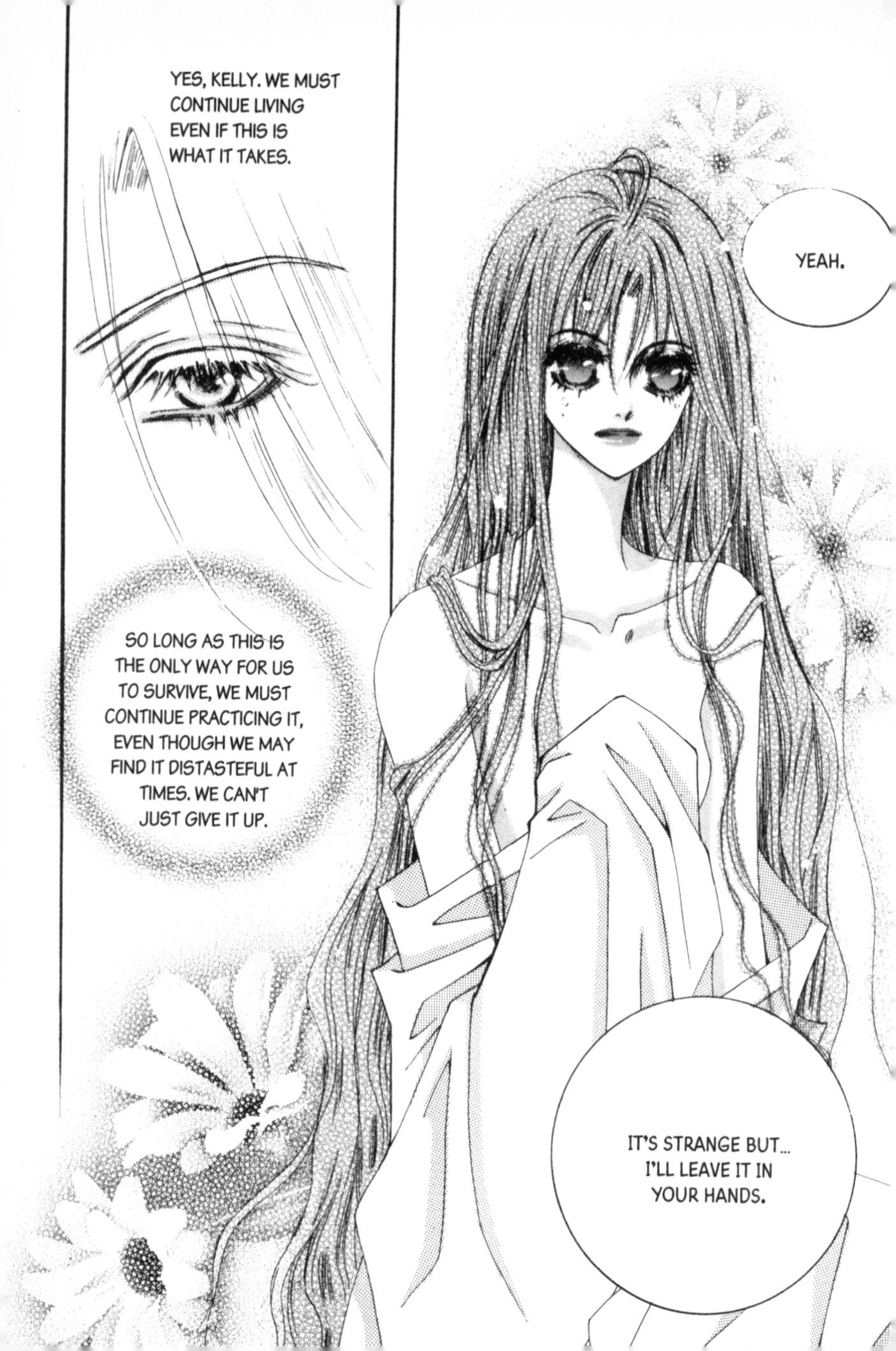
YES, KELLY. WE MUST CONTINUE LIVING EVEN IF THIS IS WHAT IT TAKES.
SO LONG AS THIS IS THE ONLY WAY FOR US TO SURVIVE, WE MUST CONTINUE PRACTICING IT, EVEN THOUGH WE MAY FIND IT DISTASTEFUL AT TIMES. WE CAN'T JUST GIVE IT UP.
YEAH.
IT'S STRANGE BUT... I'LL LEAVE IT IN YOUR HANDS.

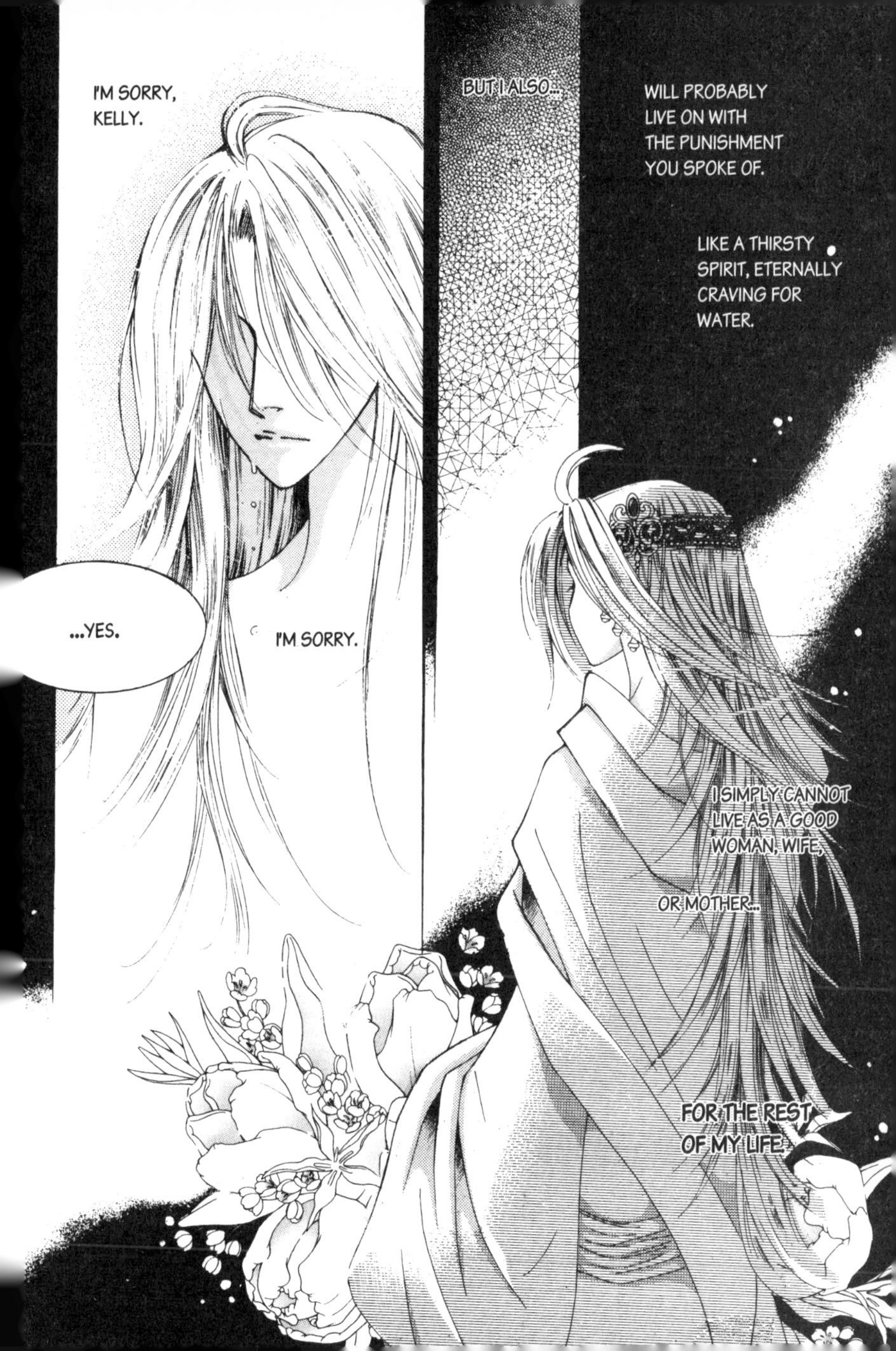
I'M SORRY, KELLY.
...YES.
I'M SORRY.
BUT I ALSO...
WILL PROBABLY LIVE ON WITH THE PUNISHMENT YOU SPOKE OF.
LIKE A THIRSTY SPIRIT, ETERNALLY CRAVING FOR WATER.
I SIMPLY CANNOT LIVE AS A GOOD WOMAN, WIFE,
OR MOTHER...
FOR THE REST OF MY LIFE.

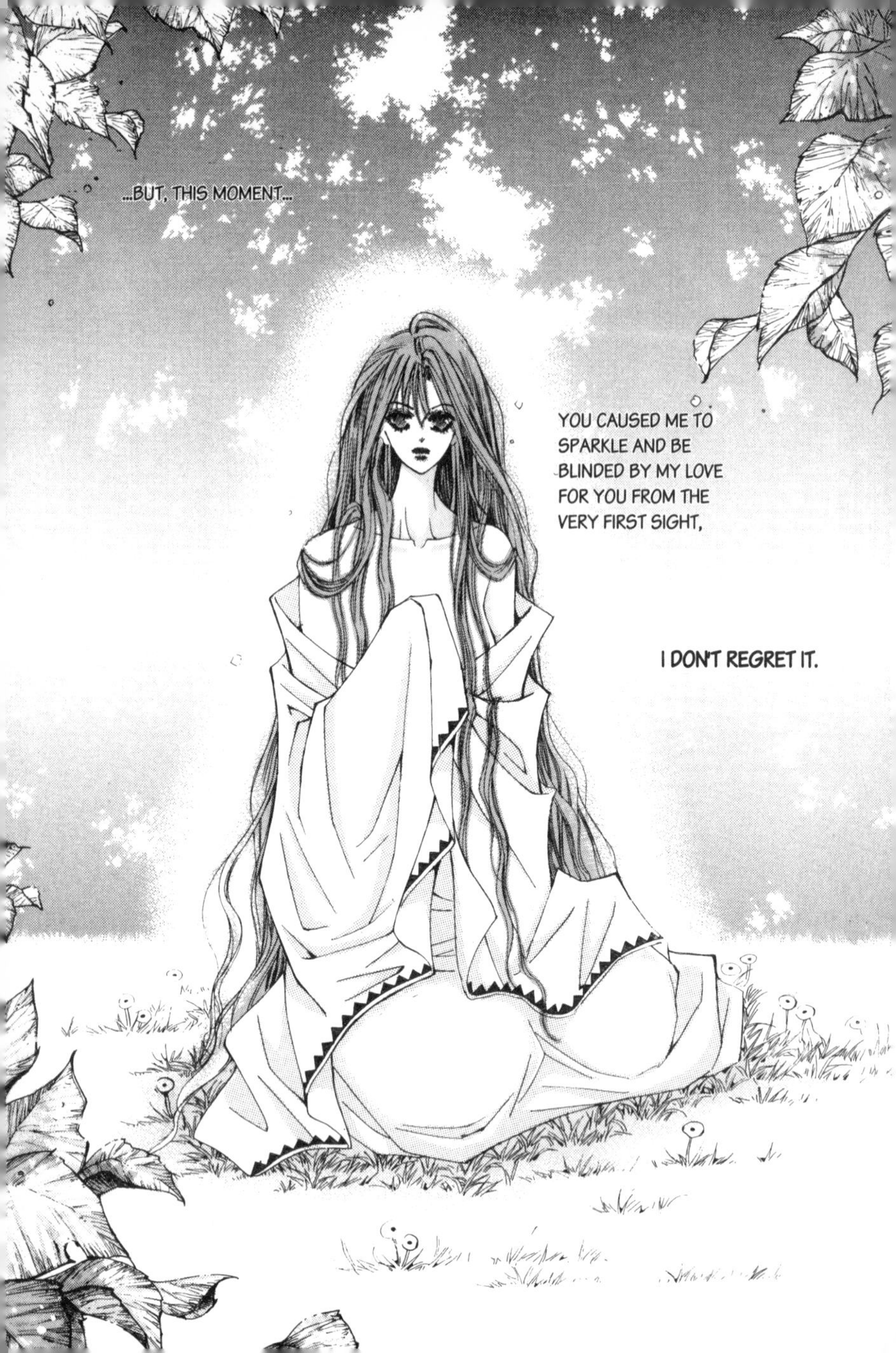
...BUT, THIS MOMENT...
YOU CAUSED ME TO SPARKLE AND BE BLINDED BY MY LOVE FOR YOU FROM THE VERY FIRST SIGHT,
I DON'T REGRET IT.

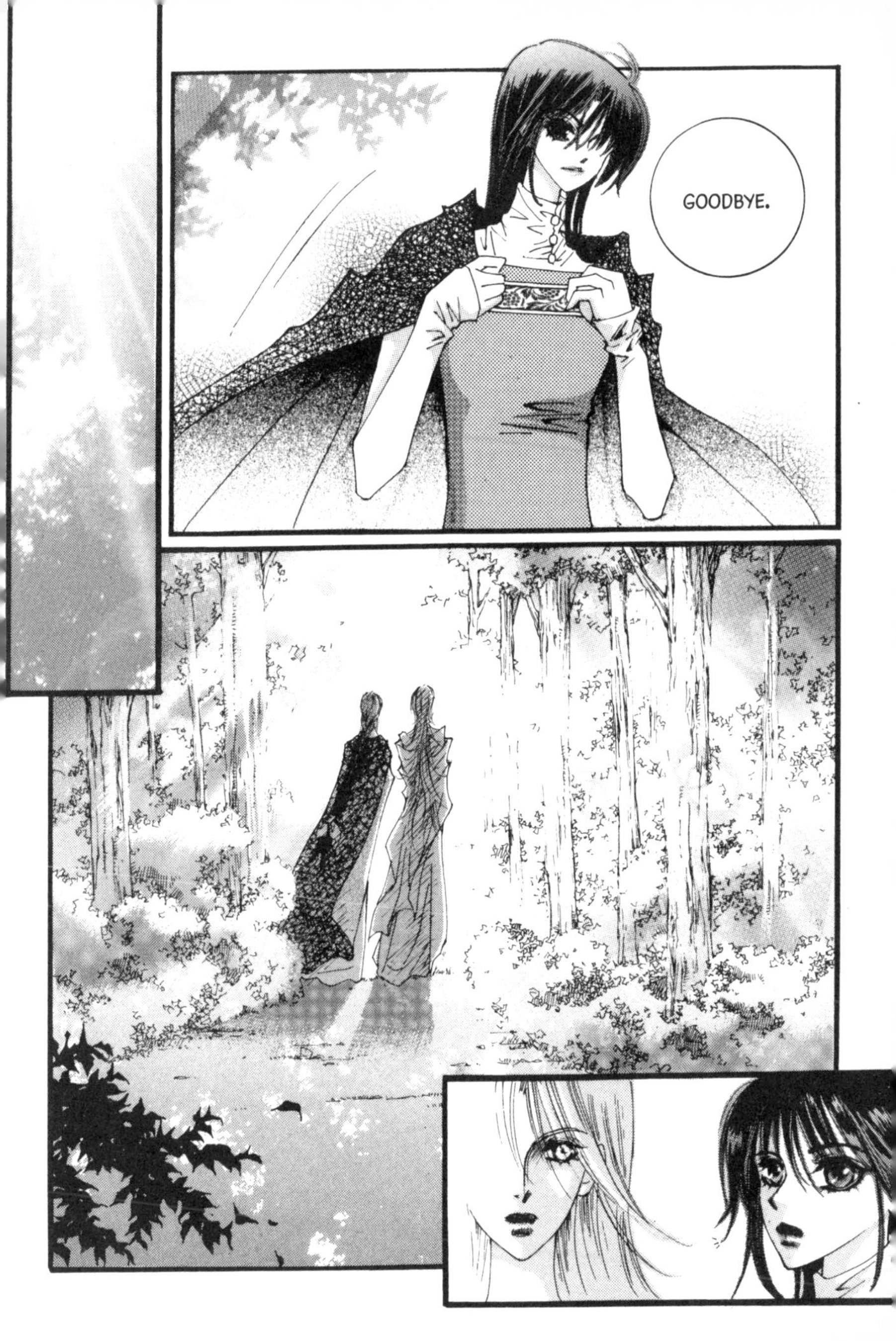
GOODBYE.

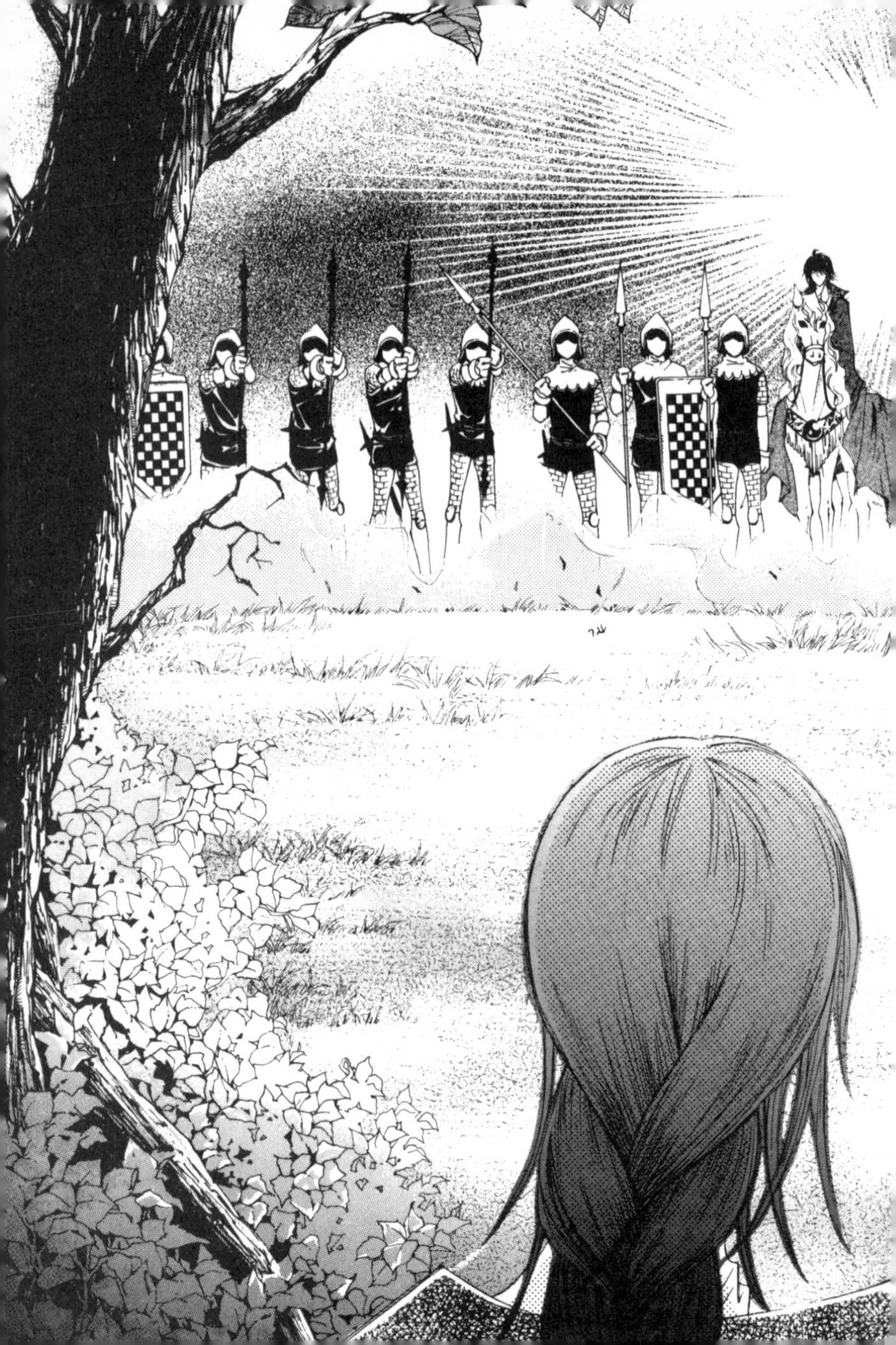

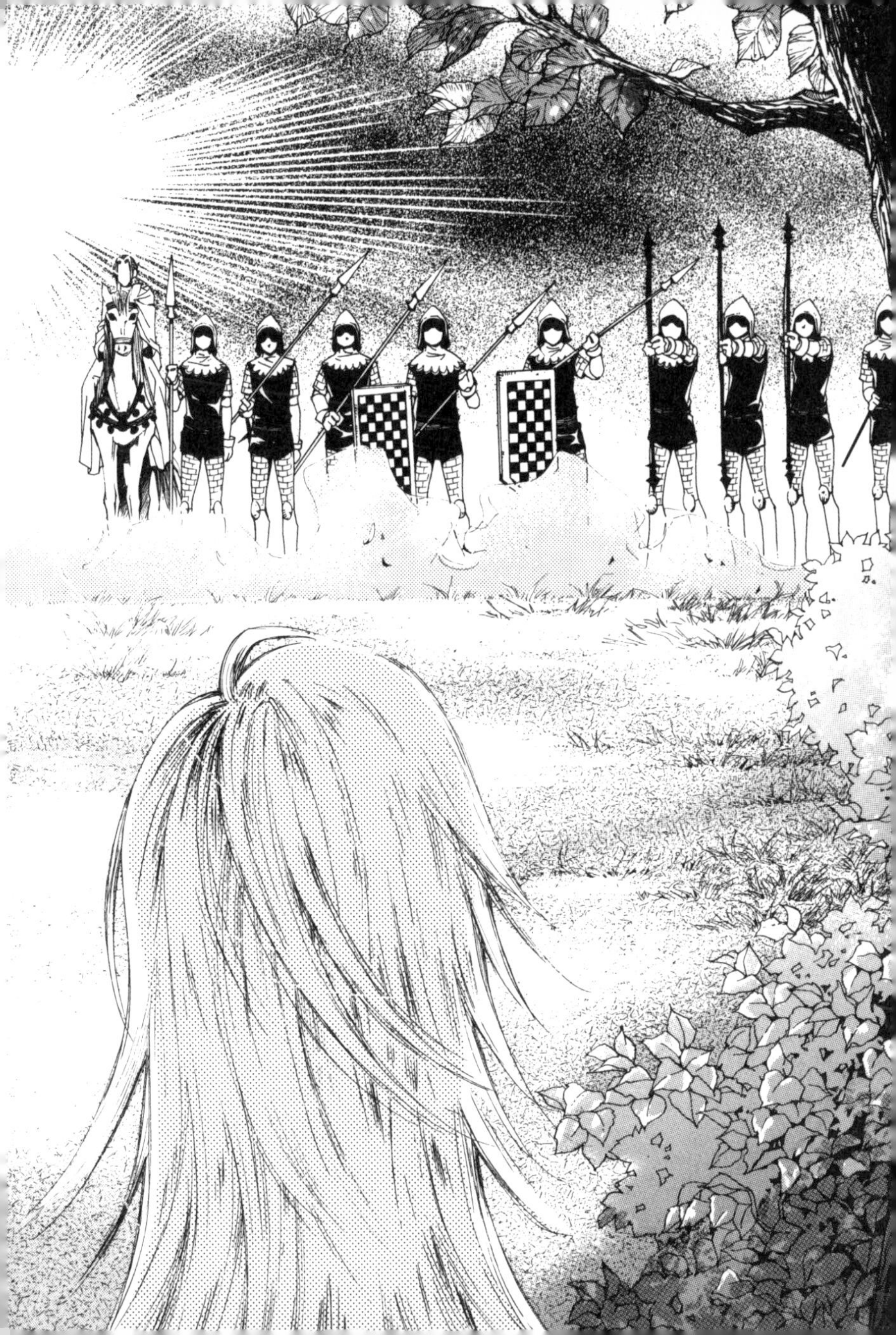

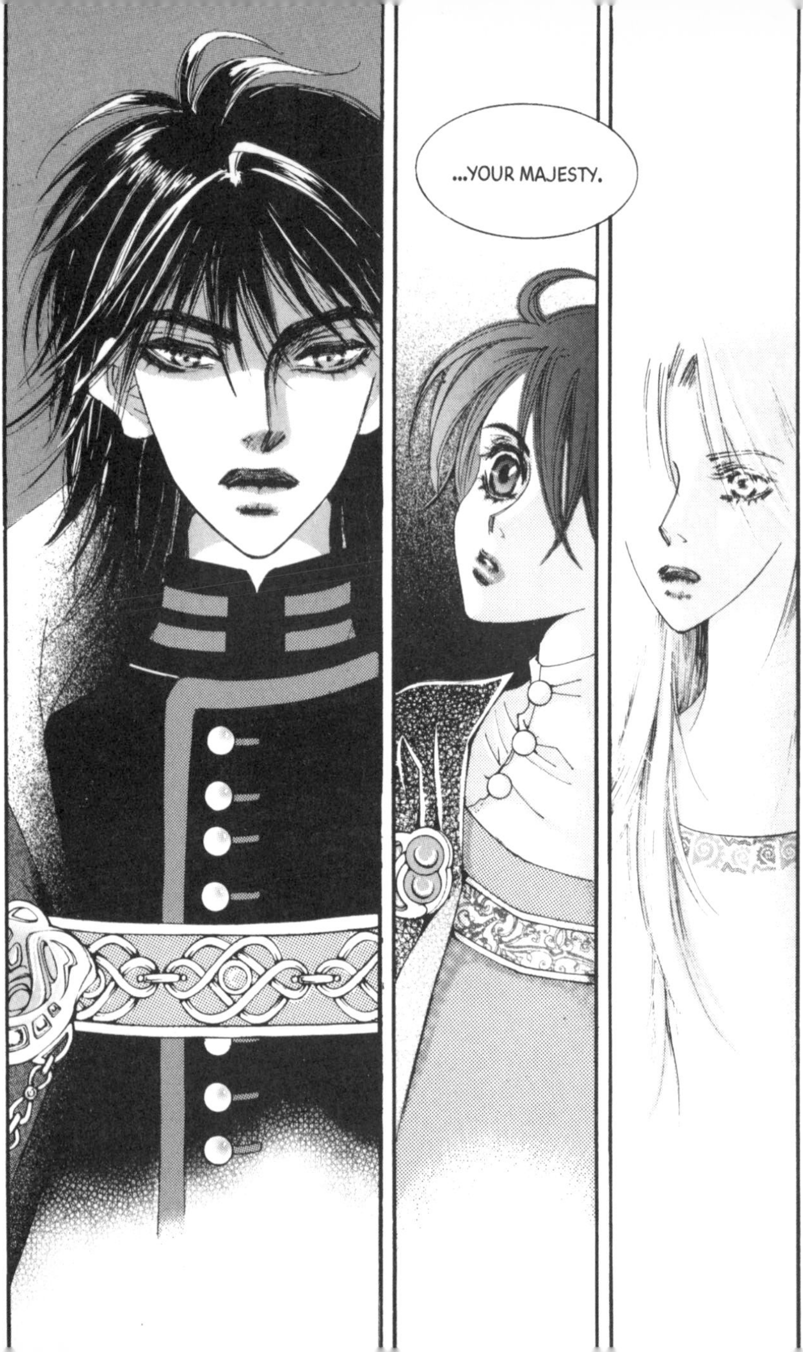
...YOUR MAJESTY.

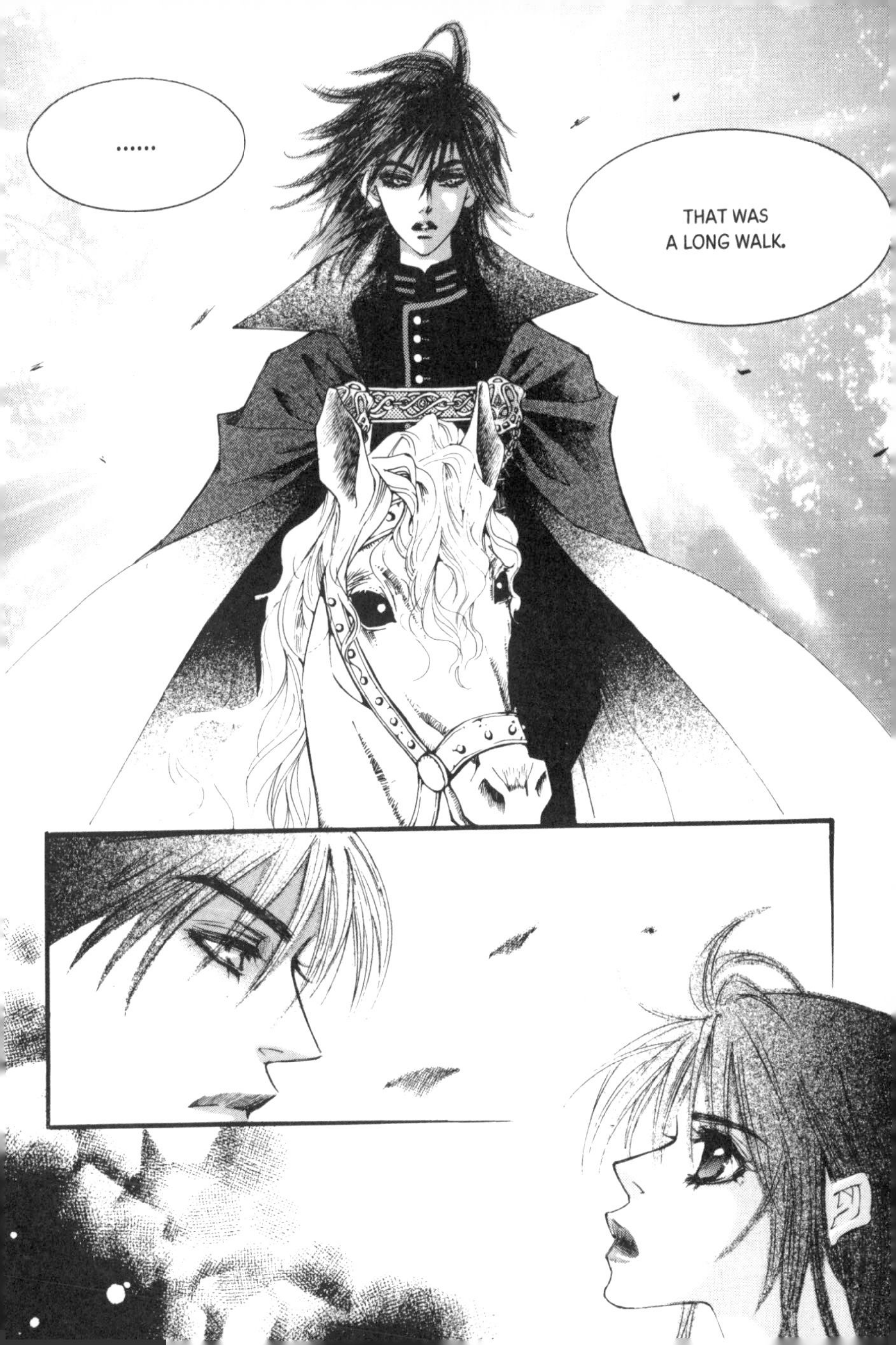
......
THAT WAS A LONG WALK.

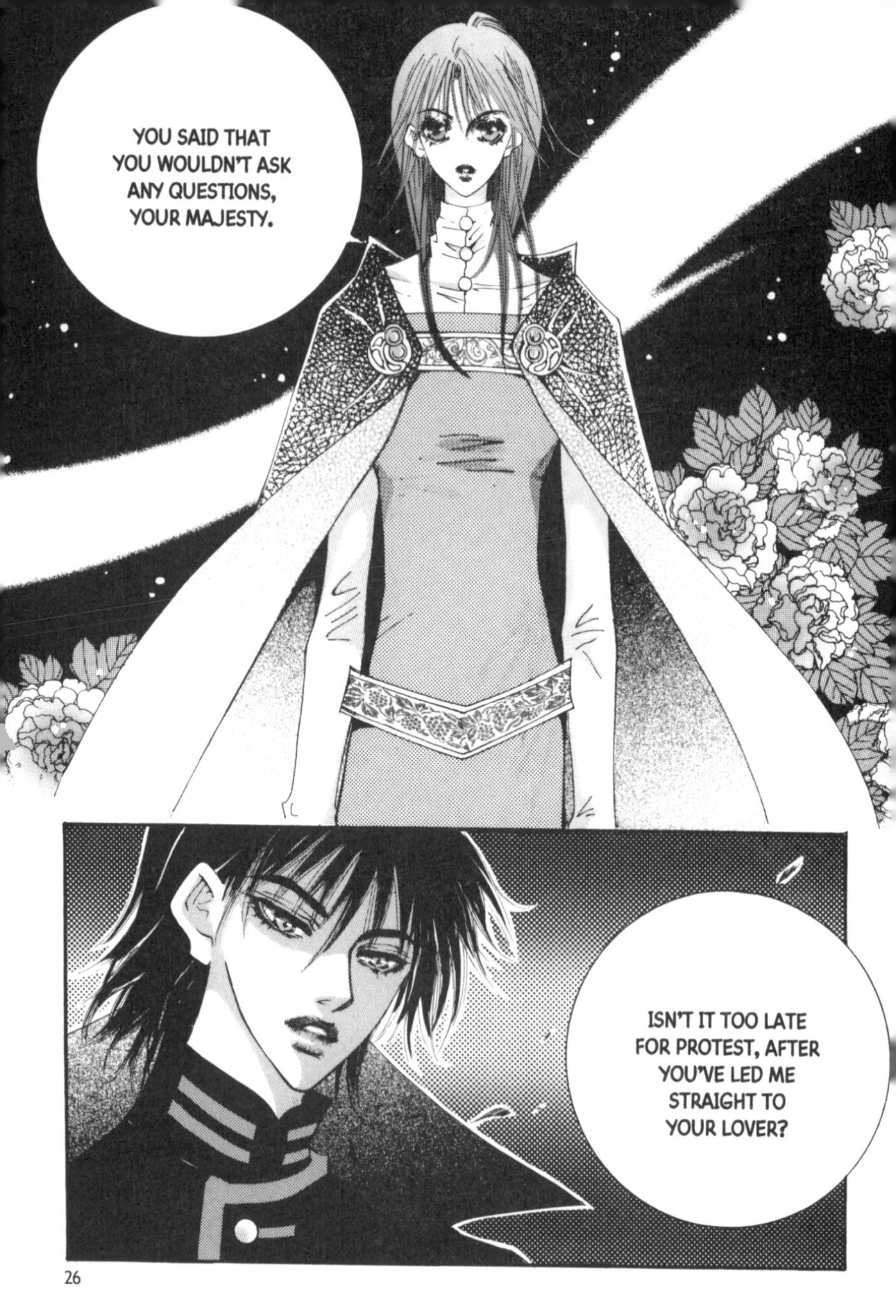
YOU SAID THAT YOU WOULDN'T ASK ANY QUESTIONS, YOUR MAJESTY.
ISN'T IT TOO LATE FOR PROTEST, AFTER YOU'VE LED ME STRAIGHT TO YOUR LOVER?

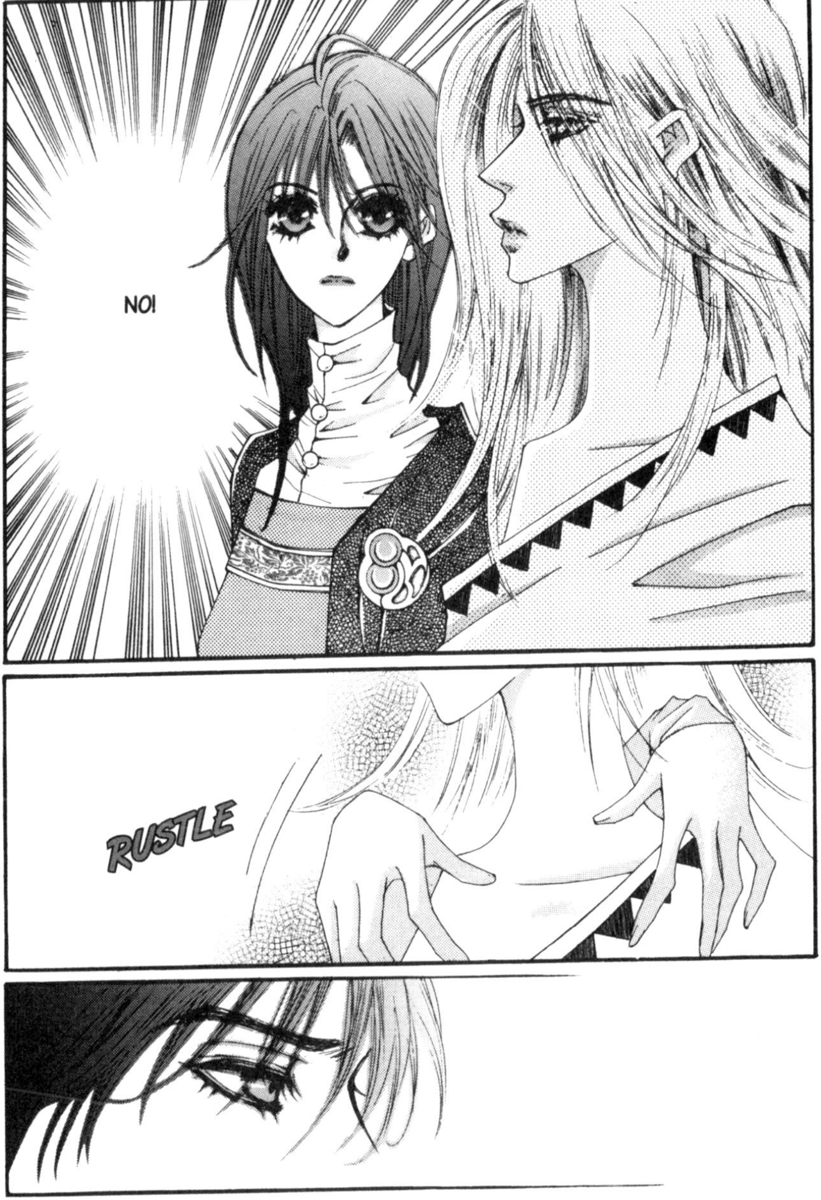
NO!
RUSTLE

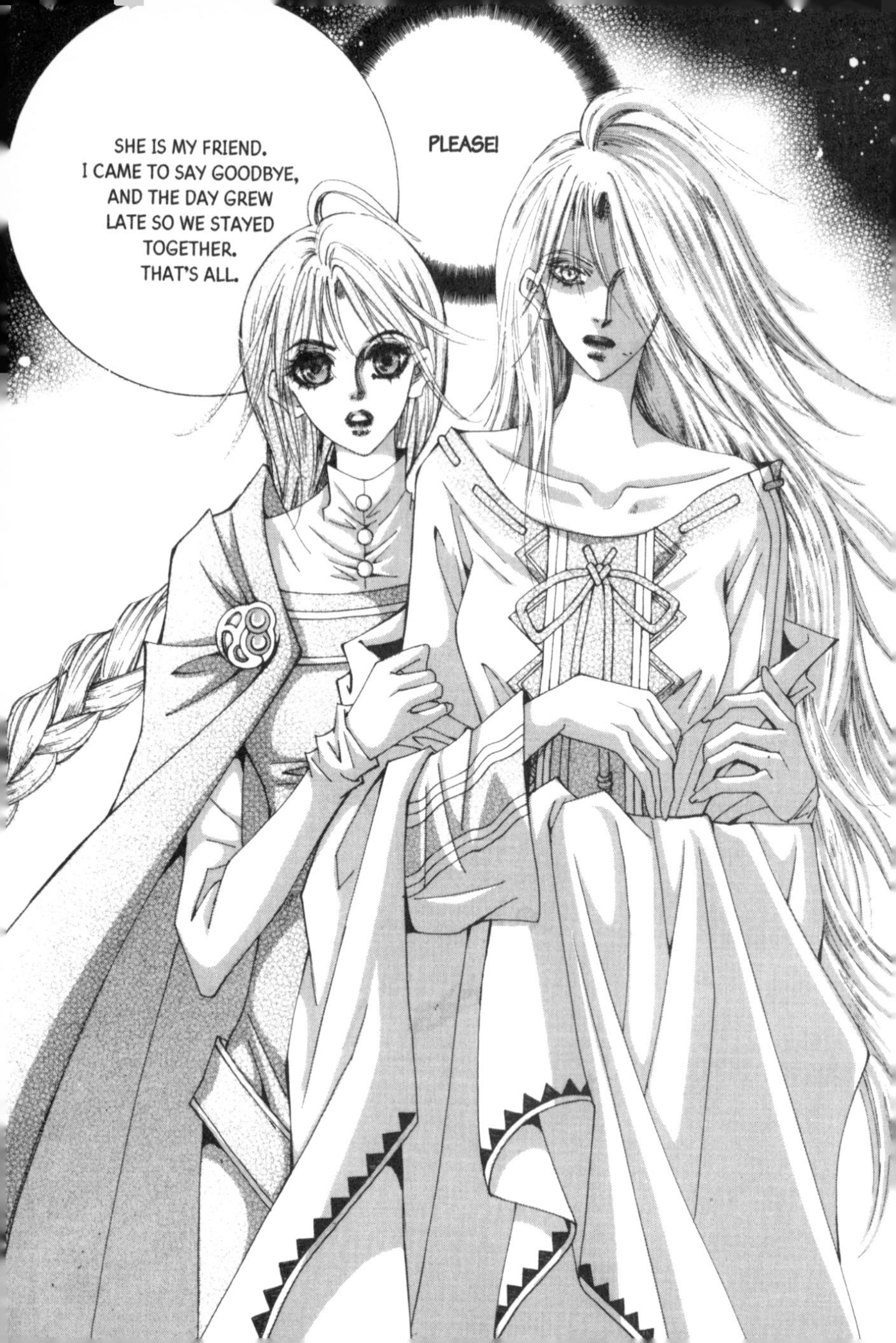
SHE IS MY FRIEND. I CAME TO SAY GOODBYE, AND THE DAY GREW LATE SO WE STAYED TOGETHER. THAT'S ALL.
PLEASE!

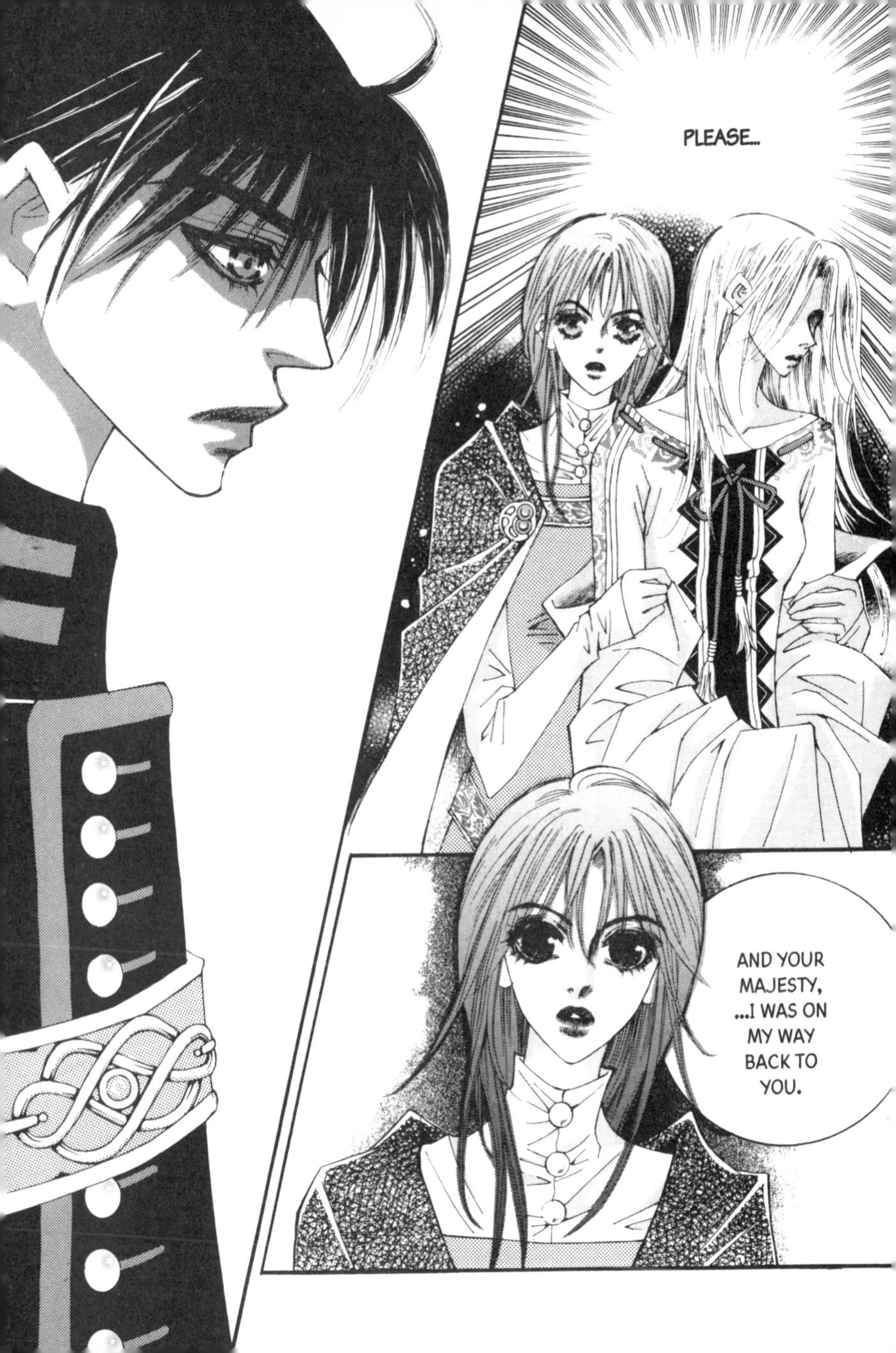
PLEASE...
AND YOUR MAJESTY, ...I WAS ON MY WAY BACK TO YOU.

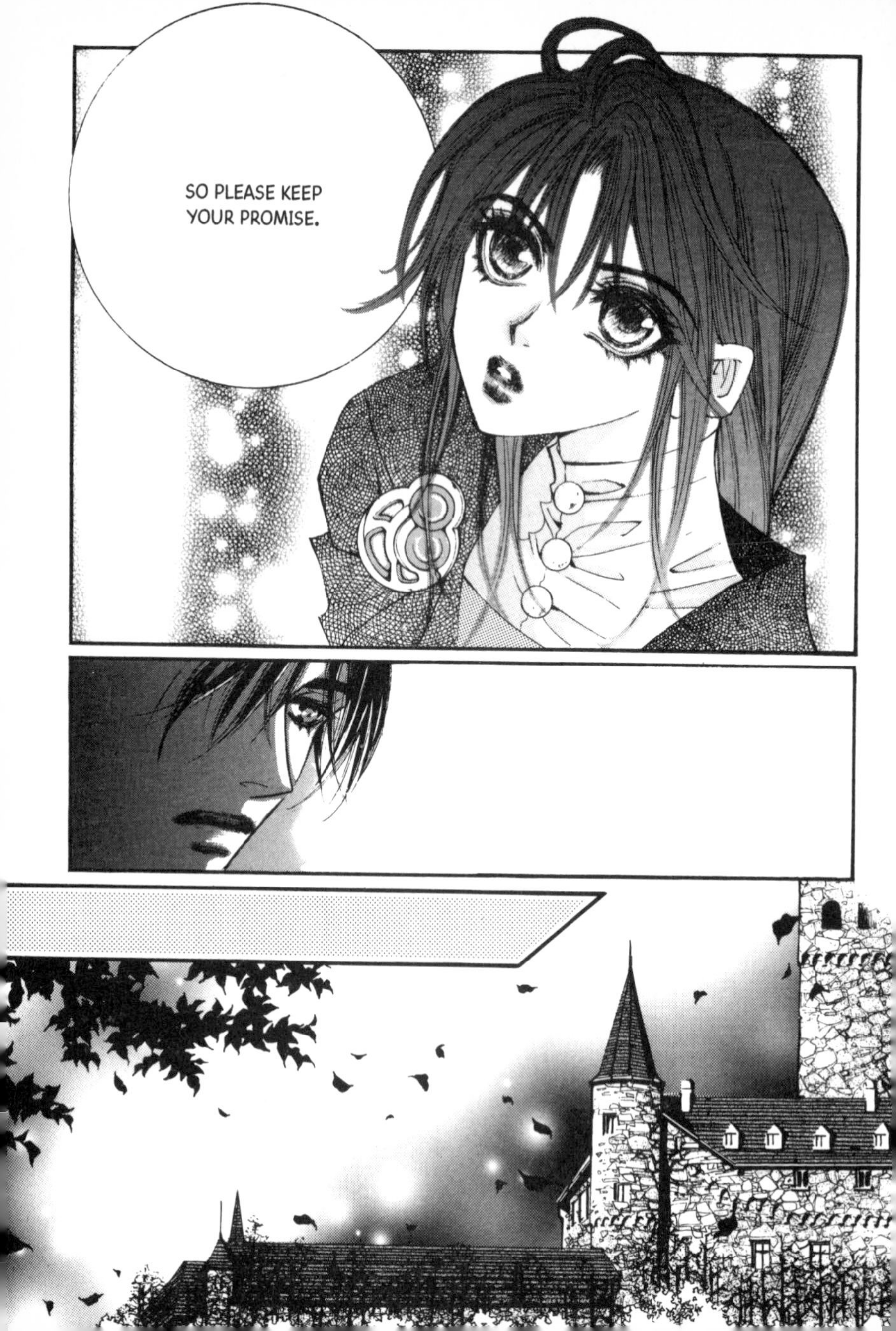
SO PLEASE KEEP YOUR PROMISE.

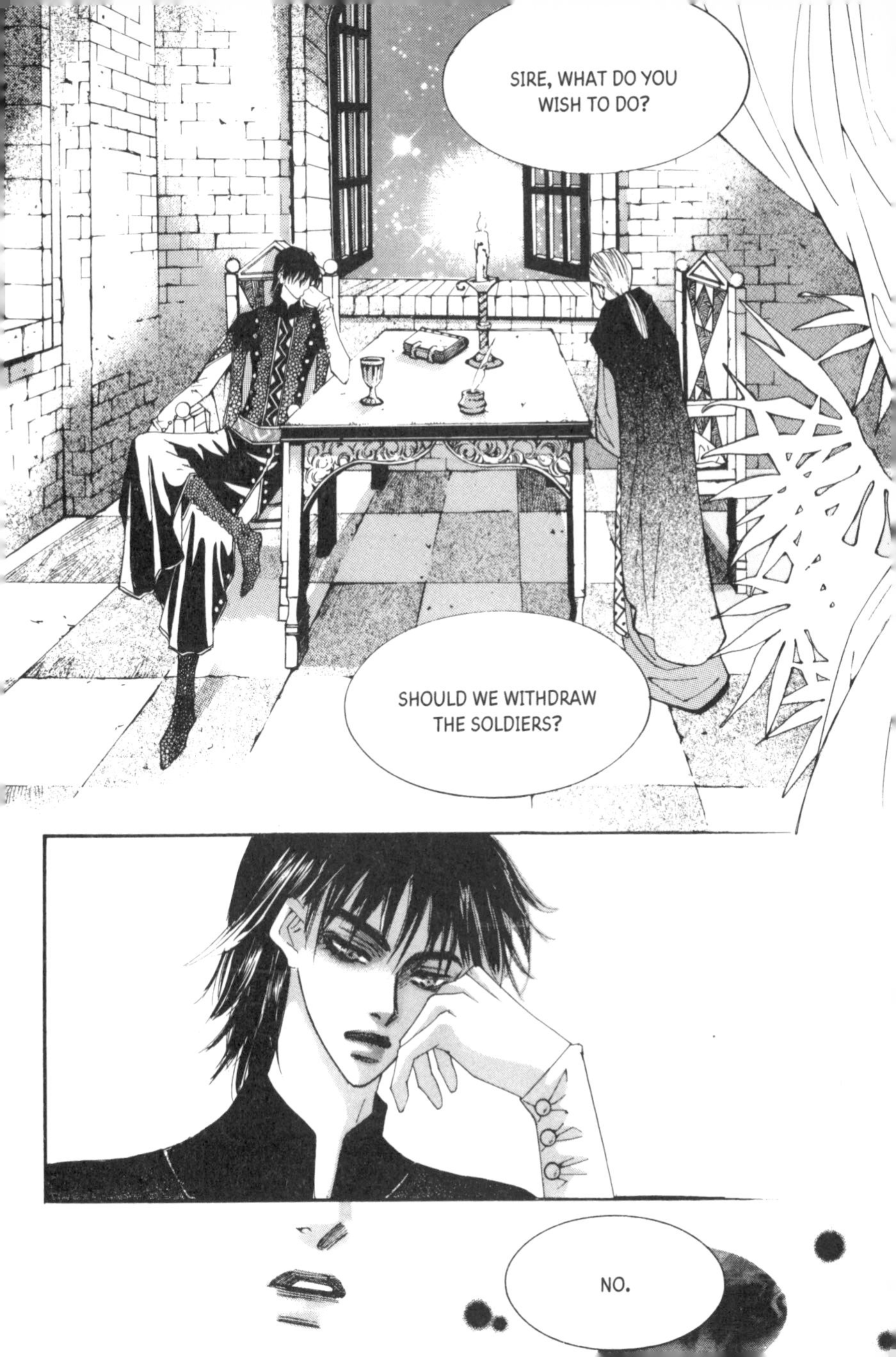
SIRE, WHAT DO YOU WISH TO DO?
SHOULD WE WITHDRAW THE SOLDIERS?
NO.

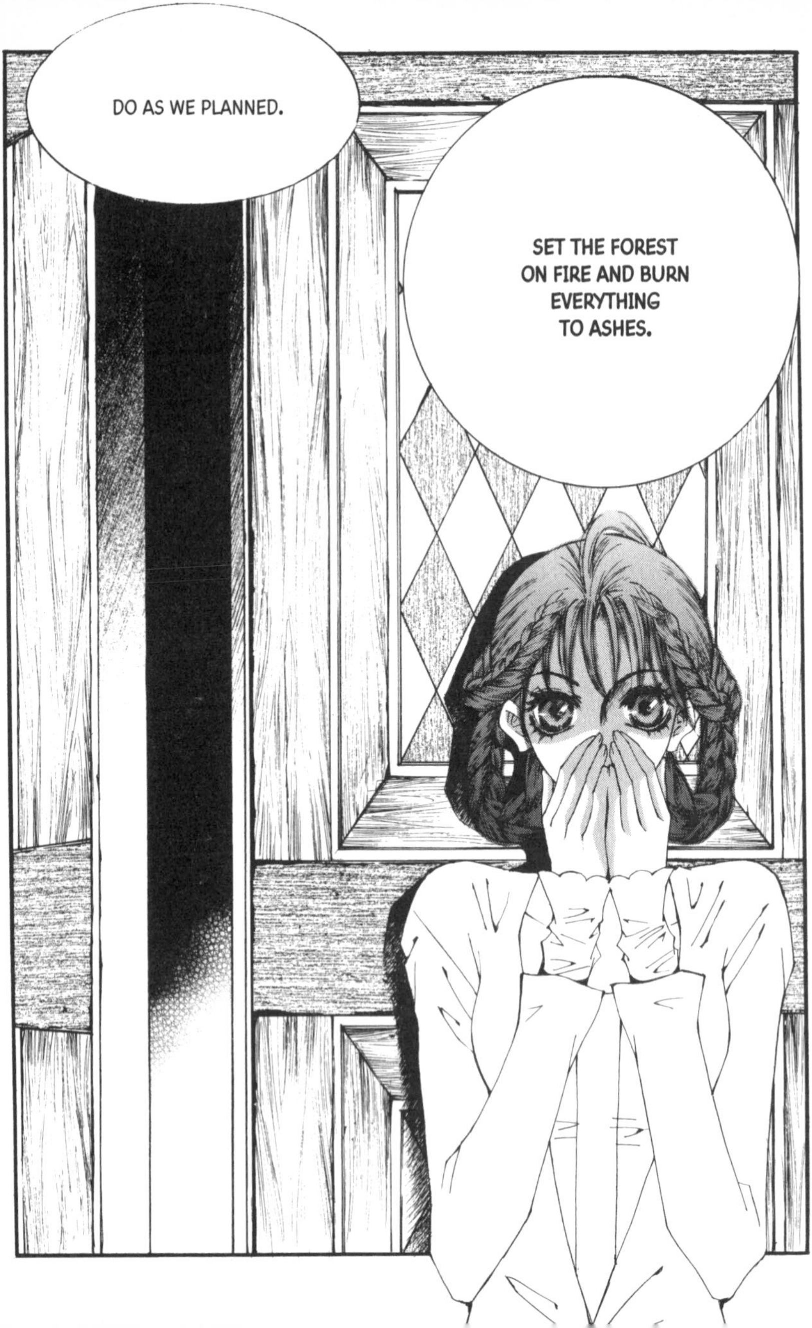
DO AS WE PLANNED.
SET THE FOREST ON FIRE AND BURN EVERYTHING TO ASHES.

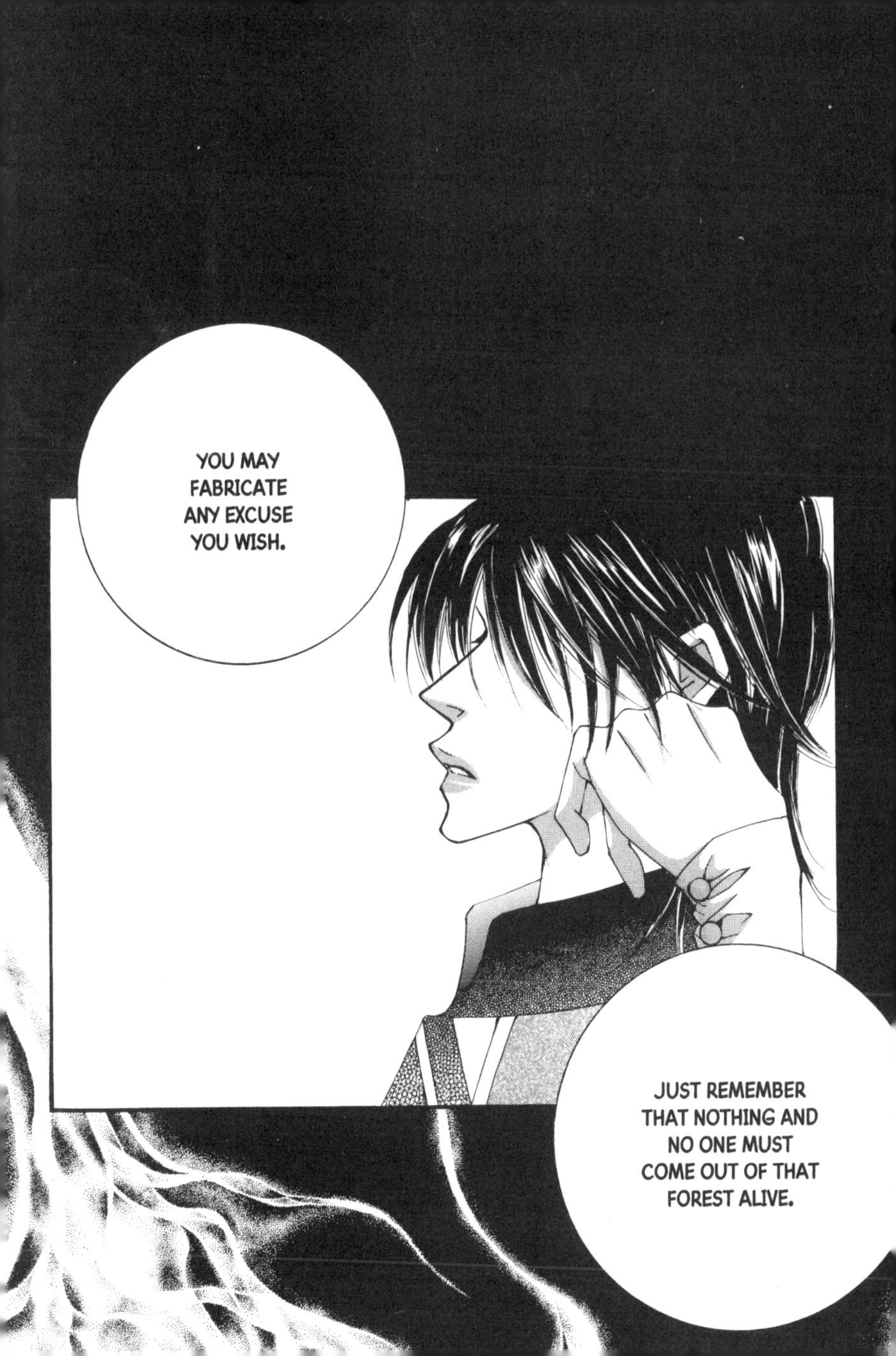
YOU MAY FABRICATE ANY EXCUSE YOU WISH.
JUST REMEMBER THAT NOTHING AND NO ONE MUST COME OUT OF THAT FOREST ALIVE.

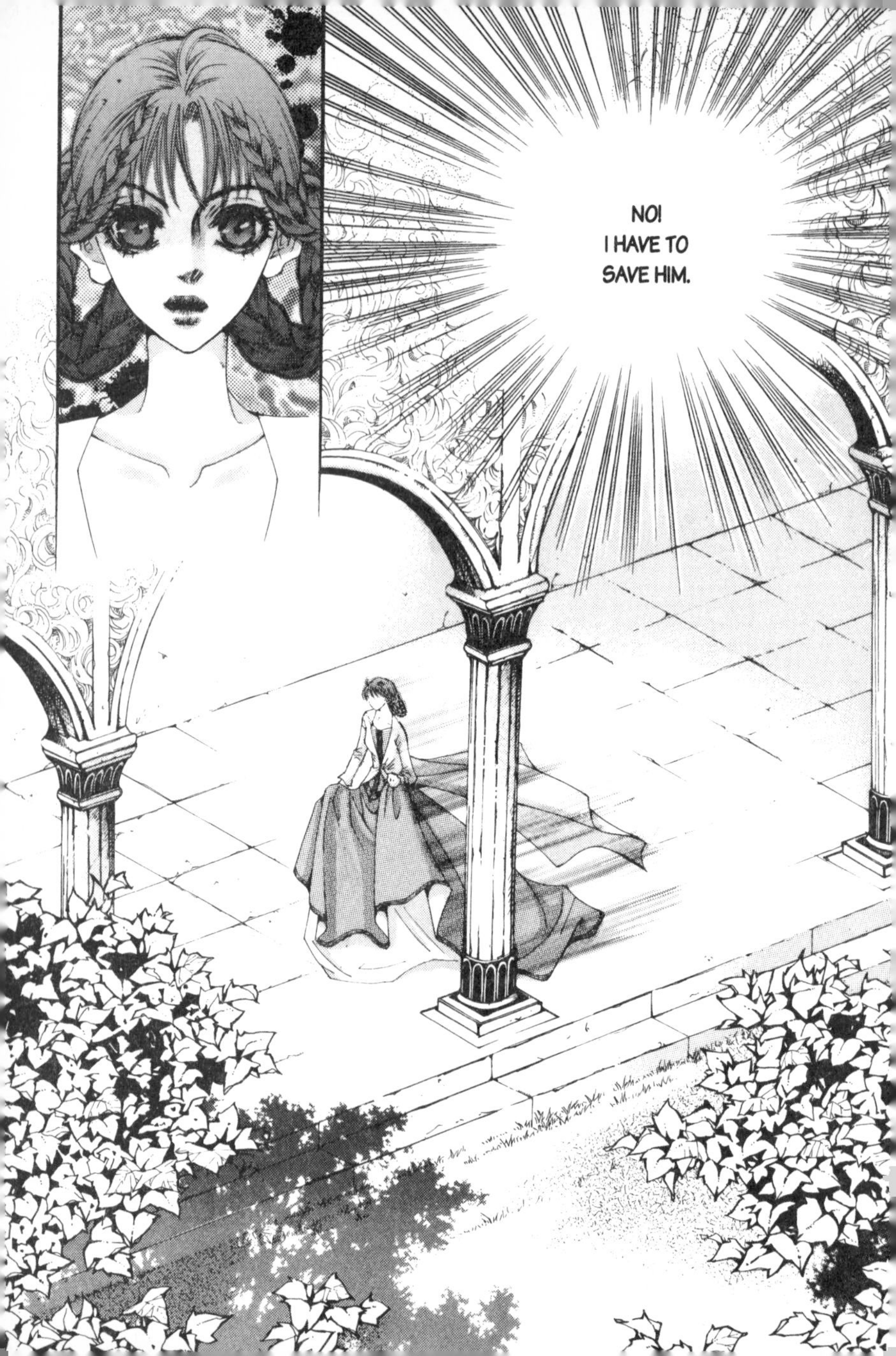
NO!
I HAVE TO
SAVE HIM.

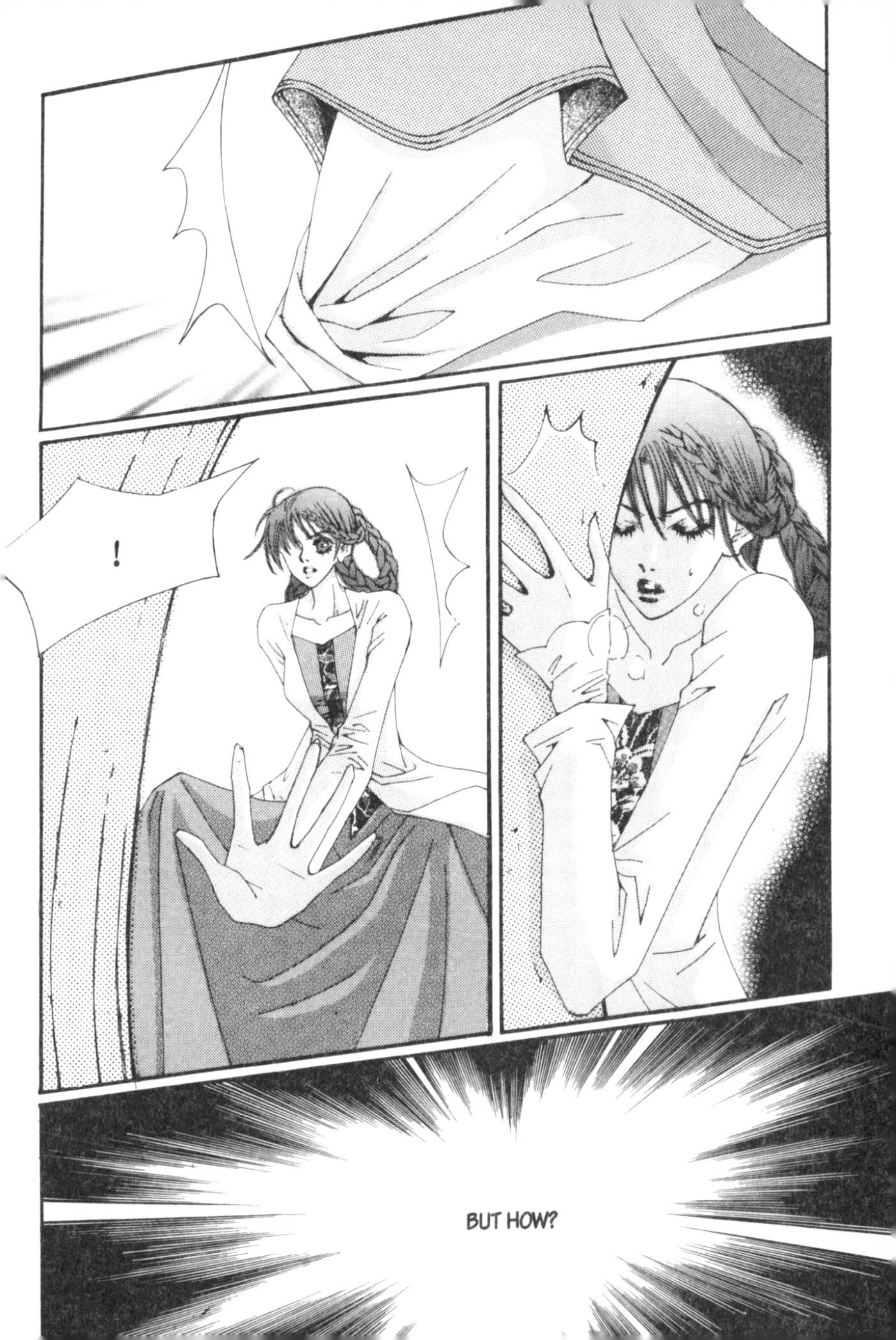
!
BUT HOW?

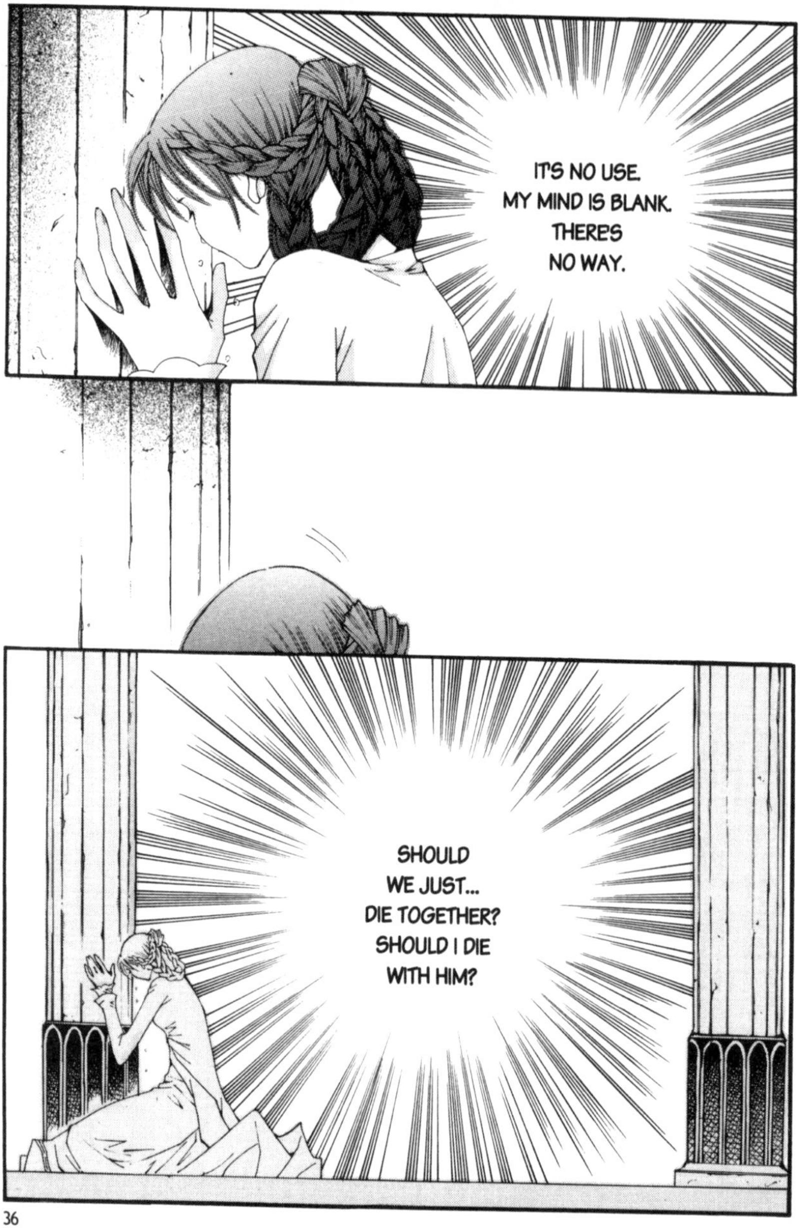
IT'S NO USE. MY MIND IS BLANK. THERE'S NO WAY.
SHOULD WE JUST... DIE TOGETHER? SHOULD I DIE WITH HIM?

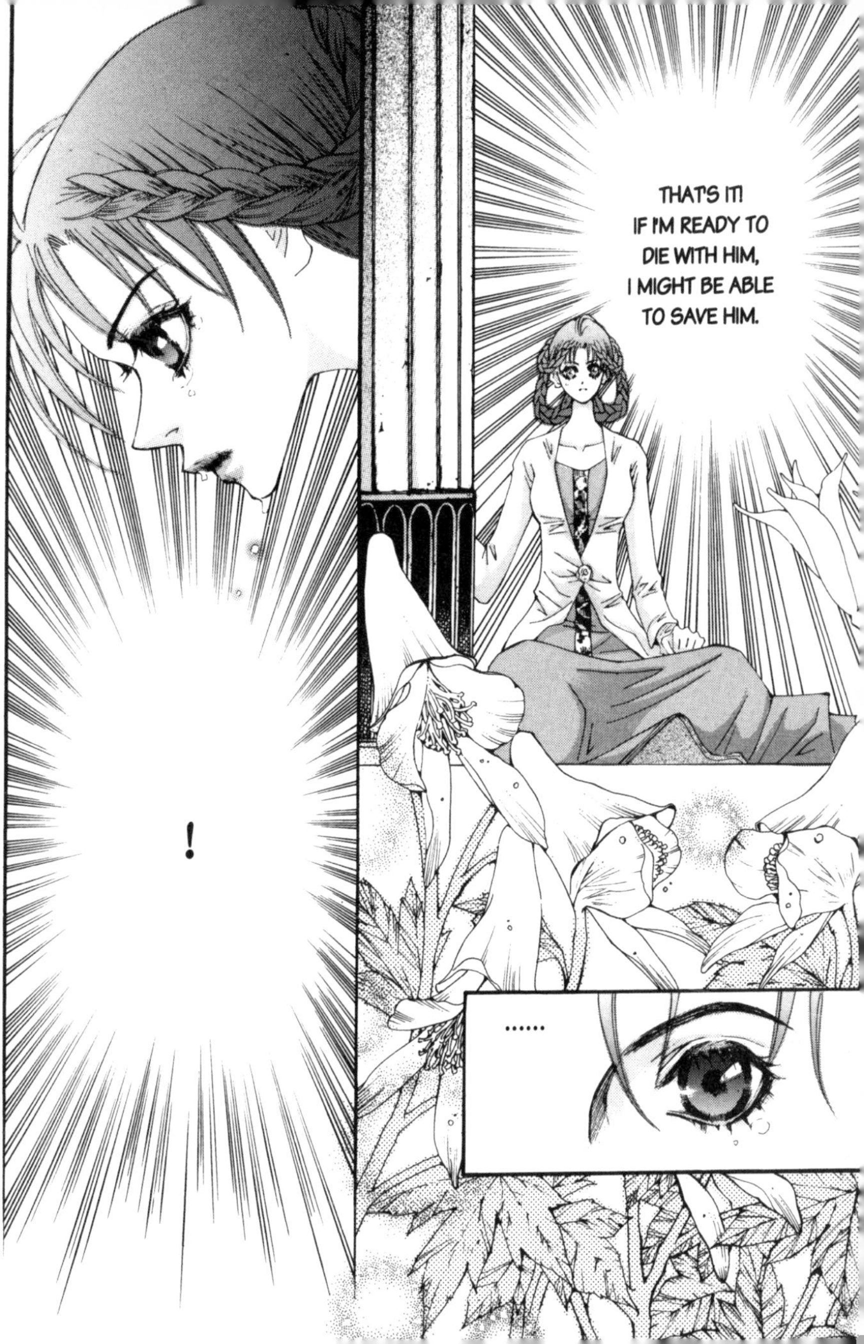
!
THAT'S IT!
IF I'M READY TO
DIE WITH HIM,
I MIGHT BE ABLE
TO SAVE HIM.
......

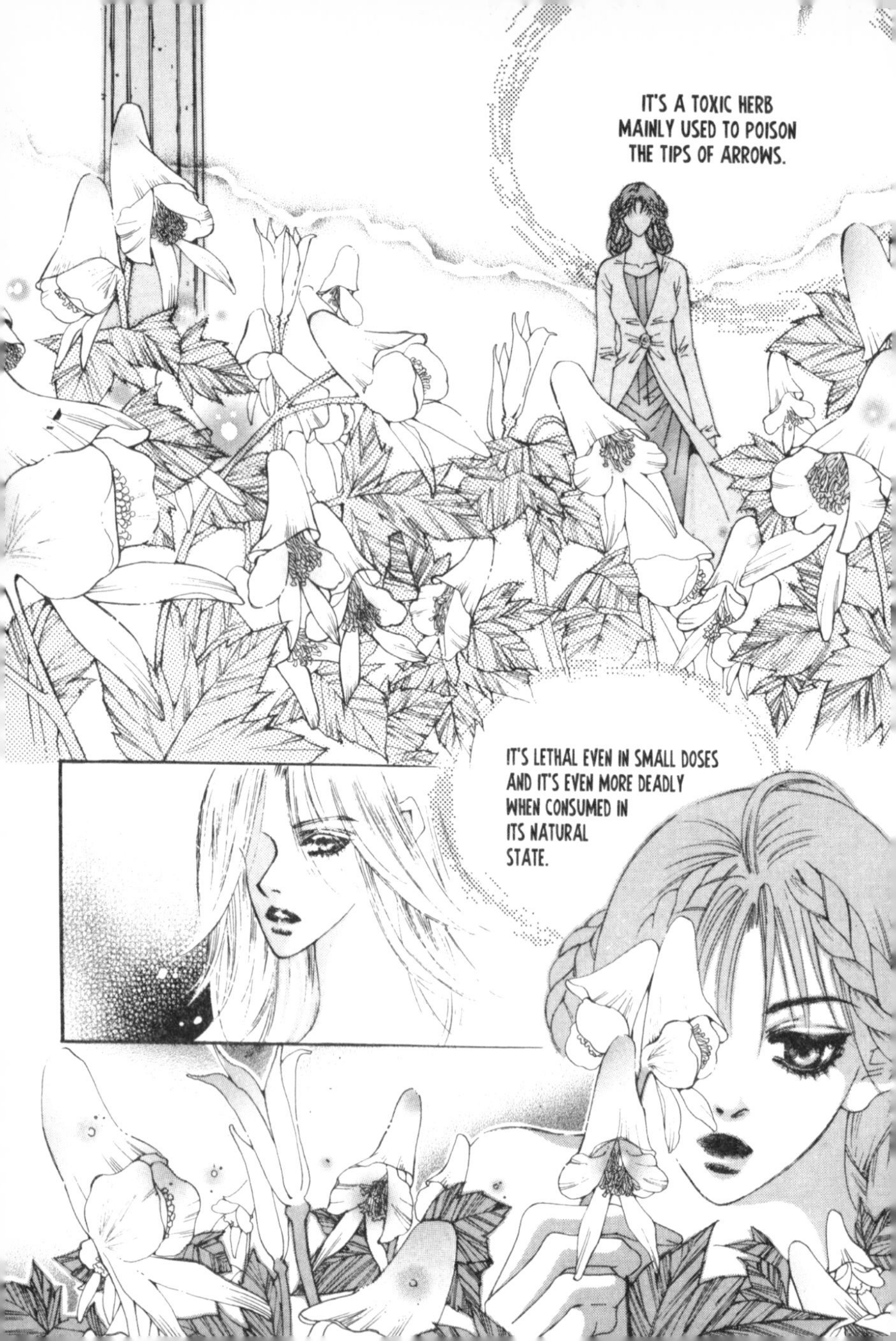
IT'S A TOXIC HERB MAINLY USED TO POISON THE TIPS OF ARROWS.
IT'S LETHAL EVEN IN SMALL DOSES AND IT'S EVEN MORE DEADLY WHEN CONSUMED IN ITS NATURAL STATE.

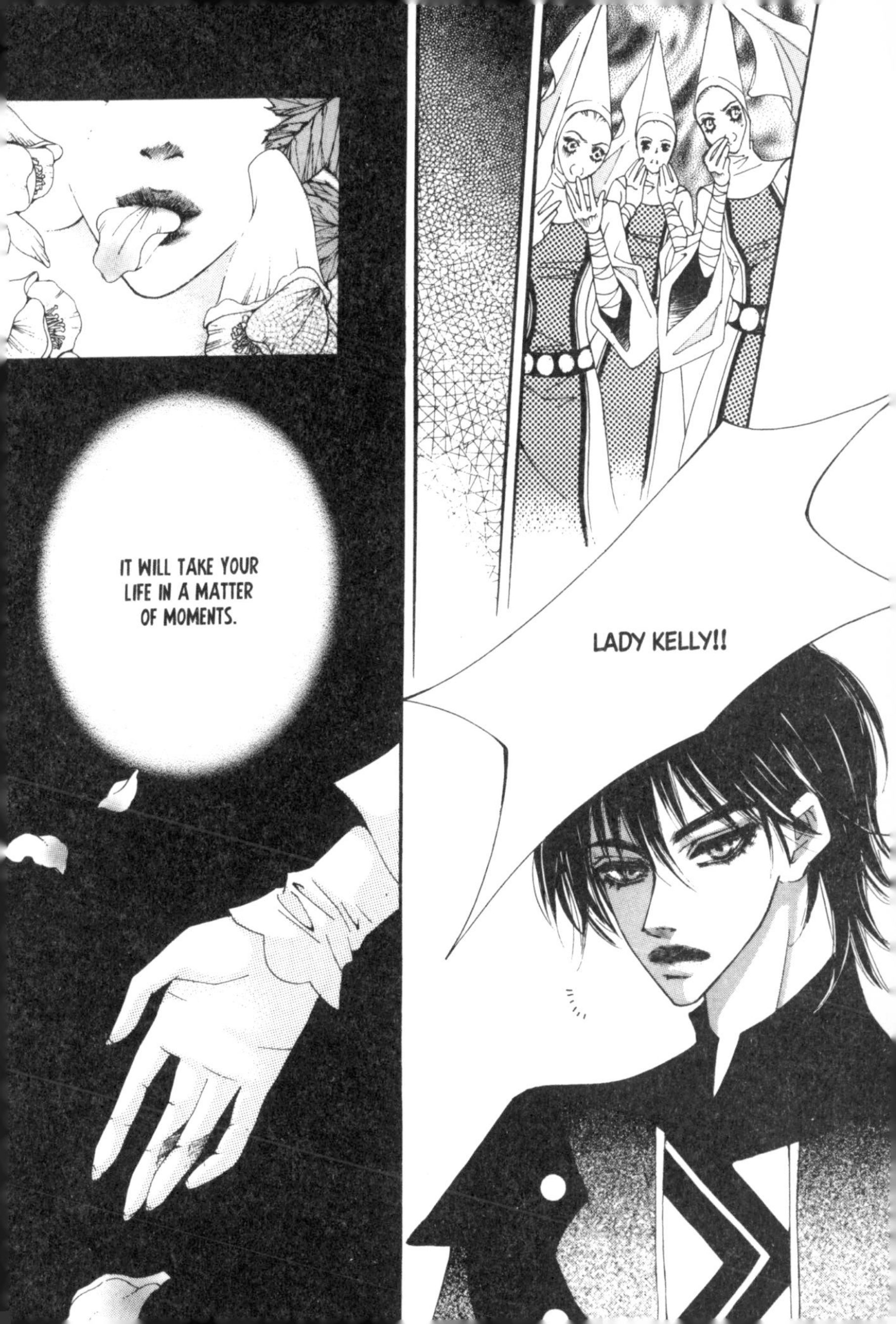
IT WILL TAKE YOUR LIFE IN A MATTER OF MOMENTS.
LADY KELLY!!

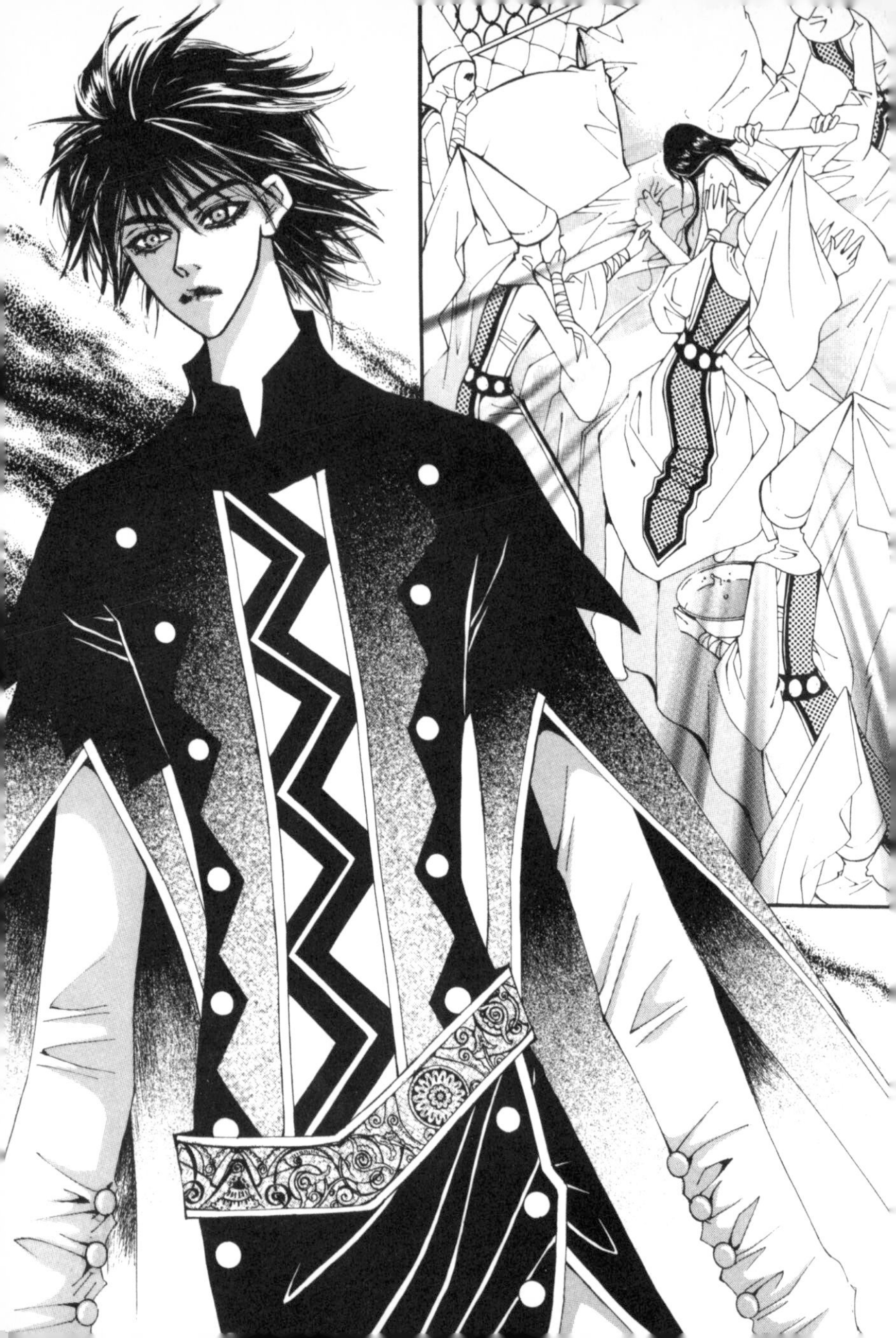

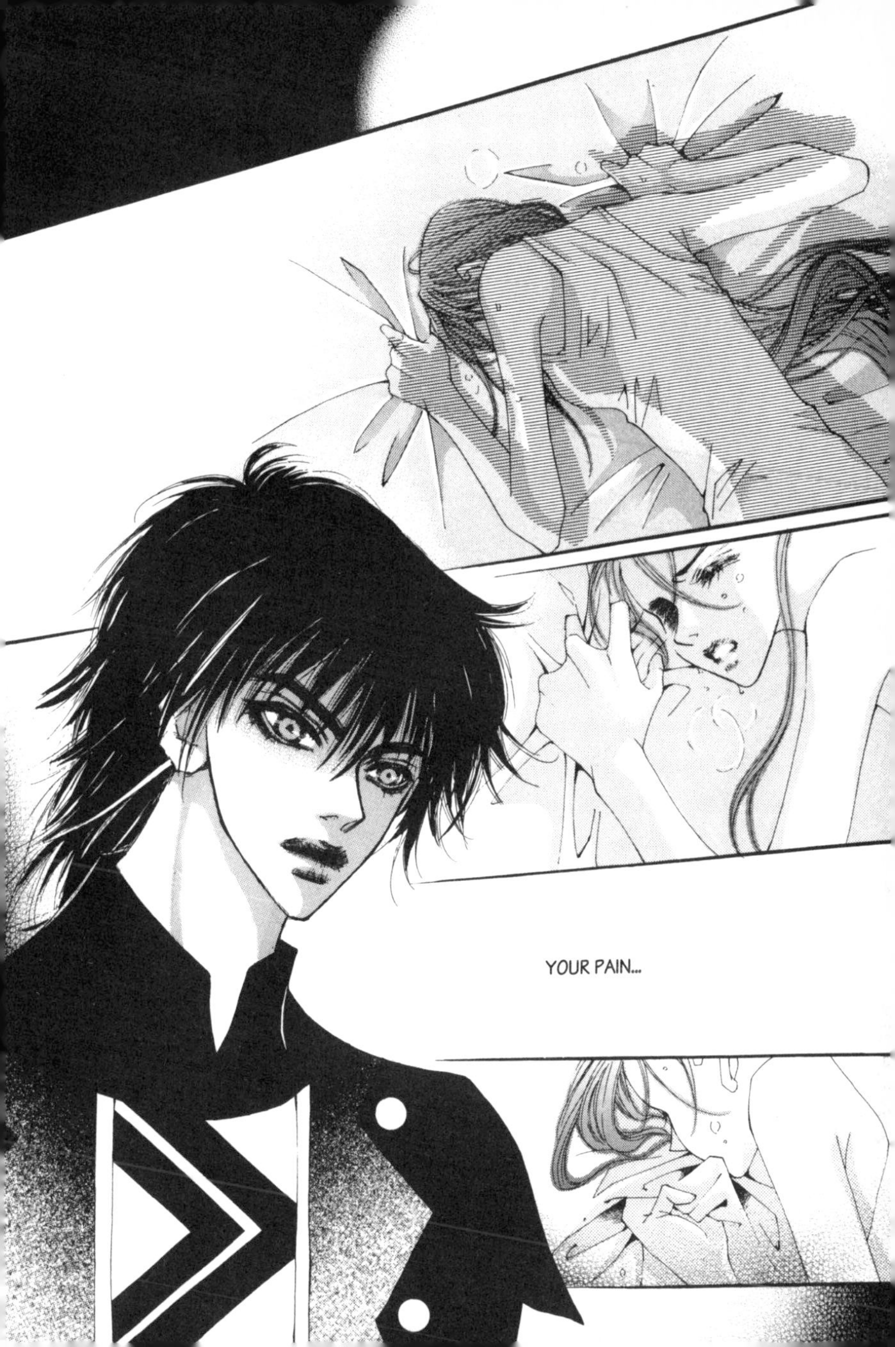
YOUR PAIN...

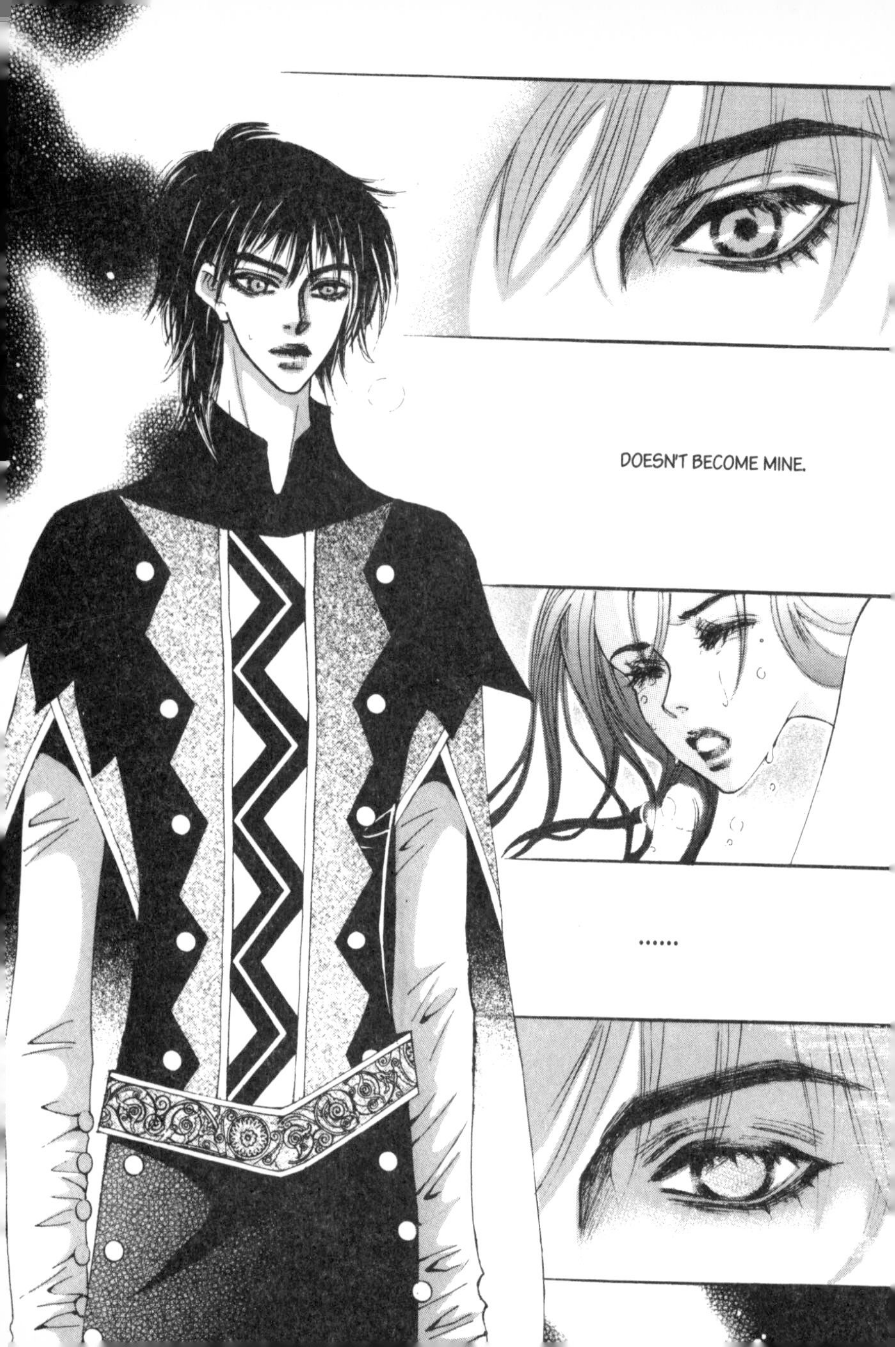
DOESN'T BECOME MINE.
......

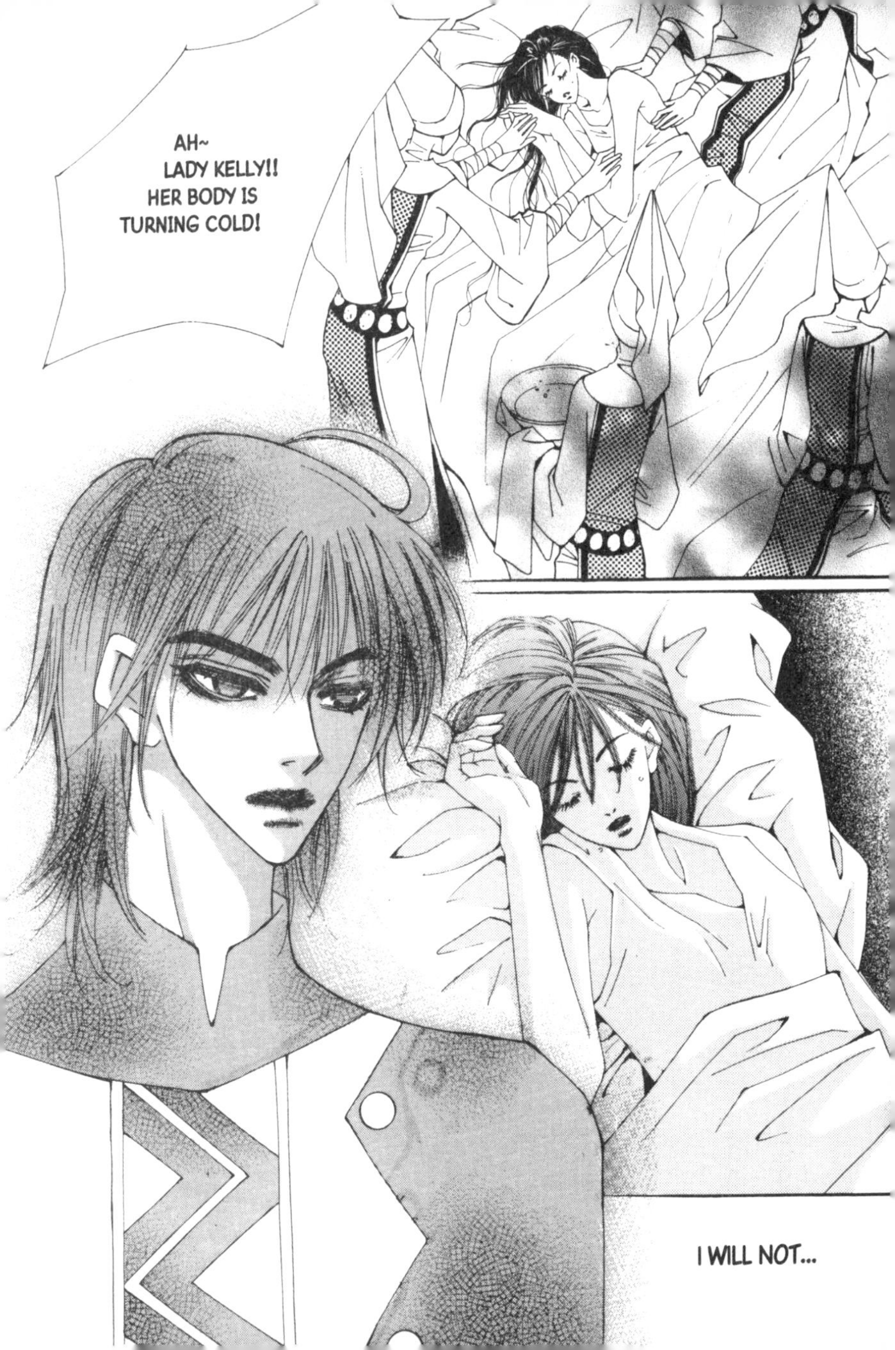
AH~
LADY KELLY!!
HER BODY IS
TURNING COLD!
I WILL NOT...

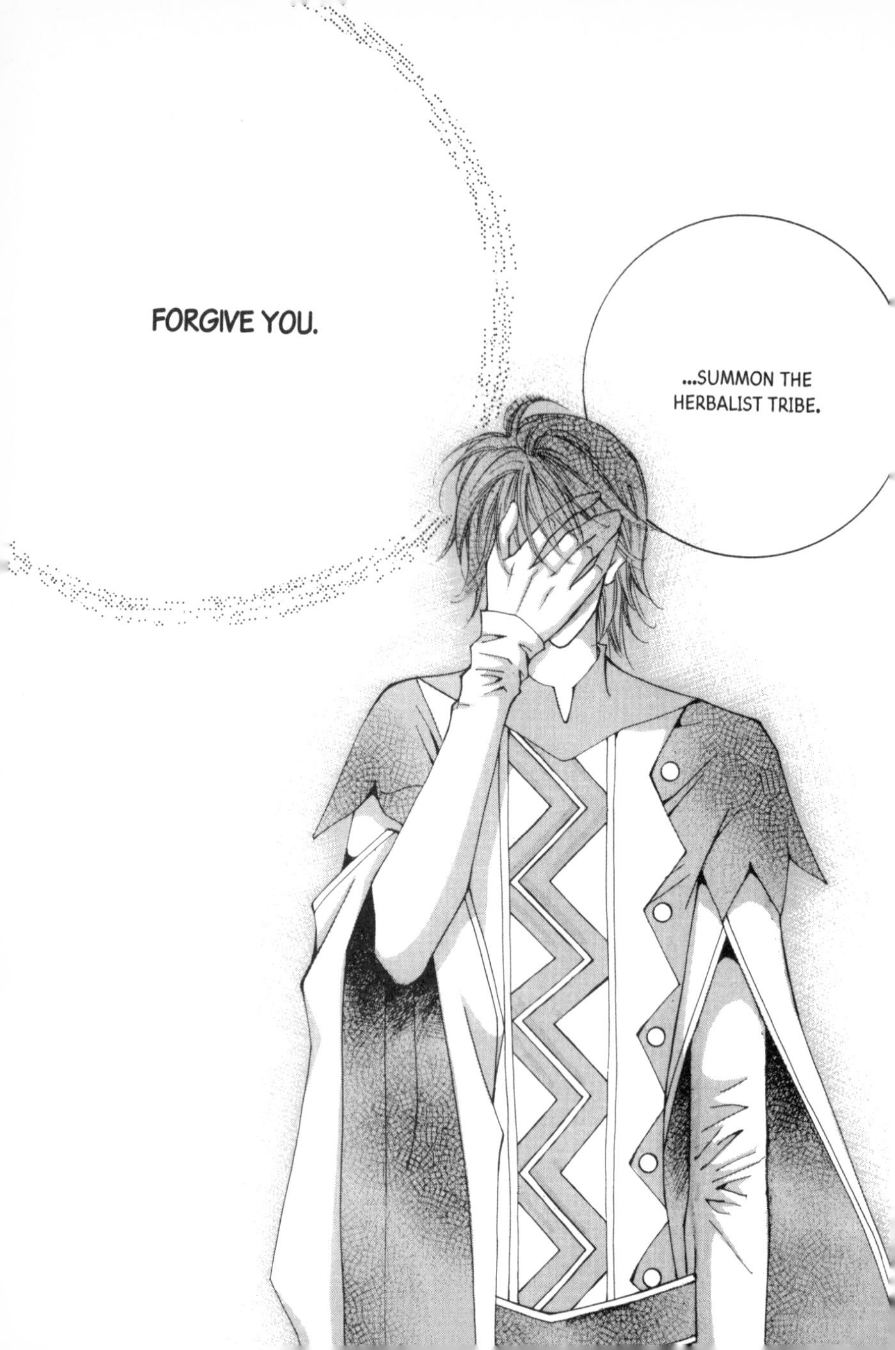
FORGIVE YOU.
...SUMMON THE HERBALIST TRIBE.

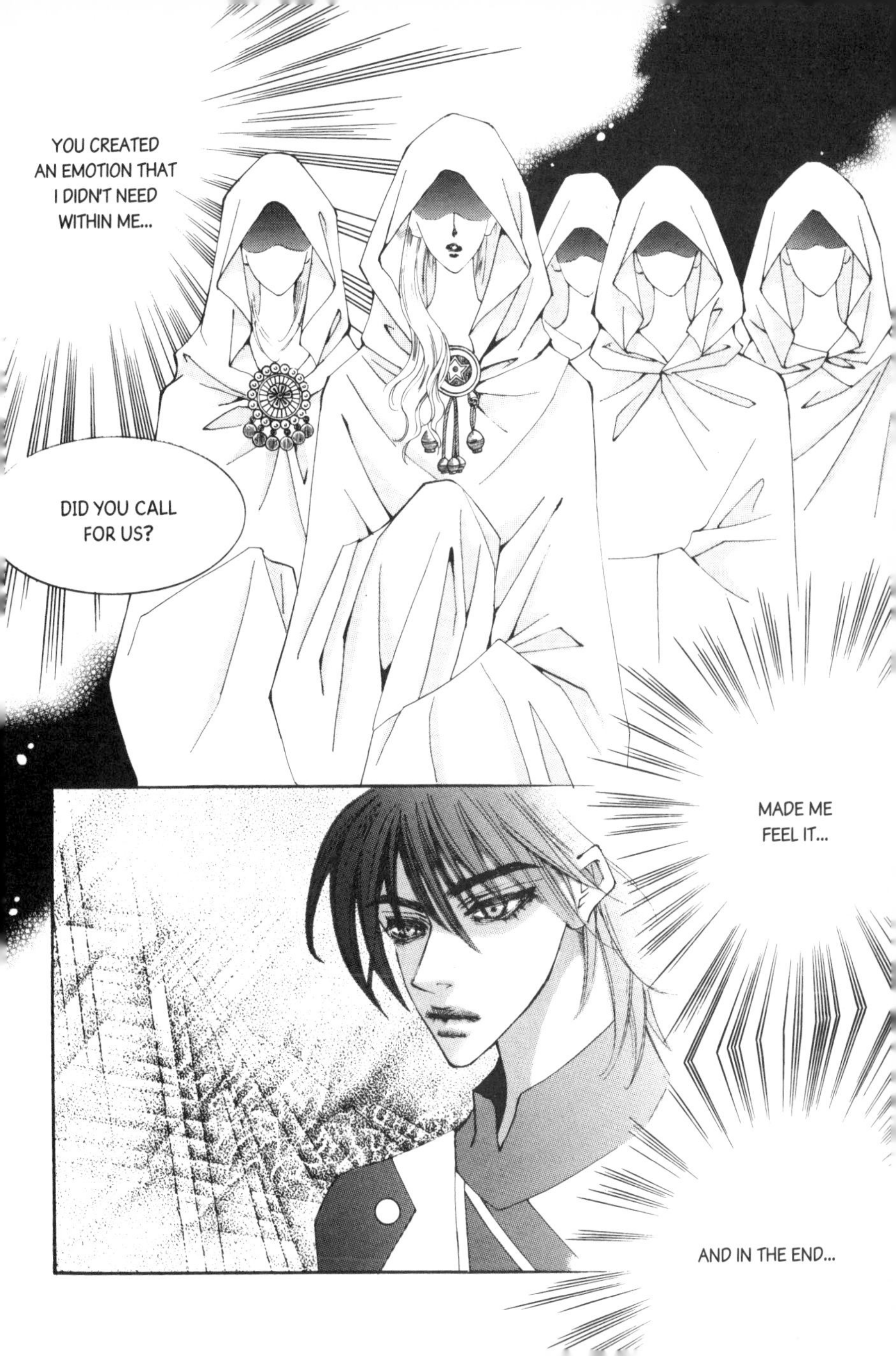
YOU CREATED AN EMOTION THAT I DIDN'T NEED WITHIN ME...
DID YOU CALL FOR US?
MADE ME FEEL IT...
AND IN THE END...

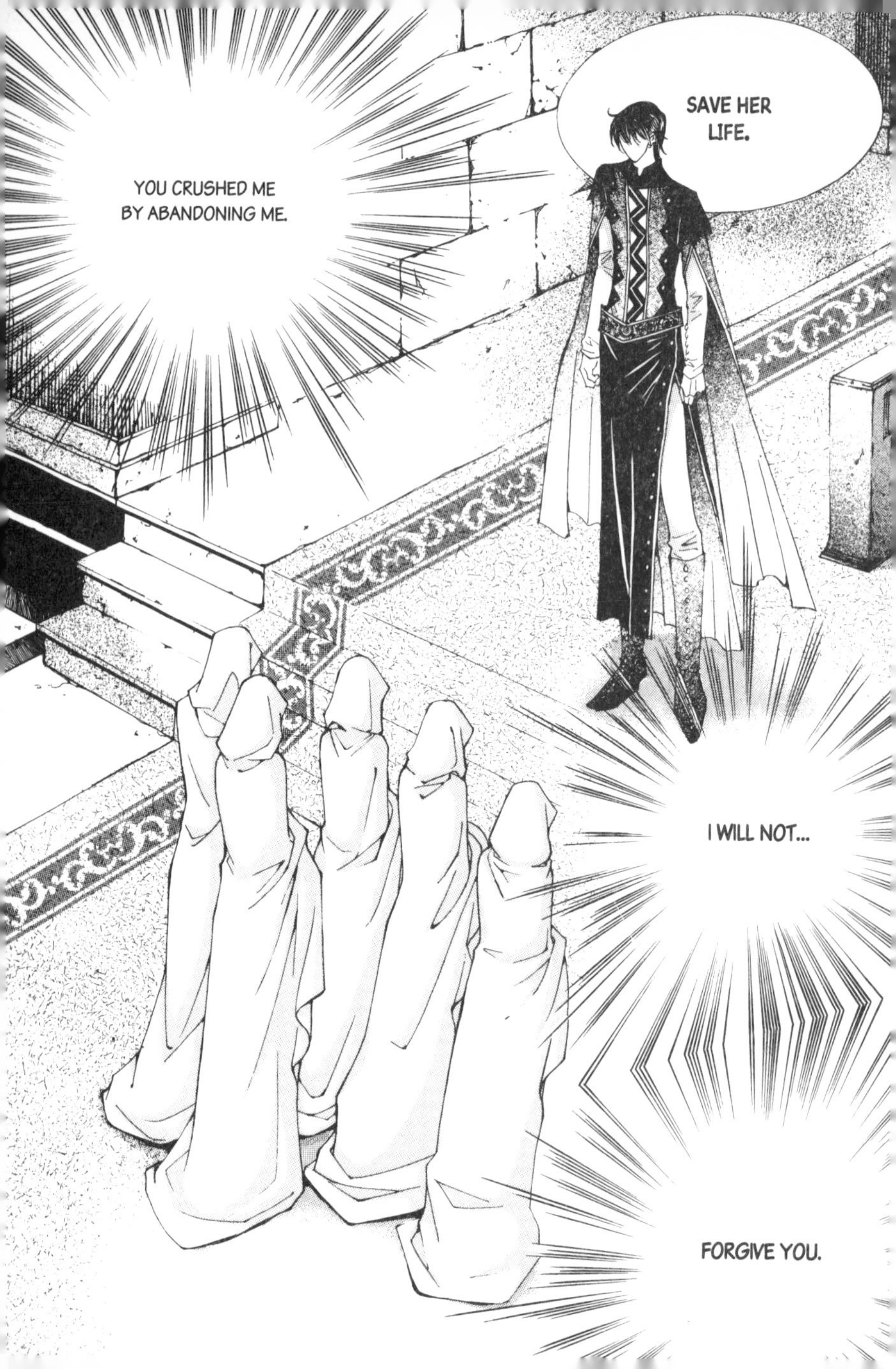
YOU CRUSHED ME BY ABANDONING ME.
SAVE HER LIFE.
I WILL NOT...
FORGIVE YOU.

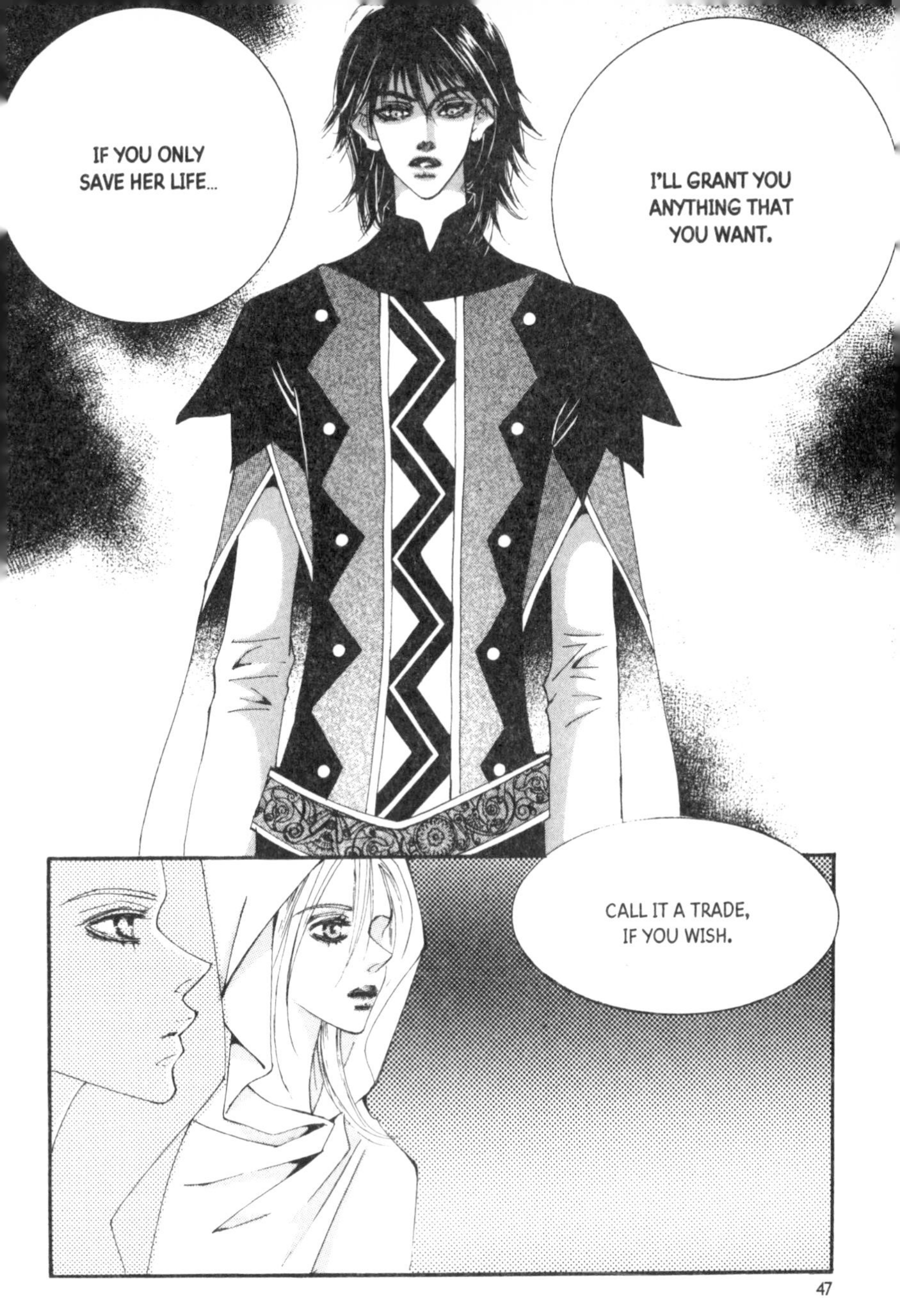
IF YOU ONLY SAVE HER LIFE...
I'LL GRANT YOU ANYTHING THAT YOU WANT.
CALL IT A TRADE, IF YOU WISH.

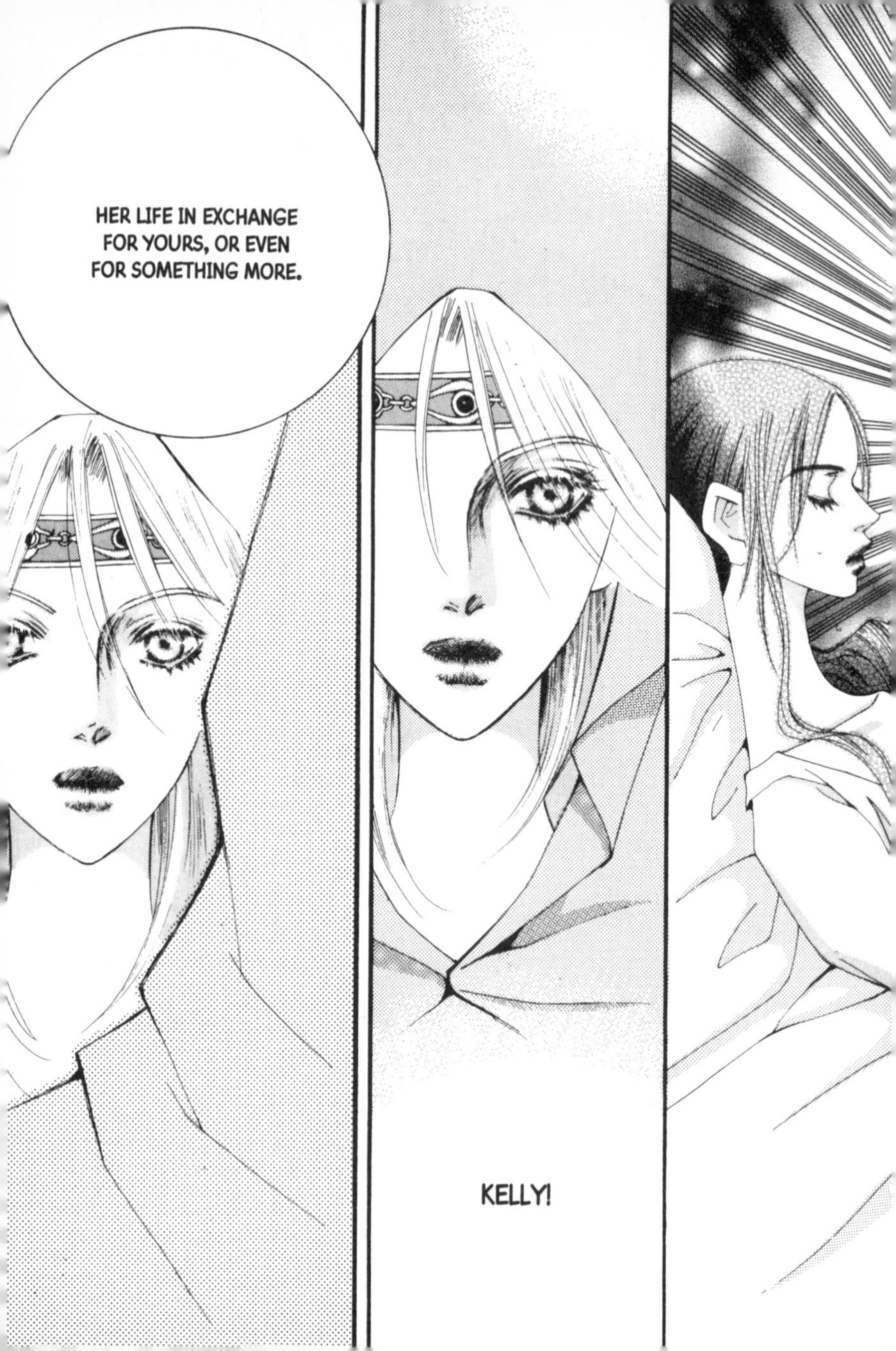
HER LIFE IN EXCHANGE FOR YOURS, OR EVEN FOR SOMETHING MORE.
KELLY!

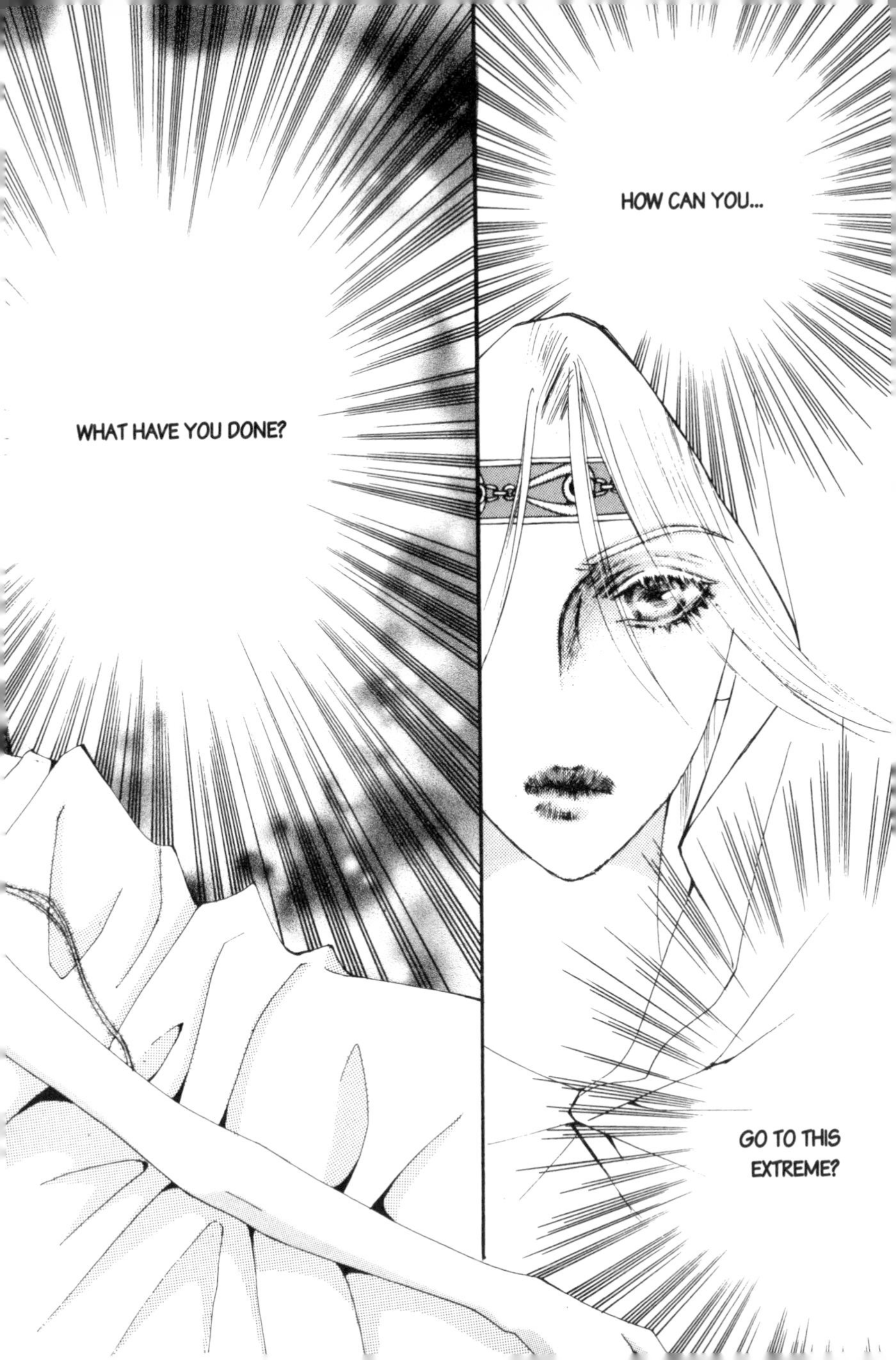
WHAT HAVE YOU DONE?
HOW CAN YOU...
GO TO THIS EXTREME?

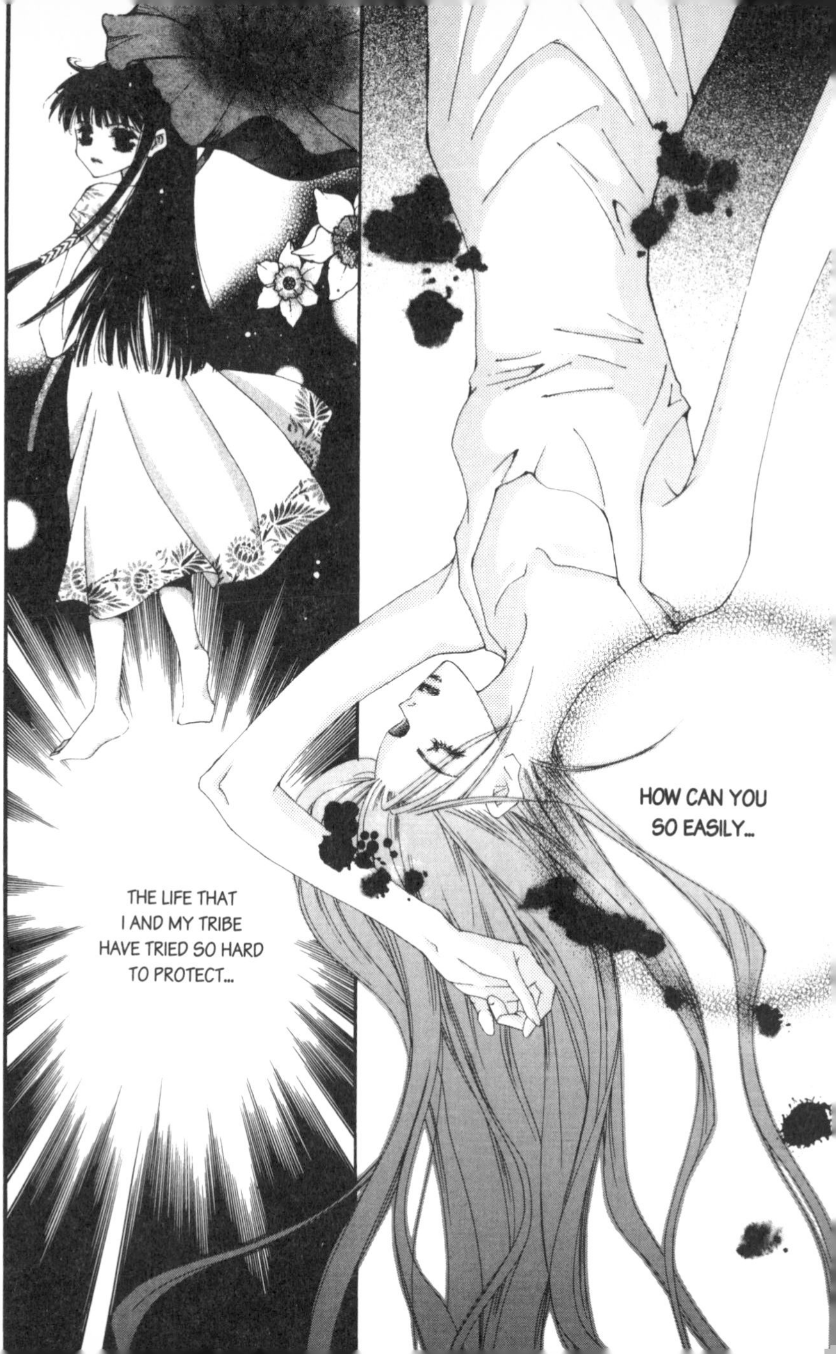
THE LIFE THAT I AND MY TRIBE HAVE TRIED SO HARD TO PROTECT...
HOW CAN YOU SO EASILY...

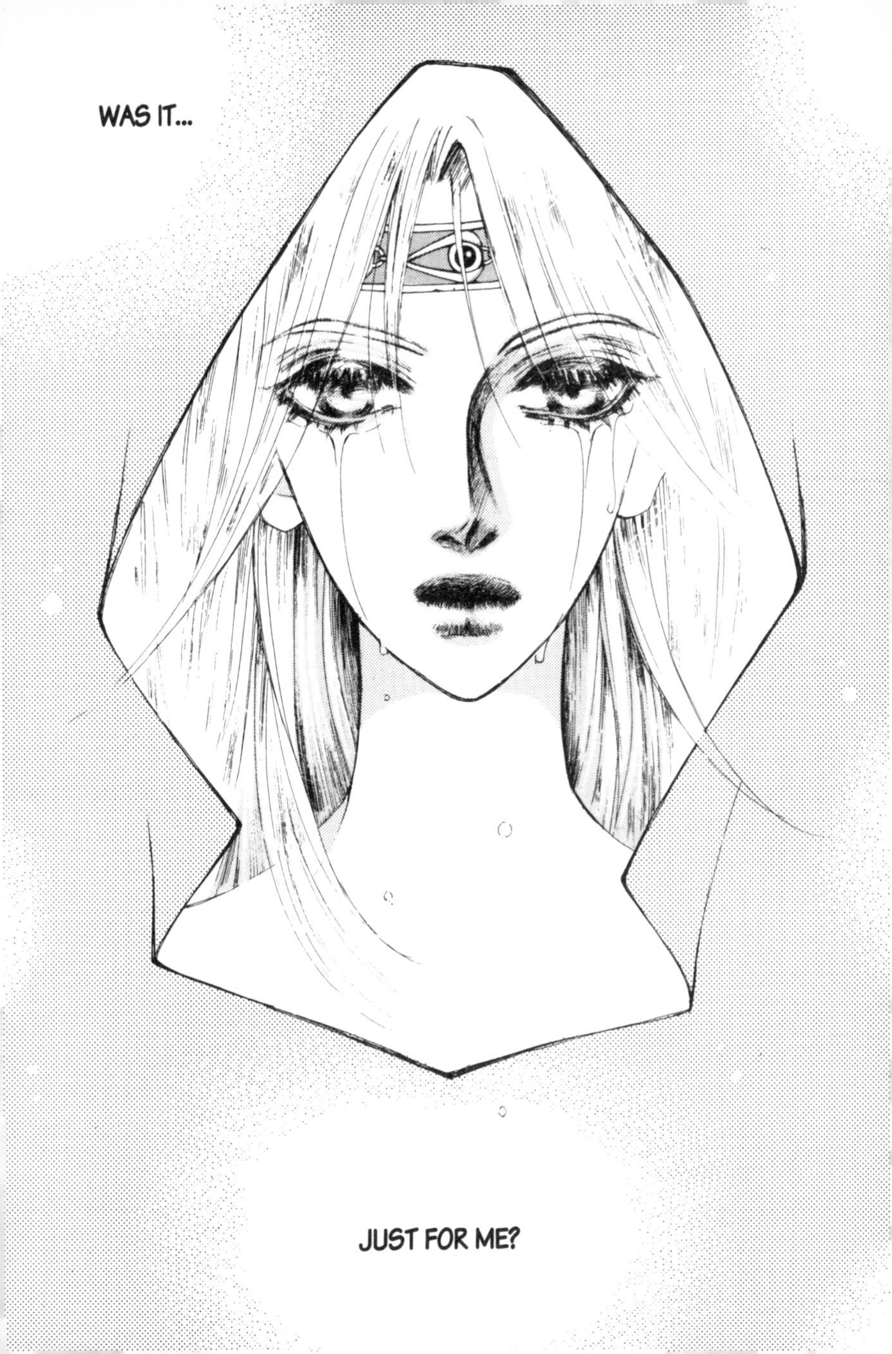
WAS IT...
JUST FOR ME?

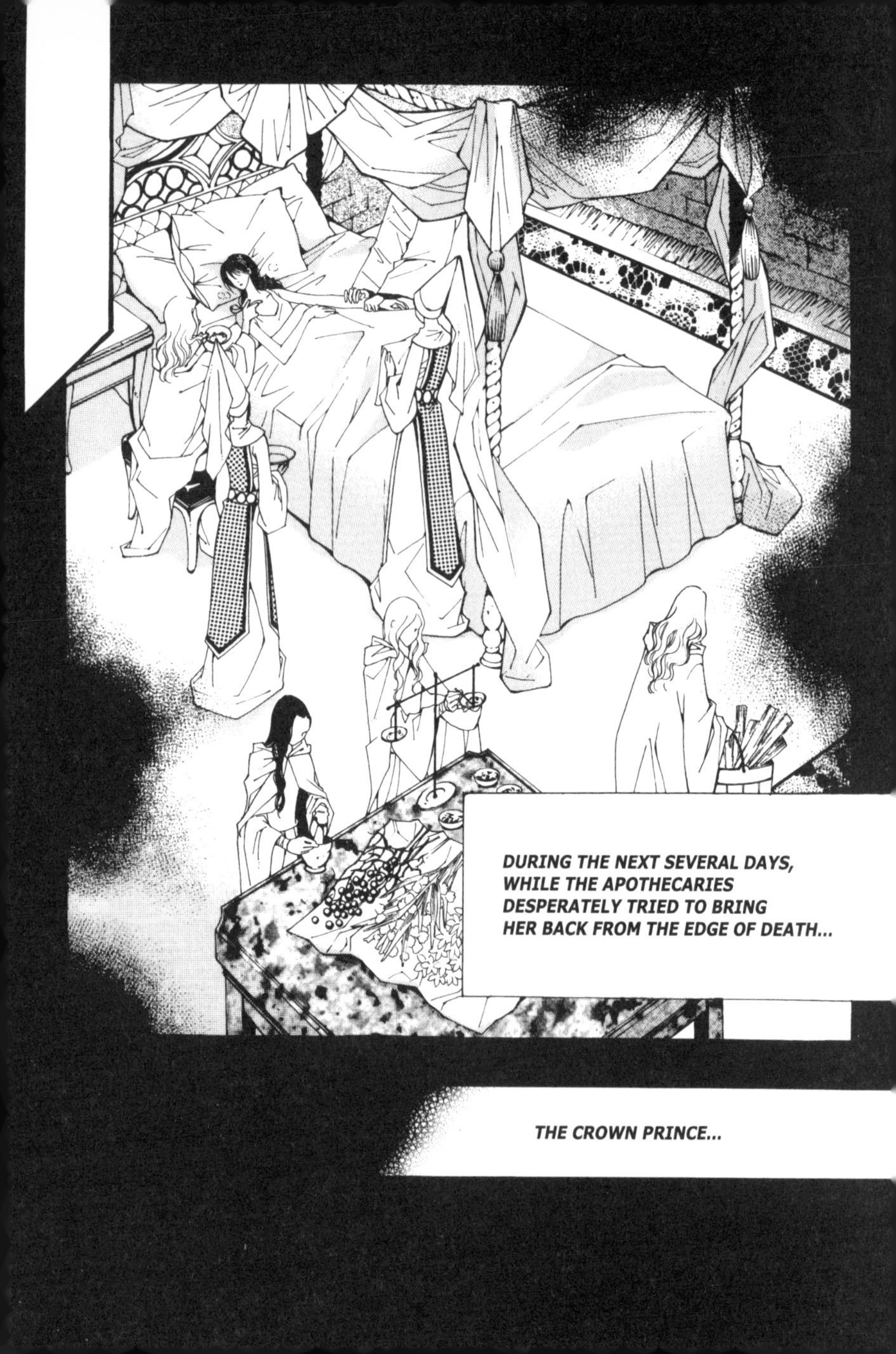
DURING THE NEXT SEVERAL DAYS, WHILE THE APOTHECARIES DESPERATELY TRIED TO BRING HER BACK FROM THE EDGE OF DEATH...
THE CROWN PRINCE...

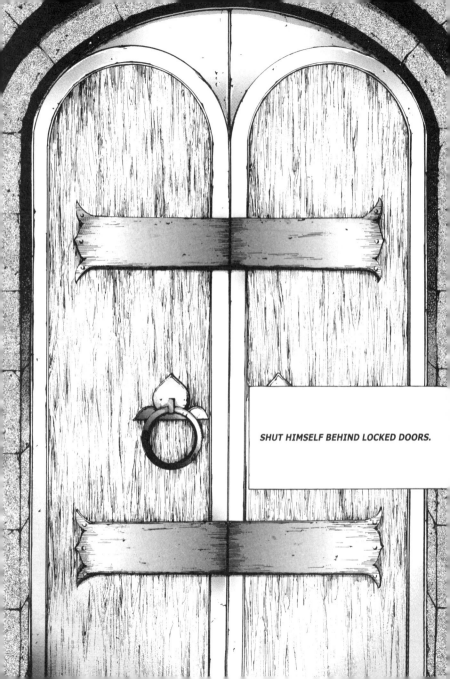

SHUT HIMSELF BEHIND LOCKED DOORS.

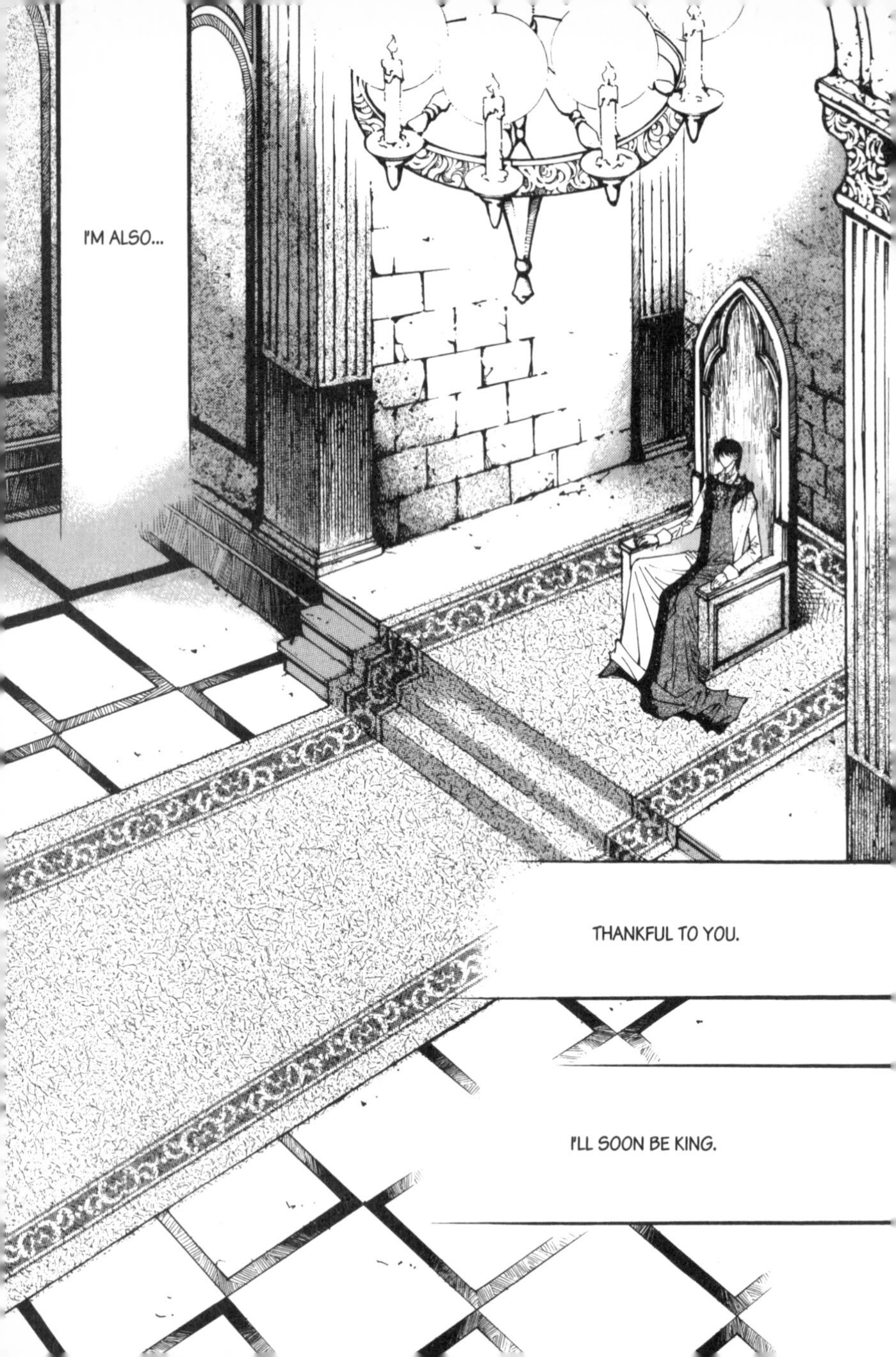
I'M ALSO...
THANKFUL TO YOU.
I'LL SOON BE KING.

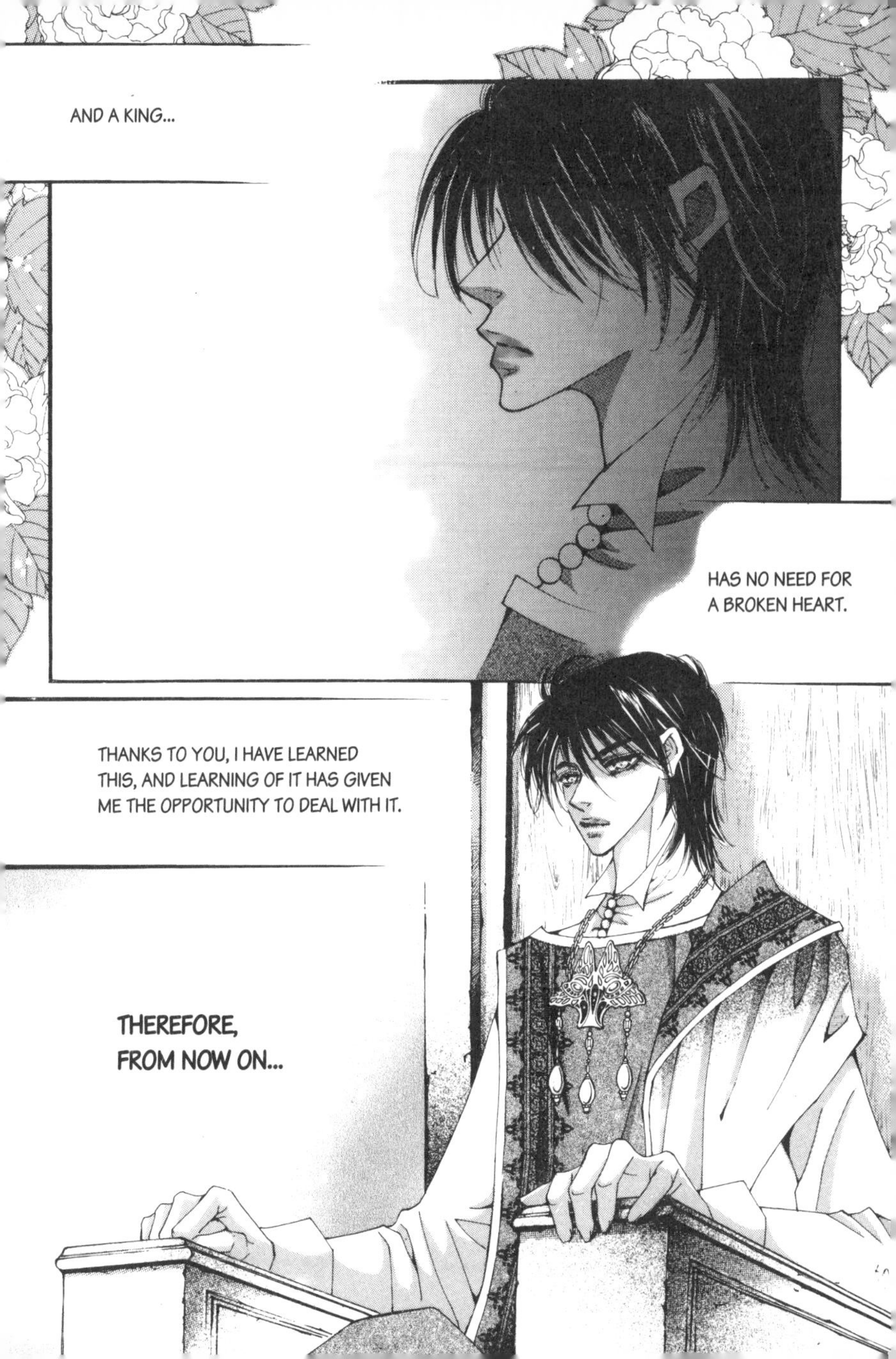
AND A KING...
HAS NO NEED FOR A BROKEN HEART.
THANKS TO YOU, I HAVE LEARNED THIS, AND LEARNING OF IT HAS GIVEN ME THE OPPORTUNITY TO DEAL WITH IT.
THEREFORE, FROM NOW ON...

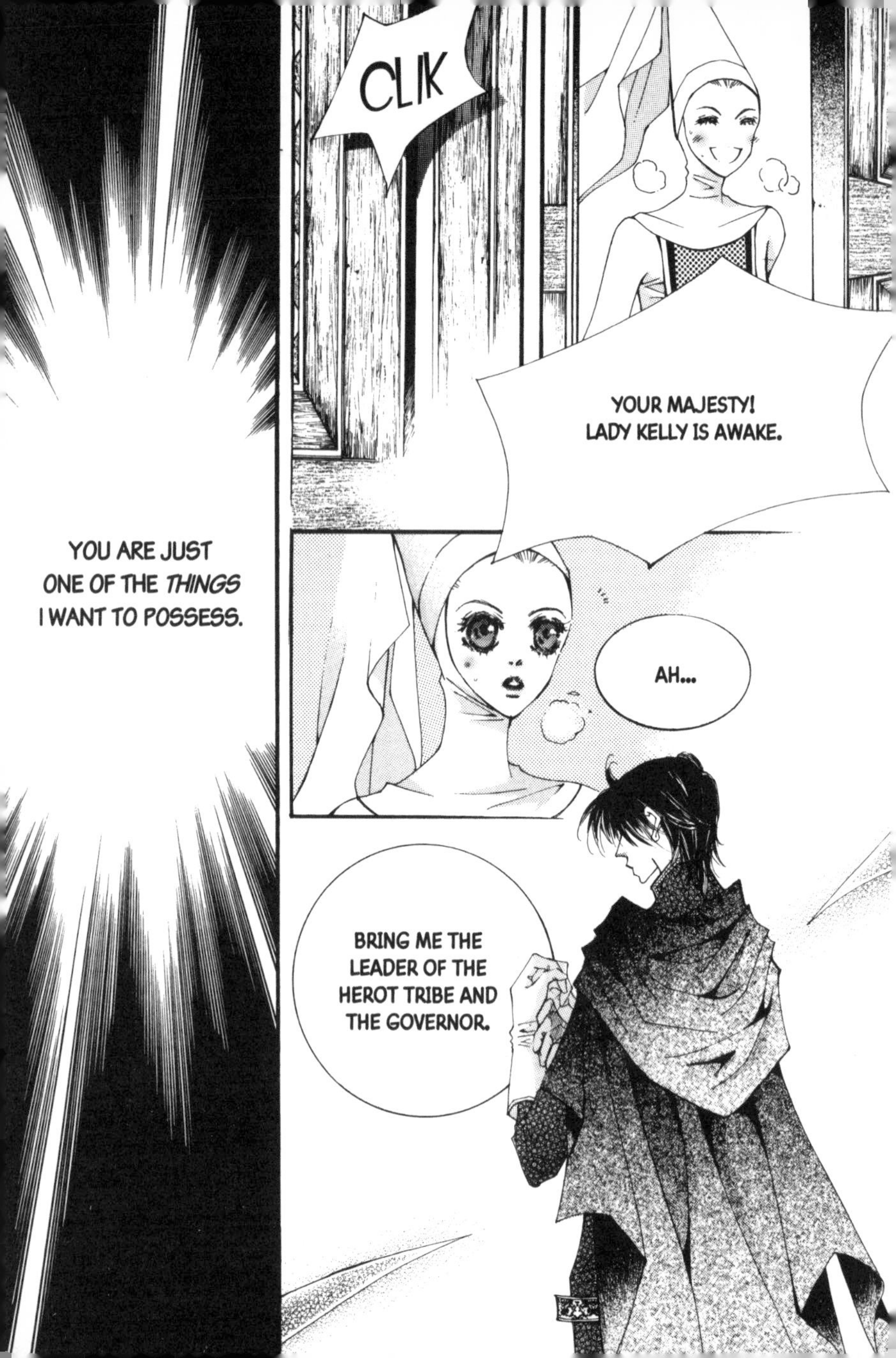
YOU ARE JUST ONE OF THE *THINGS* I WANT TO POSSESS.
CLIK
YOUR MAJESTY! LADY KELLY IS AWAKE.
AH...
BRING ME THE LEADER OF THE HEROT TRIBE AND THE GOVERNOR.

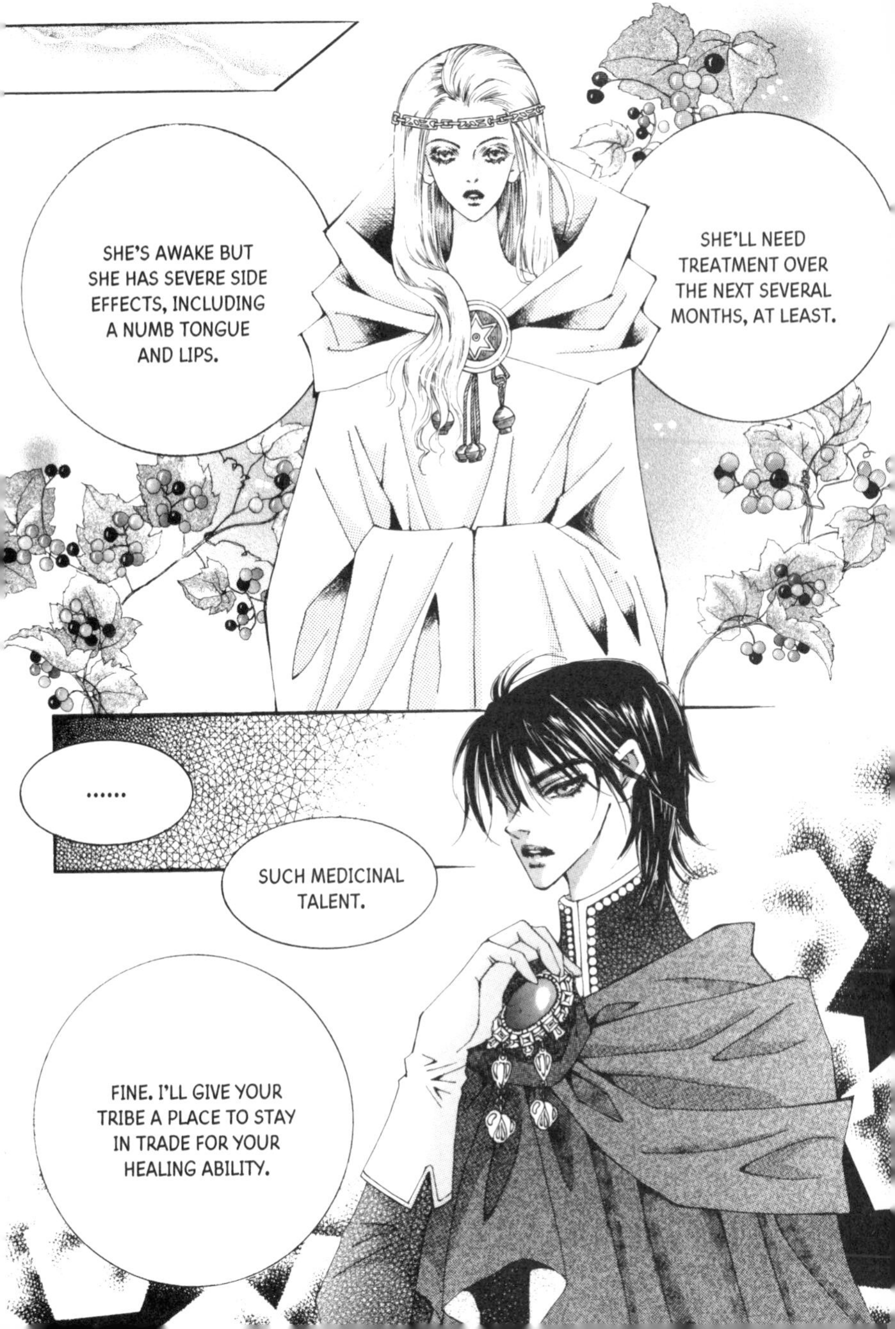
SHE'S AWAKE BUT SHE HAS SEVERE SIDE EFFECTS, INCLUDING A NUMB TONGUE AND LIPS.
SHE'LL NEED TREATMENT OVER THE NEXT SEVERAL MONTHS, AT LEAST.
......
SUCH MEDICINAL TALENT.
FINE. I'LL GIVE YOUR TRIBE A PLACE TO STAY IN TRADE FOR YOUR HEALING ABILITY.

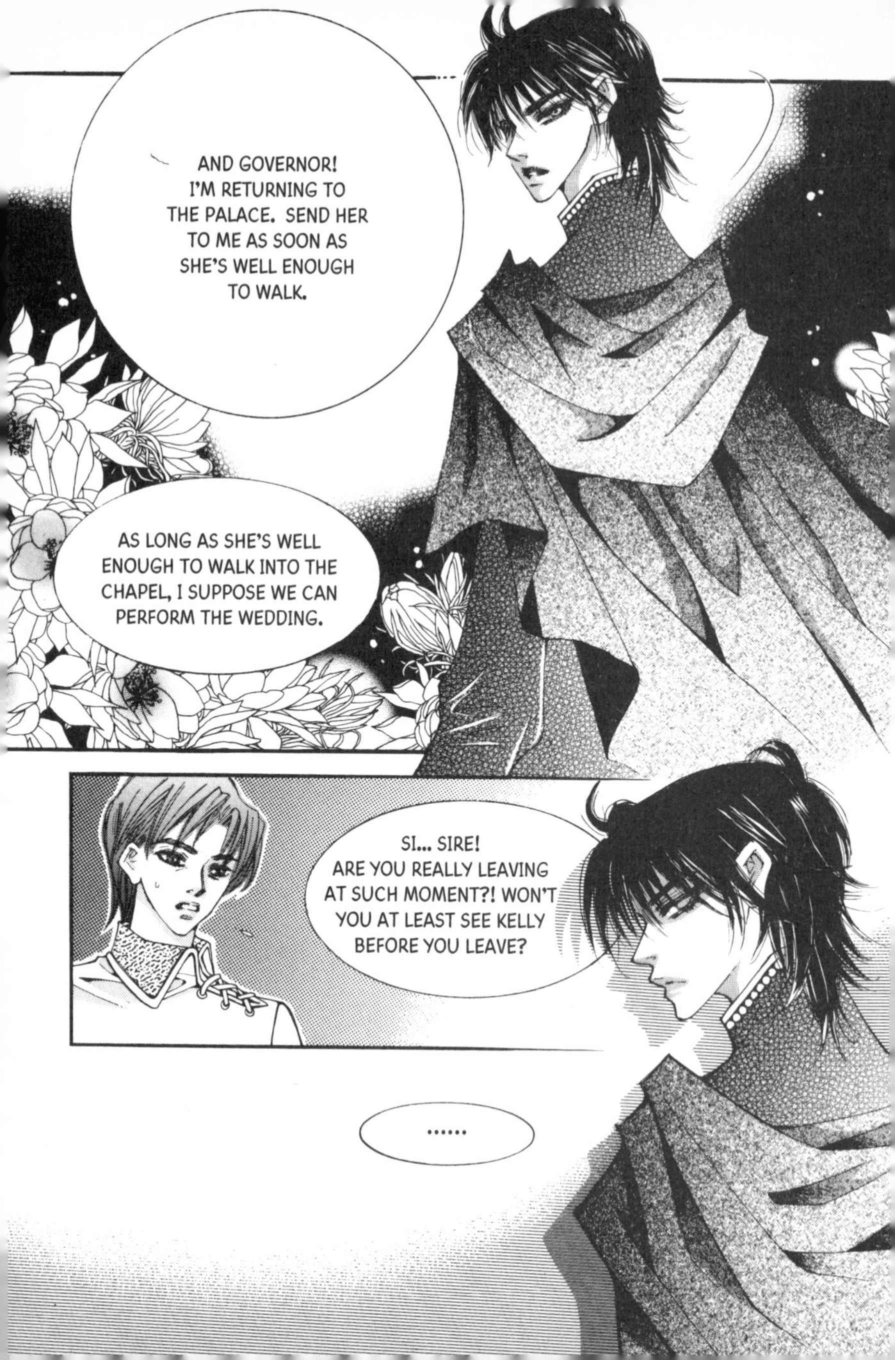
AND GOVERNOR! I'M RETURNING TO THE PALACE. SEND HER TO ME AS SOON AS SHE'S WELL ENOUGH TO WALK.
AS LONG AS SHE'S WELL ENOUGH TO WALK INTO THE CHAPEL, I SUPPOSE WE CAN PERFORM THE WEDDING.
SI... SIRE! ARE YOU REALLY LEAVING AT SUCH MOMENT?! WON'T YOU AT LEAST SEE KELLY BEFORE YOU LEAVE?
......

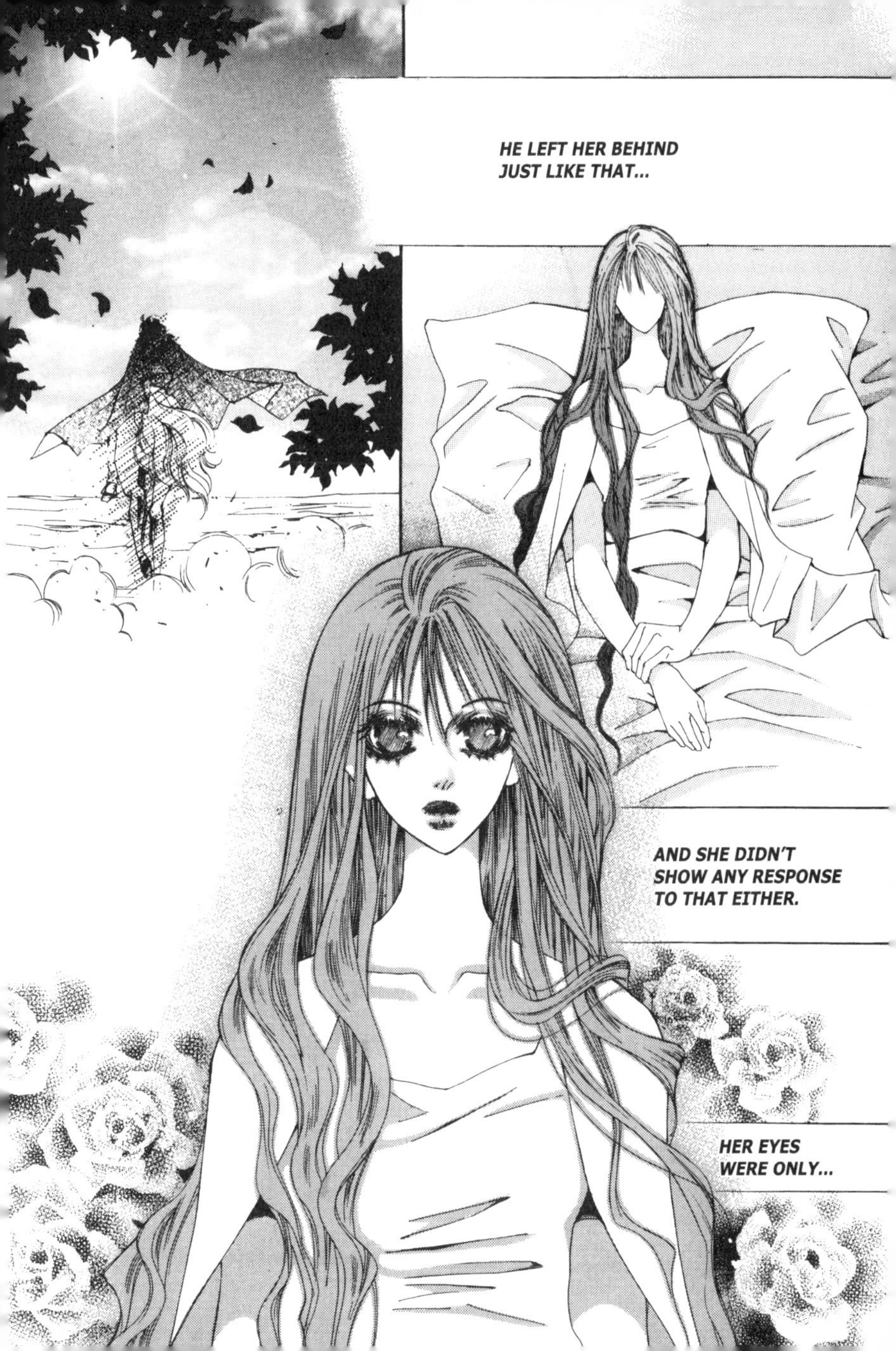
HE LEFT HER BEHIND JUST LIKE THAT...
AND SHE DIDN'T SHOW ANY RESPONSE TO THAT EITHER.
HER EYES WERE ONLY...

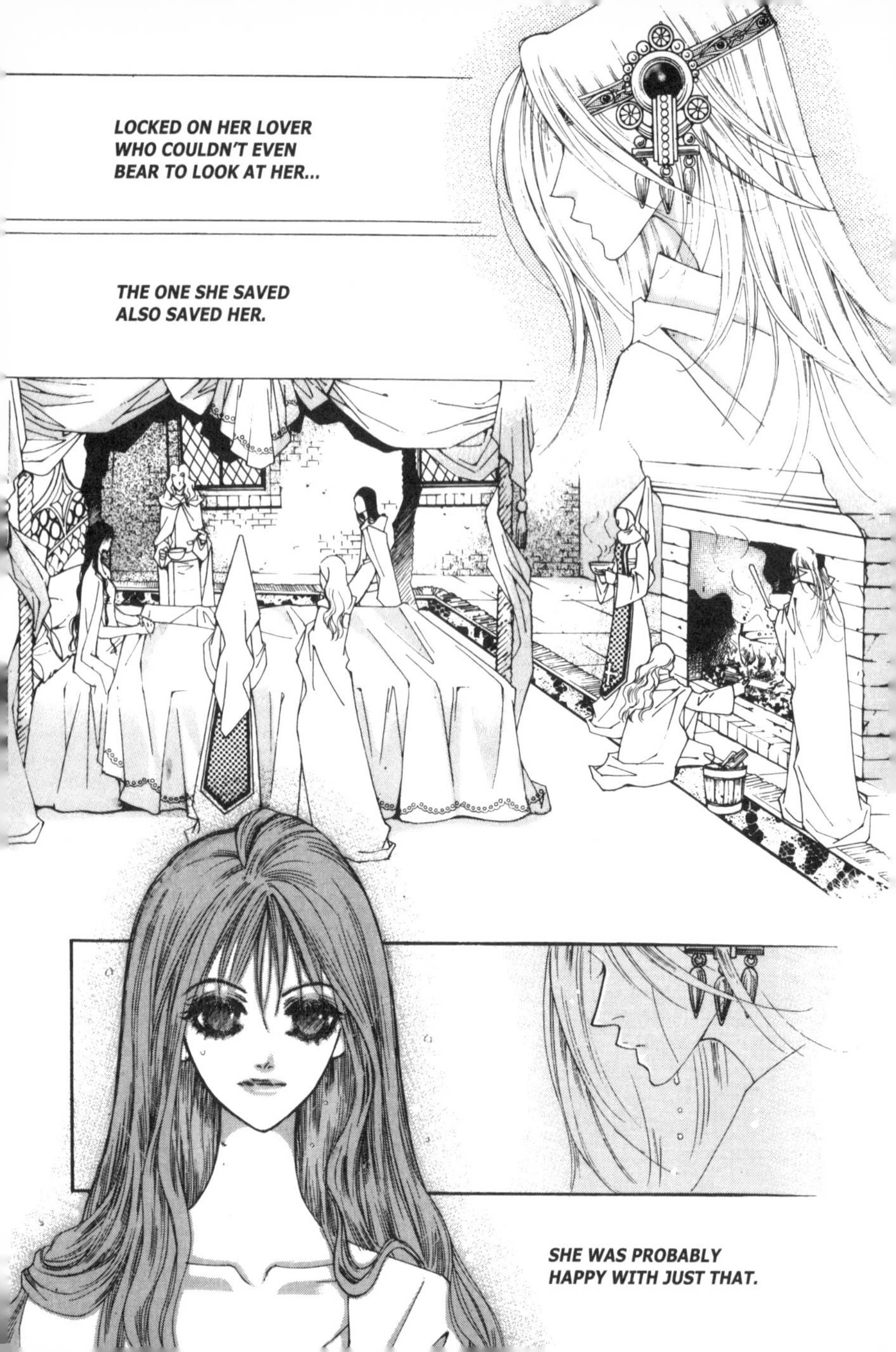
LOCKED ON HER LOVER WHO COULDN'T EVEN BEAR TO LOOK AT HER...
THE ONE SHE SAVED ALSO SAVED HER.
SHE WAS PROBABLY HAPPY WITH JUST THAT.

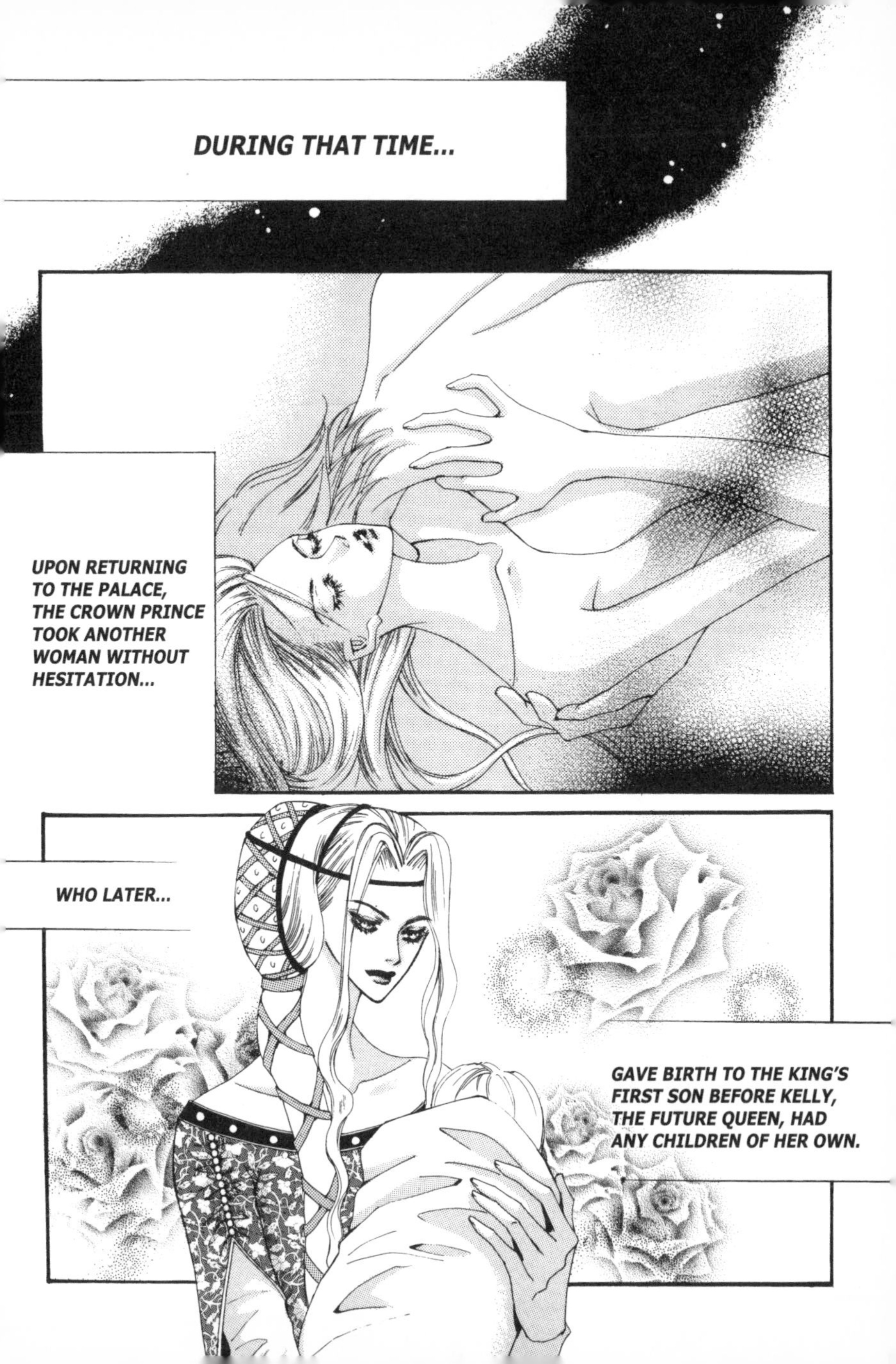
DURING THAT TIME...
UPON RETURNING TO THE PALACE, THE CROWN PRINCE TOOK ANOTHER WOMAN WITHOUT HESITATION...
WHO LATER...
GAVE BIRTH TO THE KING'S FIRST SON BEFORE KELLY, THE FUTURE QUEEN, HAD ANY CHILDREN OF HER OWN.

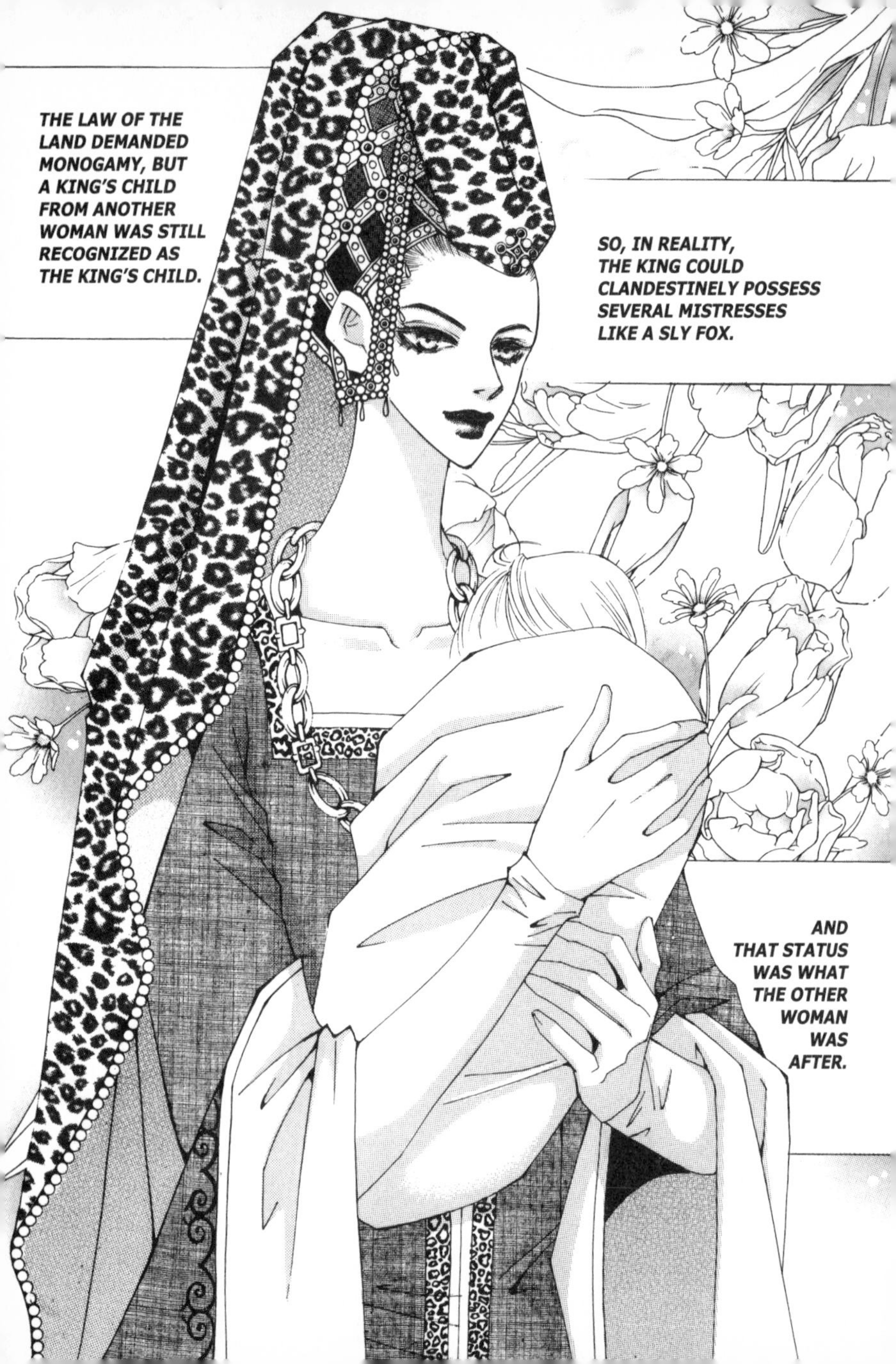
THE LAW OF THE LAND DEMANDED MONOGAMY, BUT A KING'S CHILD FROM ANOTHER WOMAN WAS STILL RECOGNIZED AS THE KING'S CHILD.
SO, IN REALITY, THE KING COULD CLANDESTINELY POSSESS SEVERAL MISTRESSES LIKE A SLY FOX.
AND THAT STATUS WAS WHAT THE OTHER WOMAN WAS AFTER.

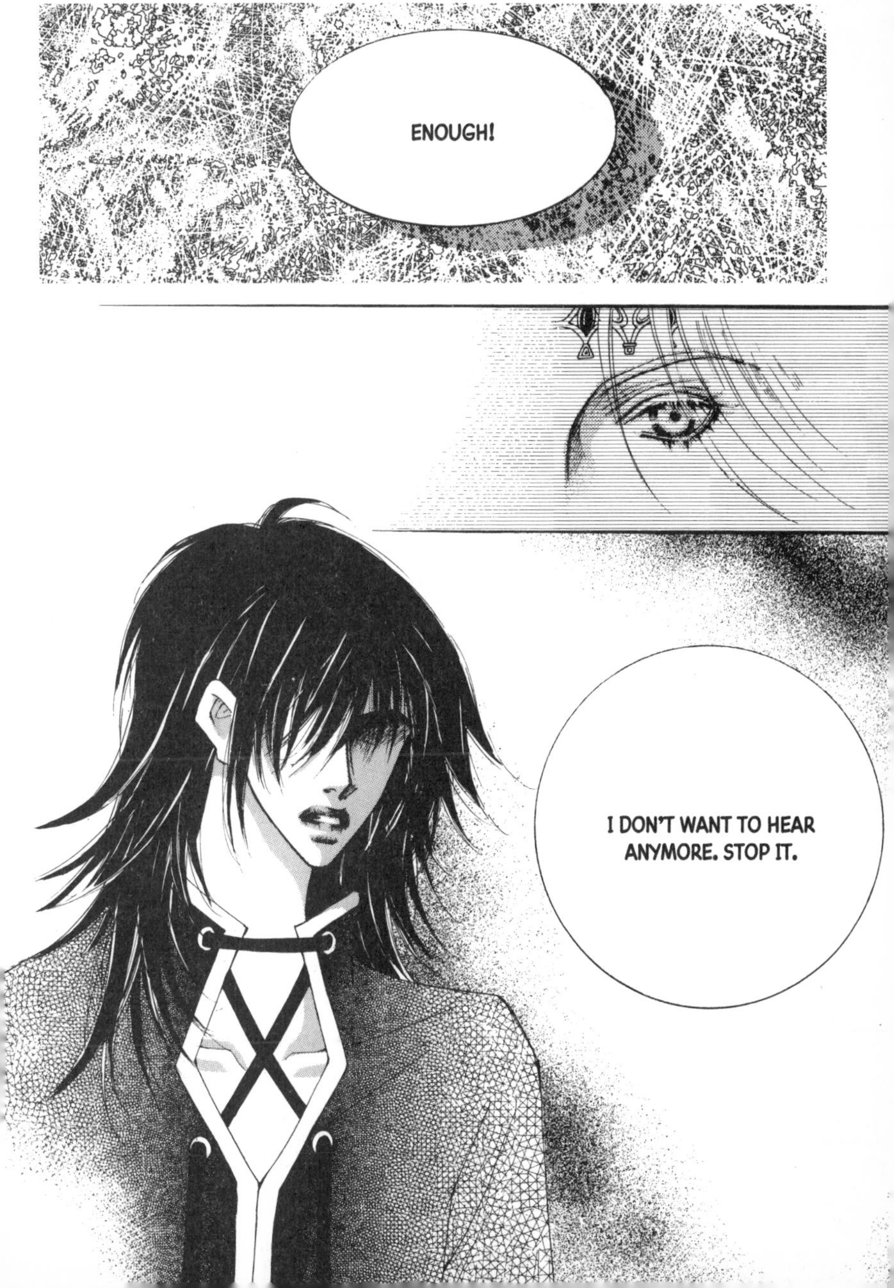
ENOUGH!
I DON'T WANT TO HEAR ANYMORE. STOP IT.

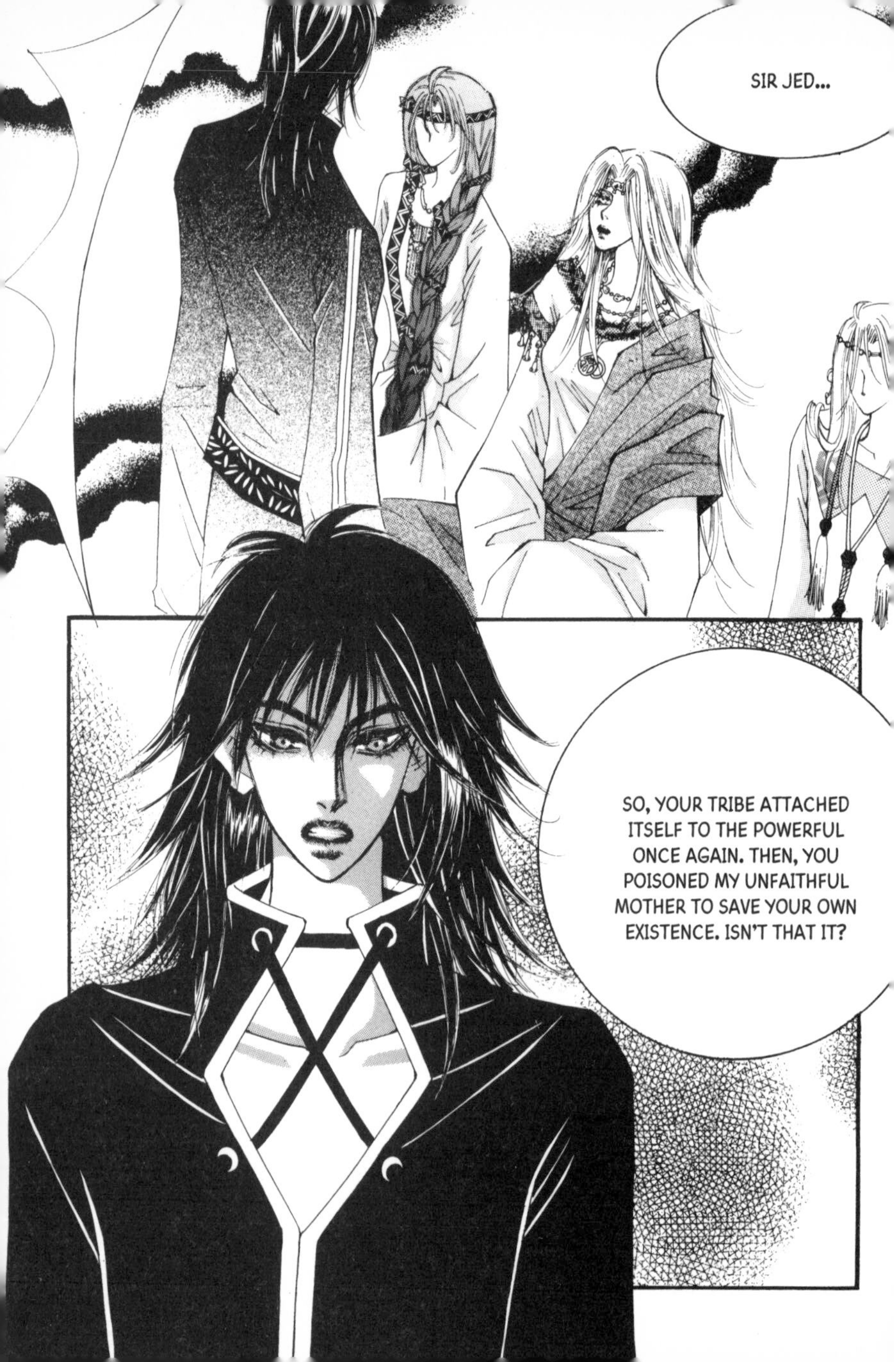
SIR JED...
SO, YOUR TRIBE ATTACHED ITSELF TO THE POWERFUL ONCE AGAIN. THEN, YOU POISONED MY UNFAITHFUL MOTHER TO SAVE YOUR OWN EXISTENCE. ISN'T THAT IT?

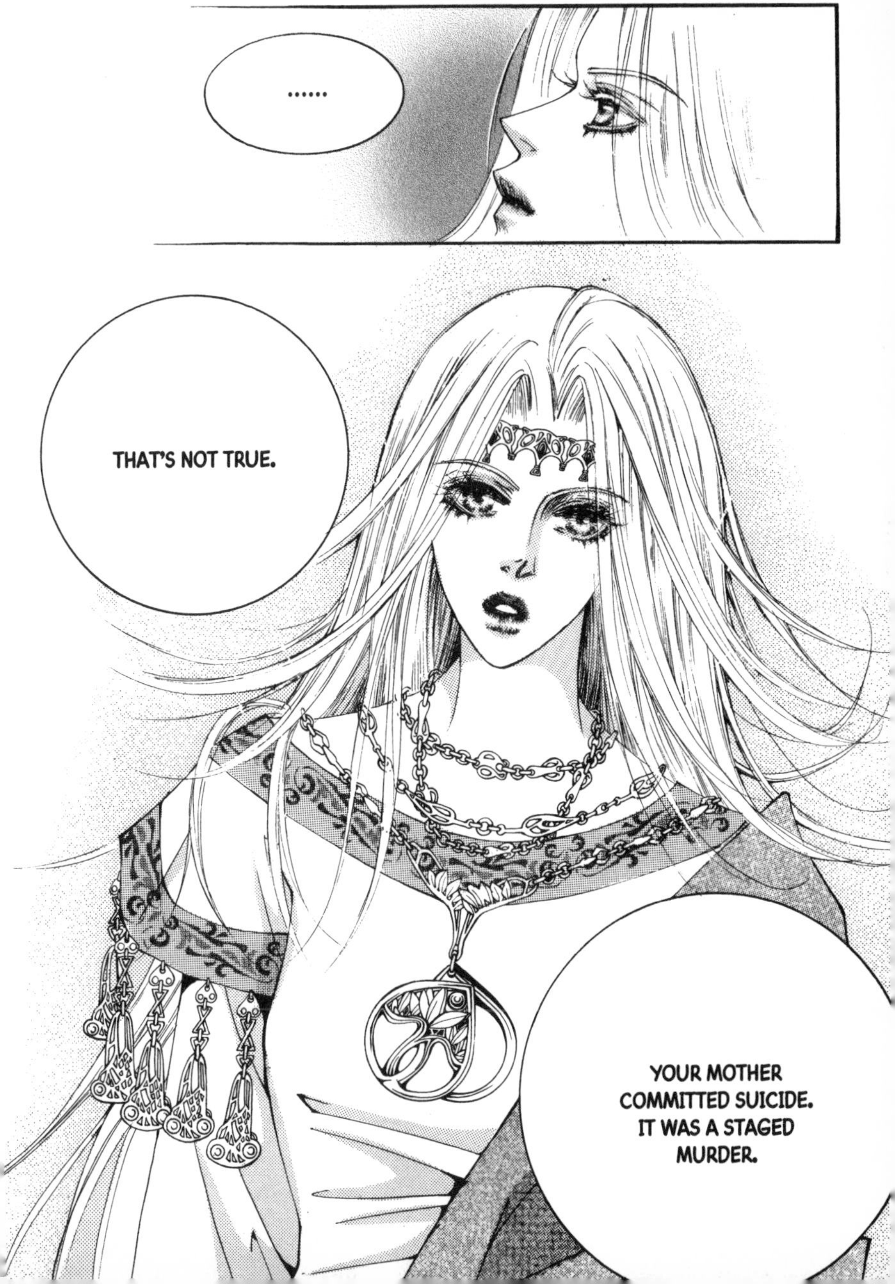
......
THAT'S NOT TRUE.
YOUR MOTHER COMMITTED SUICIDE. IT WAS A STAGED MURDER.

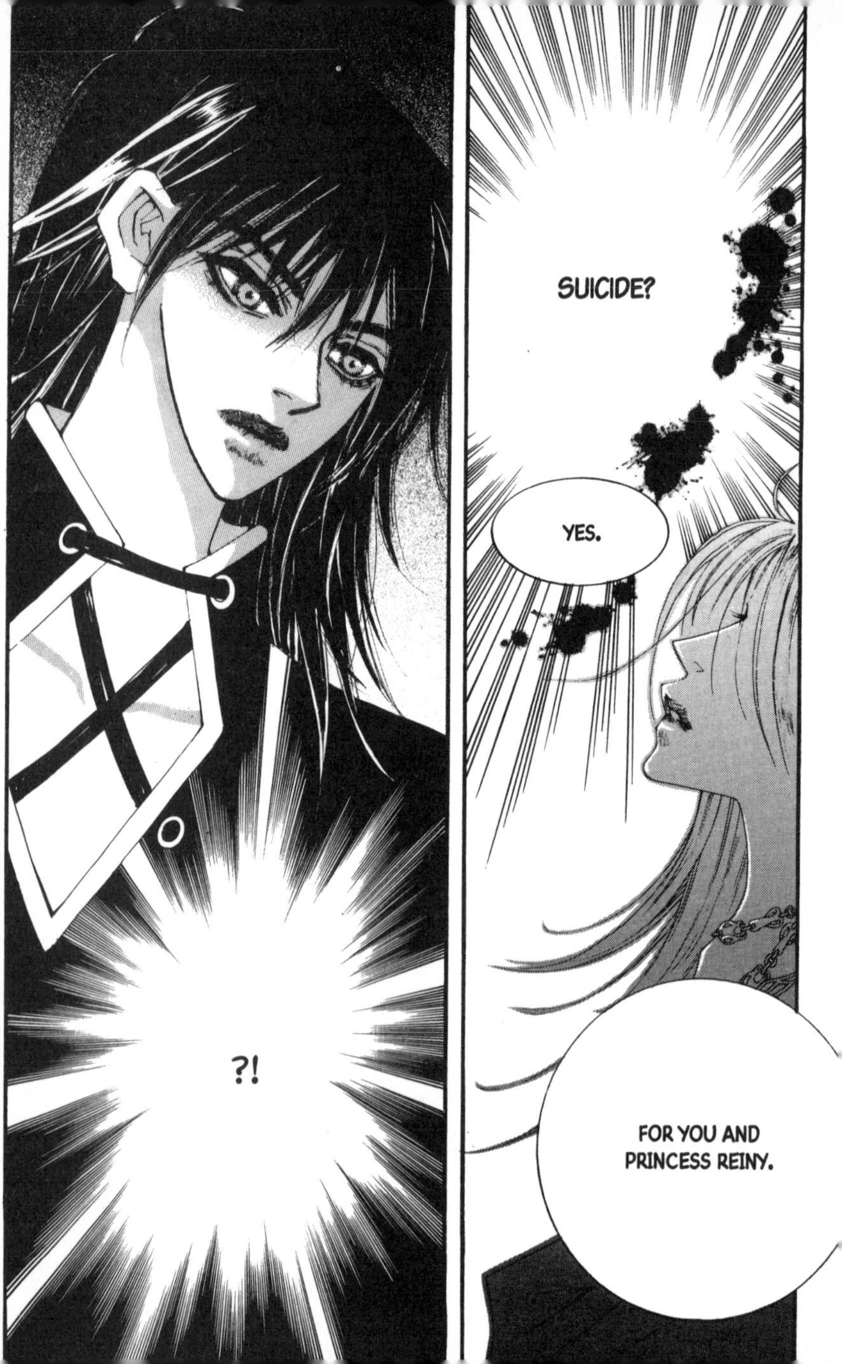
?!
SUICIDE?
YES.
FOR YOU AND PRINCESS REINY.

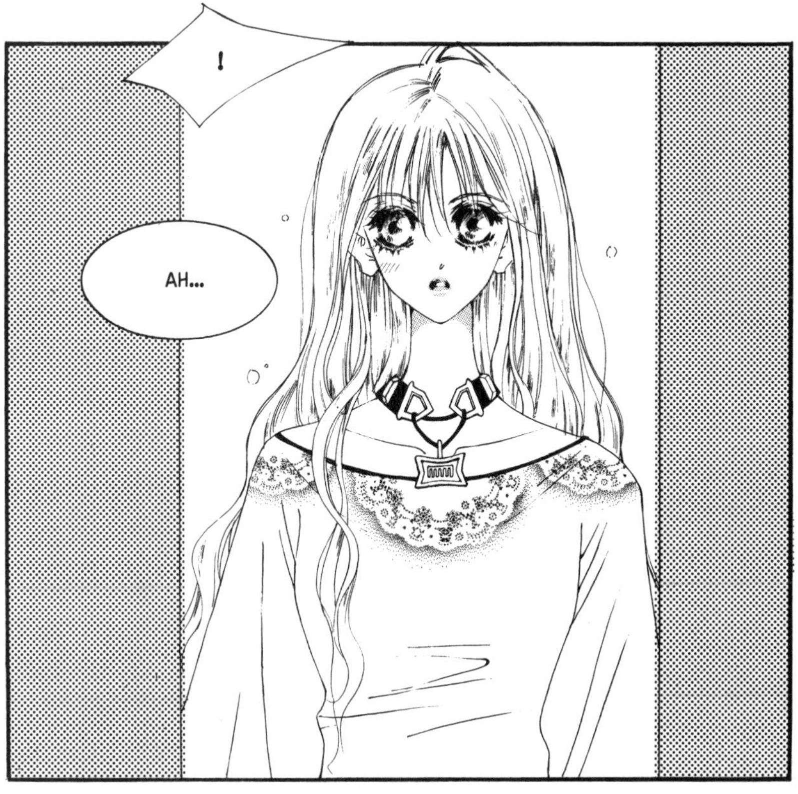
!
AH...

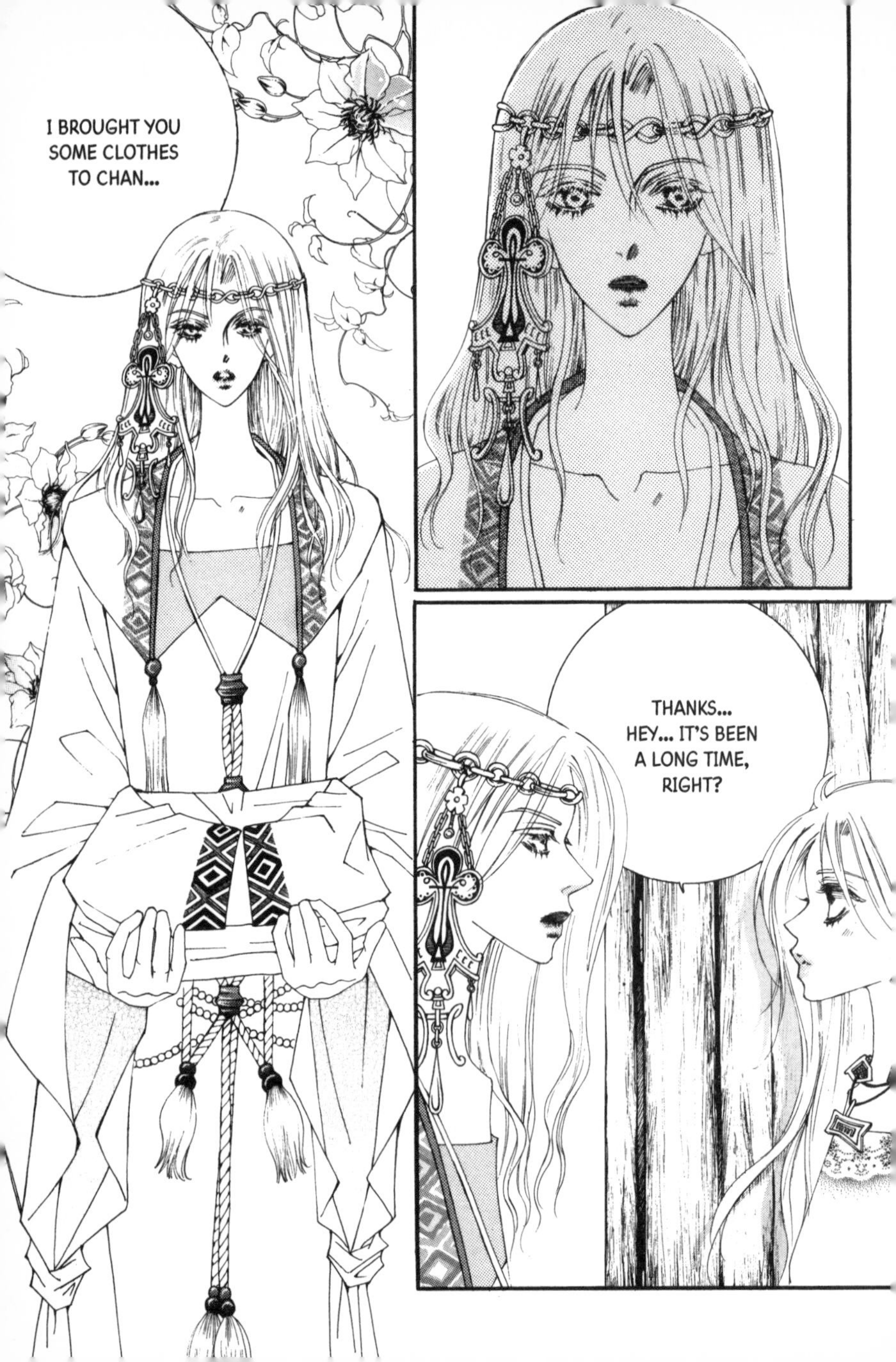
I BROUGHT YOU SOME CLOTHES TO CHAN...
THANKS... HEY... IT'S BEEN A LONG TIME, RIGHT?

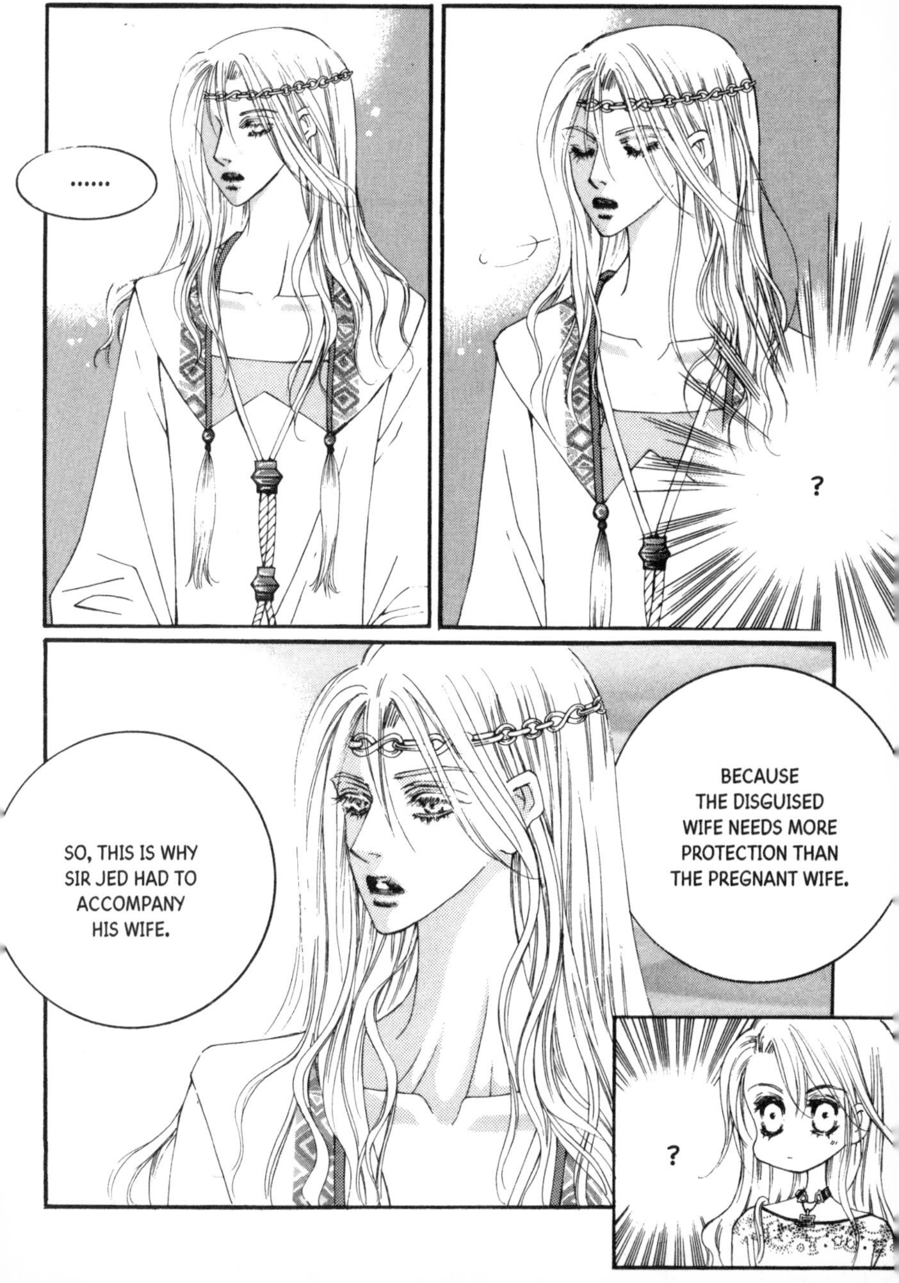

......
?
SO, THIS IS WHY SIR JED HAD TO ACCOMPANY HIS WIFE.
BECAUSE THE DISGUISED WIFE NEEDS MORE PROTECTION THAN THE PREGNANT WIFE.
?

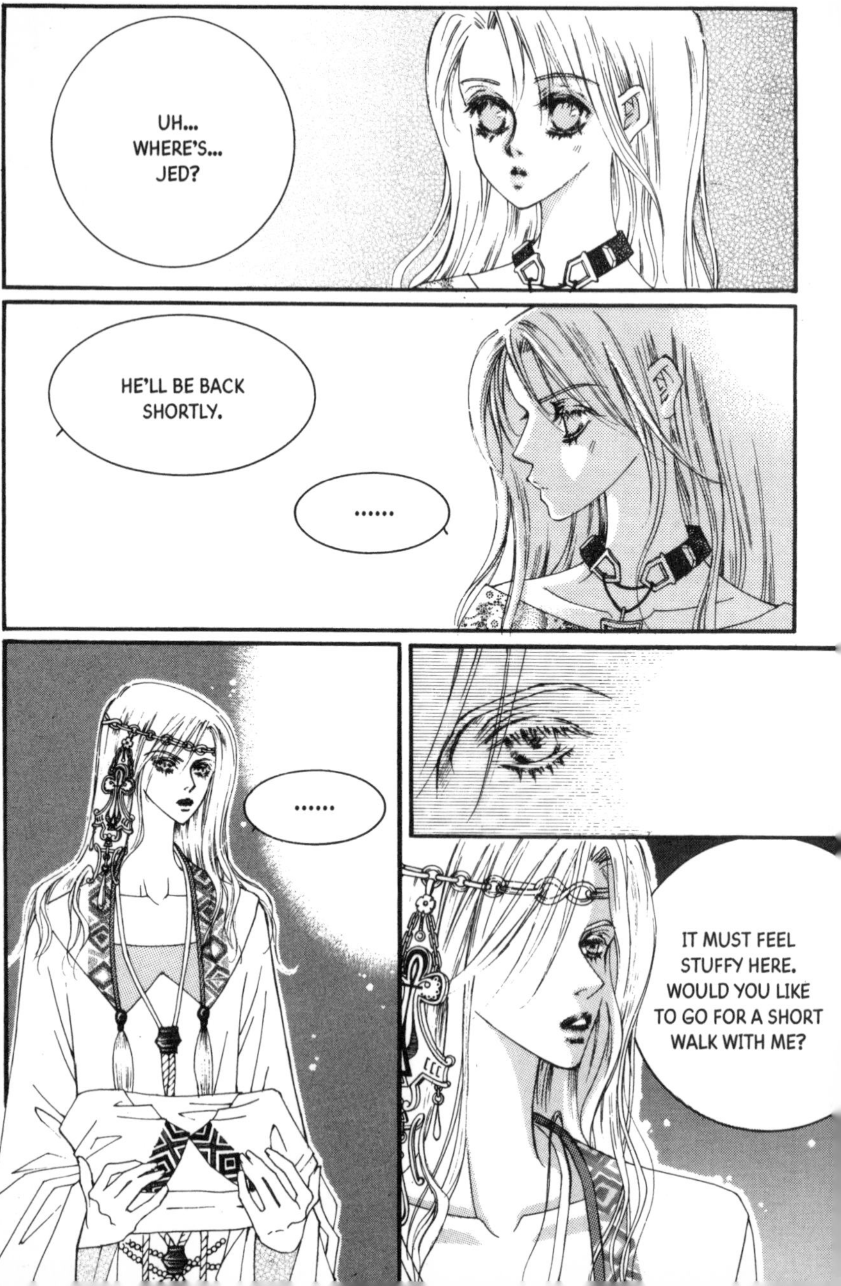
UH... WHERE'S... JED?
HE'LL BE BACK SHORTLY.
......
......
IT MUST FEEL STUFFY HERE. WOULD YOU LIKE TO GO FOR A SHORT WALK WITH ME?

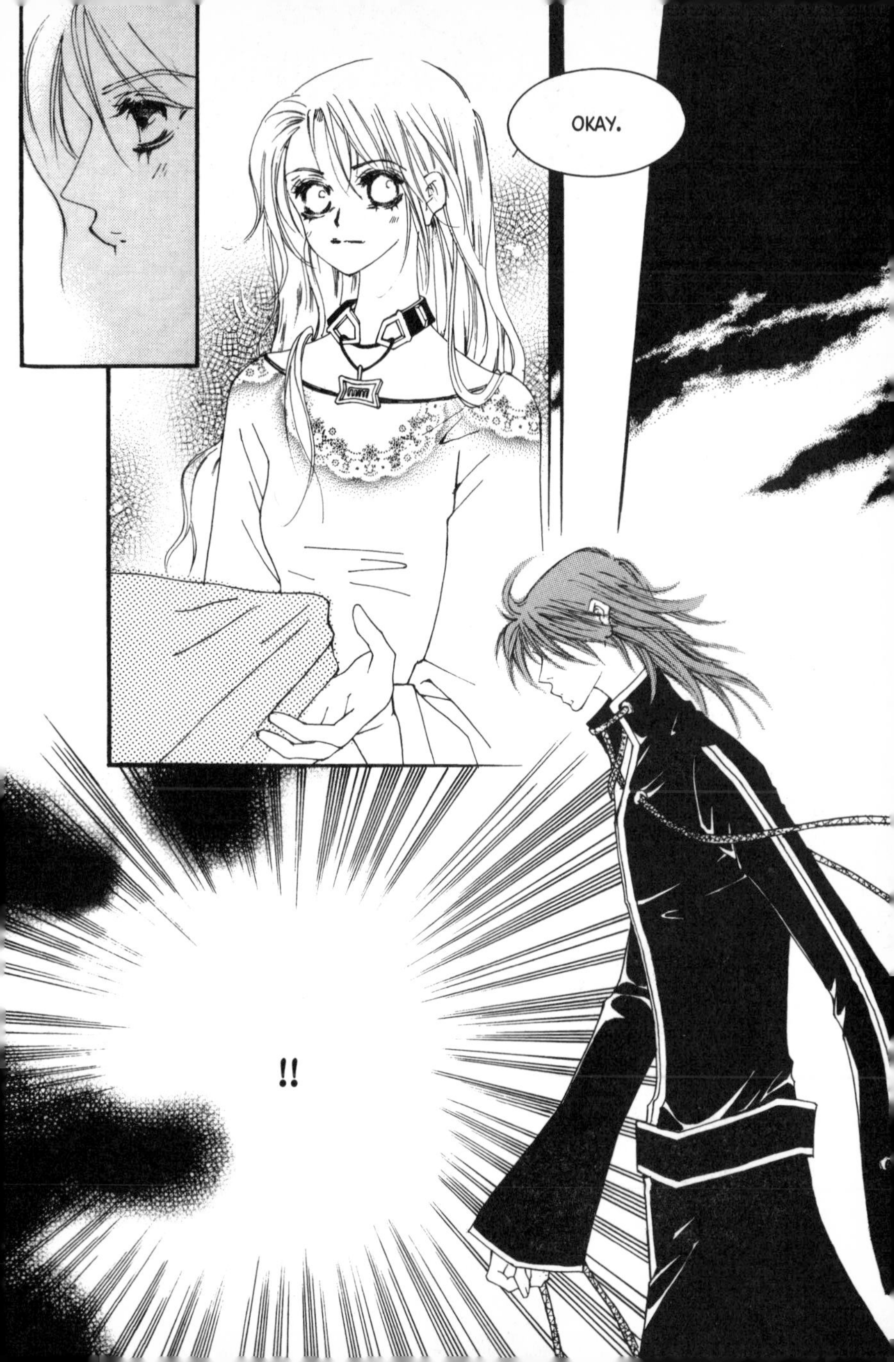
OKAY.
!!

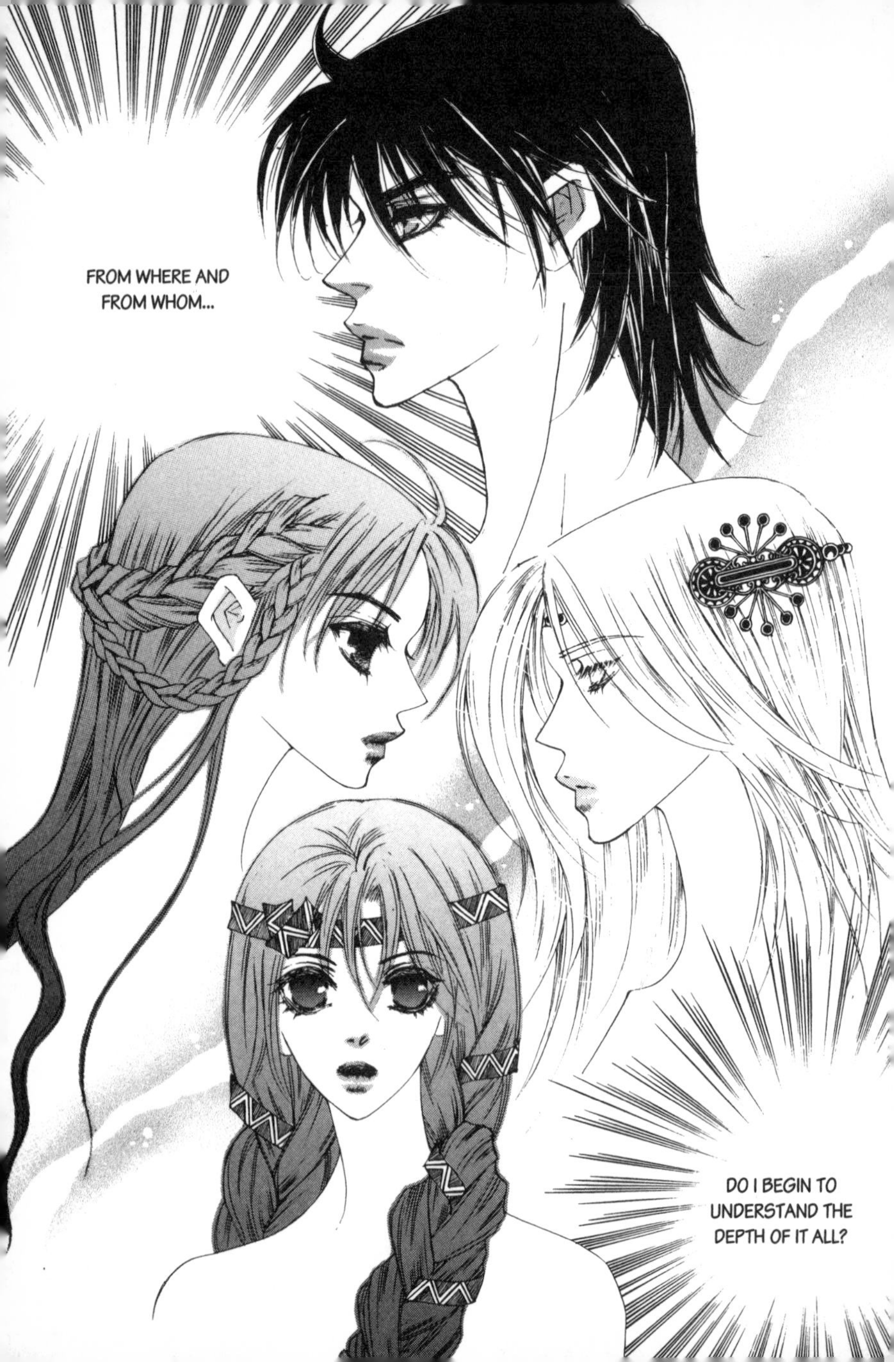
FROM WHERE AND FROM WHOM...
DO I BEGIN TO UNDERSTAND THE DEPTH OF IT ALL?

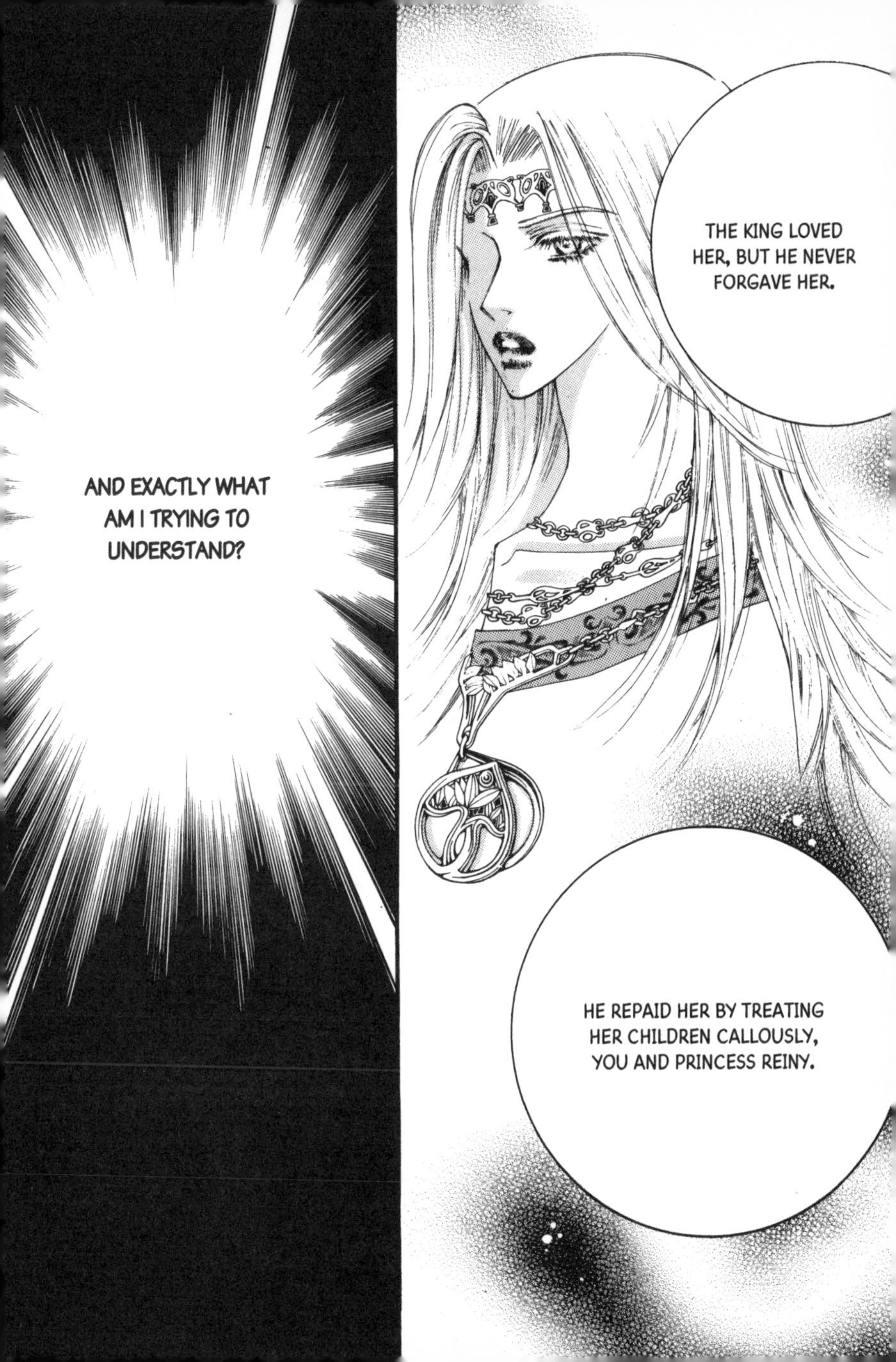
AND EXACTLY WHAT AM I TRYING TO UNDERSTAND?
THE KING LOVED HER, BUT HE NEVER FORGAVE HER.
HE REPAID HER BY TREATING HER CHILDREN CALLOUSLY, YOU AND PRINCESS REINY.

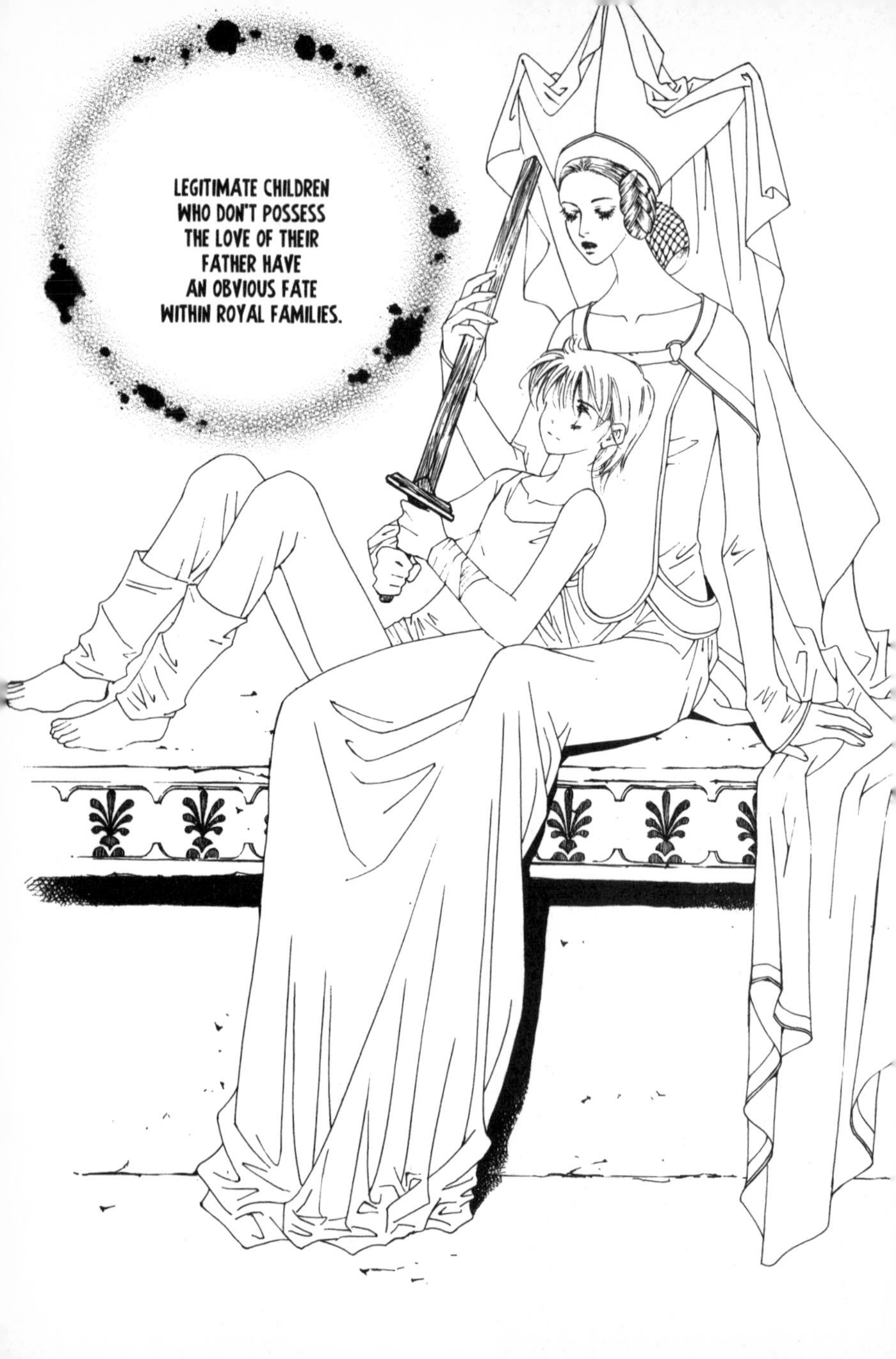
LEGITIMATE CHILDREN WHO DON'T POSSESS THE LOVE OF THEIR FATHER HAVE AN OBVIOUS FATE WITHIN ROYAL FAMILIES.

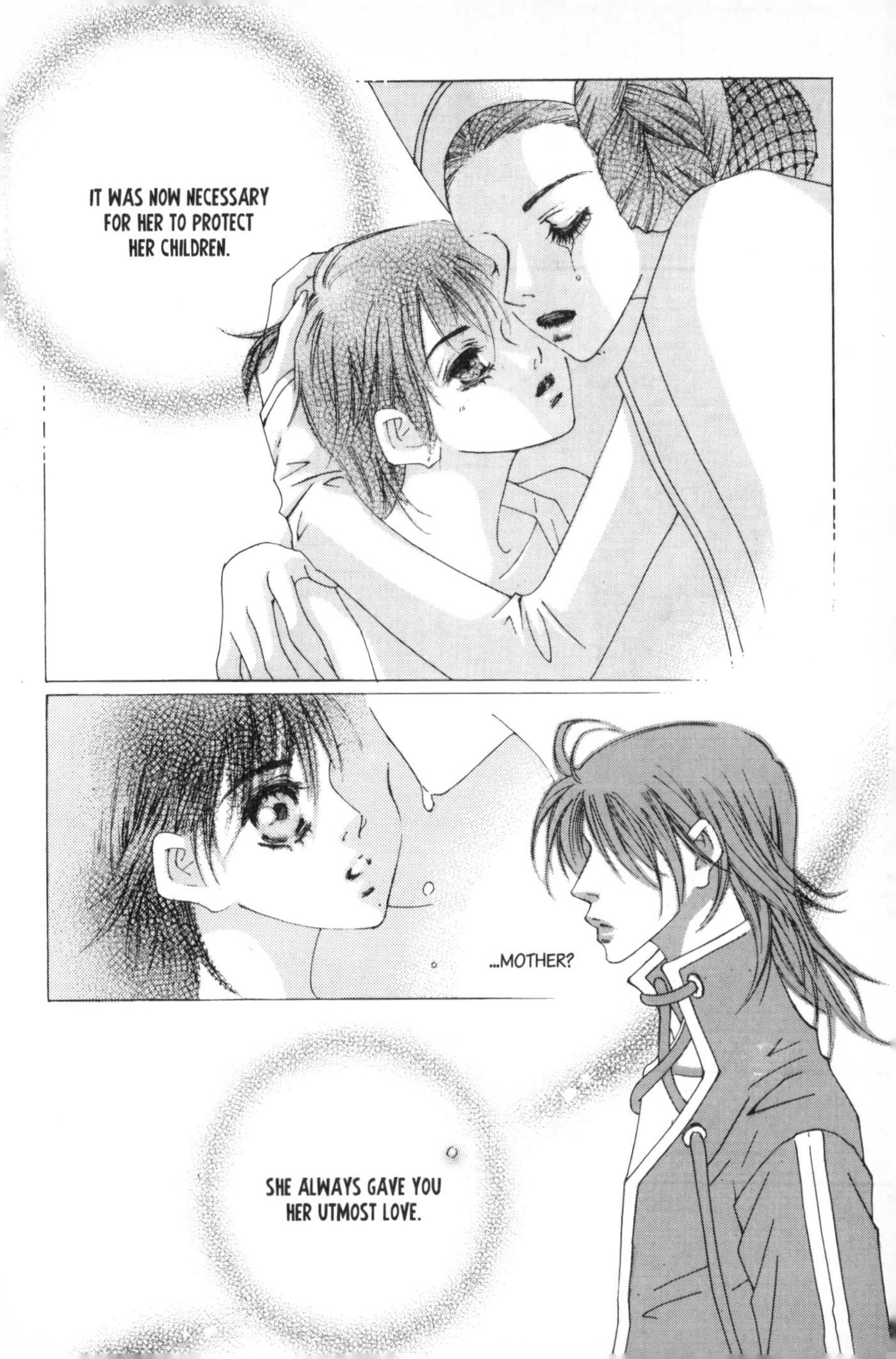
IT WAS NOW NECESSARY FOR HER TO PROTECT HER CHILDREN.
...MOTHER?
SHE ALWAYS GAVE YOU HER UTMOST LOVE.

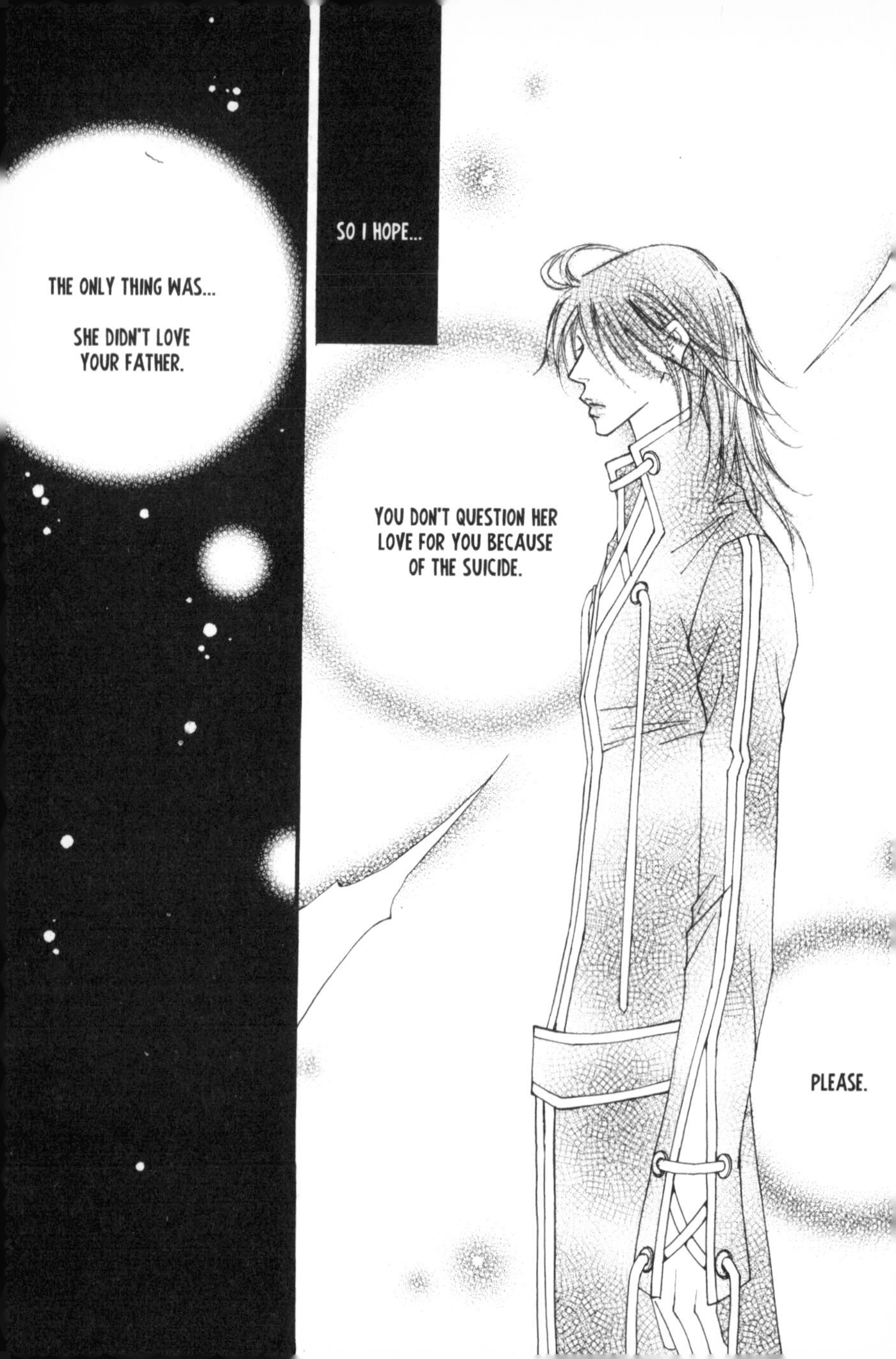
THE ONLY THING WAS...
SHE DIDN'T LOVE YOUR FATHER.
SO I HOPE...
YOU DON'T QUESTION HER LOVE FOR YOU BECAUSE OF THE SUICIDE.
PLEASE.

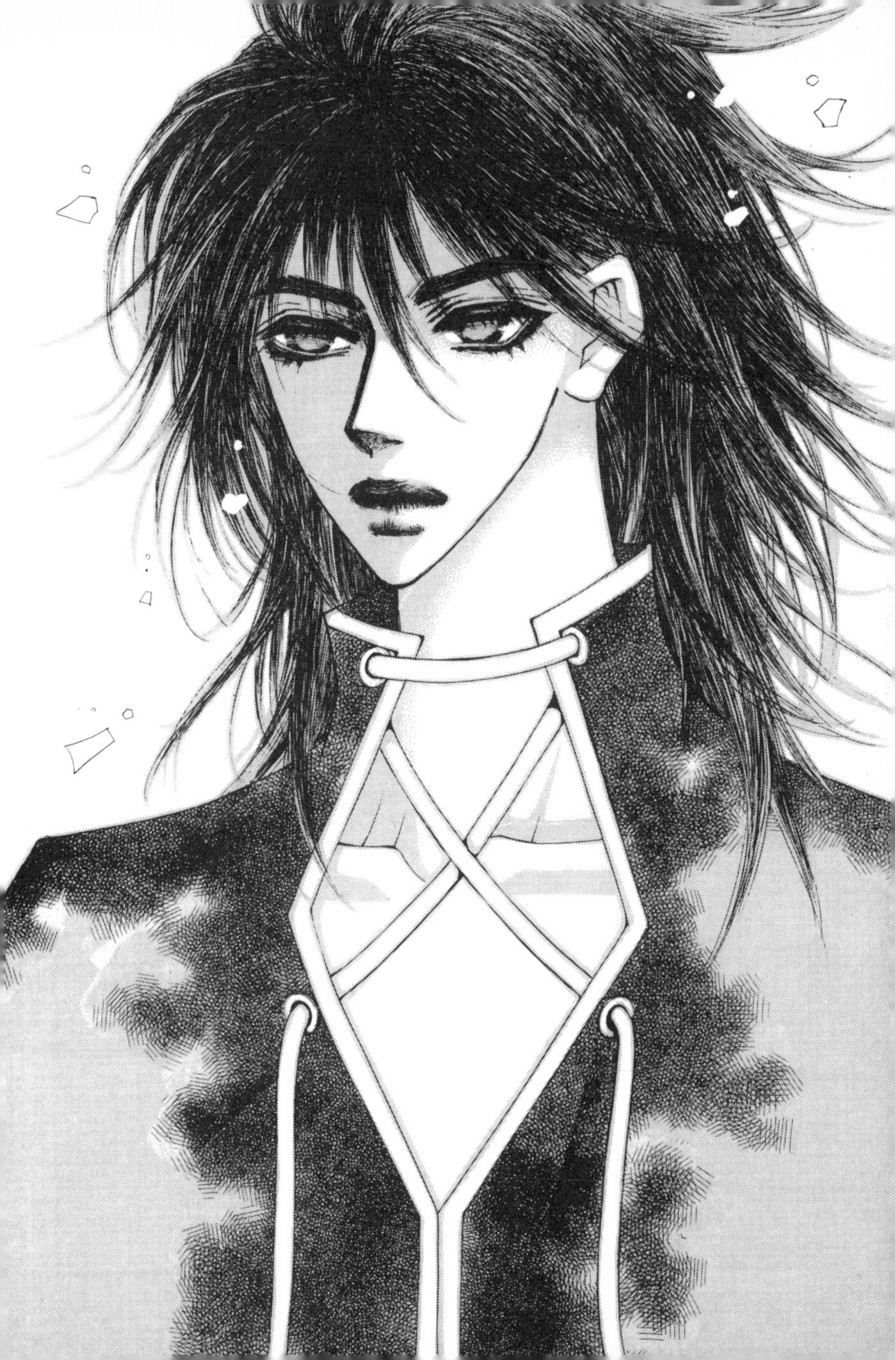

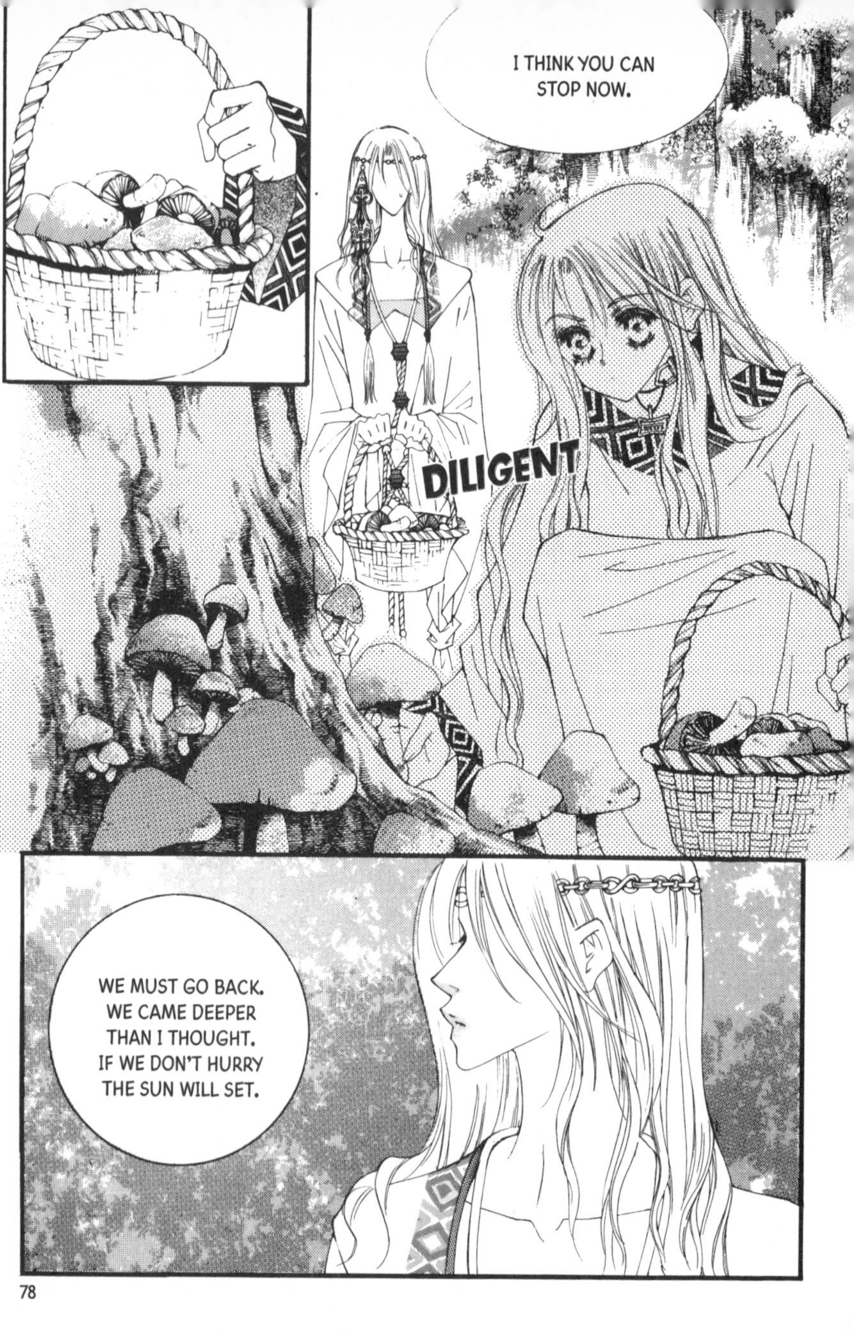
I THINK YOU CAN STOP NOW.
DILIGENT
WE MUST GO BACK. WE CAME DEEPER THAN I THOUGHT. IF WE DON'T HURRY THE SUN WILL SET.

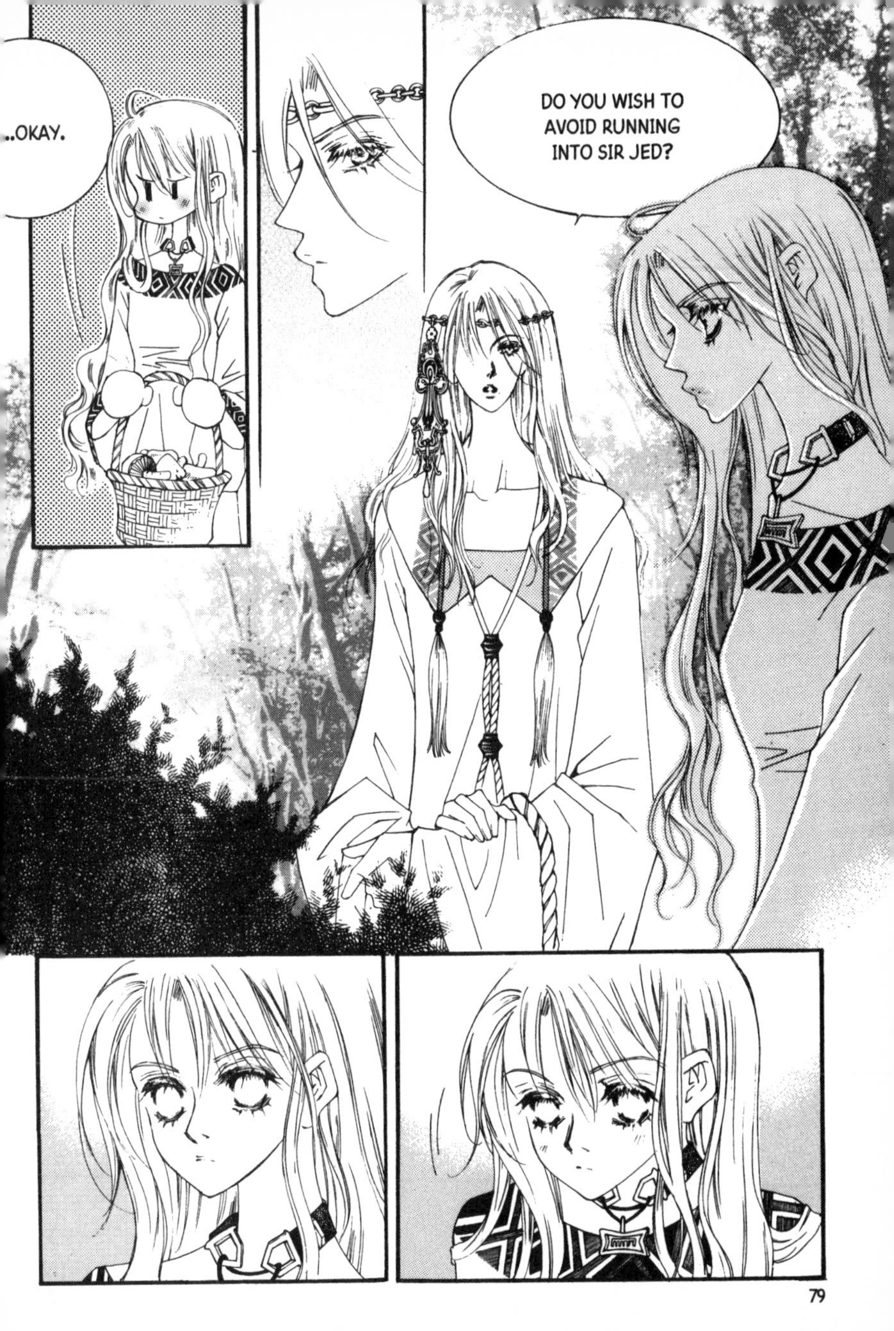
..OKAY.
DO YOU WISH TO AVOID RUNNING INTO SIR JED?

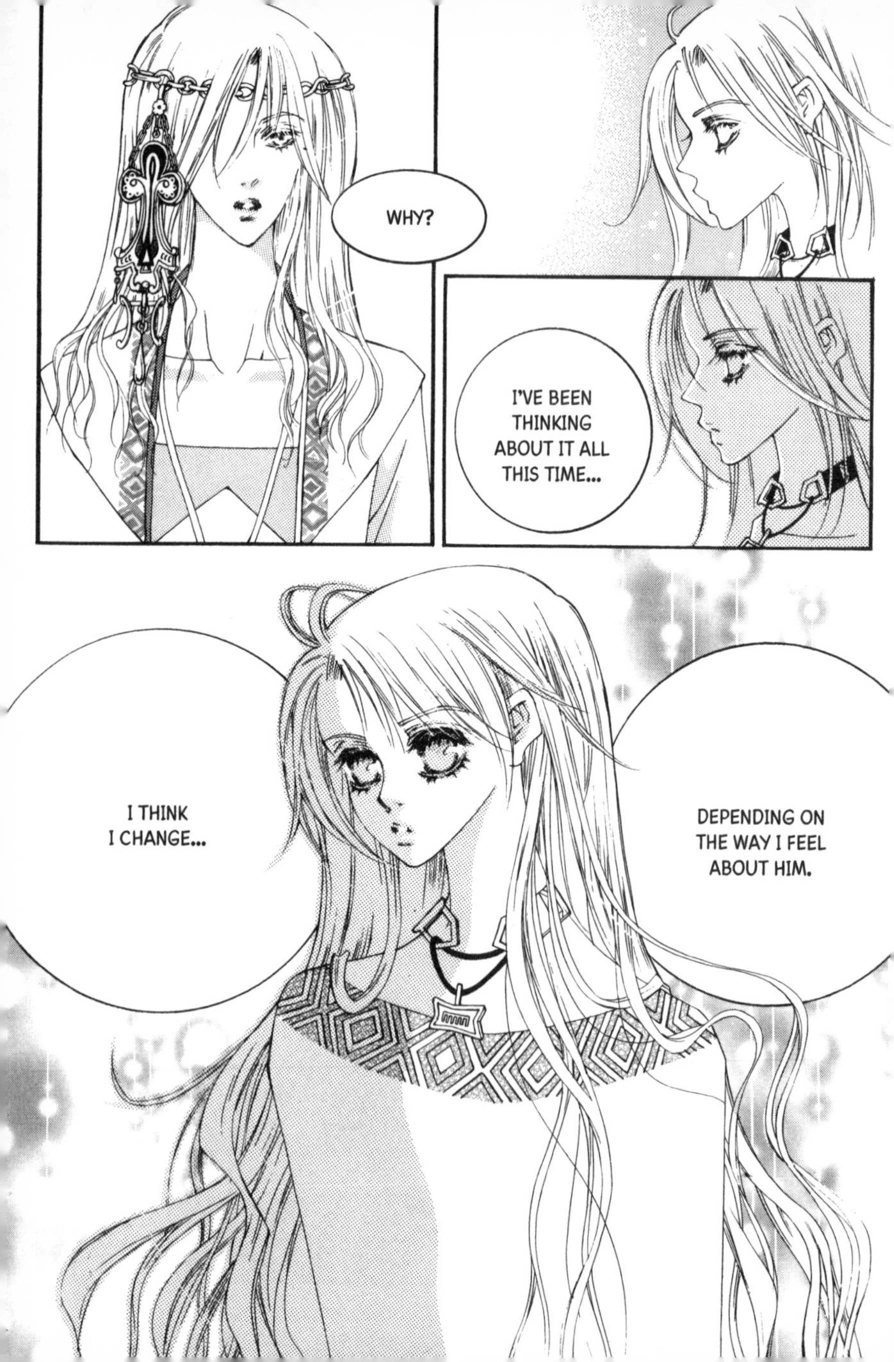
WHY?
I'VE BEEN THINKING ABOUT IT ALL THIS TIME...
I THINK I CHANGE...
DEPENDING ON THE WAY I FEEL ABOUT HIM.

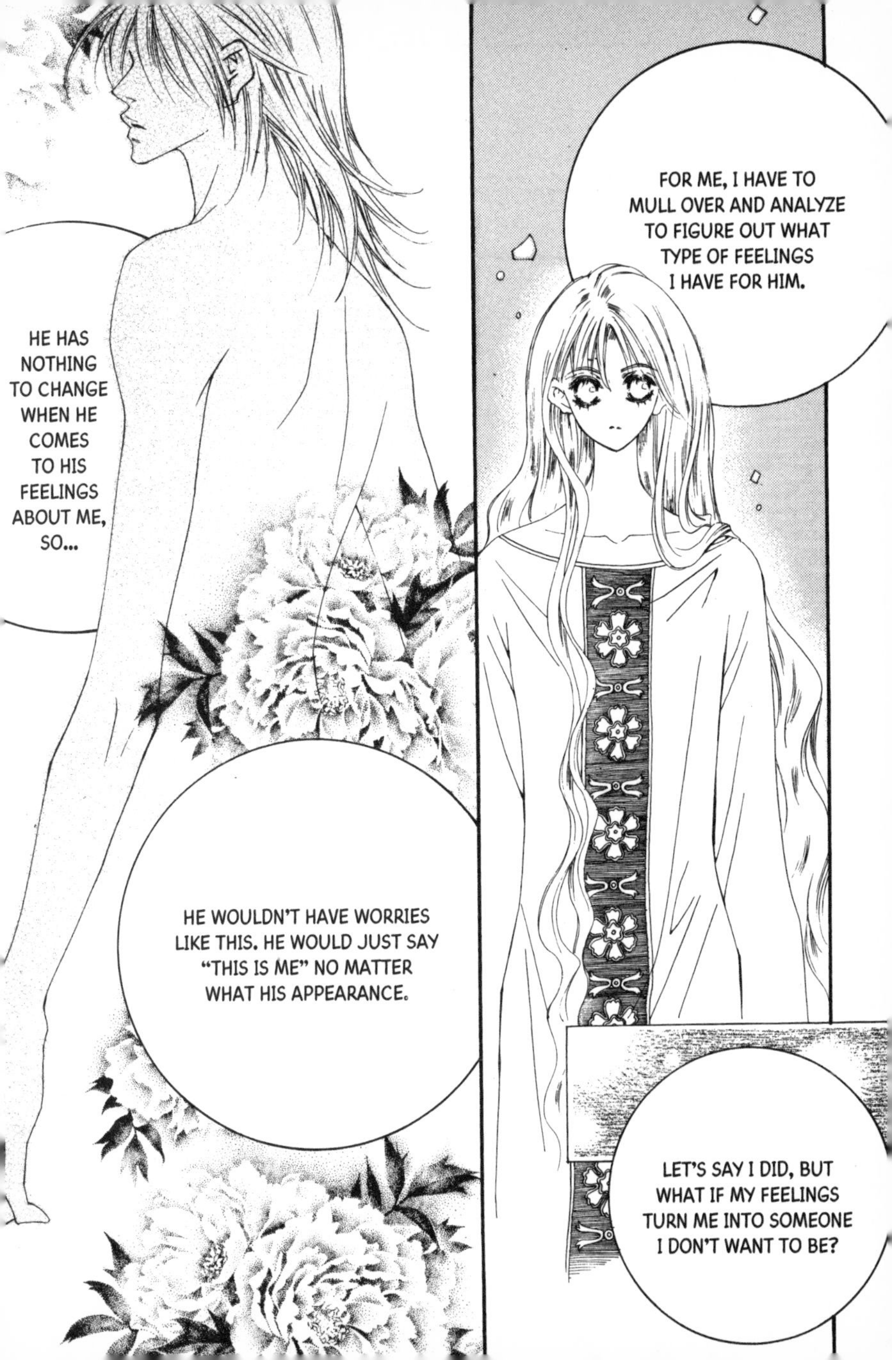
HE HAS NOTHING TO CHANGE WHEN HE COMES TO HIS FEELINGS ABOUT ME, SO...
HE WOULDN'T HAVE WORRIES LIKE THIS. HE WOULD JUST SAY "THIS IS ME" NO MATTER WHAT HIS APPEARANCE.
FOR ME, I HAVE TO MULL OVER AND ANALYZE TO FIGURE OUT WHAT TYPE OF FEELINGS I HAVE FOR HIM.
LET'S SAY I DID, BUT WHAT IF MY FEELINGS TURN ME INTO SOMEONE I DON'T WANT TO BE?

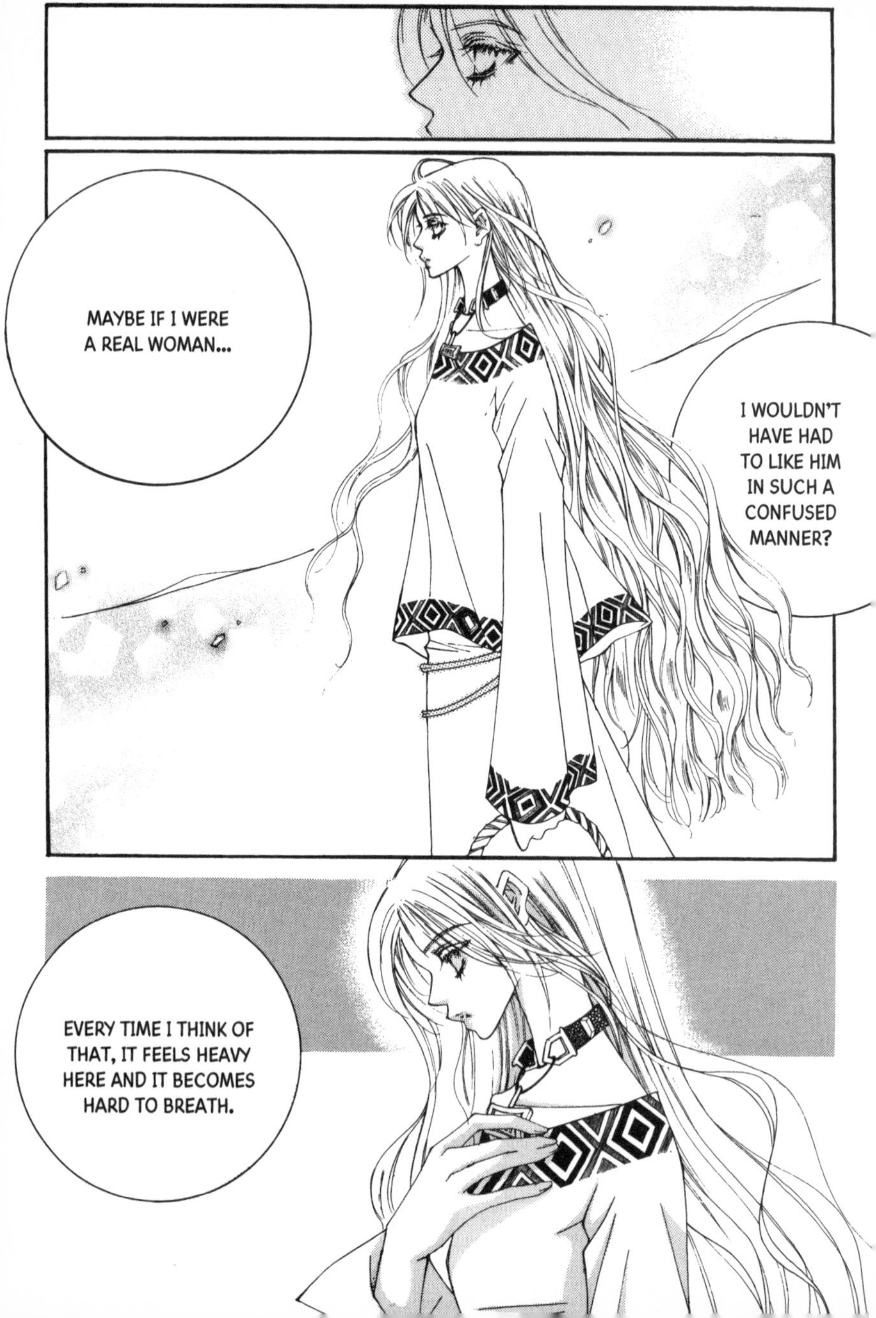
MAYBE IF I WERE A REAL WOMAN...
I WOULDN'T HAVE HAD TO LIKE HIM IN SUCH A CONFUSED MANNER?
EVERY TIME I THINK OF THAT, IT FEELS HEAVY HERE AND IT BECOMES HARD TO BREATH.

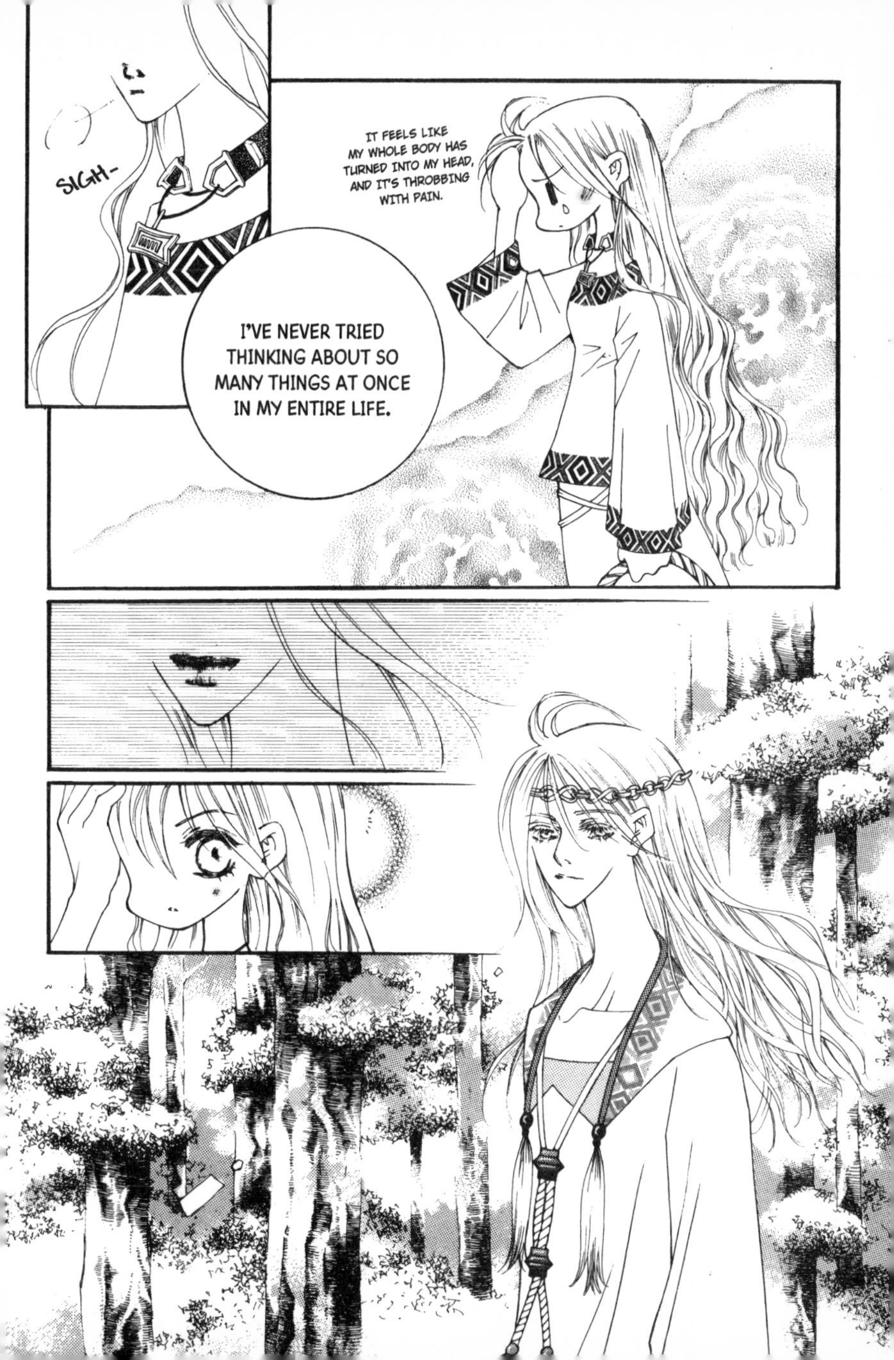
SIGH-
IT FEELS LIKE MY WHOLE BODY HAS TURNED INTO MY HEAD, AND IT'S THROBBING WITH PAIN.
I'VE NEVER TRIED THINKING ABOUT SO MANY THINGS AT ONCE IN MY ENTIRE LIFE.

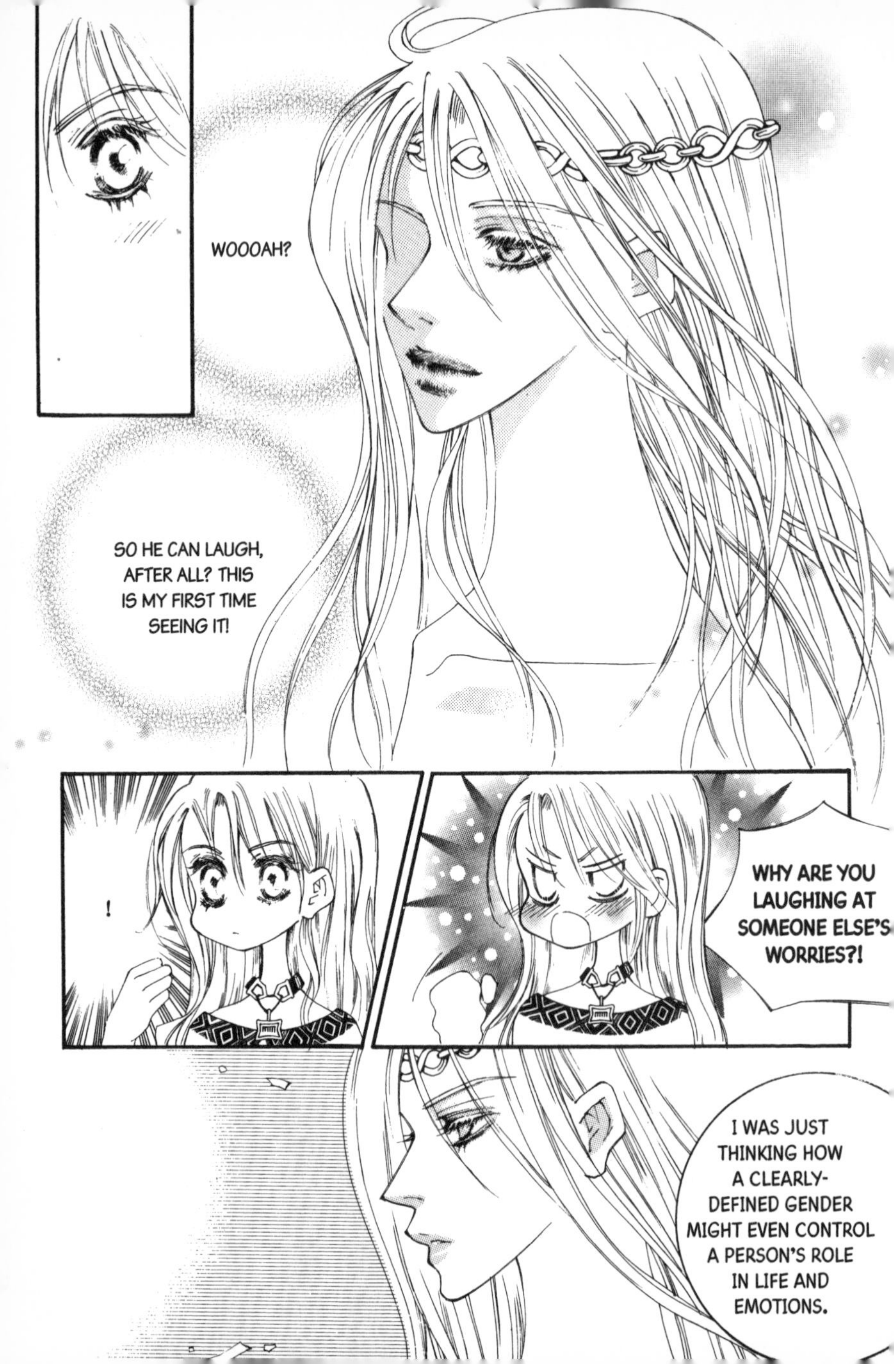
WOOOAH?
SO HE CAN LAUGH, AFTER ALL? THIS IS MY FIRST TIME SEEING IT!
WHY ARE YOU LAUGHING AT SOMEONE ELSE'S WORRIES?!
!
I WAS JUST THINKING HOW A CLEARLY-DEFINED GENDER MIGHT EVEN CONTROL A PERSON'S ROLE IN LIFE AND EMOTIONS.

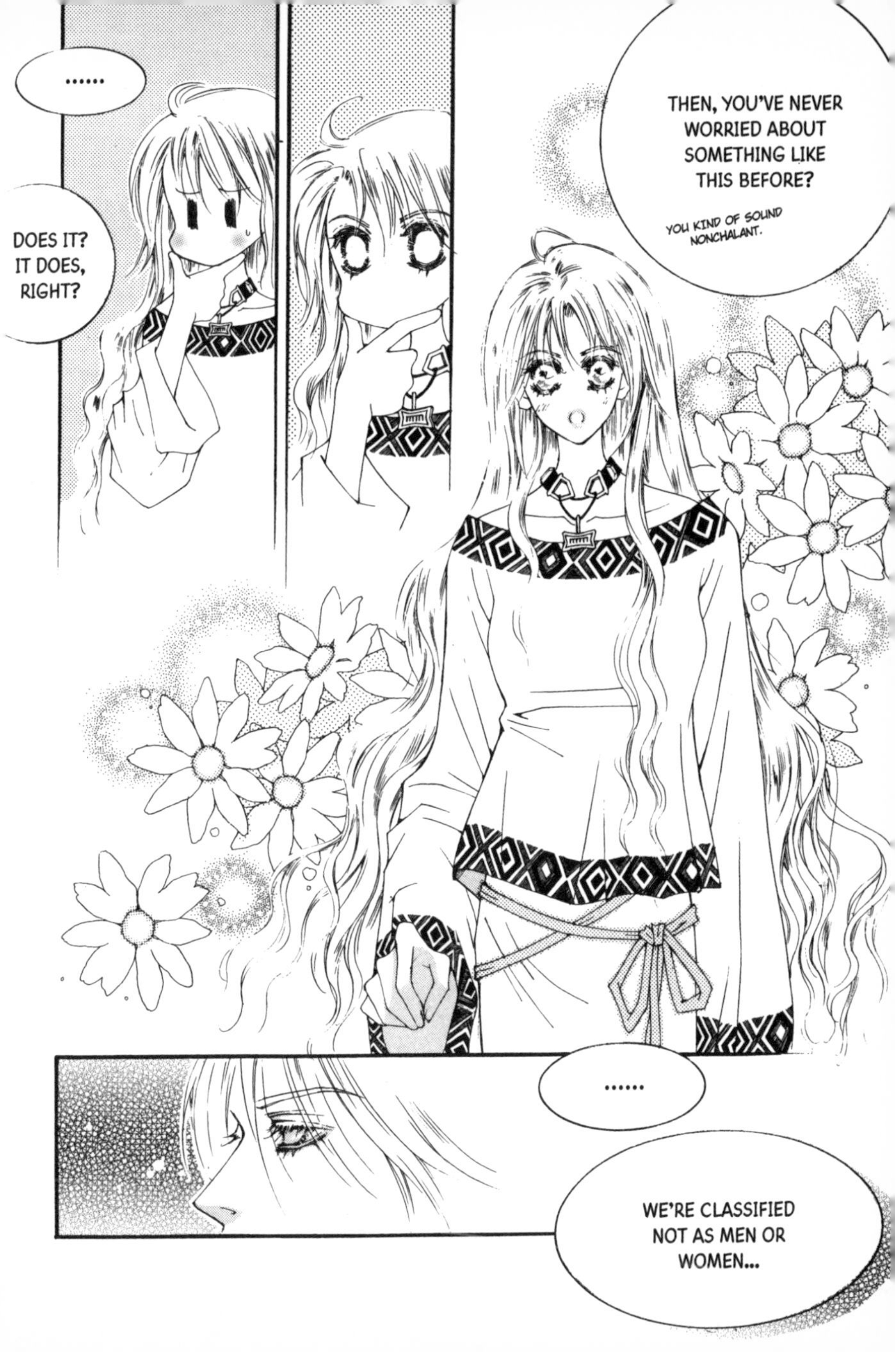
......
DOES IT? IT DOES, RIGHT?
THEN, YOU'VE NEVER WORRIED ABOUT SOMETHING LIKE THIS BEFORE?
YOU KIND OF SOUND NONCHALANT.
......
WE'RE CLASSIFIED NOT AS MEN OR WOMEN...

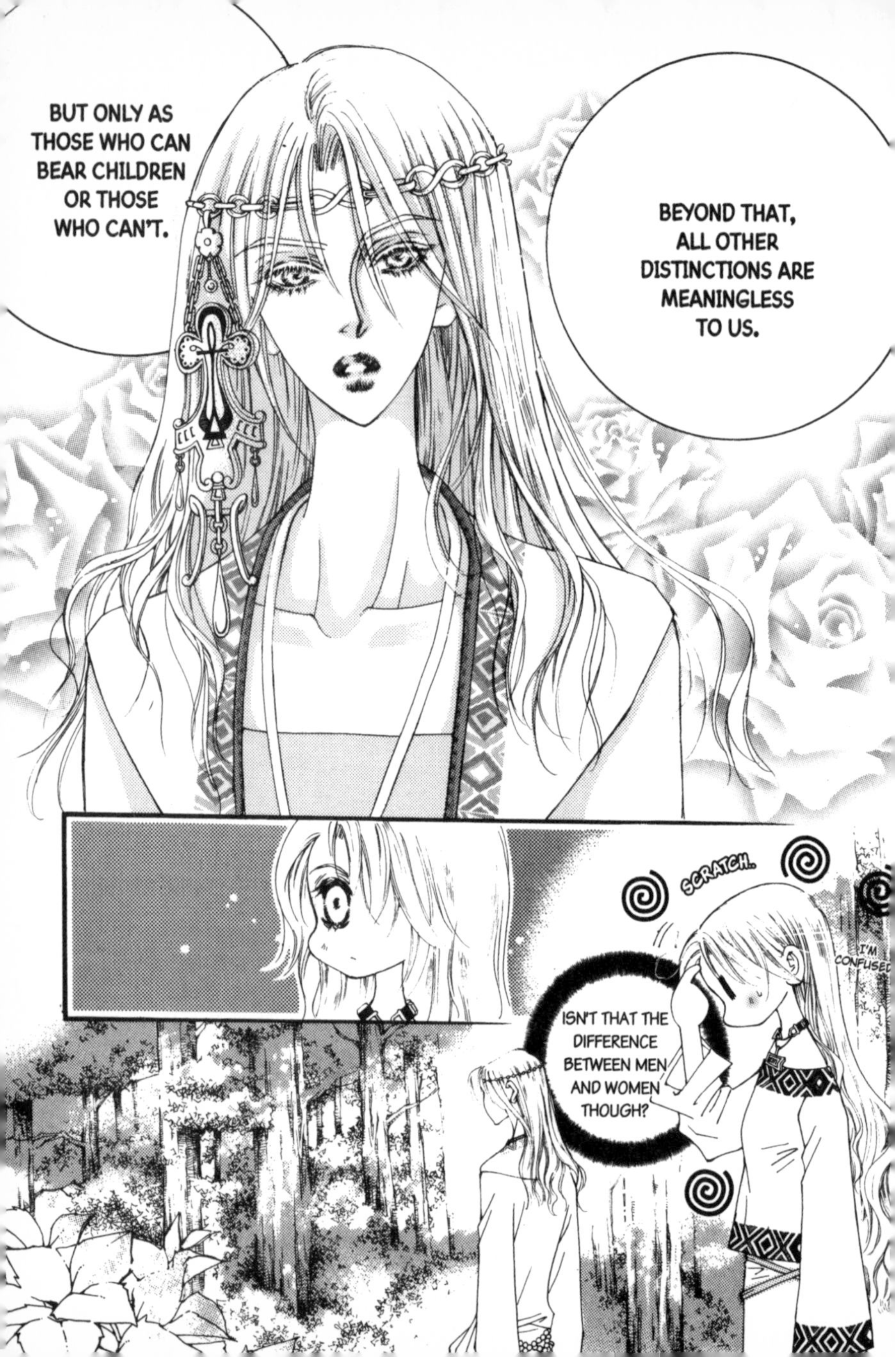
BUT ONLY AS THOSE WHO CAN BEAR CHILDREN OR THOSE WHO CAN'T.
BEYOND THAT, ALL OTHER DISTINCTIONS ARE MEANINGLESS TO US.
SCRATCH..
I'M CONFUSED
ISN'T THAT THE DIFFERENCE BETWEEN MEN AND WOMEN THOUGH?

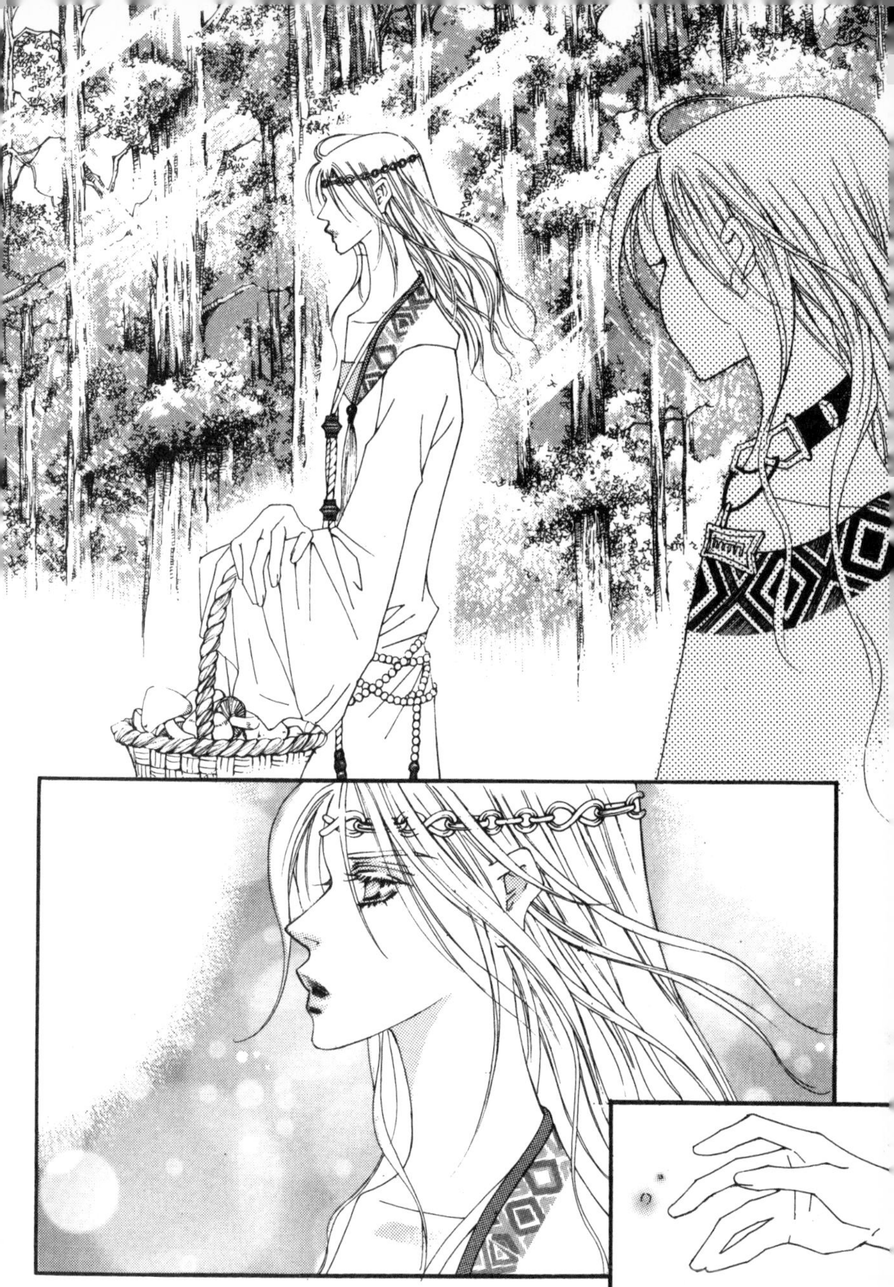

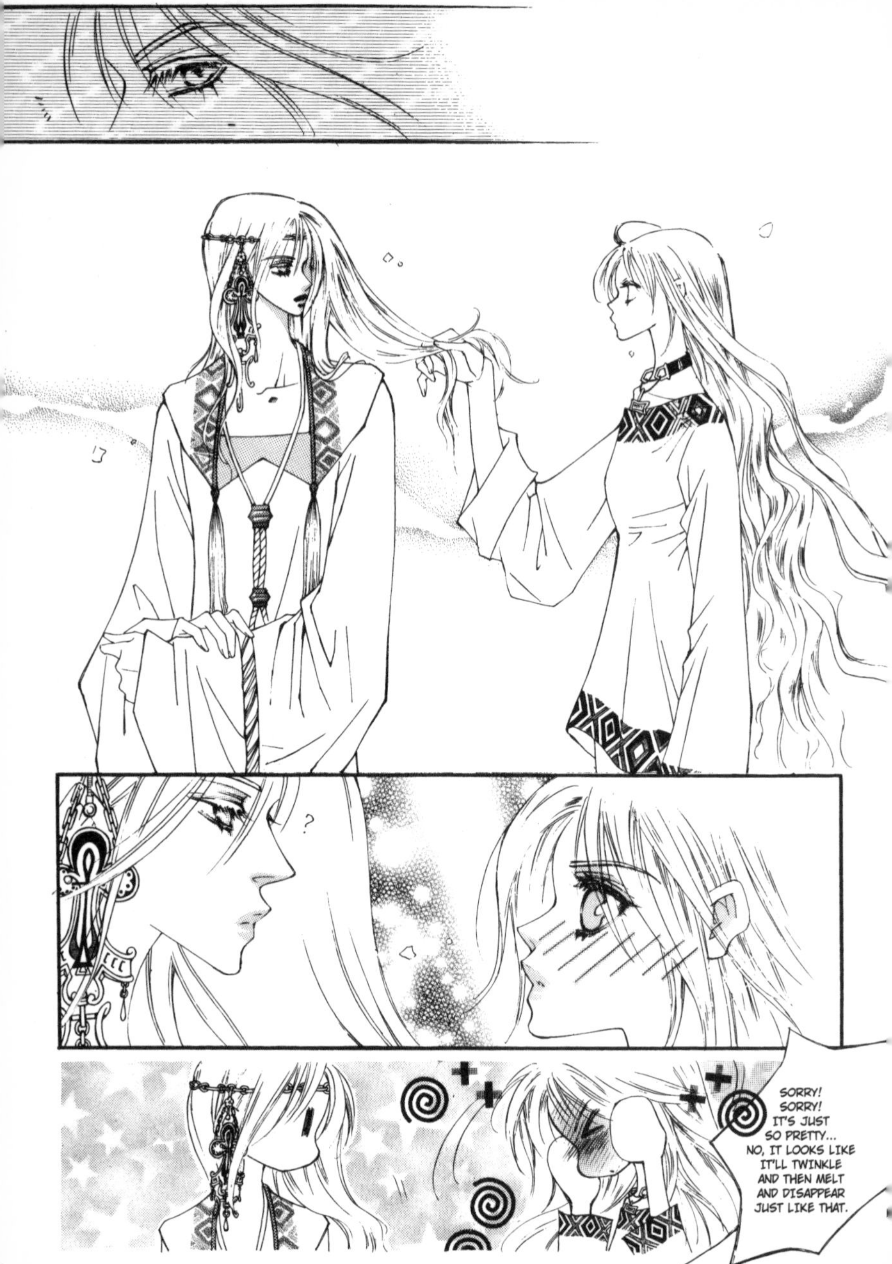
...
?
SORRY! SORRY! IT'S JUST SO PRETTY... NO, IT LOOKS LIKE IT'LL TWINKLE AND THEN MELT AND DISAPPEAR JUST LIKE THAT.
NO~, I MEAN...

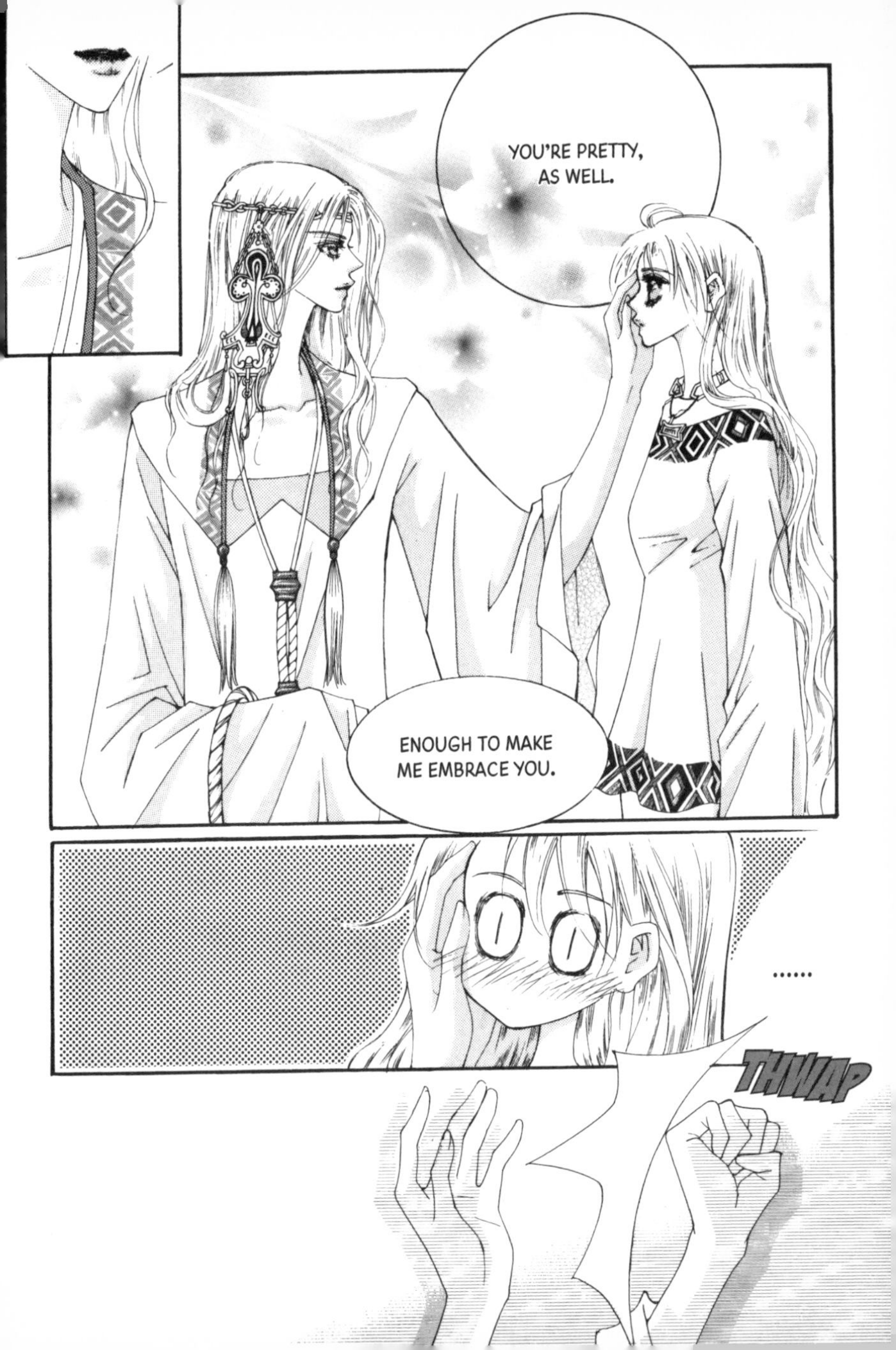
YOU'RE PRETTY, AS WELL.
ENOUGH TO MAKE ME EMBRACE YOU.
......
THWAP

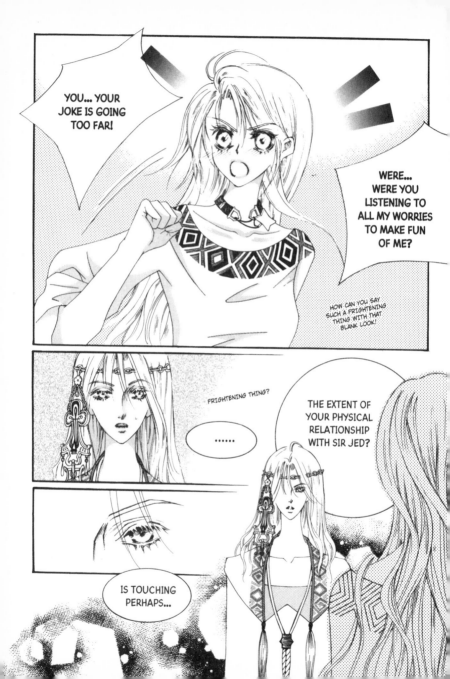

YOU... YOUR JOKE IS GOING TOO FAR!

WERE... WERE YOU LISTENING TO ALL MY WORRIES TO MAKE FUN OF ME?

HOW CAN YOU SAY SUCH A FRIGHTENING THING WITH THAT BLANK LOOK!

FRIGHTENING THING?

......

THE EXTENT OF YOUR PHYSICAL RELATIONSHIP WITH SIR JED?

IS TOUCHING PERHAPS...

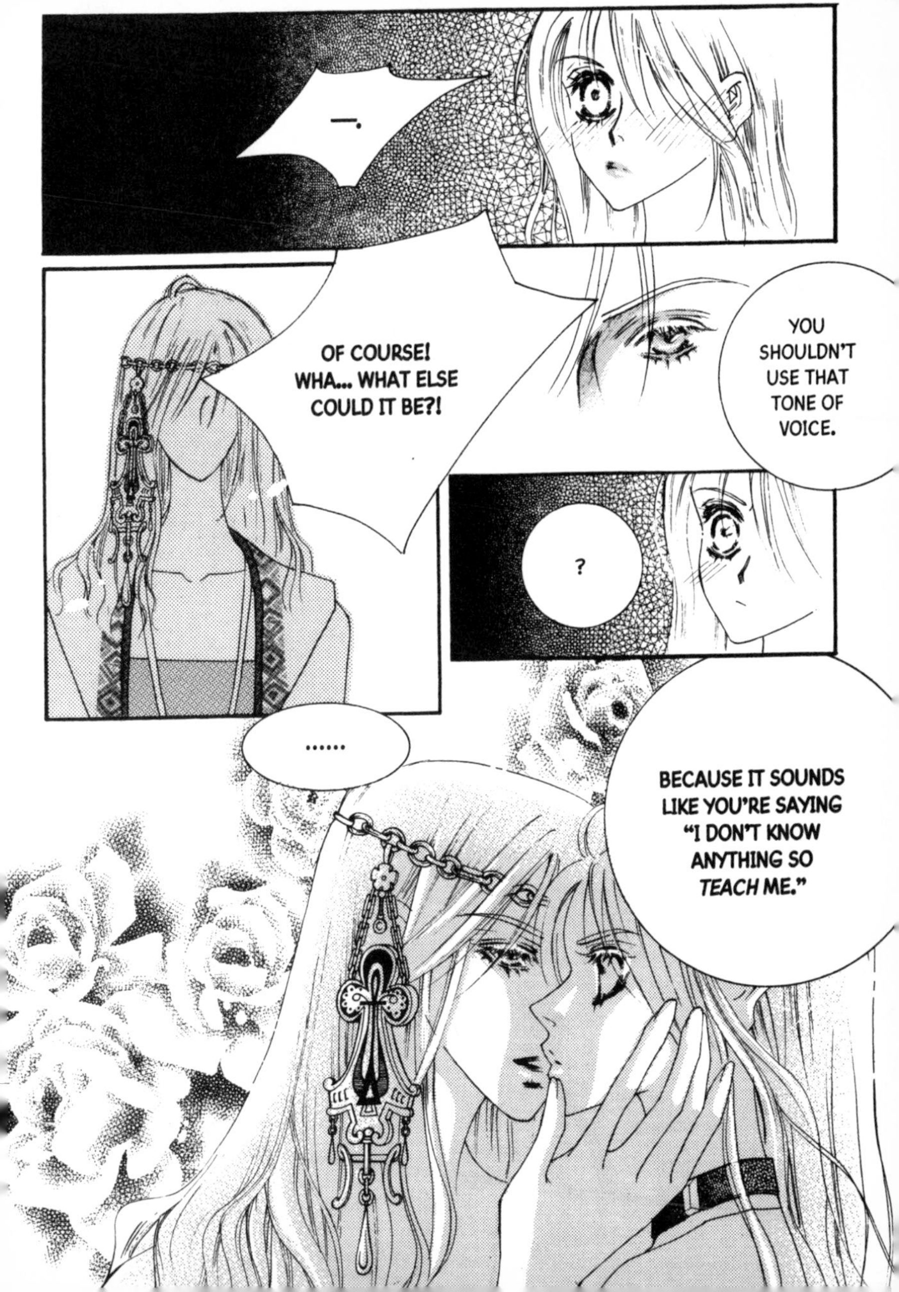
—.
OF COURSE! WHA... WHAT ELSE COULD IT BE?!
YOU SHOULDN'T USE THAT TONE OF VOICE.
?
......
BECAUSE IT SOUNDS LIKE YOU'RE SAYING "I DON'T KNOW ANYTHING SO *TEACH* ME."

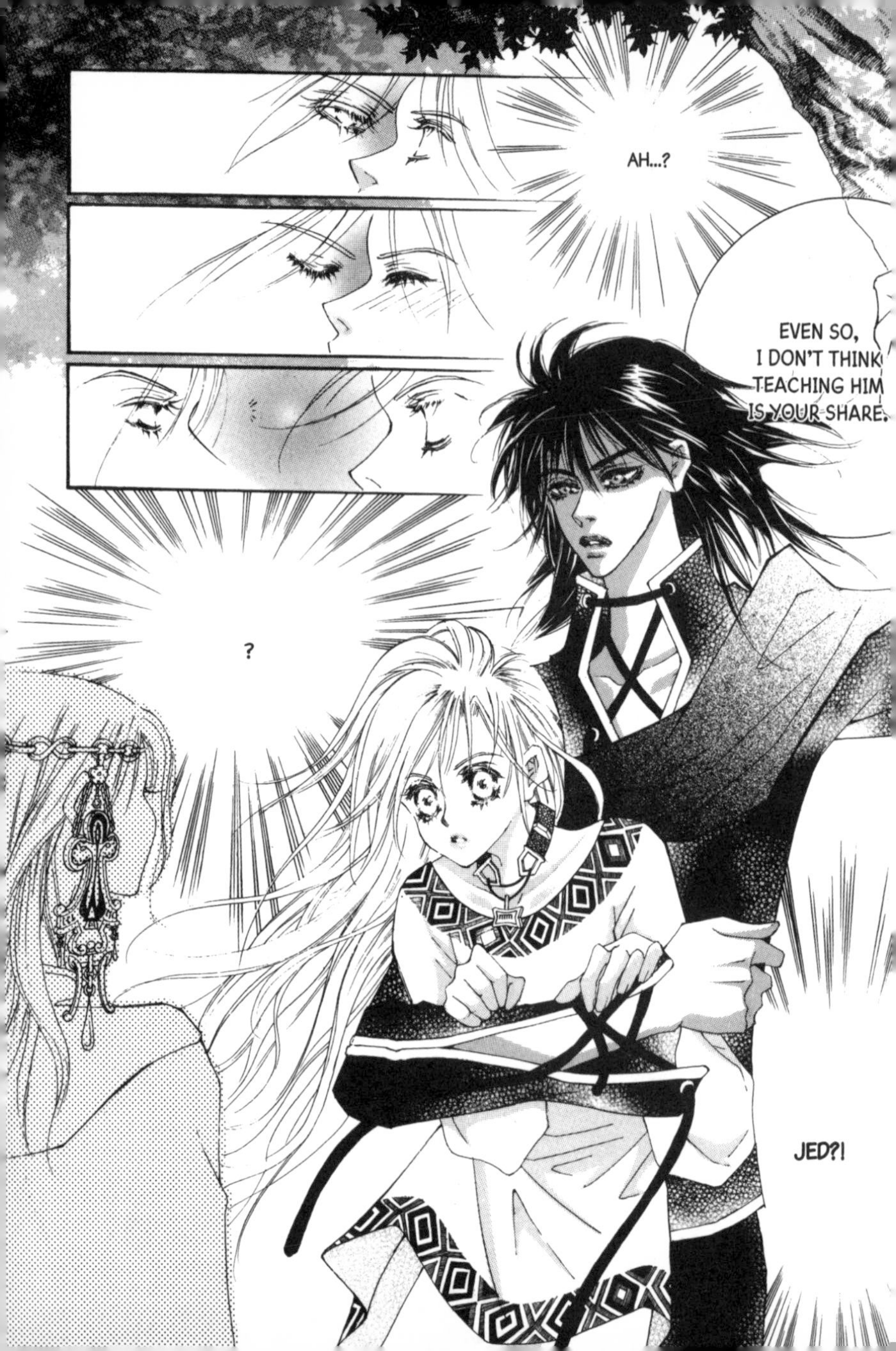
AH...?
EVEN SO, I DON'T THINK TEACHING HIM IS YOUR SHARE.
?
JED?!

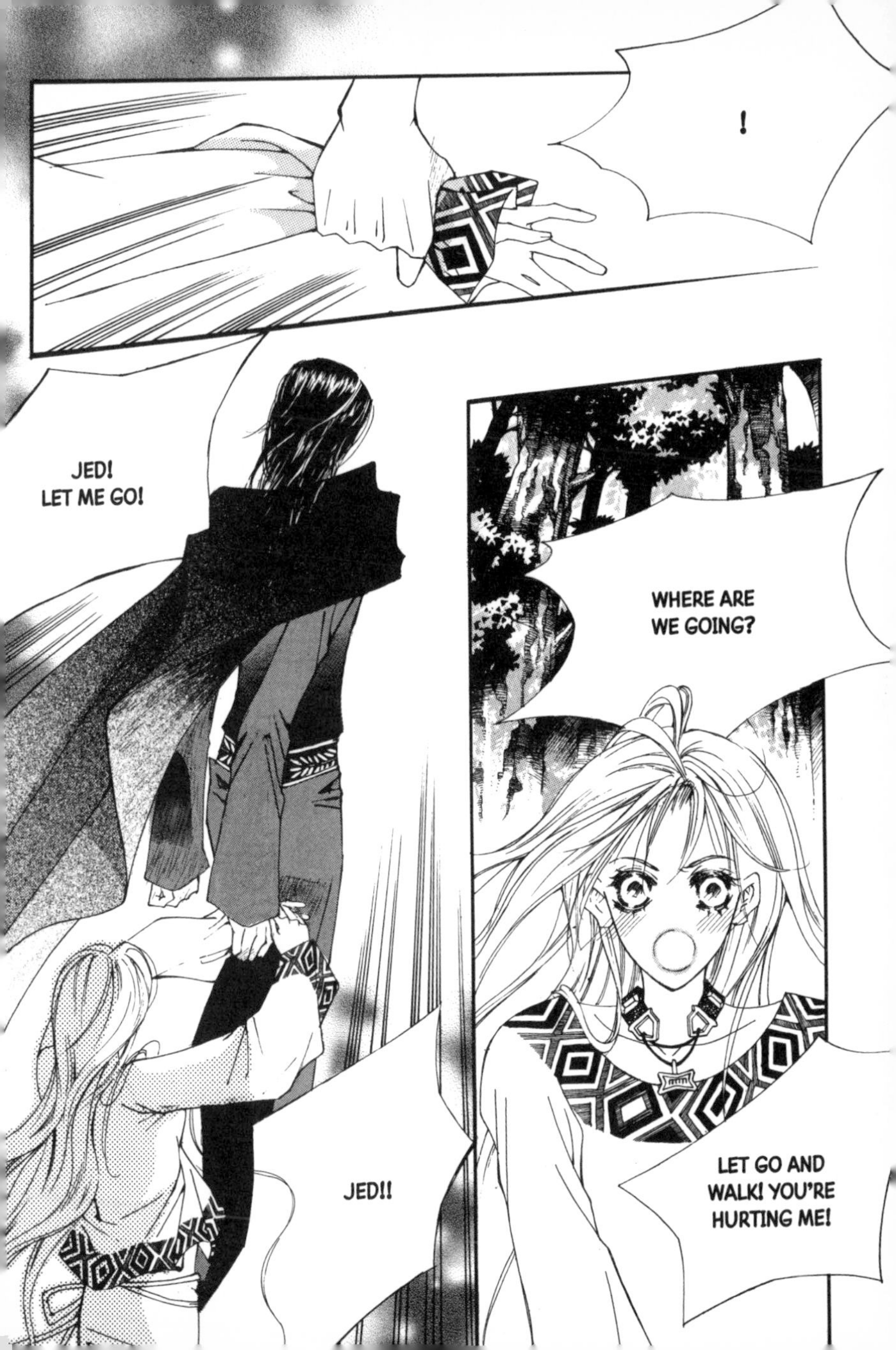
!
JED! LET ME GO!
JED!!
WHERE ARE WE GOING?
LET GO AND WALK! YOU'RE HURTING ME!

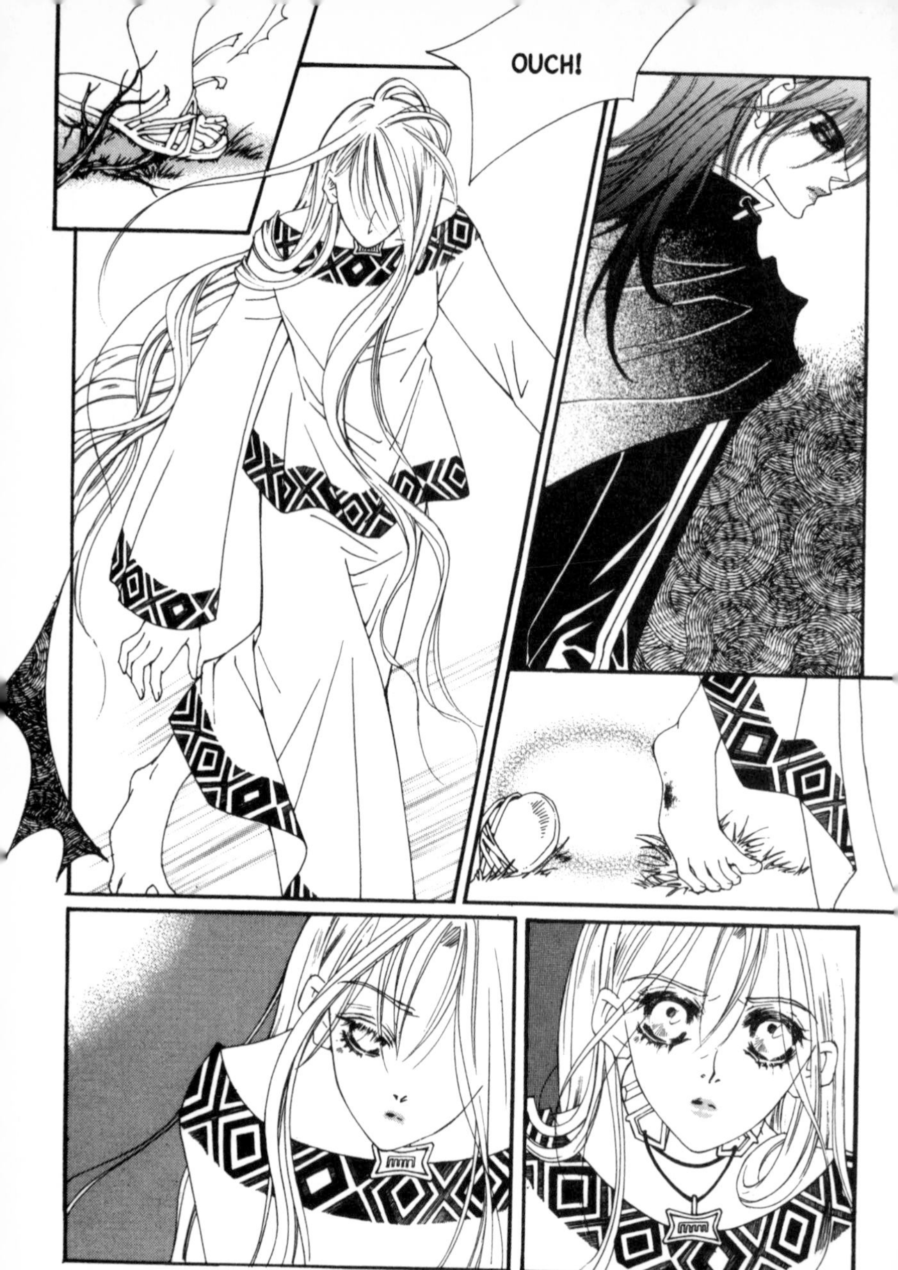
OUCH!

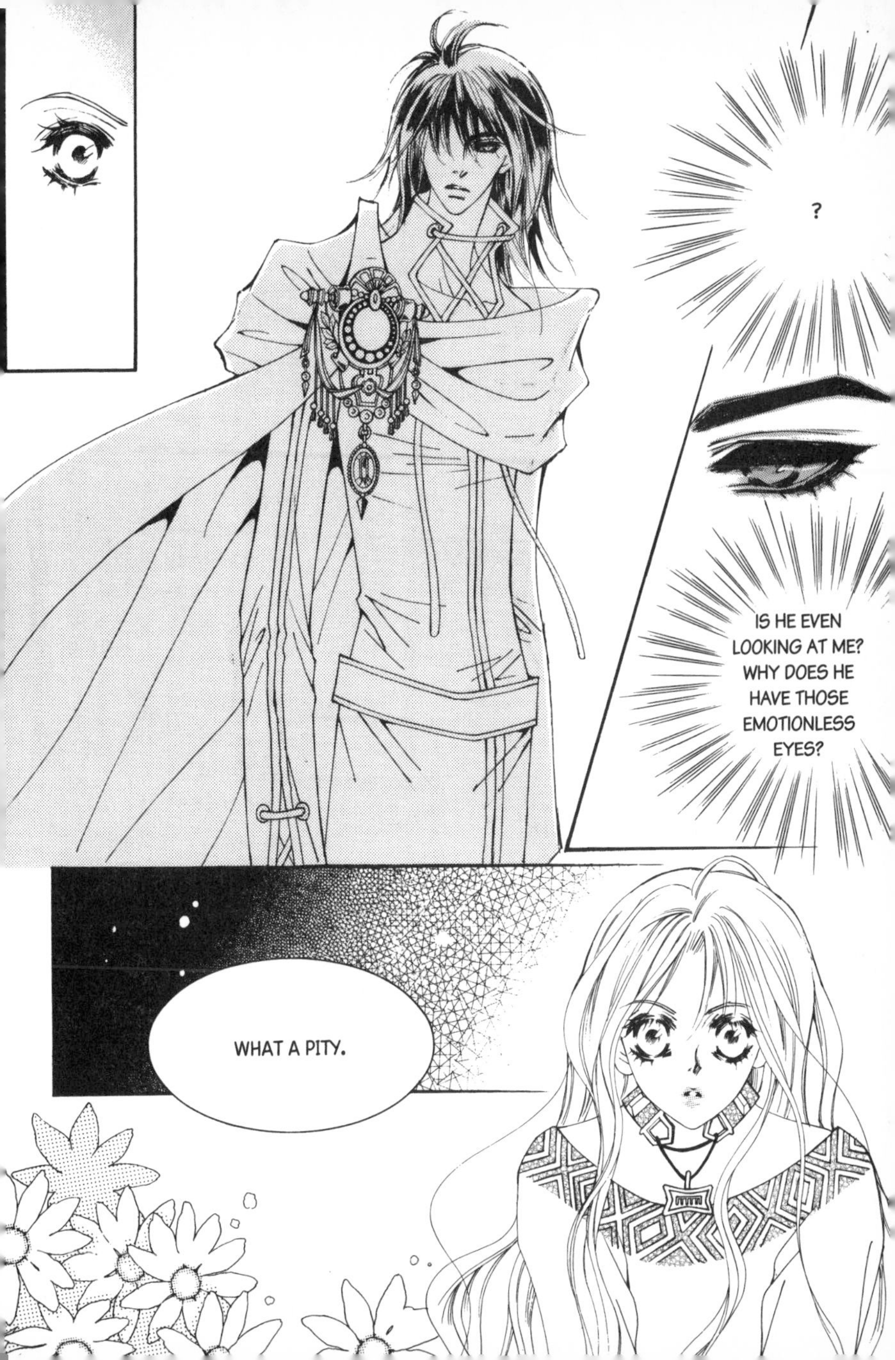
?
IS HE EVEN LOOKING AT ME? WHY DOES HE HAVE THOSE EMOTIONLESS EYES?
WHAT A PITY.

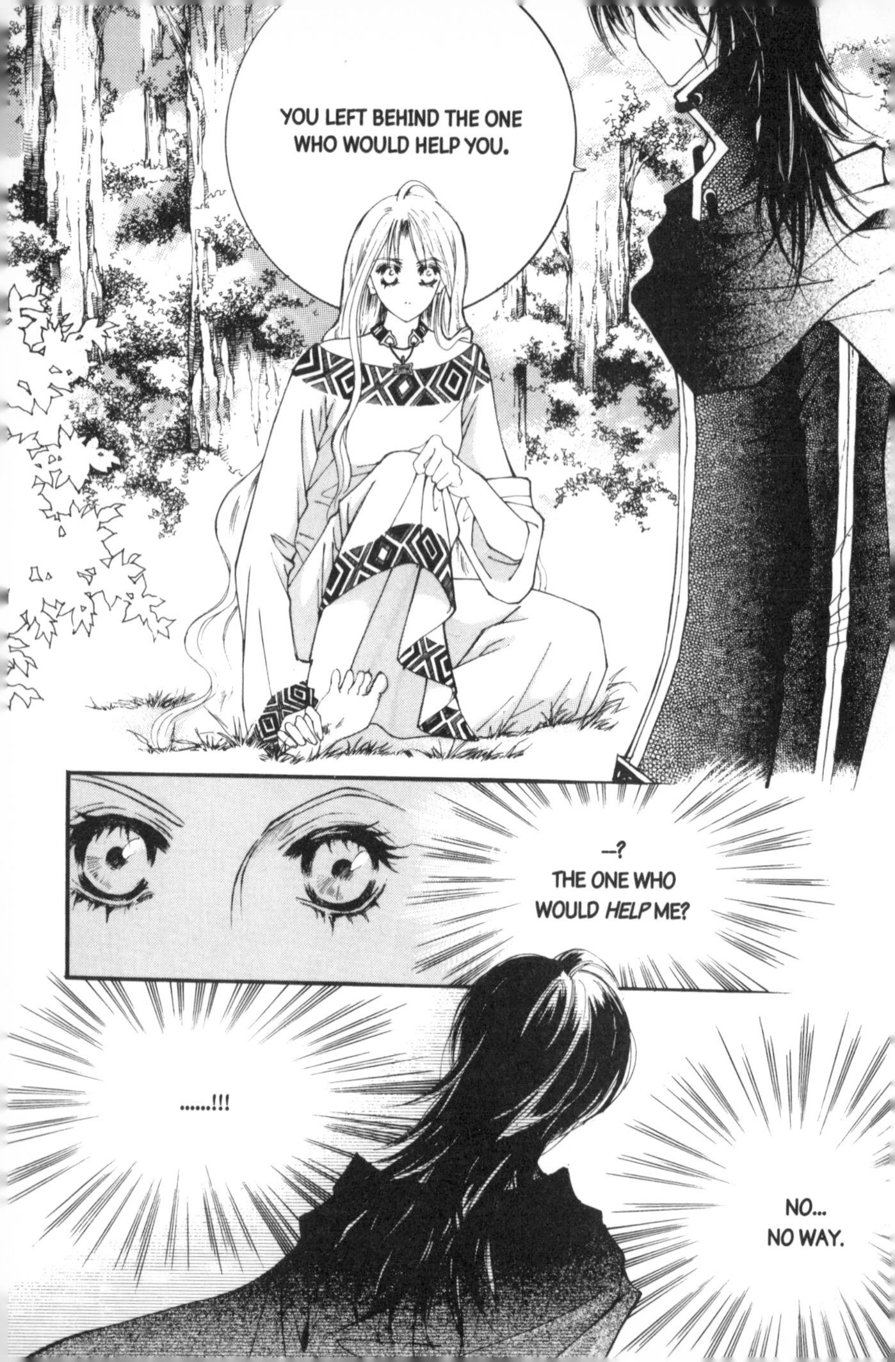
YOU LEFT BEHIND THE ONE WHO WOULD HELP YOU.
--? THE ONE WHO WOULD *HELP* ME?
......!!!
NO... NO WAY.

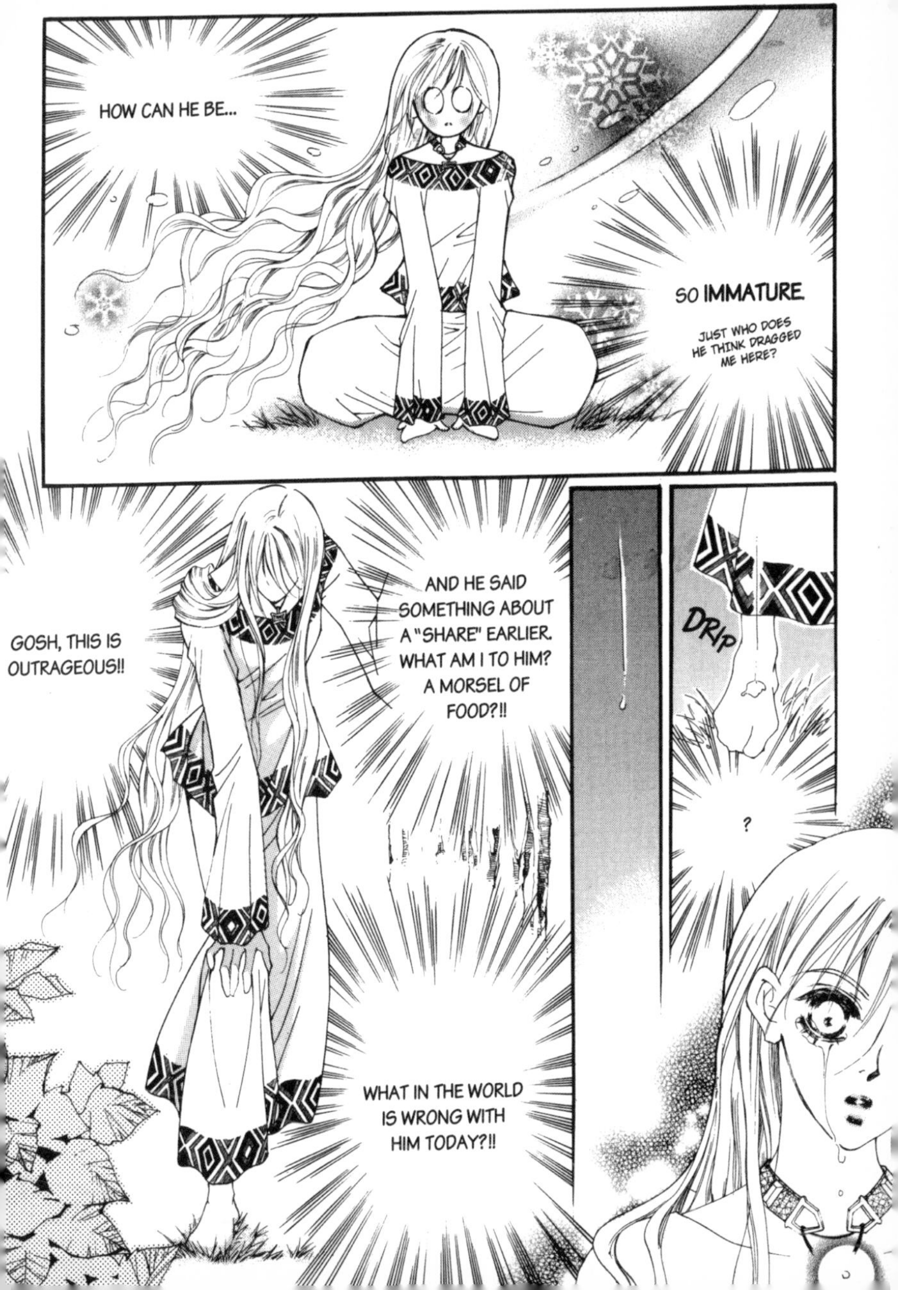
HOW CAN HE BE...
SO IMMATURE.
JUST WHO DOES HE THINK DRAGGED ME HERE?
GOSH, THIS IS OUTRAGEOUS!!
AND HE SAID SOMETHING ABOUT A "SHARE" EARLIER. WHAT AM I TO HIM? A MORSEL OF FOOD?!!
WHAT IN THE WORLD IS WRONG WITH HIM TODAY?!!
DRIP
?

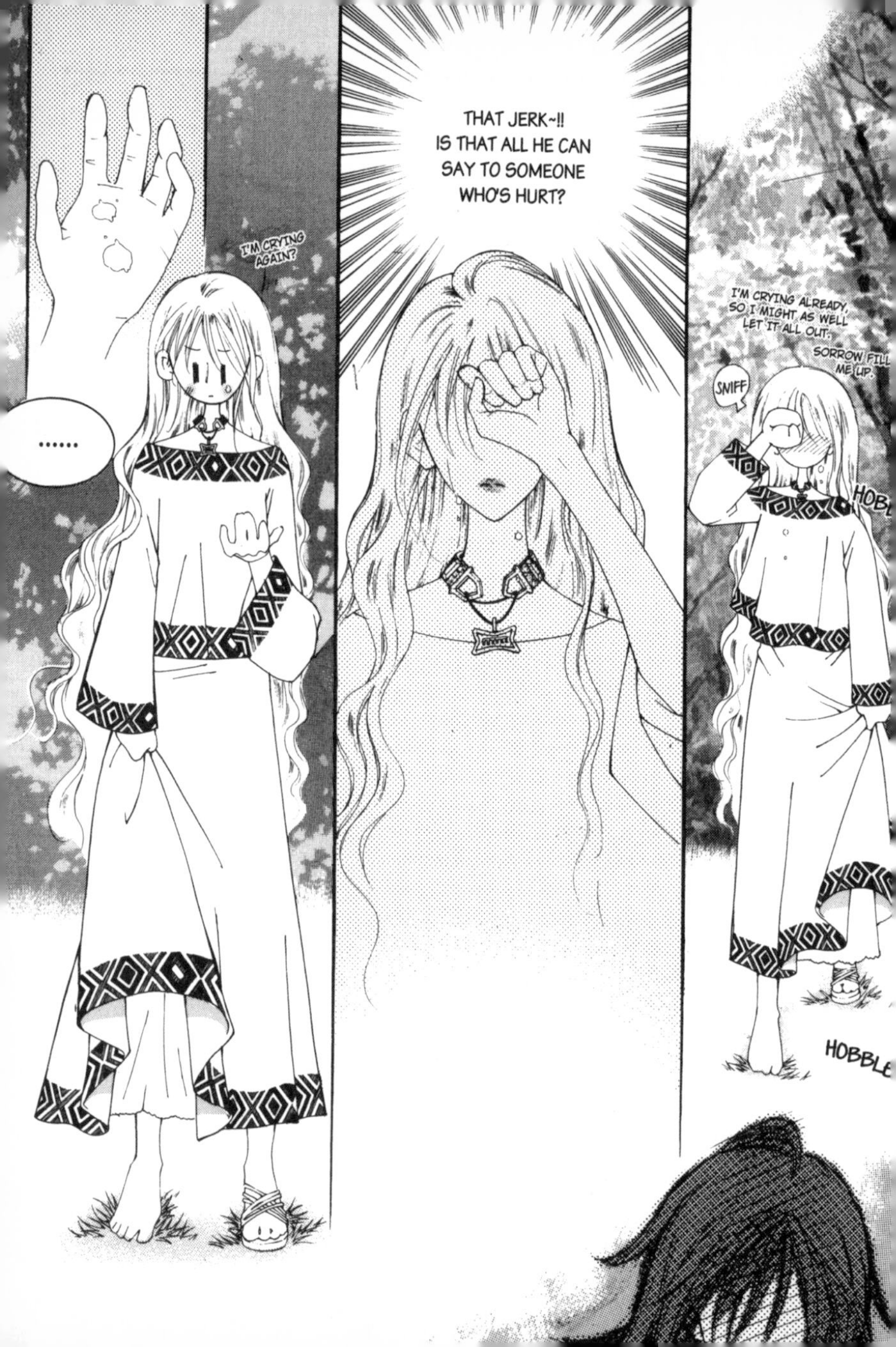
I'M CRYING AGAIN?
......
THAT JERK~!!
IS THAT ALL HE CAN SAY TO SOMEONE WHO'S HURT?
I'M CRYING ALREADY, SO I MIGHT AS WELL LET IT ALL OUT.
SORROW FILL ME UP.
SNIFF
HOBBLE
HOBBLE

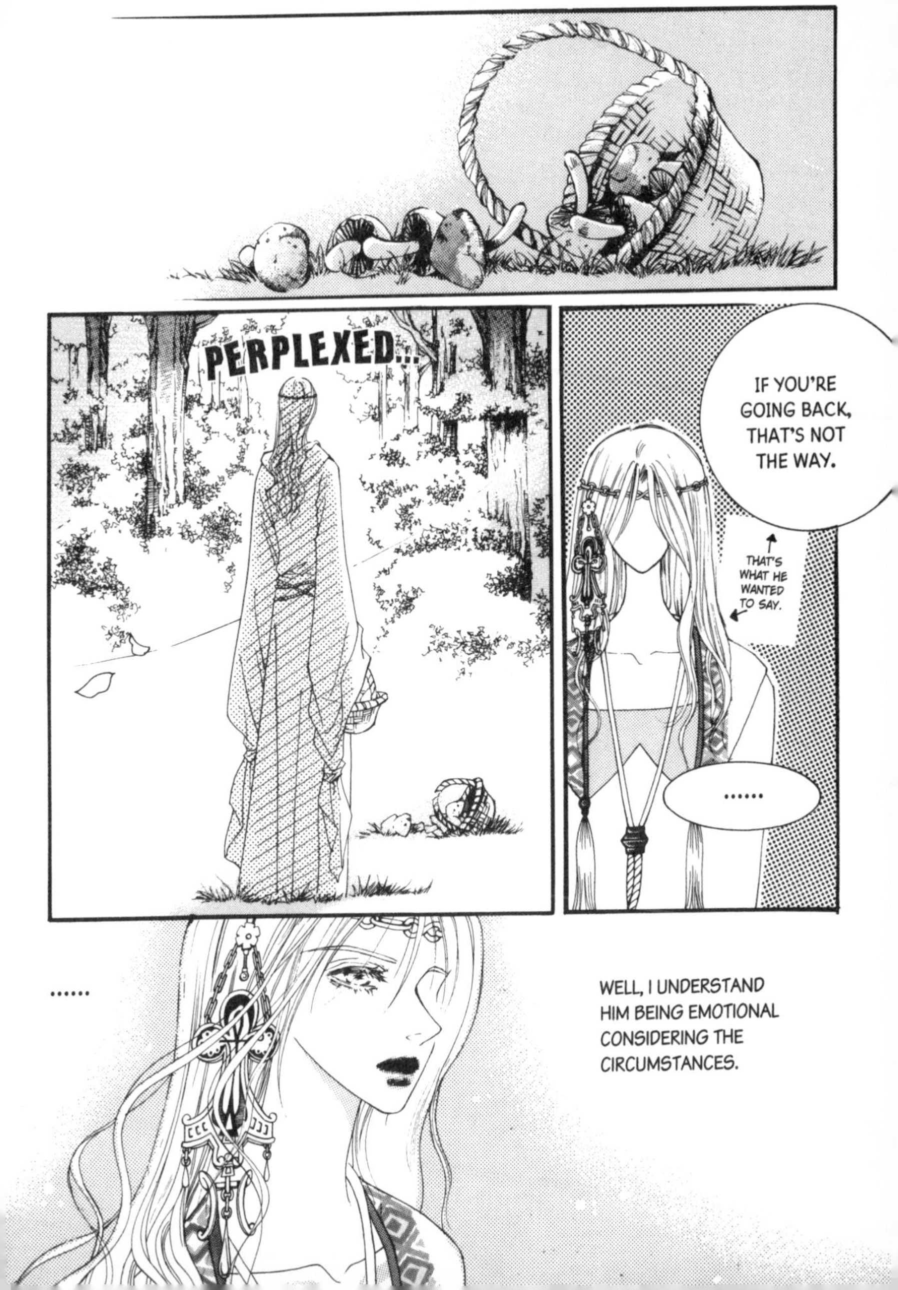
PERPLEXED...
IF YOU'RE GOING BACK, THAT'S NOT THE WAY.
THAT'S WHAT HE WANTED TO SAY.
......
......
WELL, I UNDERSTAND HIM BEING EMOTIONAL CONSIDERING THE CIRCUMSTANCES.

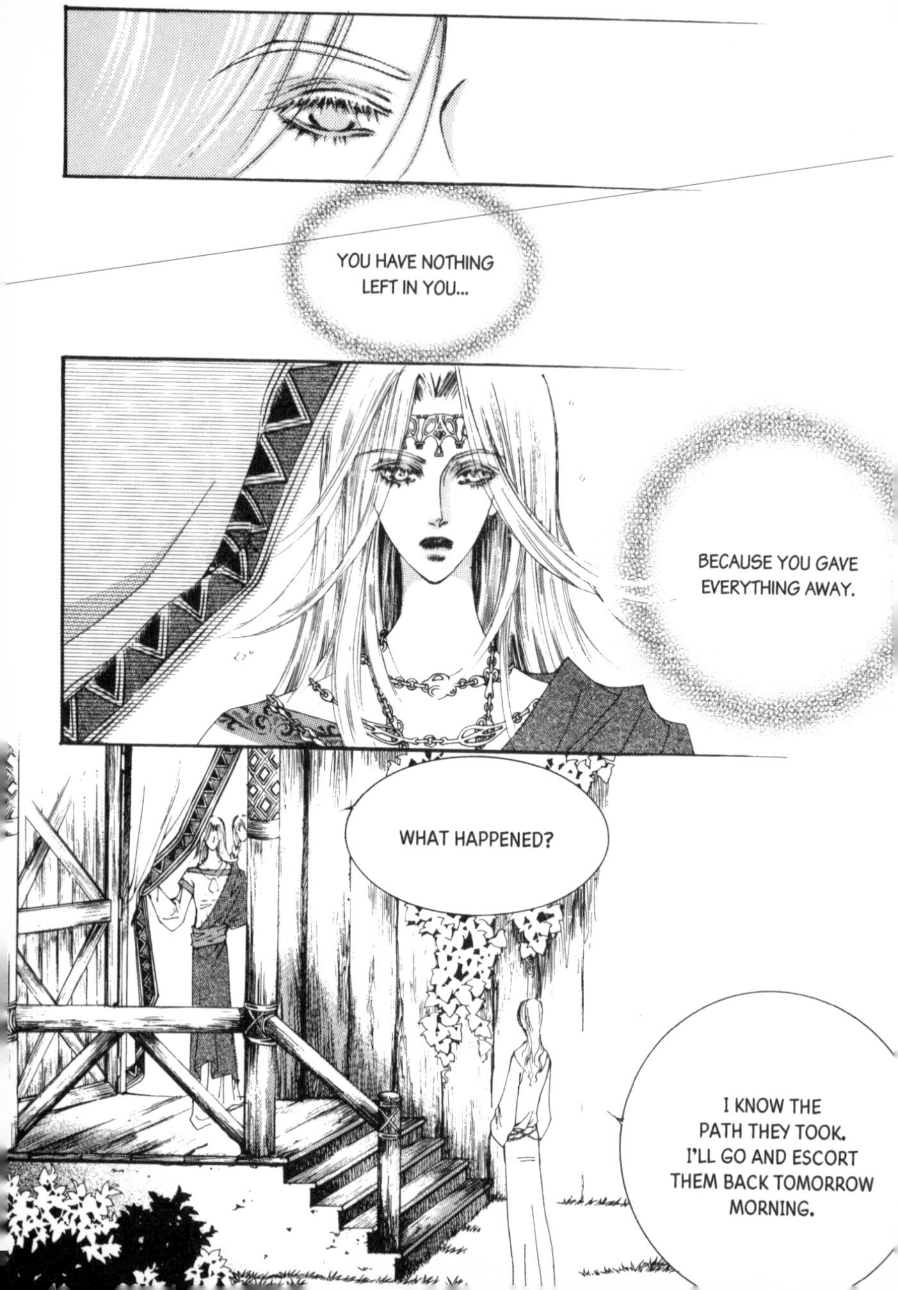
YOU HAVE NOTHING LEFT IN YOU...
BECAUSE YOU GAVE EVERYTHING AWAY.
WHAT HAPPENED?
I KNOW THE PATH THEY TOOK. I'LL GO AND ESCORT THEM BACK TOMORROW MORNING.

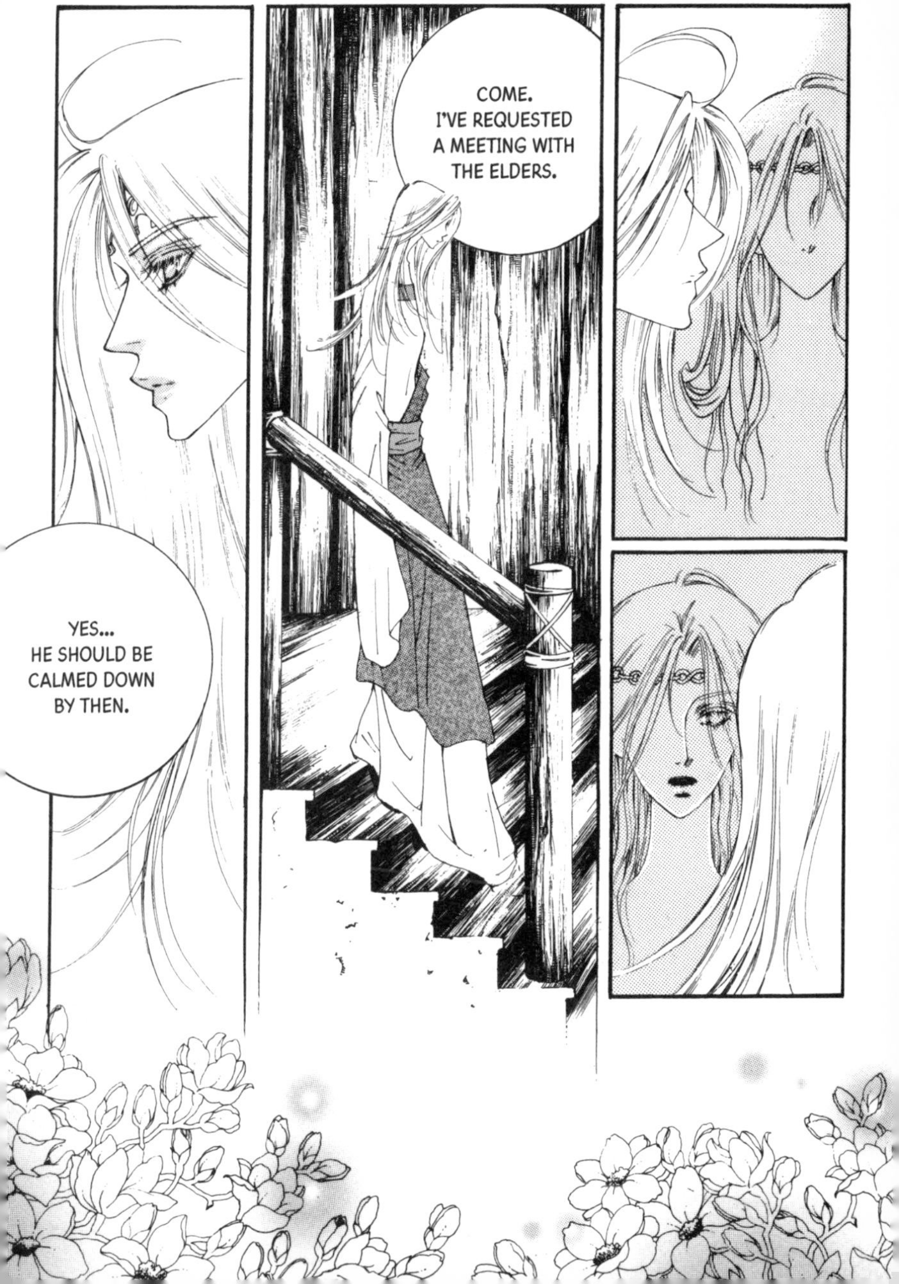
YES... HE SHOULD BE CALMED DOWN BY THEN.
COME. I'VE REQUESTED A MEETING WITH THE ELDERS.

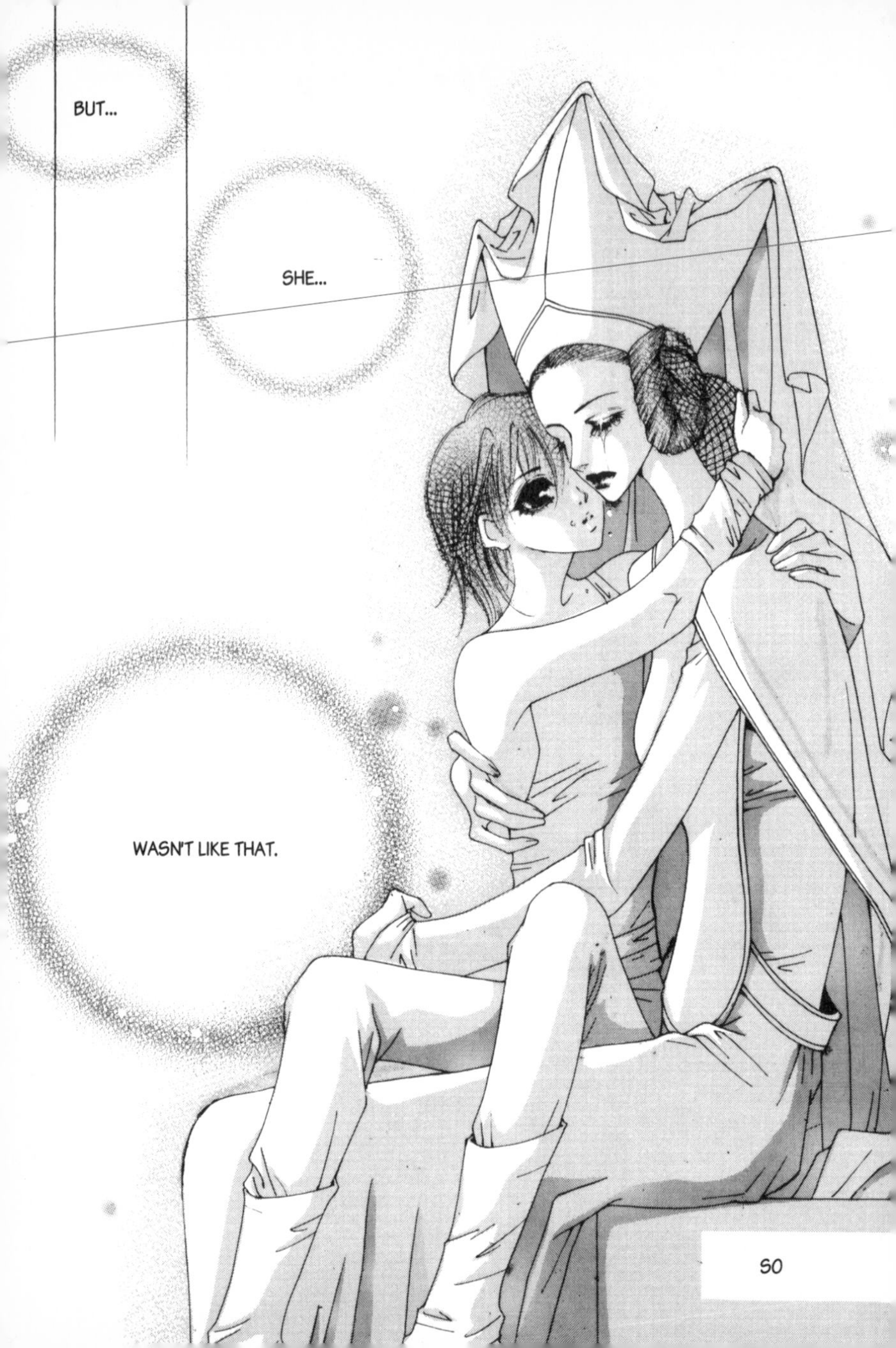
BUT...
SHE...
WASN'T LIKE THAT.
SO

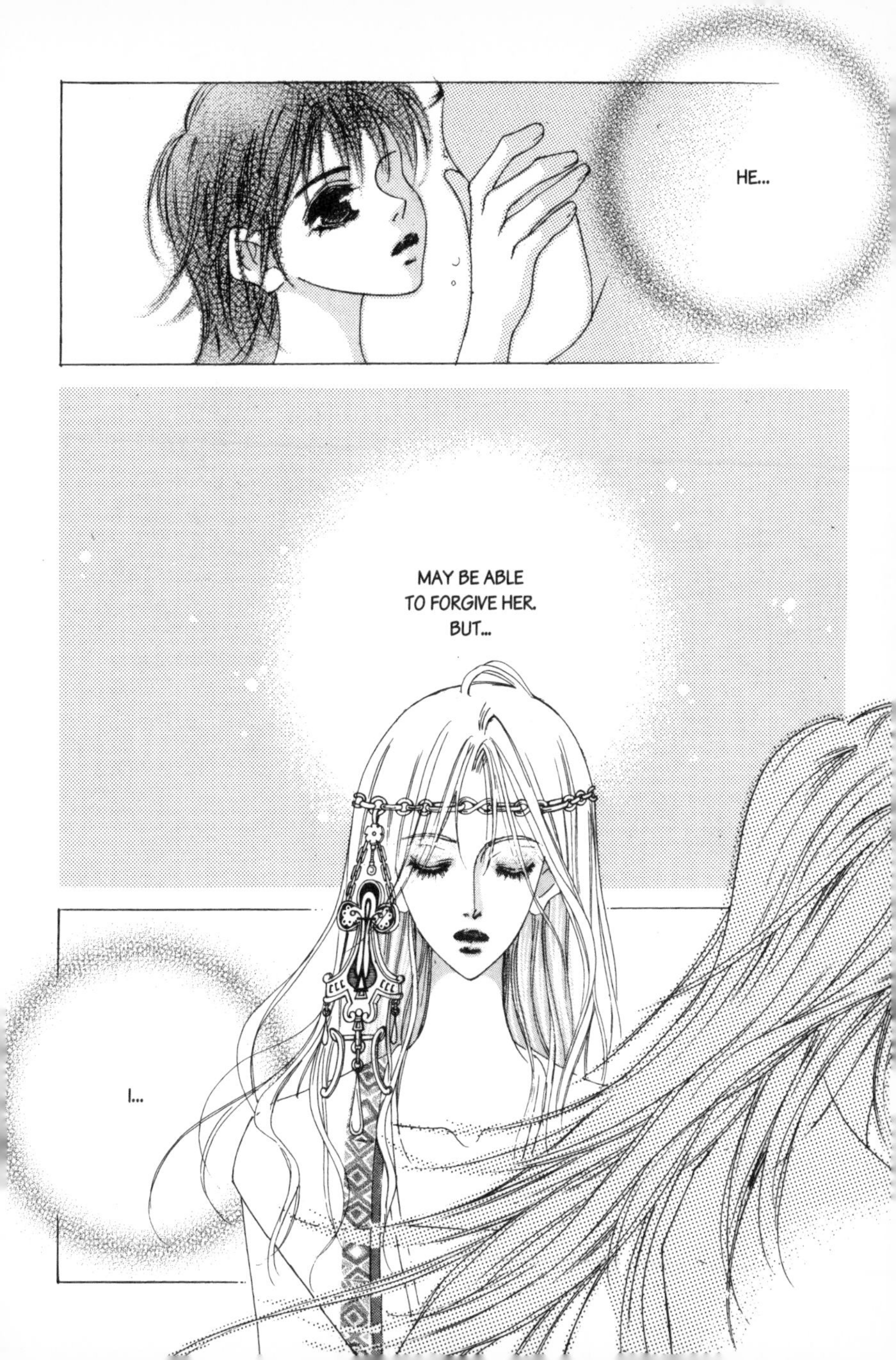
HE...
MAY BE ABLE
TO FORGIVE HER.
BUT...
I...

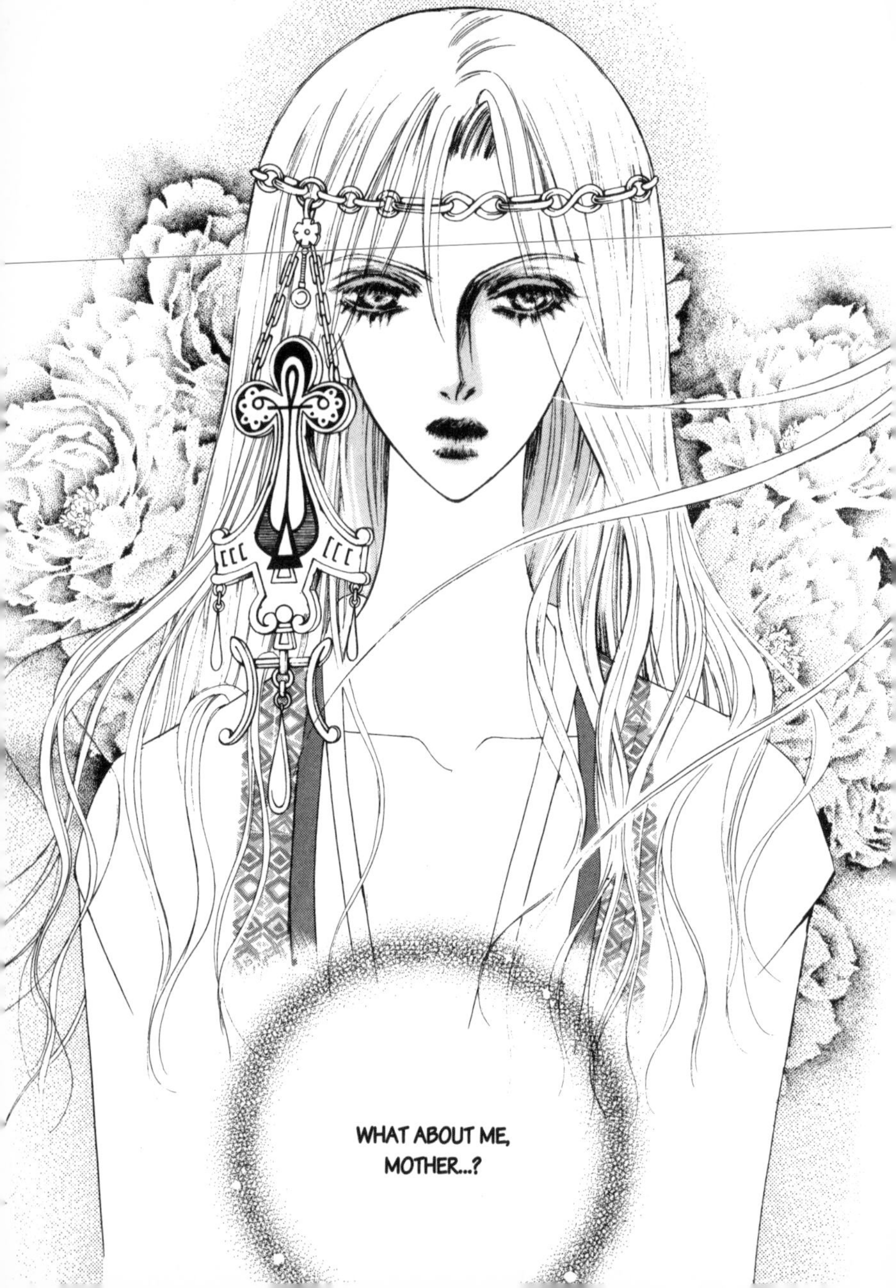
WHAT ABOUT ME,
MOTHER...?

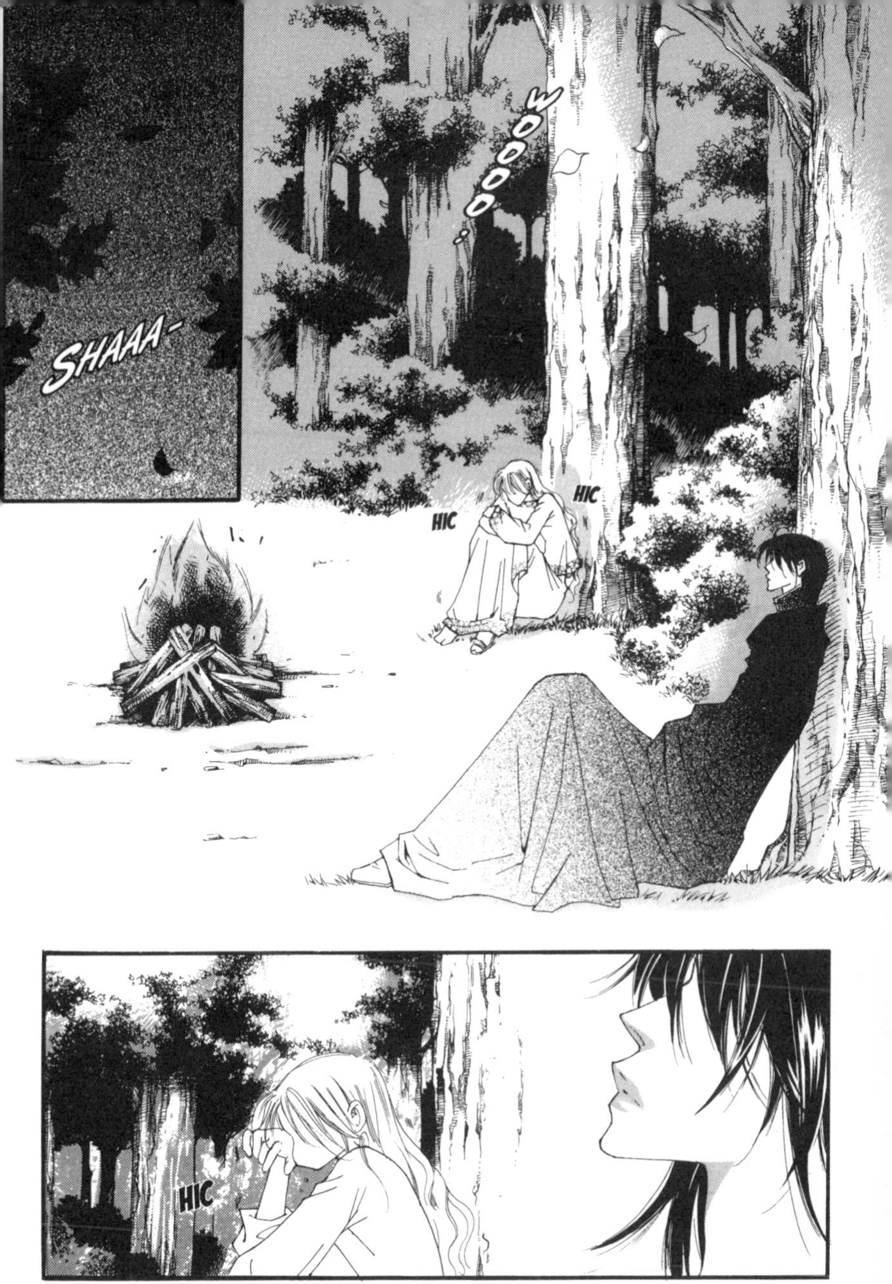
SHAAA-
WOOOO..
HIC
HIC
HIC

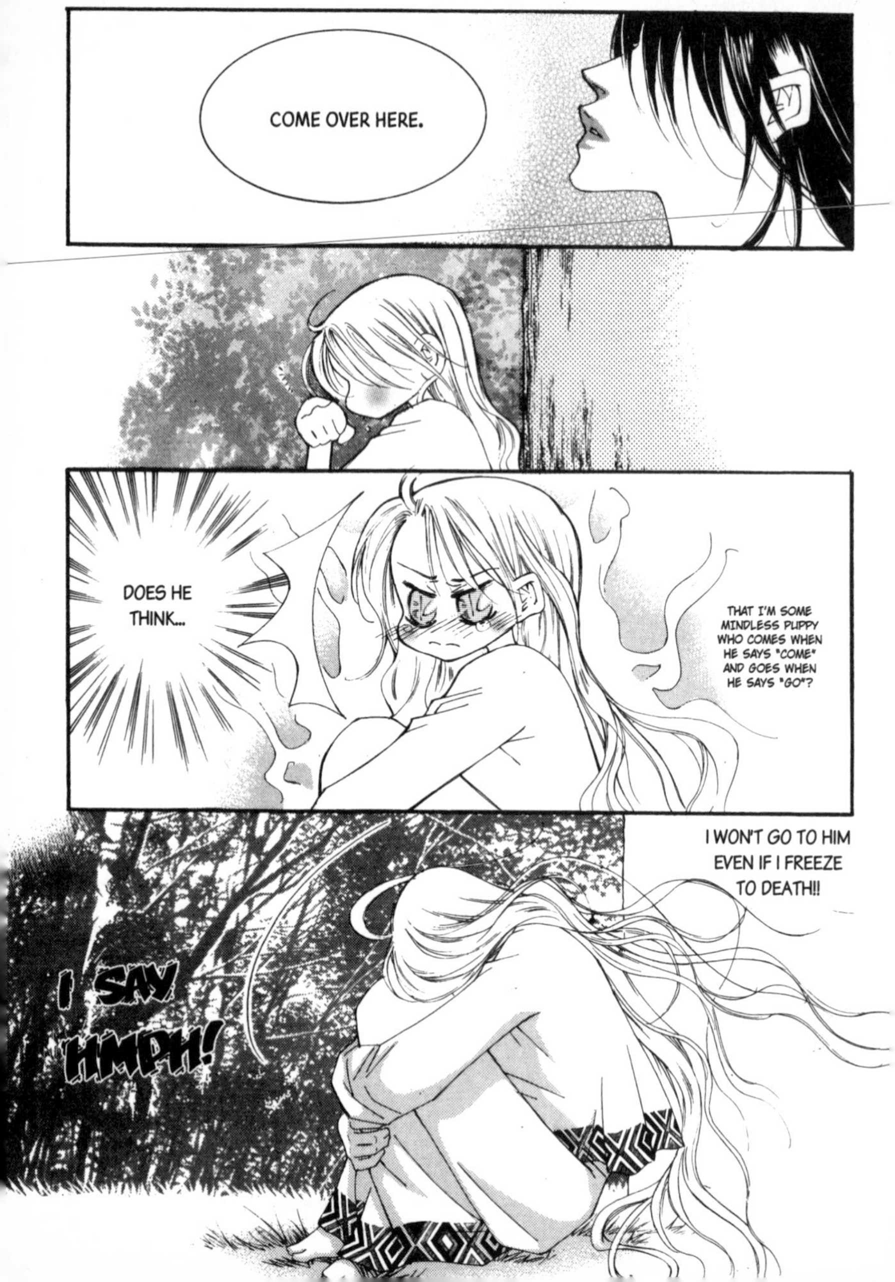
COME OVER HERE.
DOES HE THINK...
THAT I'M SOME MINDLESS PUPPY WHO COMES WHEN HE SAYS "COME" AND GOES WHEN HE SAYS "GO"?
I SAY HMPH!
I WON'T GO TO HIM EVEN IF I FREEZE TO DEATH!!

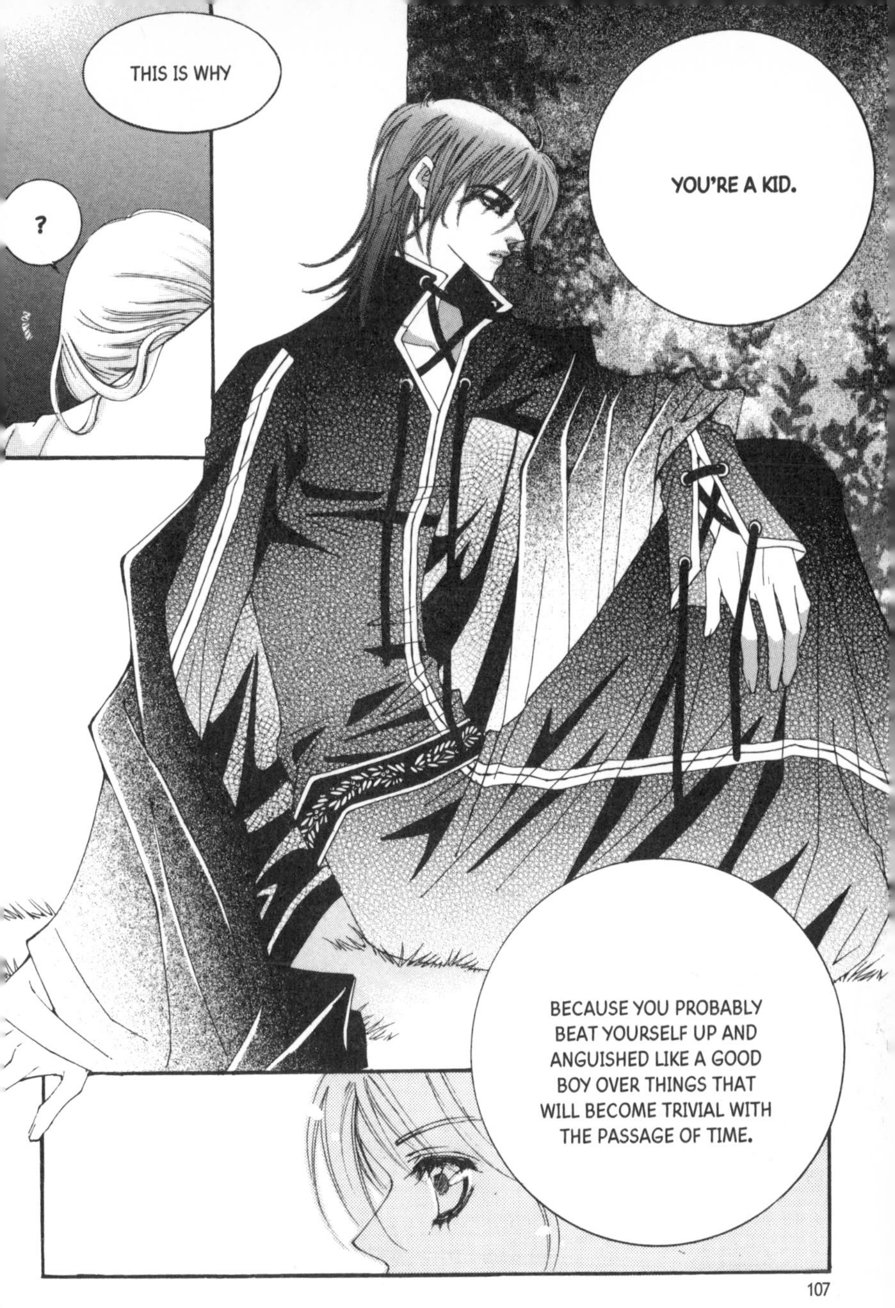
THIS IS WHY
?
YOU'RE A KID.
BECAUSE YOU PROBABLY BEAT YOURSELF UP AND ANGUISHED LIKE A GOOD BOY OVER THINGS THAT WILL BECOME TRIVIAL WITH THE PASSAGE OF TIME.

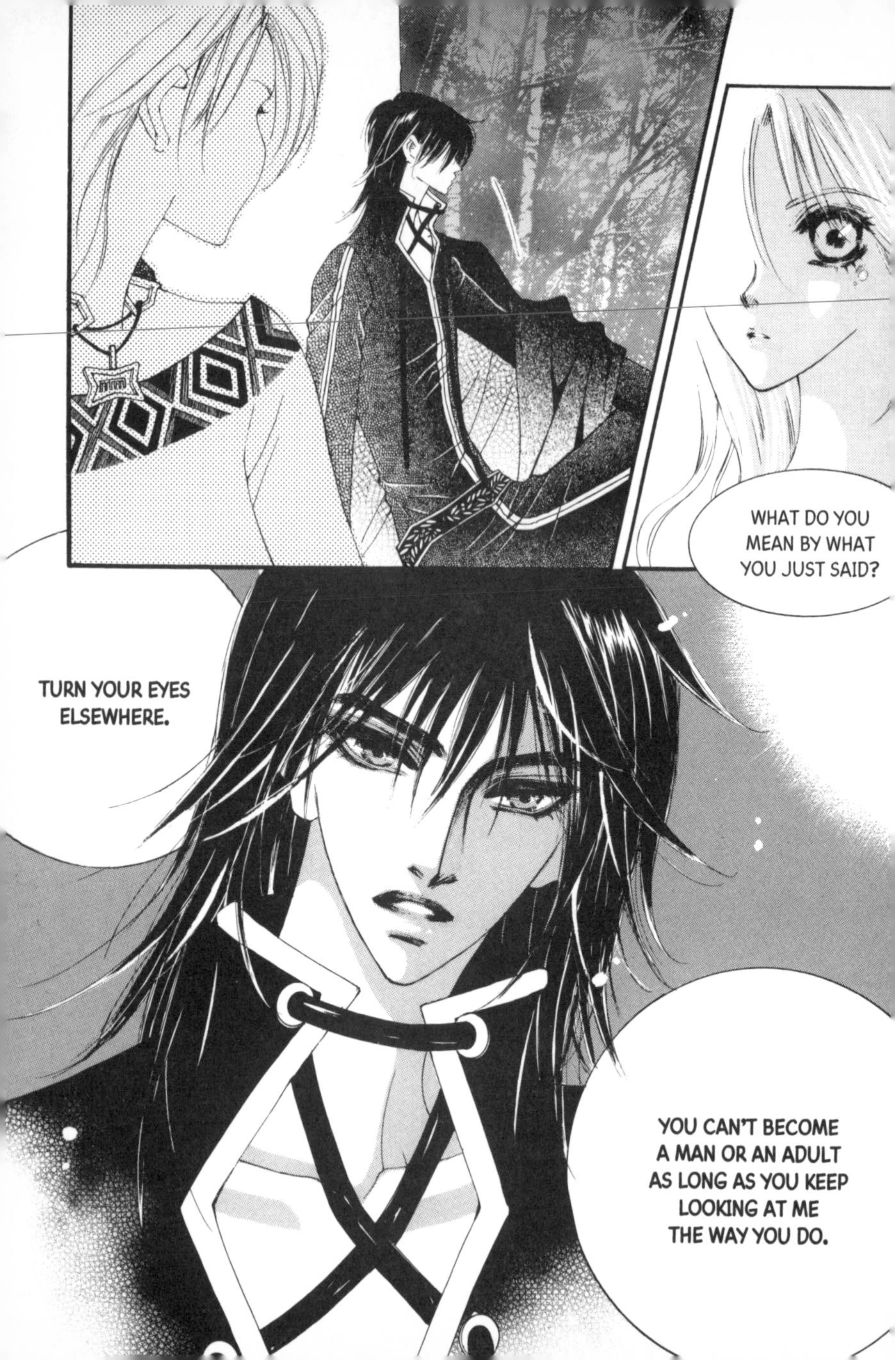
WHAT DO YOU MEAN BY WHAT YOU JUST SAID?
TURN YOUR EYES ELSEWHERE.
YOU CAN'T BECOME A MAN OR AN ADULT AS LONG AS YOU KEEP LOOKING AT ME THE WAY YOU DO.

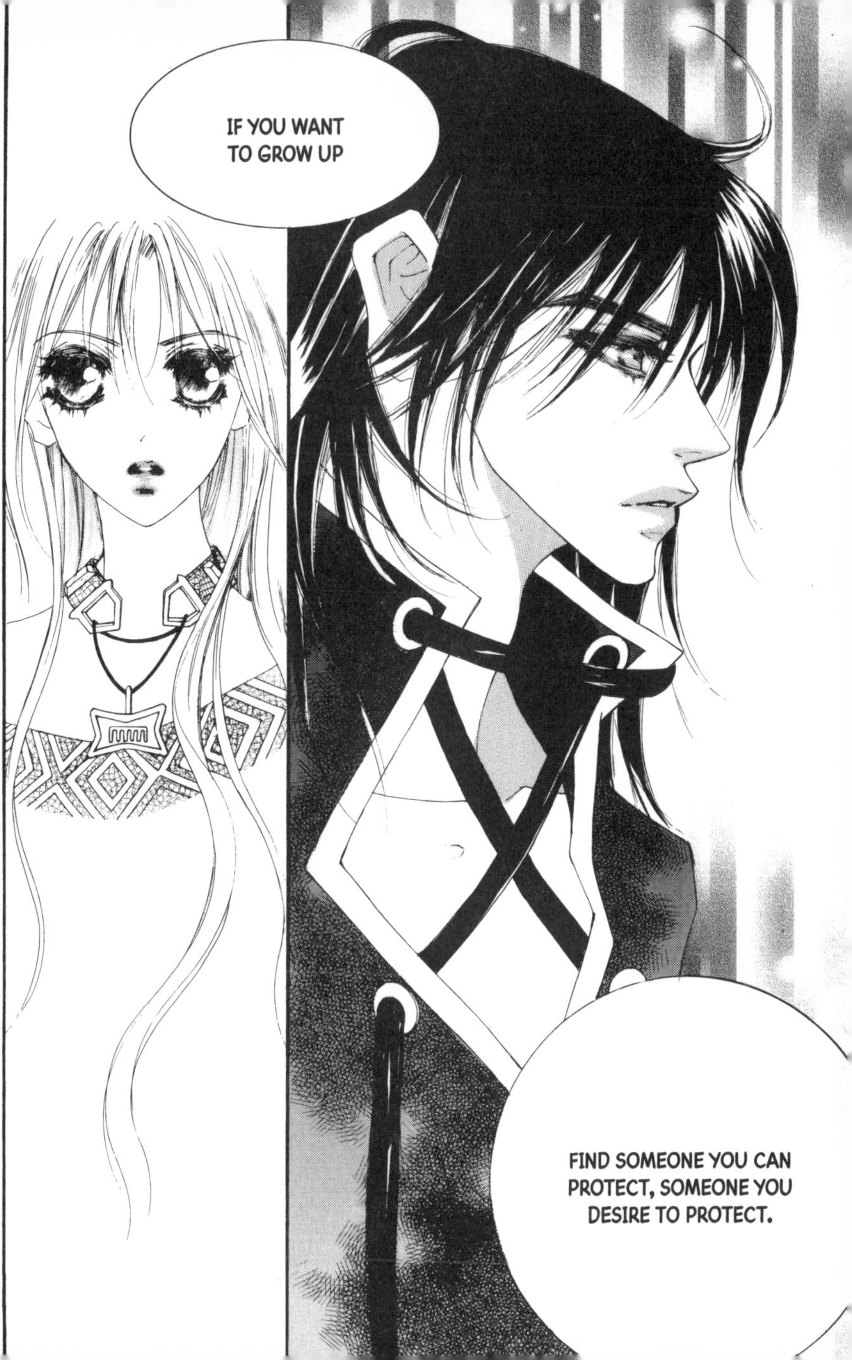
IF YOU WANT TO GROW UP
FIND SOMEONE YOU CAN PROTECT, SOMEONE YOU DESIRE TO PROTECT.

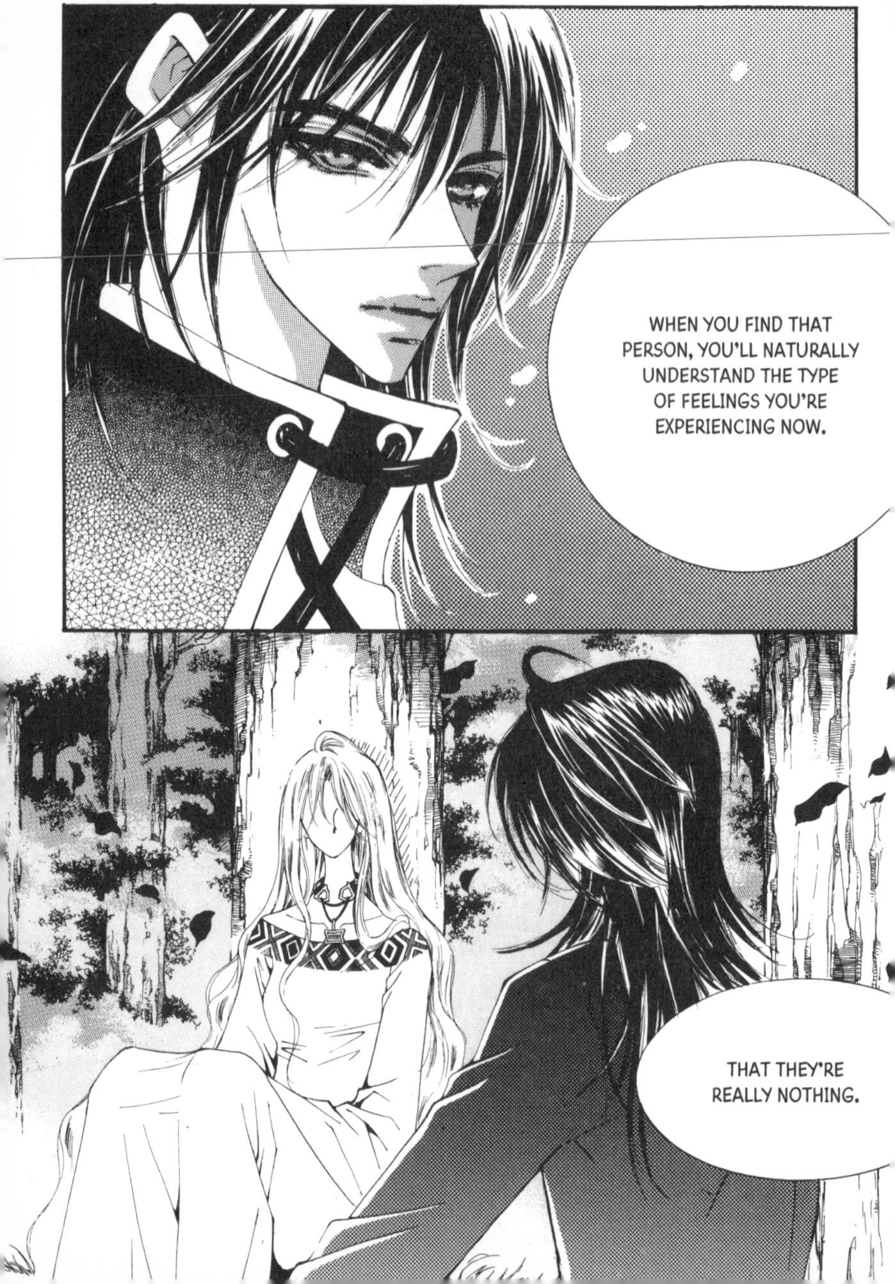
WHEN YOU FIND THAT PERSON, YOU'LL NATURALLY UNDERSTAND THE TYPE OF FEELINGS YOU'RE EXPERIENCING NOW.
THAT THEY'RE REALLY NOTHING.

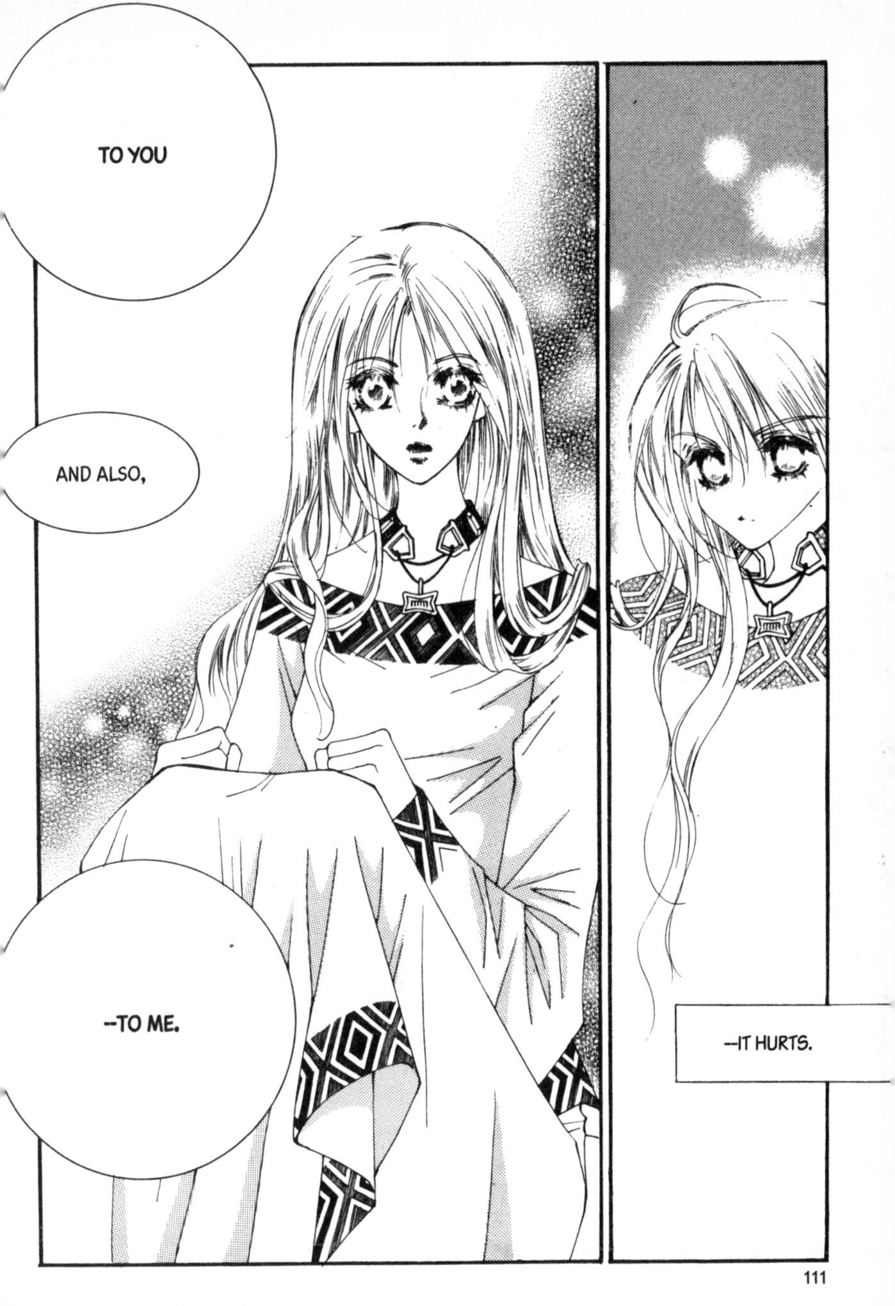
TO YOU
AND ALSO,
--TO ME.
--IT HURTS.

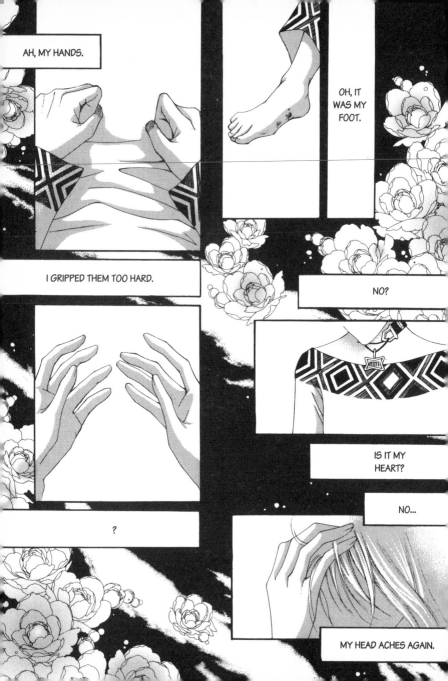

AH, MY HANDS.

OH, IT WAS MY FOOT.

I GRIPPED THEM TOO HARD.

NO?

?

IS IT MY HEART?

NO...

MY HEAD ACHES AGAIN.

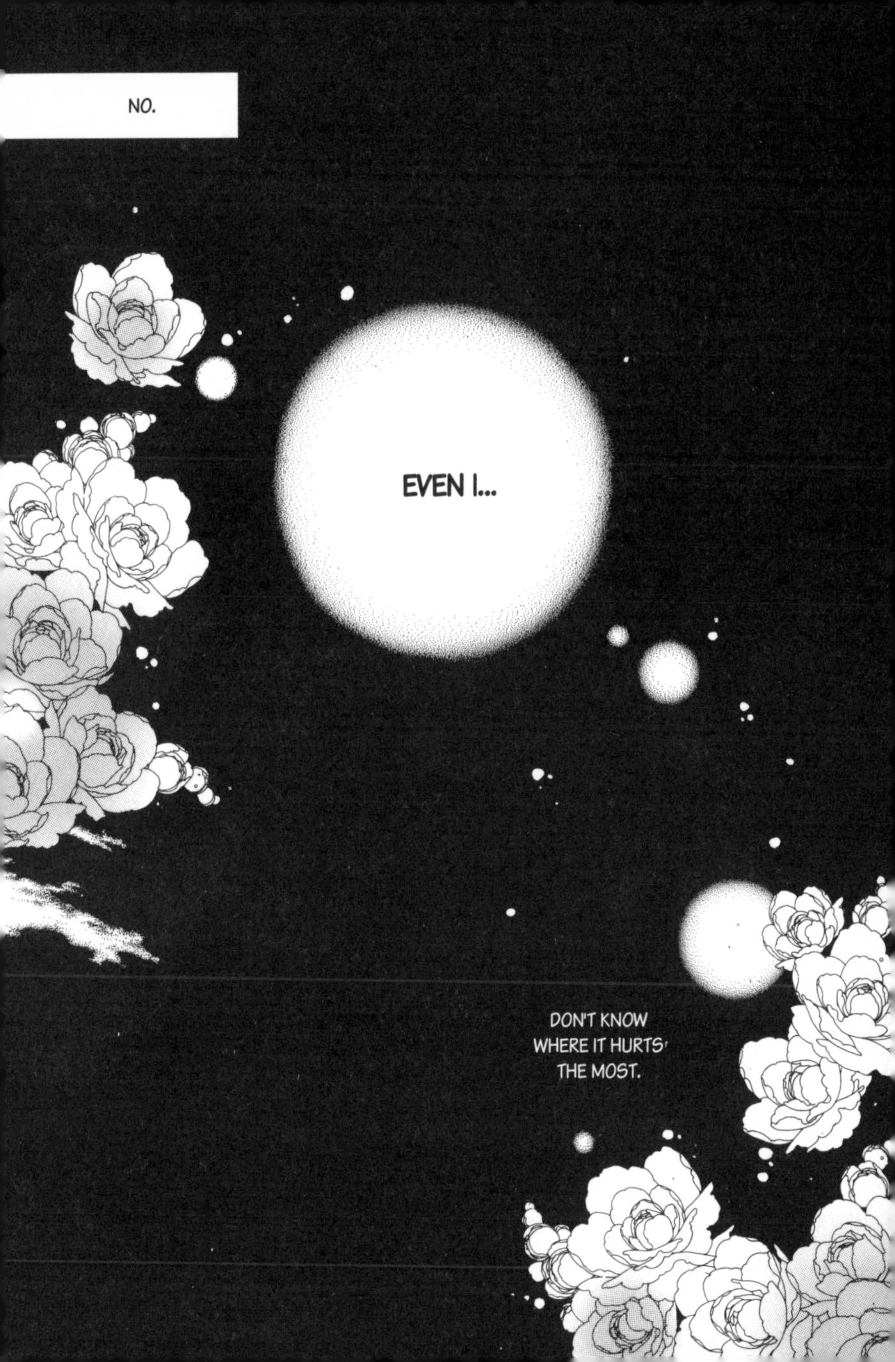
NO.
EVEN I...
DON'T KNOW WHERE IT HURTS THE MOST.

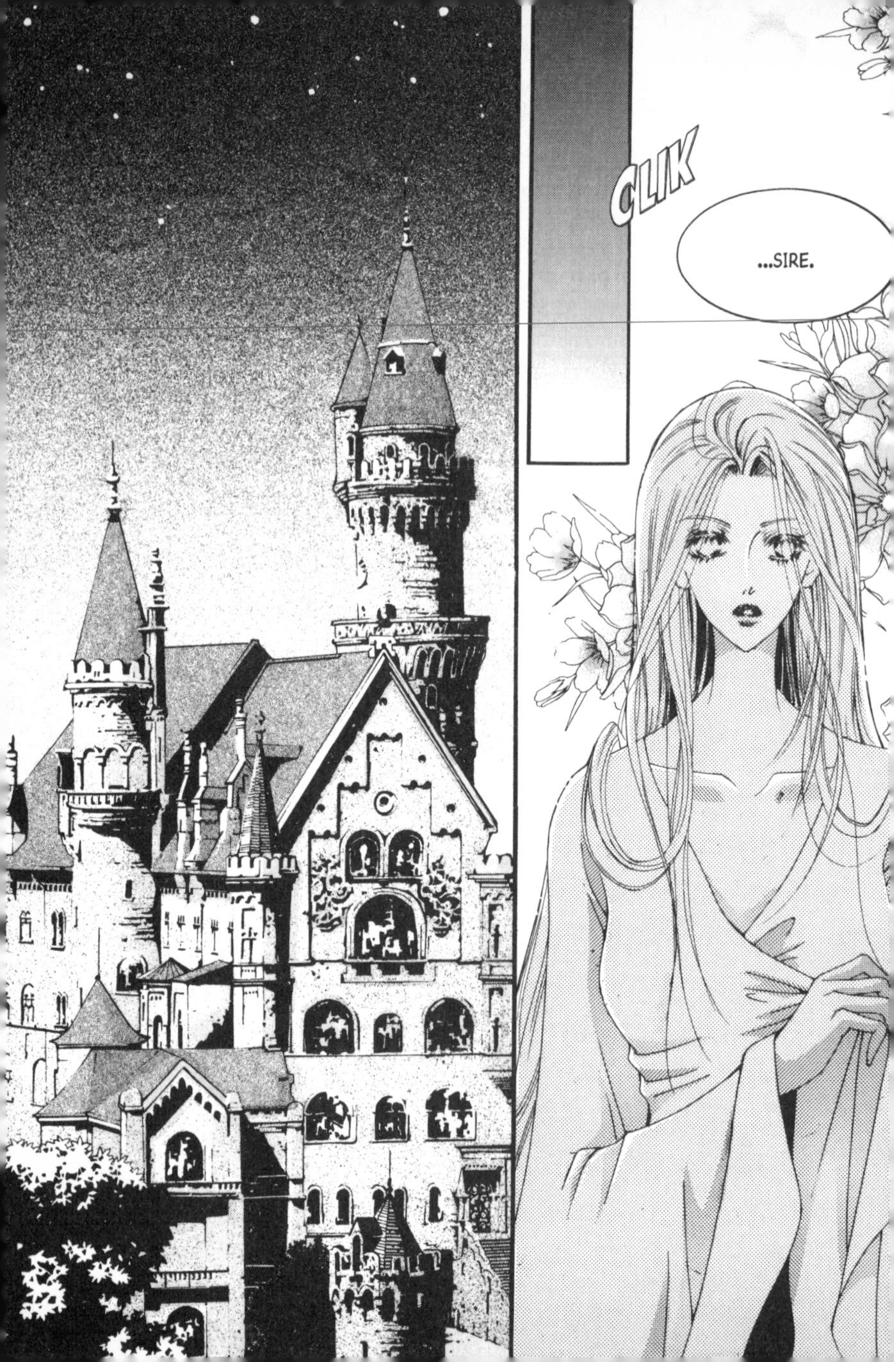
CLIK
...SIRE.

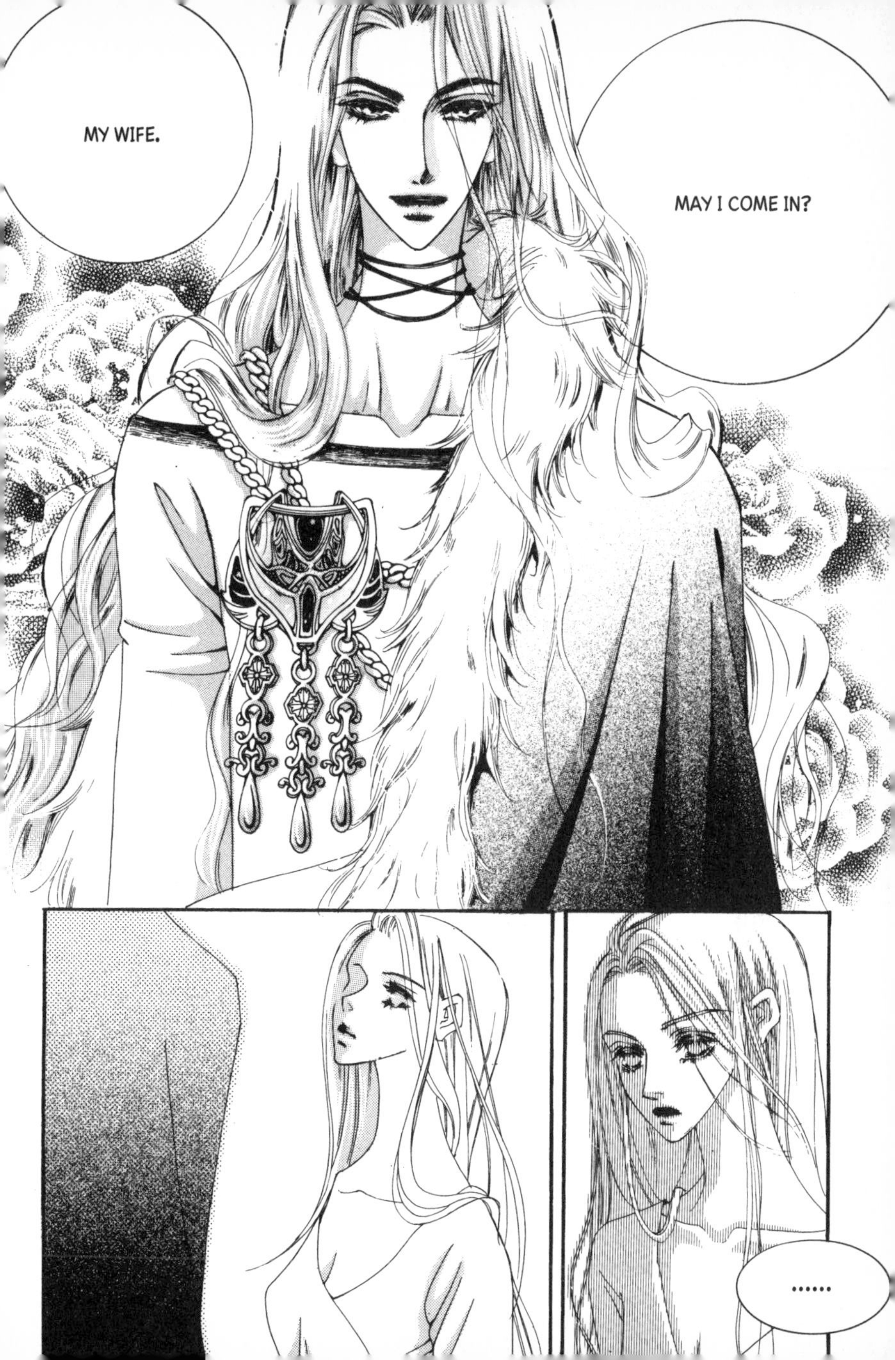
MY WIFE.
MAY I COME IN?
......

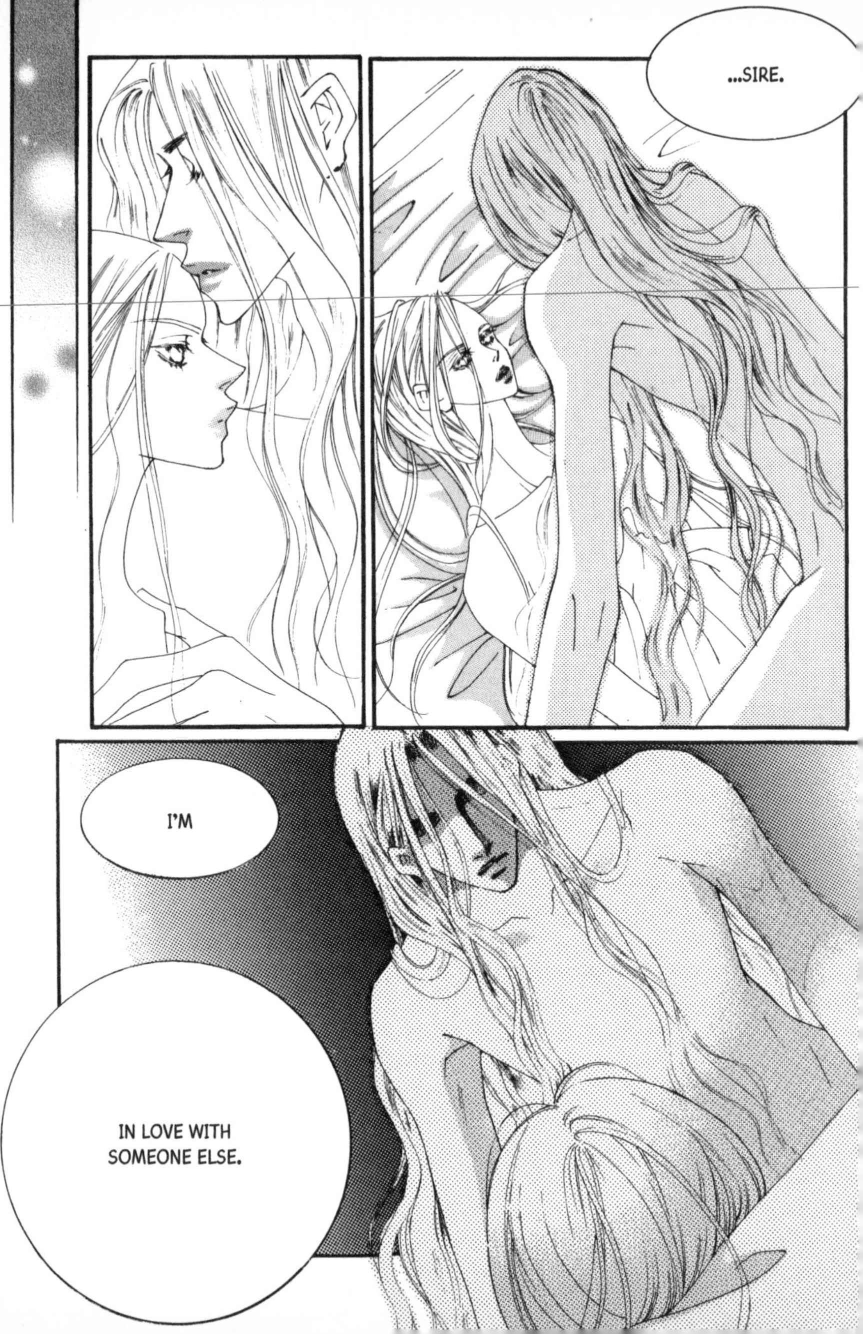
...SIRE.
I'M
IN LOVE WITH SOMEONE ELSE.

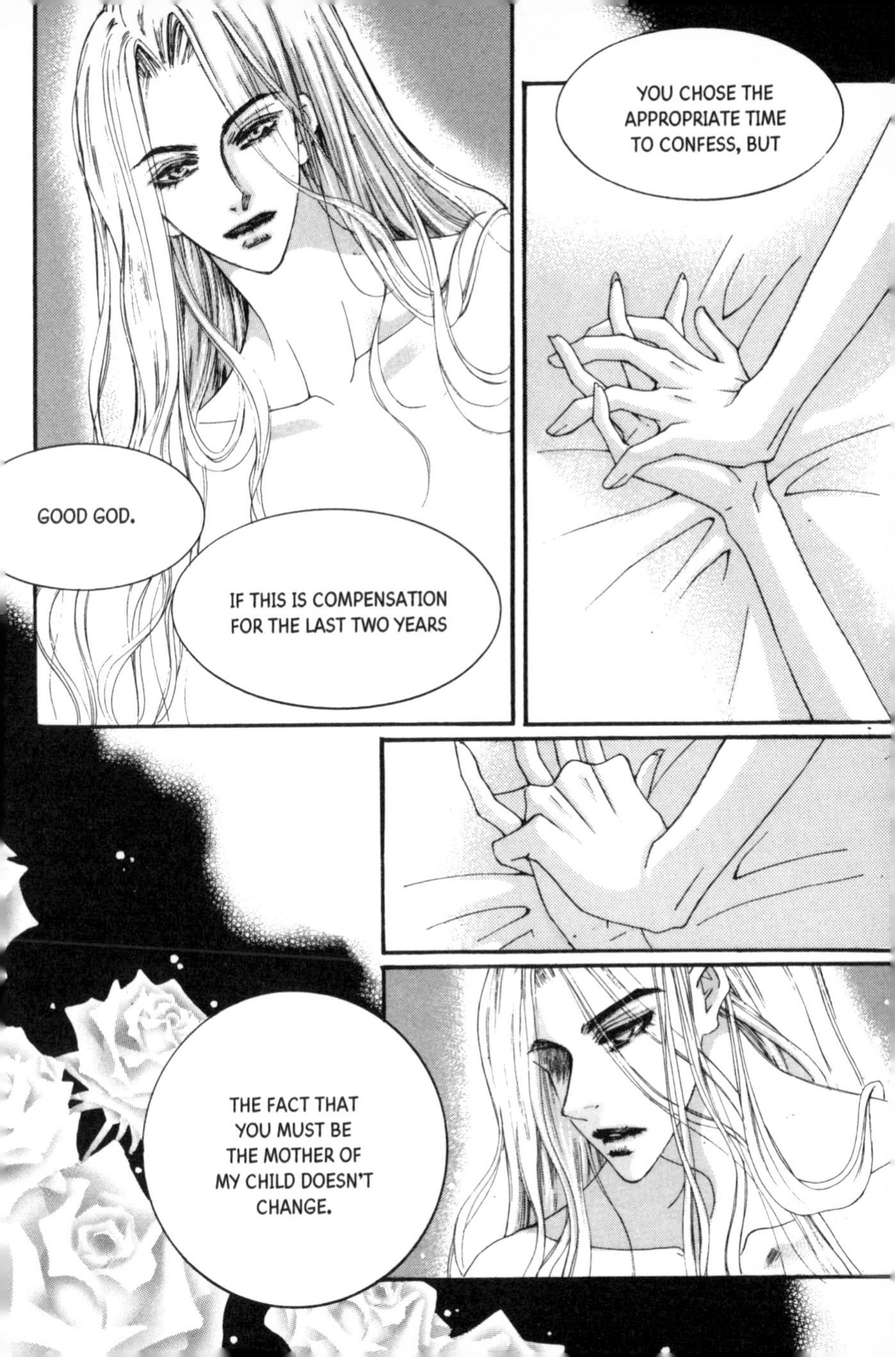
GOOD GOD.
IF THIS IS COMPENSATION FOR THE LAST TWO YEARS
YOU CHOSE THE APPROPRIATE TIME TO CONFESS, BUT
THE FACT THAT YOU MUST BE THE MOTHER OF MY CHILD DOESN'T CHANGE.

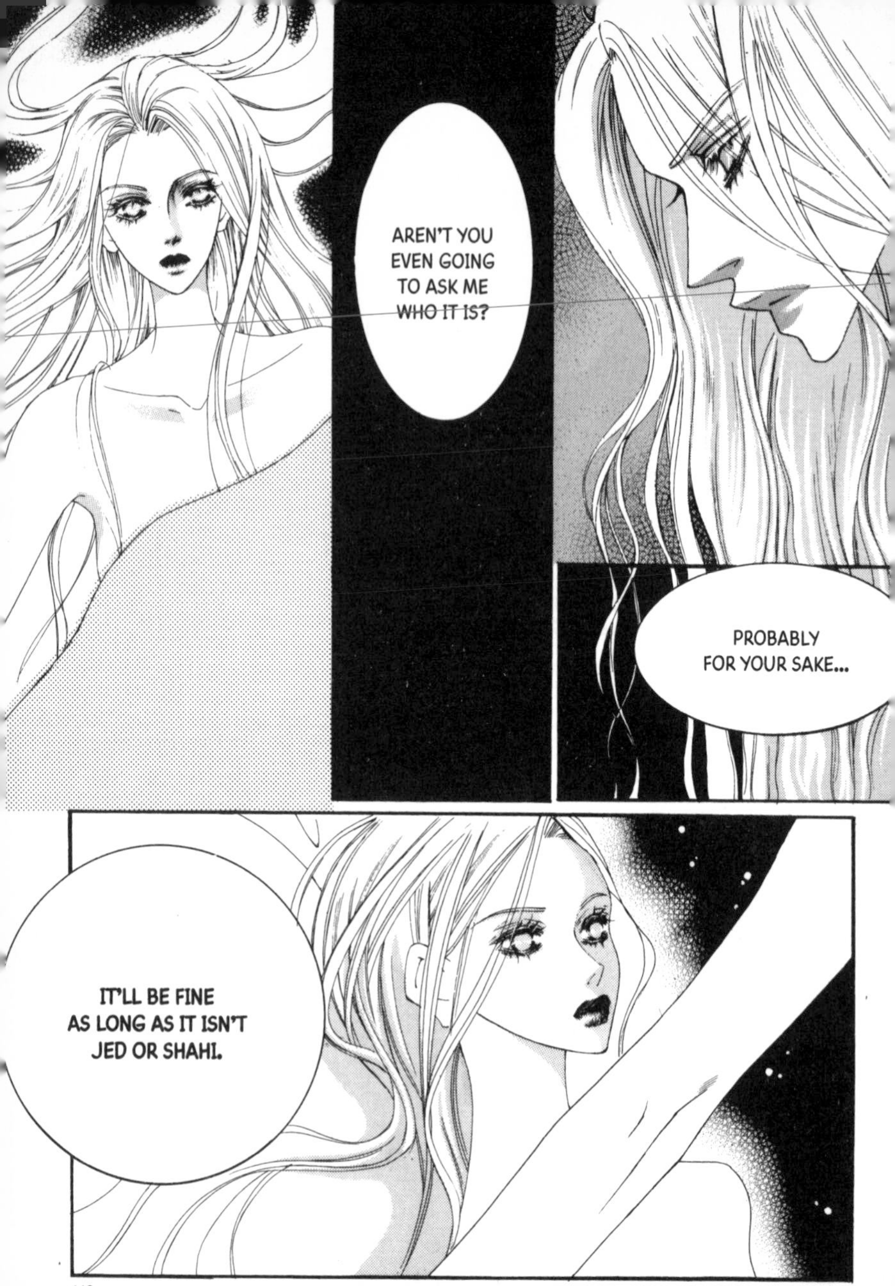
AREN'T YOU EVEN GOING TO ASK ME WHO IT IS?
PROBABLY FOR YOUR SAKE...
IT'LL BE FINE AS LONG AS IT ISN'T JED OR SHAHI.

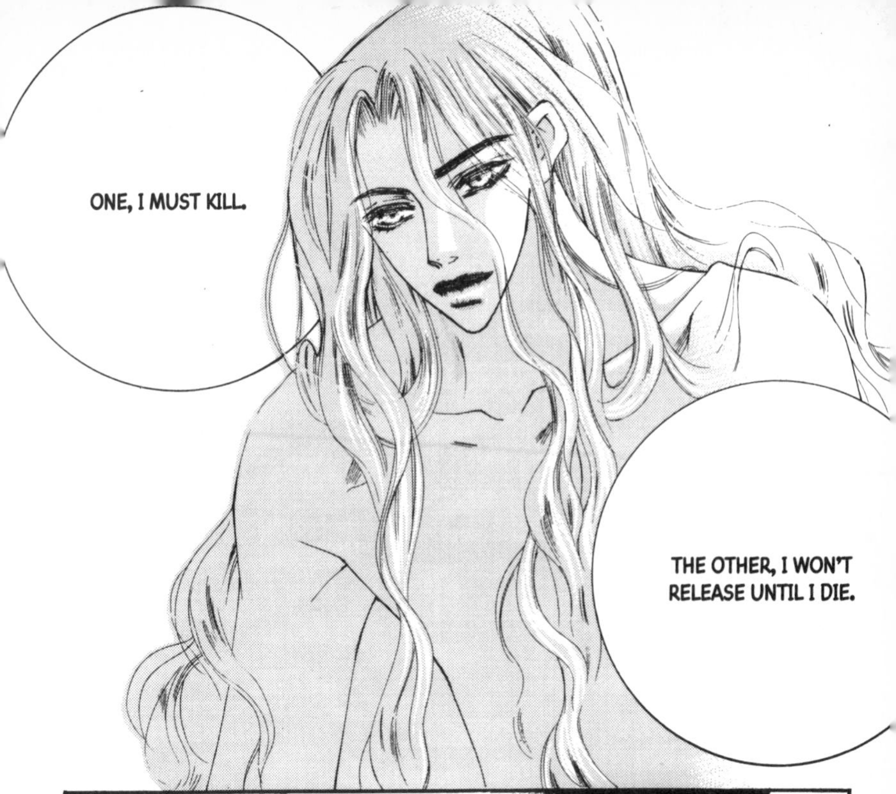
ONE, I MUST KILL.
THE OTHER, I WON'T RELEASE UNTIL I DIE.

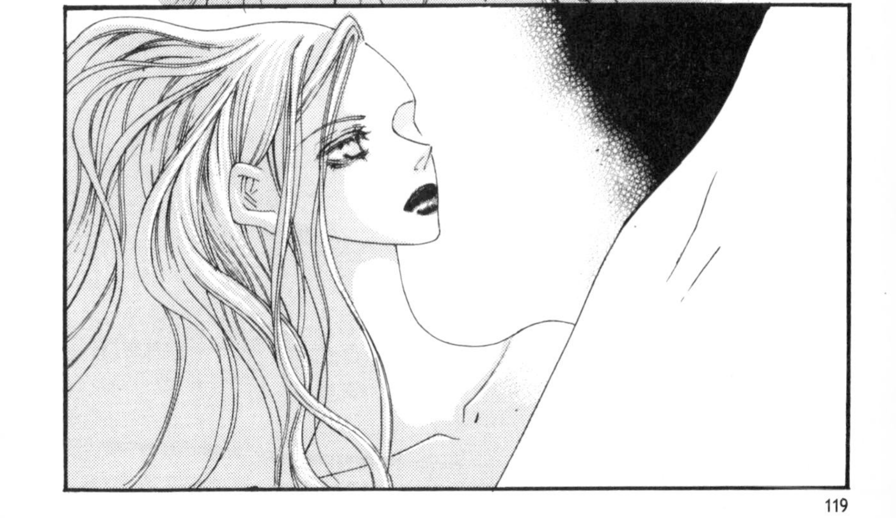

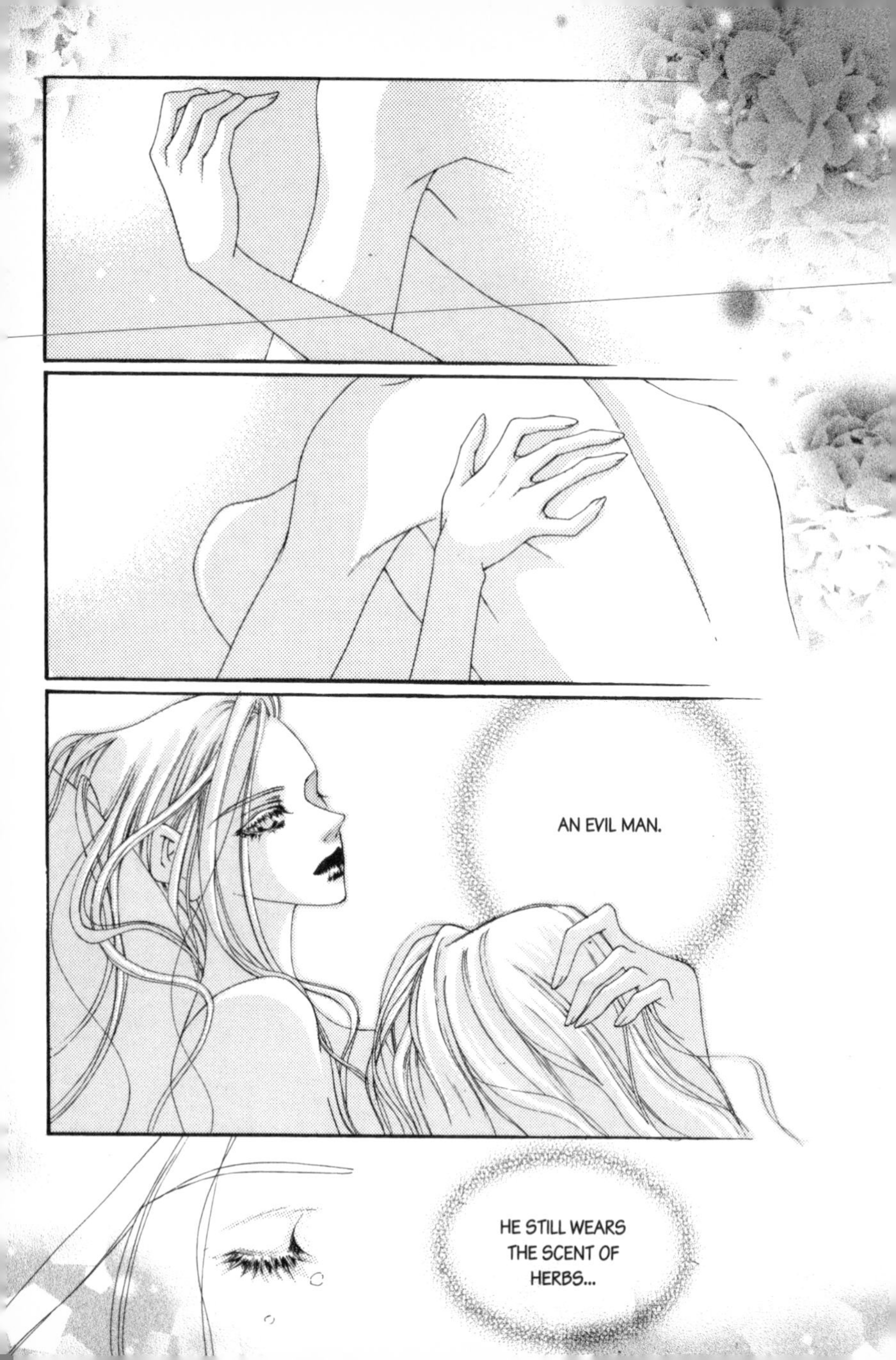
AN EVIL MAN.
HE STILL WEARS THE SCENT OF HERBS...

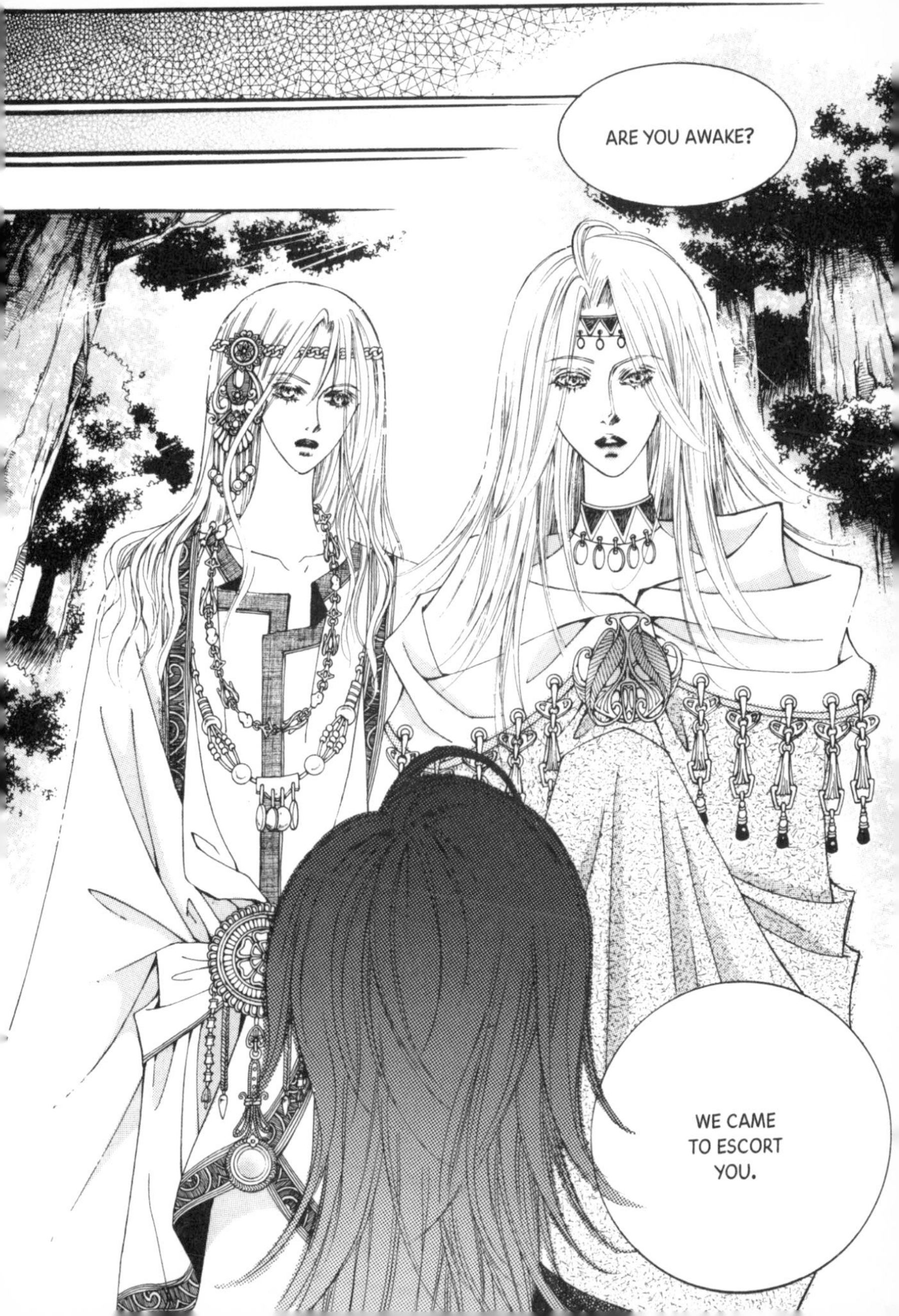
ARE YOU AWAKE?
WE CAME TO ESCORT YOU.

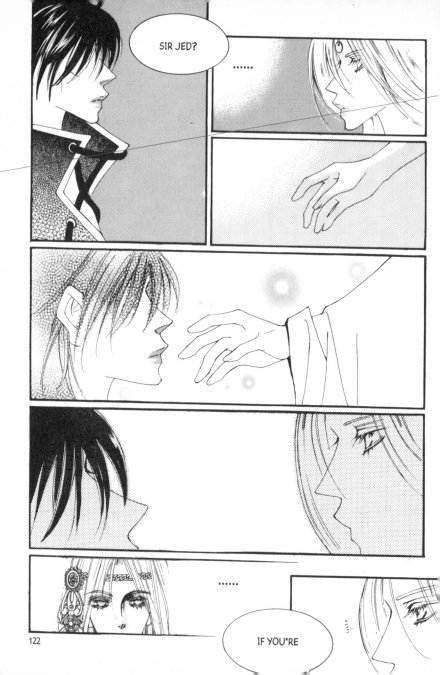

SIR JED?

......

......

IF YOU'RE

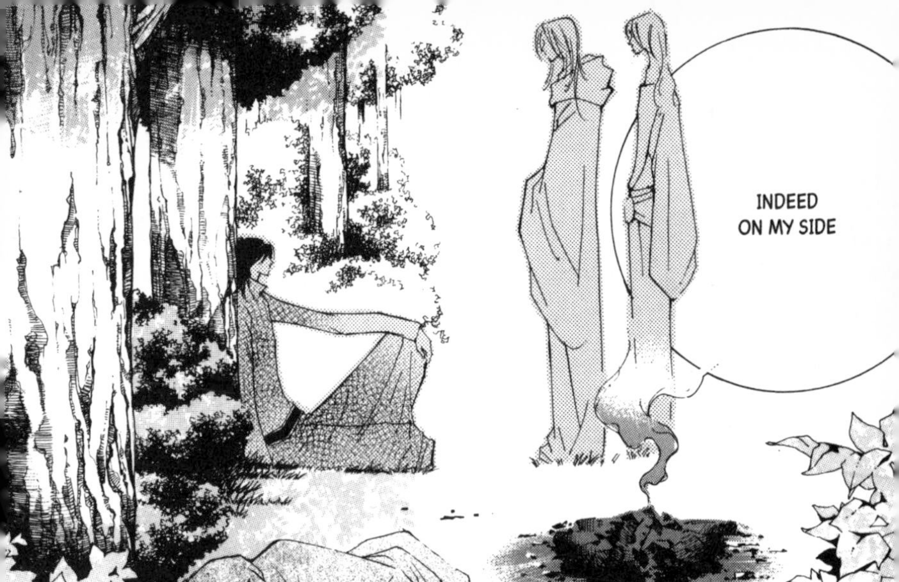
INDEED
ON MY SIDE
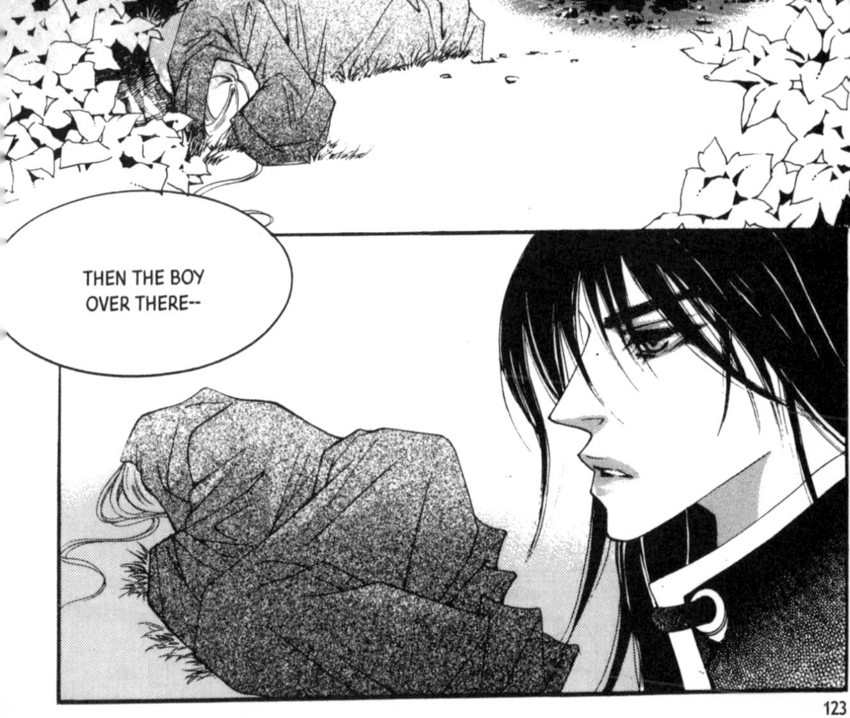
THEN THE BOY
OVER THERE--

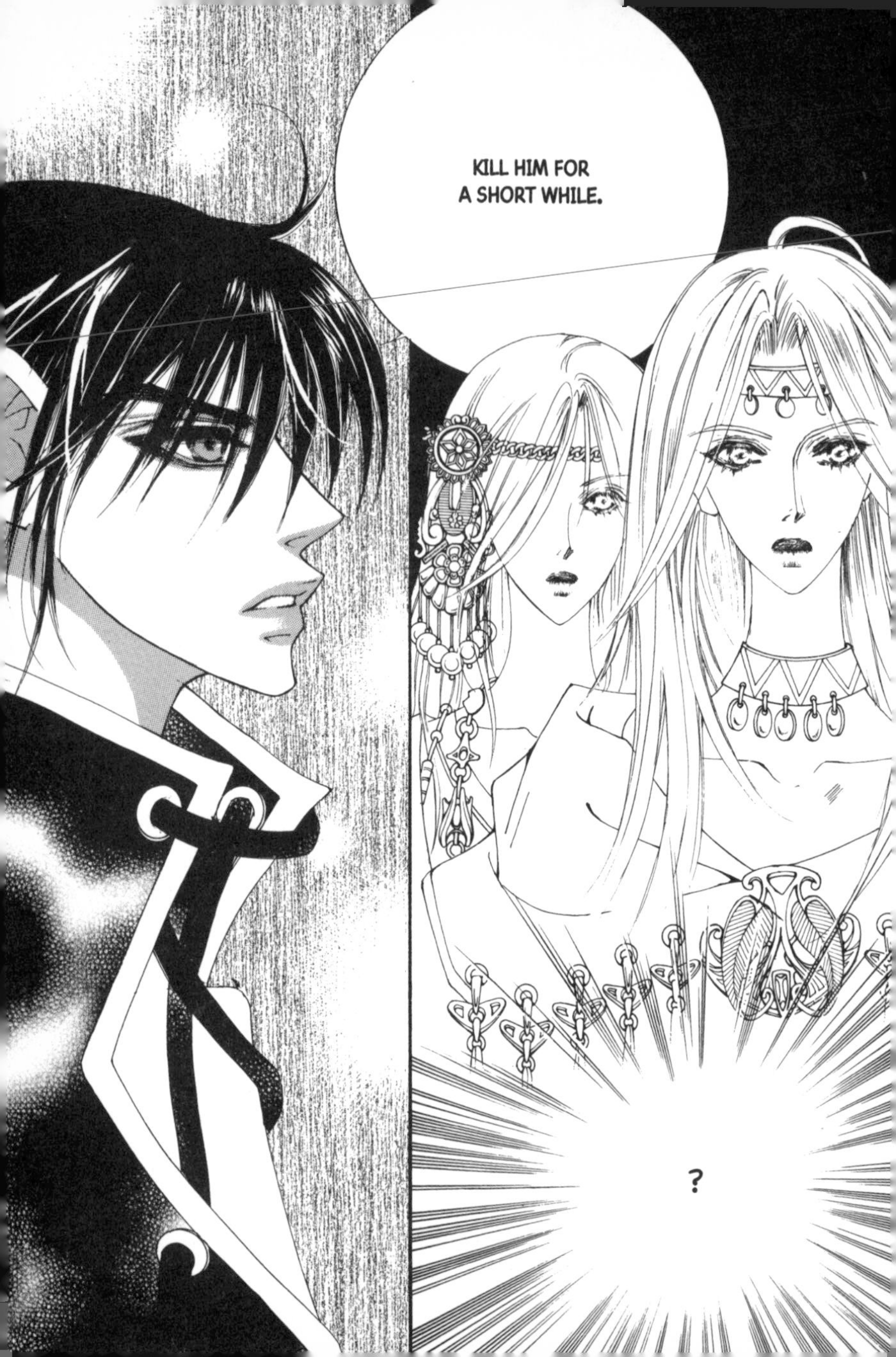
KILL HIM FOR
A SHORT WHILE.
?

......

UM...
BROTHER-.

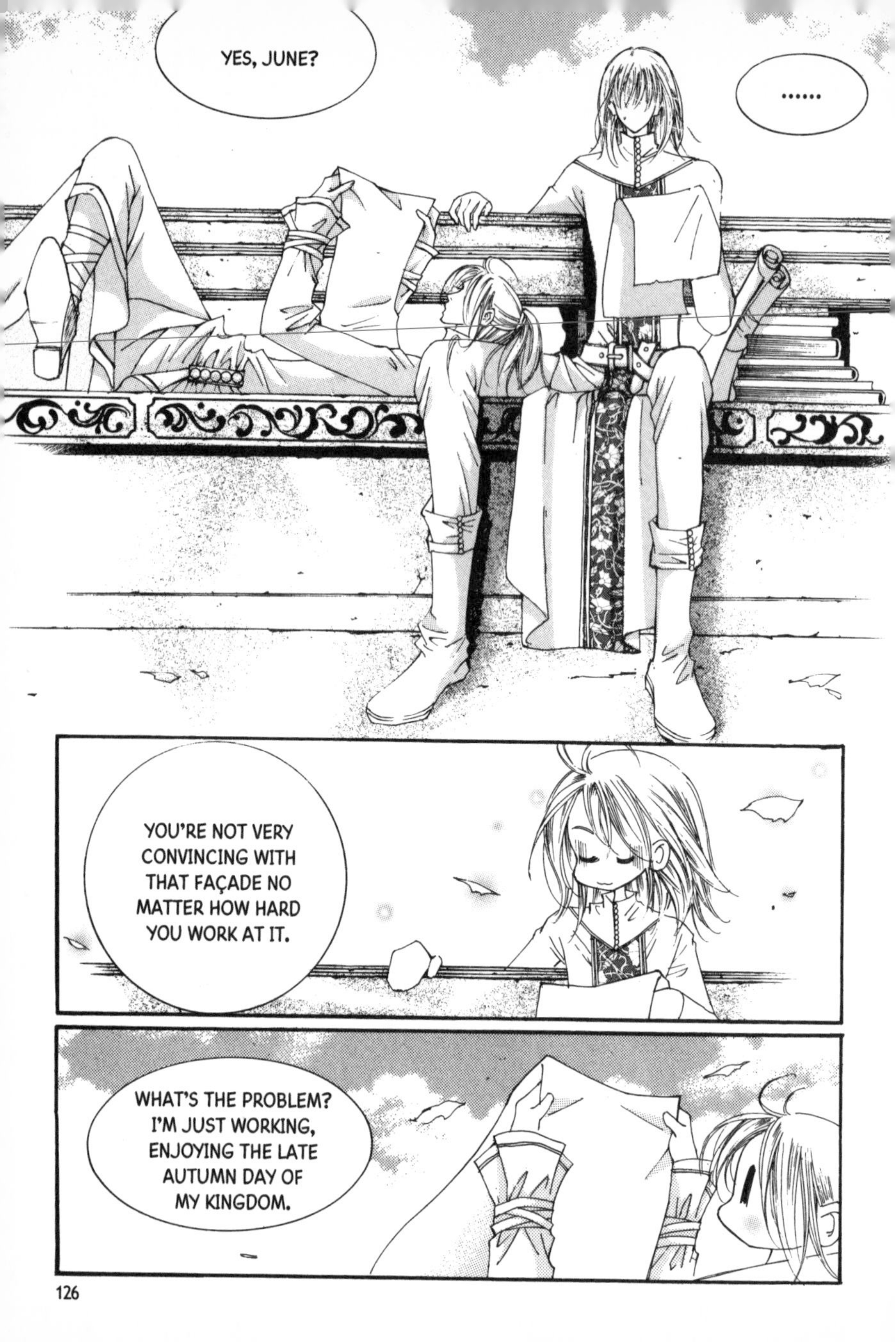
YES, JUNE?
......
YOU'RE NOT VERY CONVINCING WITH THAT FAÇADE NO MATTER HOW HARD YOU WORK AT IT.
WHAT'S THE PROBLEM? I'M JUST WORKING, ENJOYING THE LATE AUTUMN DAY OF MY KINGDOM.

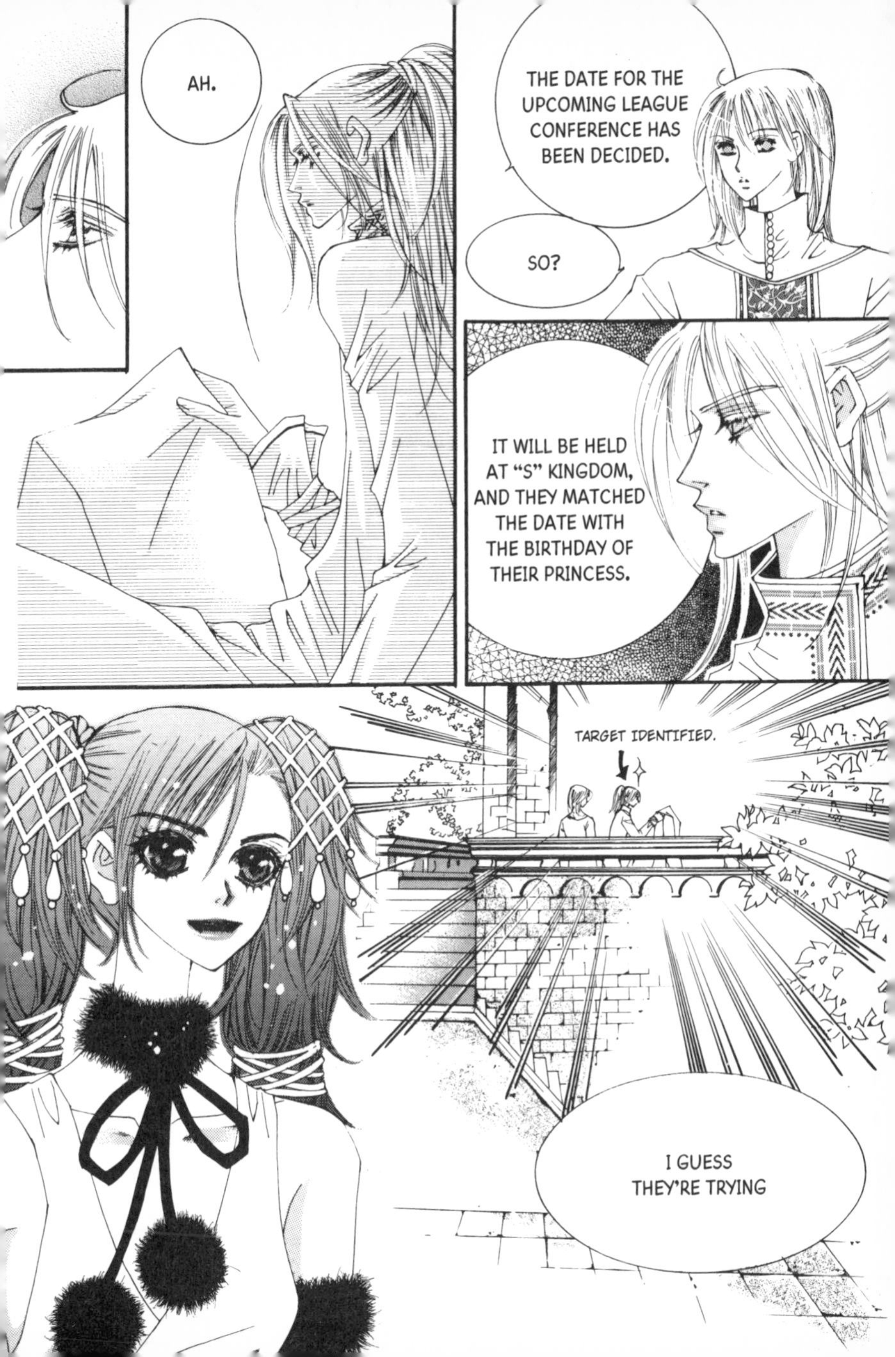
AH.
THE DATE FOR THE UPCOMING LEAGUE CONFERENCE HAS BEEN DECIDED.
SO?
IT WILL BE HELD AT "S" KINGDOM, AND THEY MATCHED THE DATE WITH THE BIRTHDAY OF THEIR PRINCESS.
TARGET IDENTIFIED.
I GUESS THEY'RE TRYING

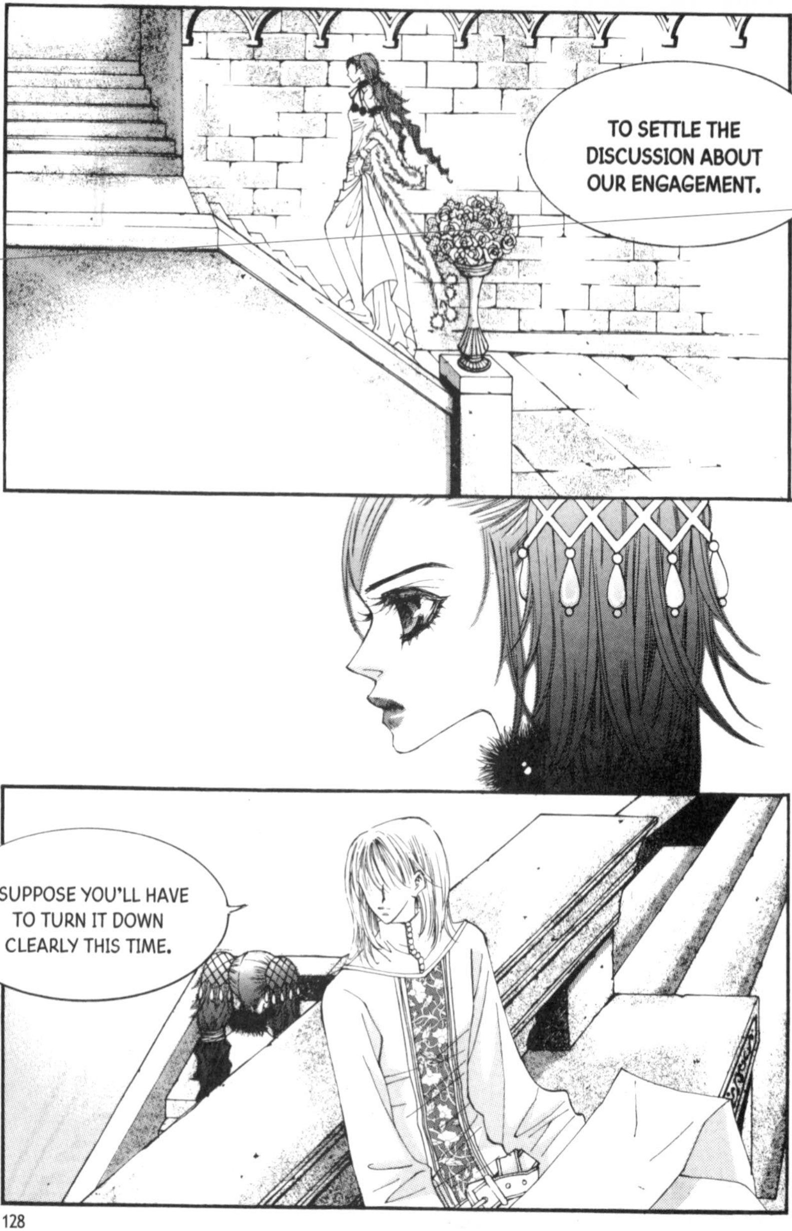
TO SETTLE THE DISCUSSION ABOUT OUR ENGAGEMENT.
I SUPPOSE YOU'LL HAVE TO TURN IT DOWN CLEARLY THIS TIME.

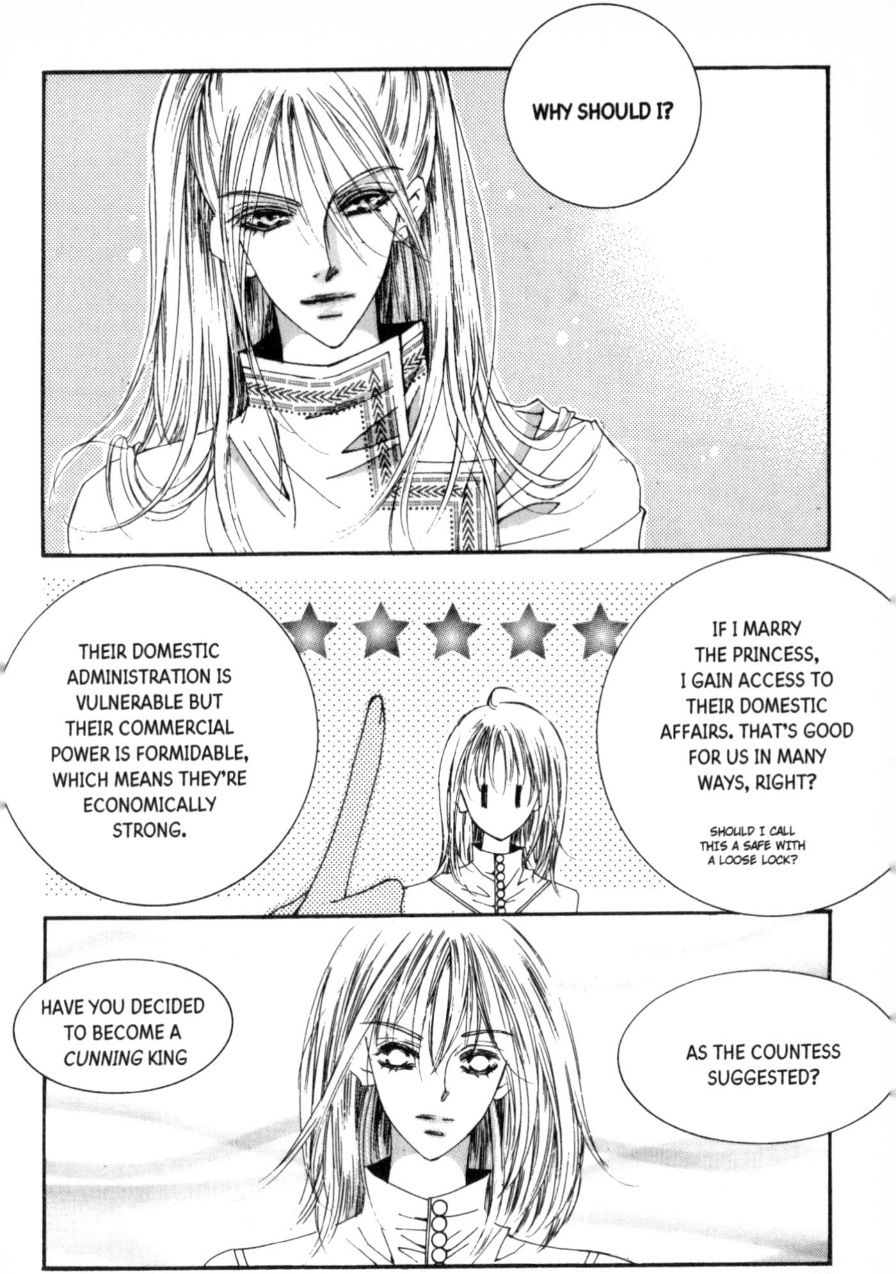
WHY SHOULD I?
THEIR DOMESTIC ADMINISTRATION IS VULNERABLE BUT THEIR COMMERCIAL POWER IS FORMIDABLE, WHICH MEANS THEY'RE ECONOMICALLY STRONG.
IF I MARRY THE PRINCESS, I GAIN ACCESS TO THEIR DOMESTIC AFFAIRS. THAT'S GOOD FOR US IN MANY WAYS, RIGHT?
SHOULD I CALL THIS A SAFE WITH A LOOSE LOCK?
HAVE YOU DECIDED TO BECOME A *CUNNING* KING
AS THE COUNTESS SUGGESTED?

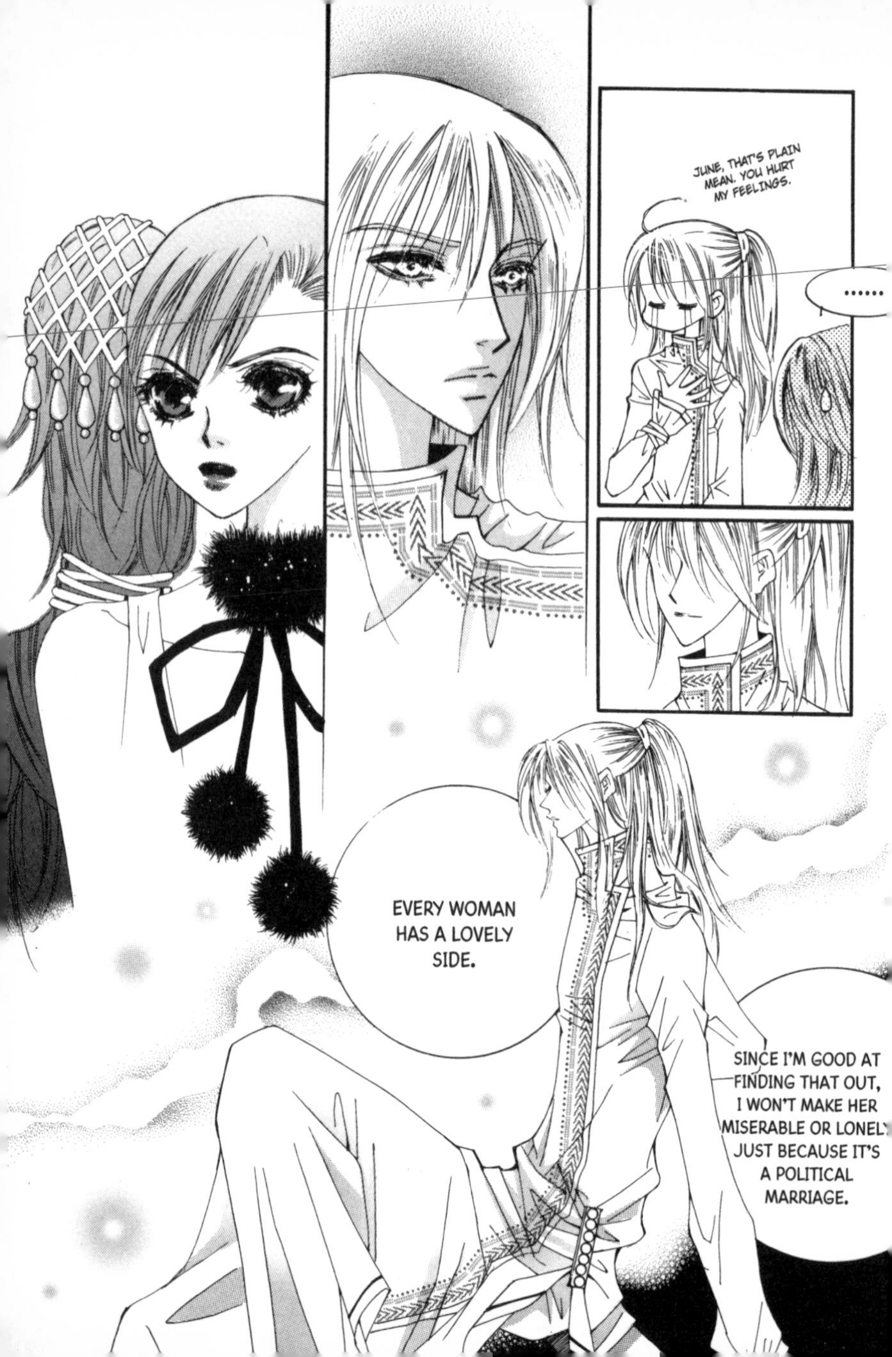

JUNE, THAT'S PLAIN MEAN. YOU HURT MY FEELINGS.
......
EVERY WOMAN HAS A LOVELY SIDE.
SINCE I'M GOOD AT FINDING THAT OUT, I WON'T MAKE HER MISERABLE OR LONEL JUST BECAUSE IT'S A POLITICAL MARRIAGE.

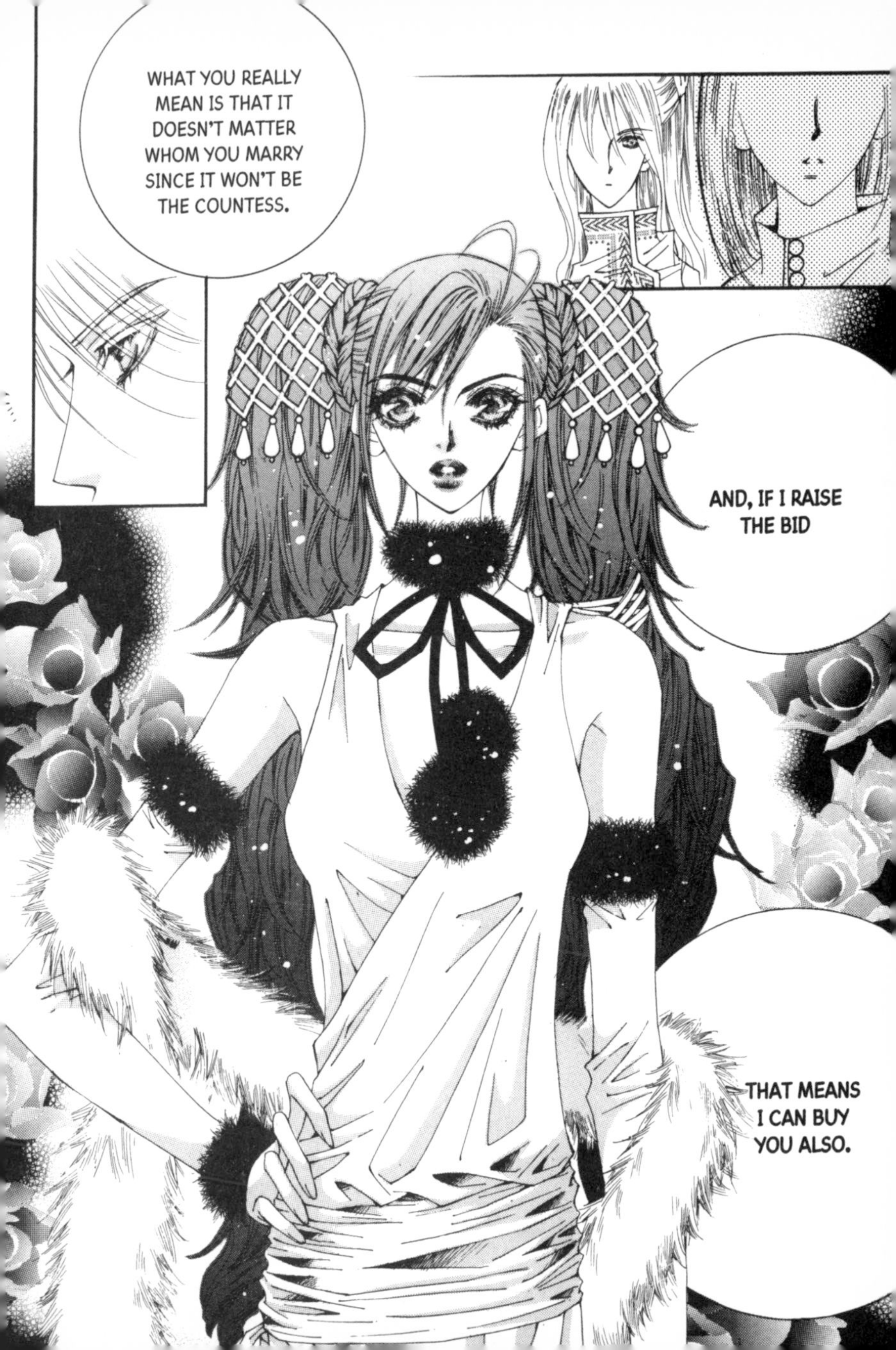
WHAT YOU REALLY MEAN IS THAT IT DOESN'T MATTER WHOM YOU MARRY SINCE IT WON'T BE THE COUNTESS.
AND, IF I RAISE THE BID
THAT MEANS I CAN BUY YOU ALSO.

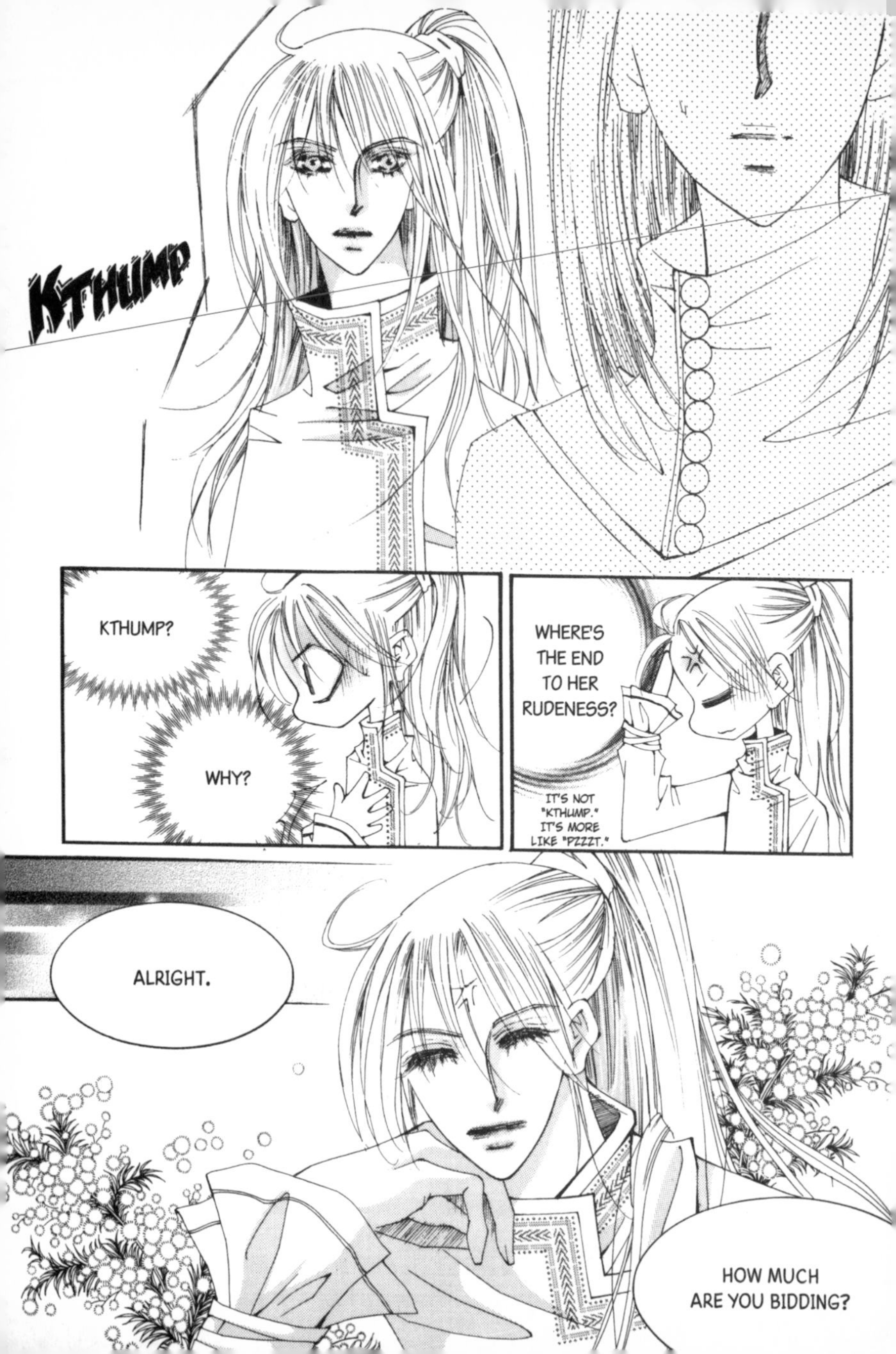
KTHUMP
KTHUMP?
WHY?
WHERE'S THE END TO HER RUDENESS?
IT'S NOT "KTHUMP." IT'S MORE LIKE "PZZZT."
ALRIGHT.
HOW MUCH ARE YOU BIDDING?

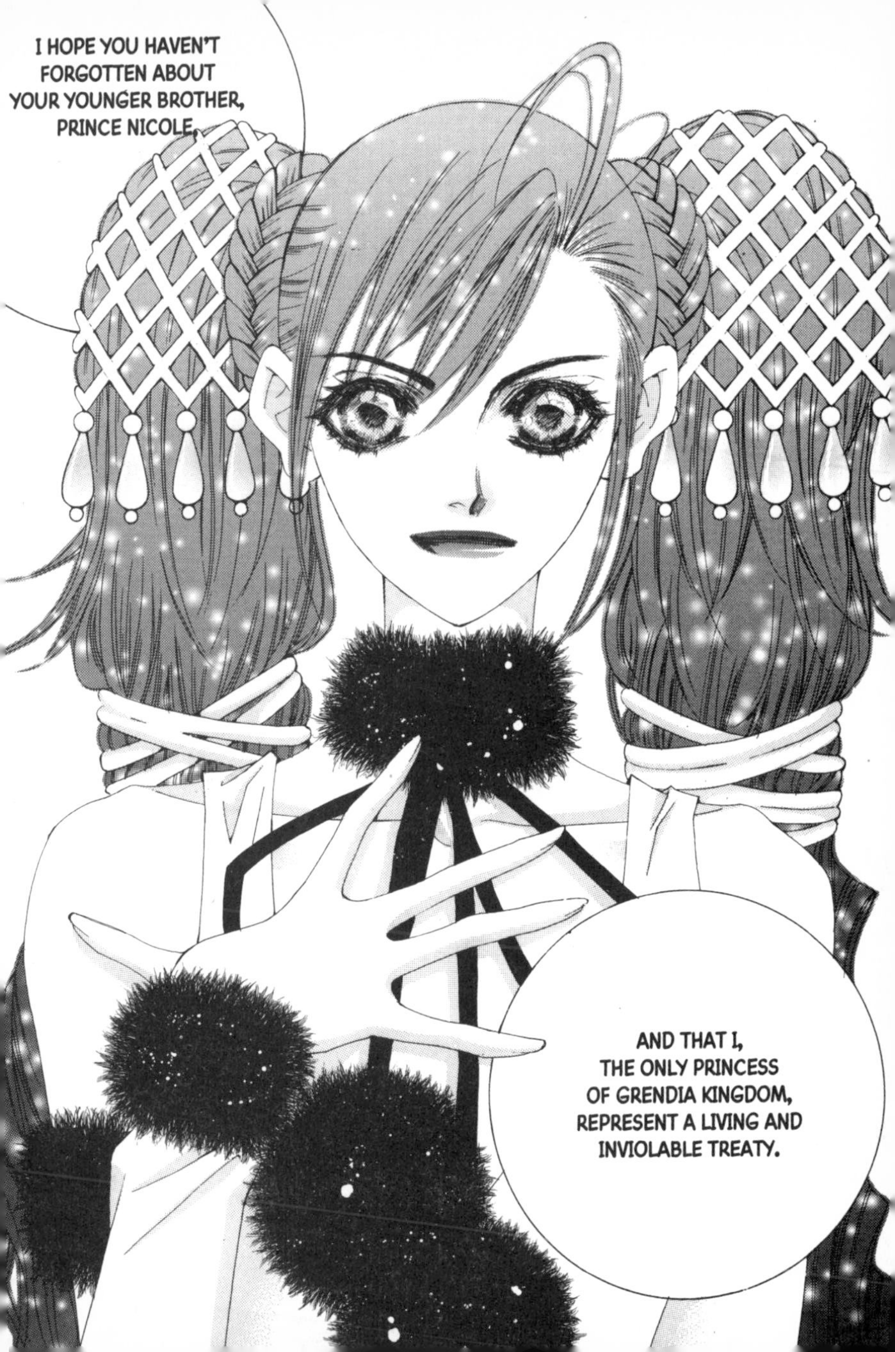
I HOPE YOU HAVEN'T FORGOTTEN ABOUT YOUR YOUNGER BROTHER, PRINCE NICOLE,
AND THAT I, THE ONLY PRINCESS OF GRENDIA KINGDOM, REPRESENT A LIVING AND INVIOLABLE TREATY.

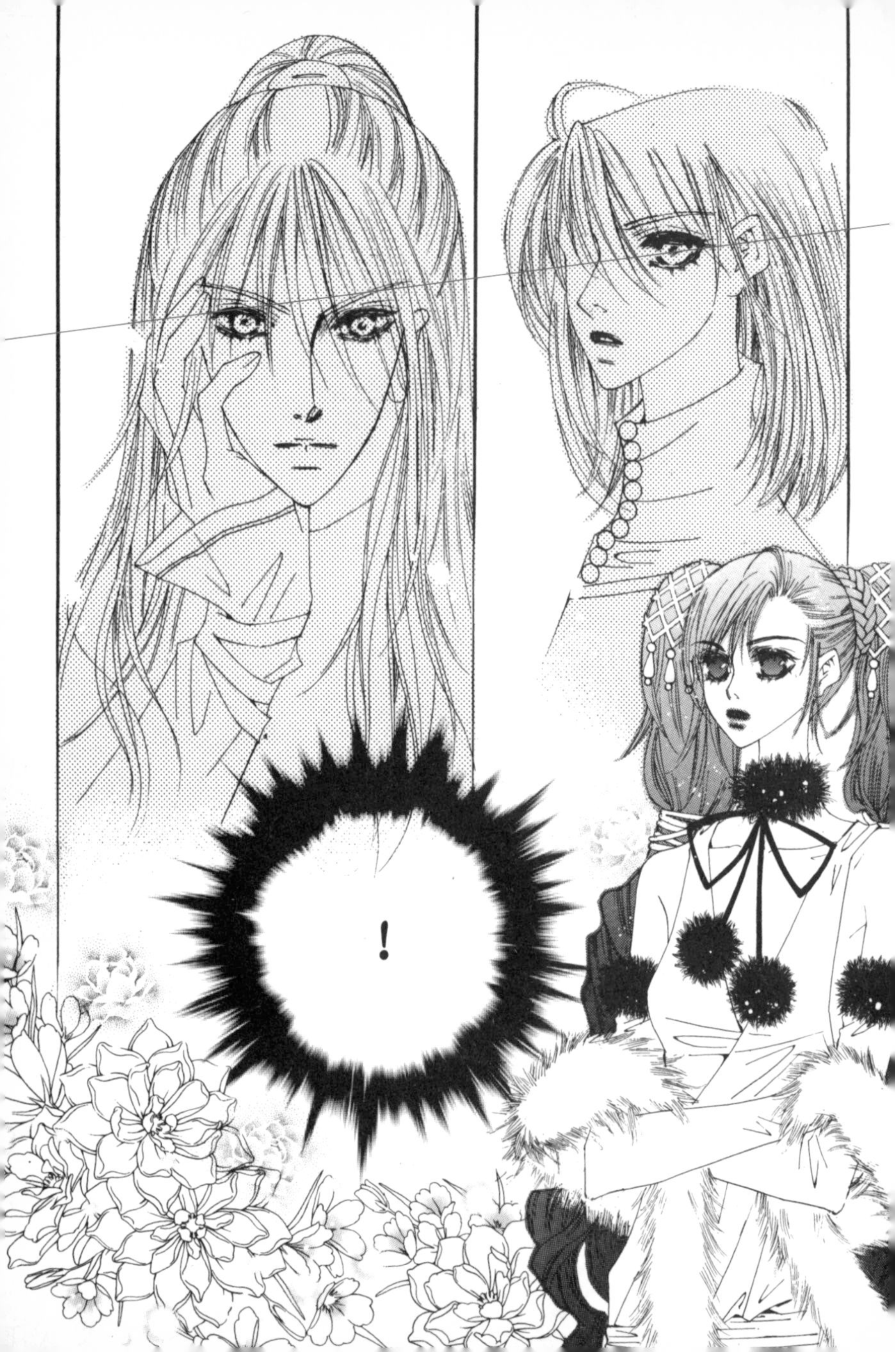
!

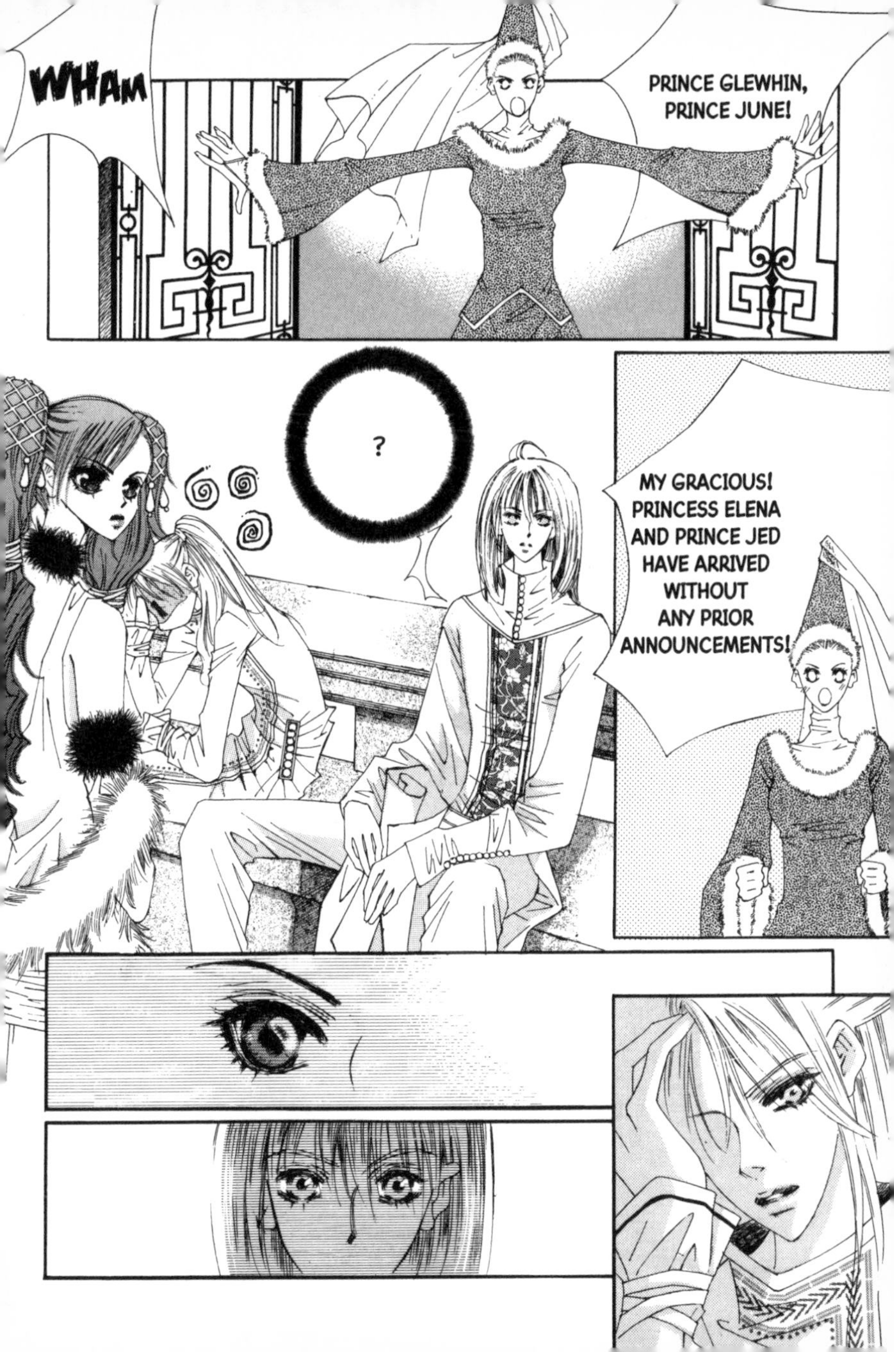
WHAM
PRINCE GLEWHIN, PRINCE JUNE!
?
MY GRACIOUS! PRINCESS ELENA AND PRINCE JED HAVE ARRIVED WITHOUT ANY PRIOR ANNOUNCEMENTS!

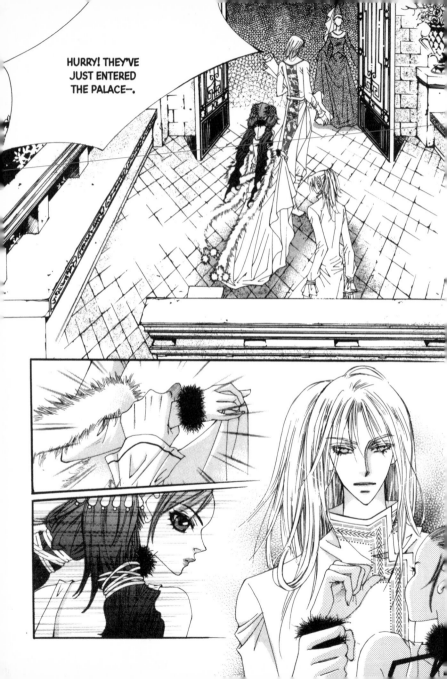

HURRY! THEY'VE
JUST ENTERED
THE PALACE--.

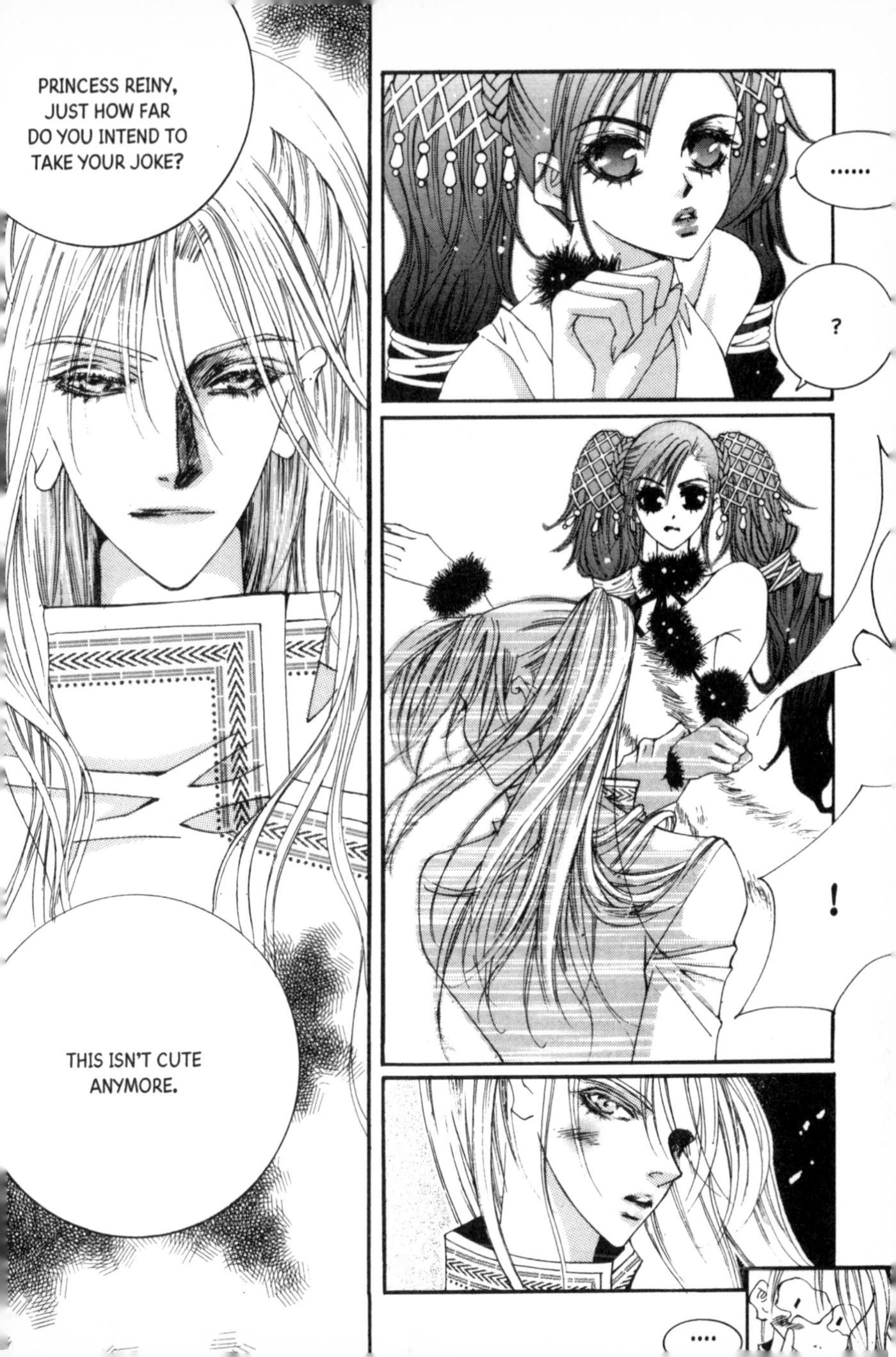
PRINCESS REINY, JUST HOW FAR DO YOU INTEND TO TAKE YOUR JOKE?
THIS ISN'T CUTE ANYMORE.
......
?
!
....

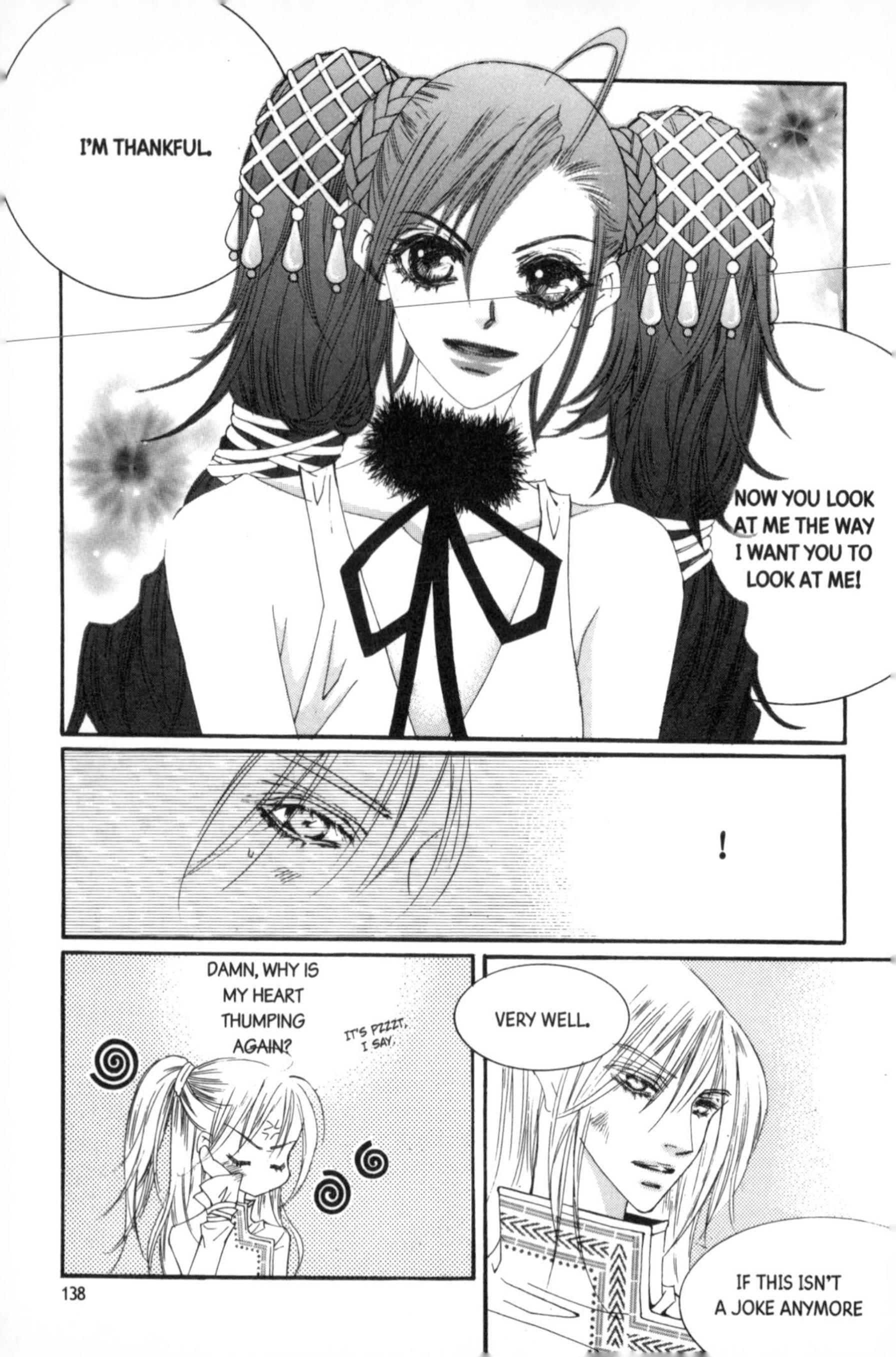
I'M THANKFUL.
NOW YOU LOOK AT ME THE WAY I WANT YOU TO LOOK AT ME!
!
DAMN, WHY IS MY HEART THUMPING AGAIN?
IT'S PZZZT, I SAY.
VERY WELL.
IF THIS ISN'T A JOKE ANYMORE

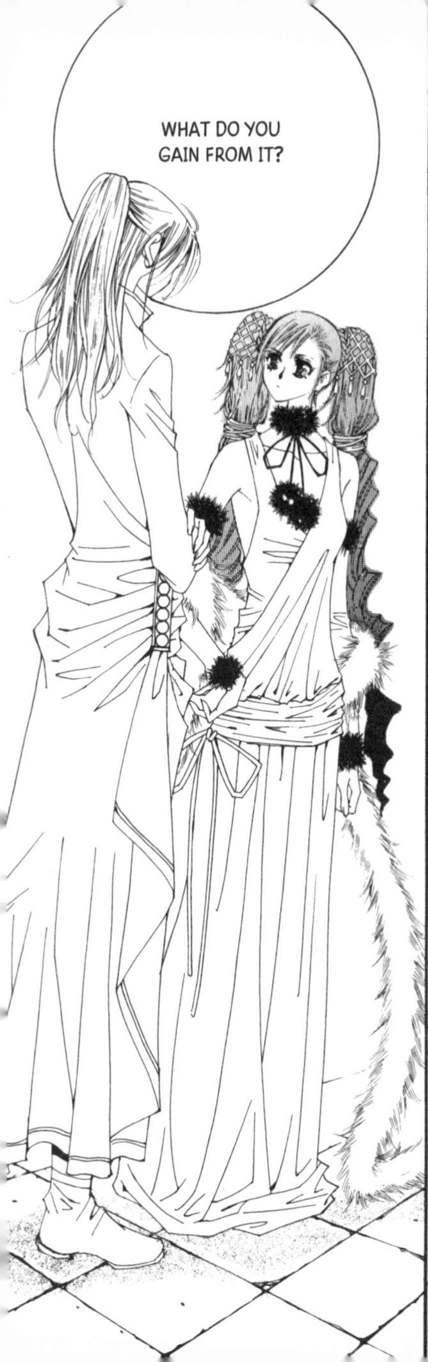
WHAT DO YOU
GAIN FROM IT?
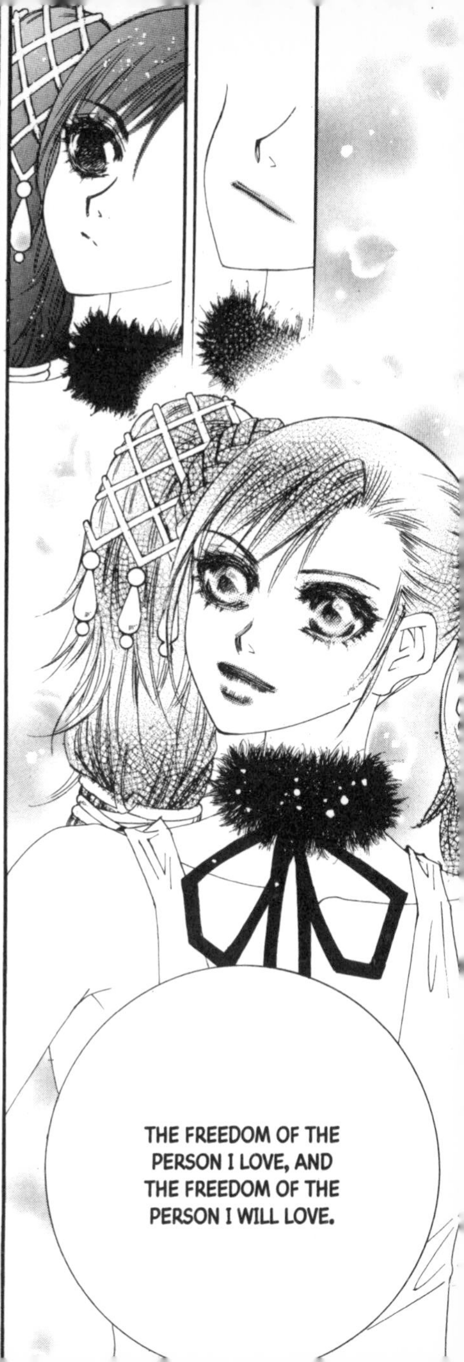
THE FREEDOM OF THE
PERSON I LOVE, AND
THE FREEDOM OF THE
PERSON I WILL LOVE.

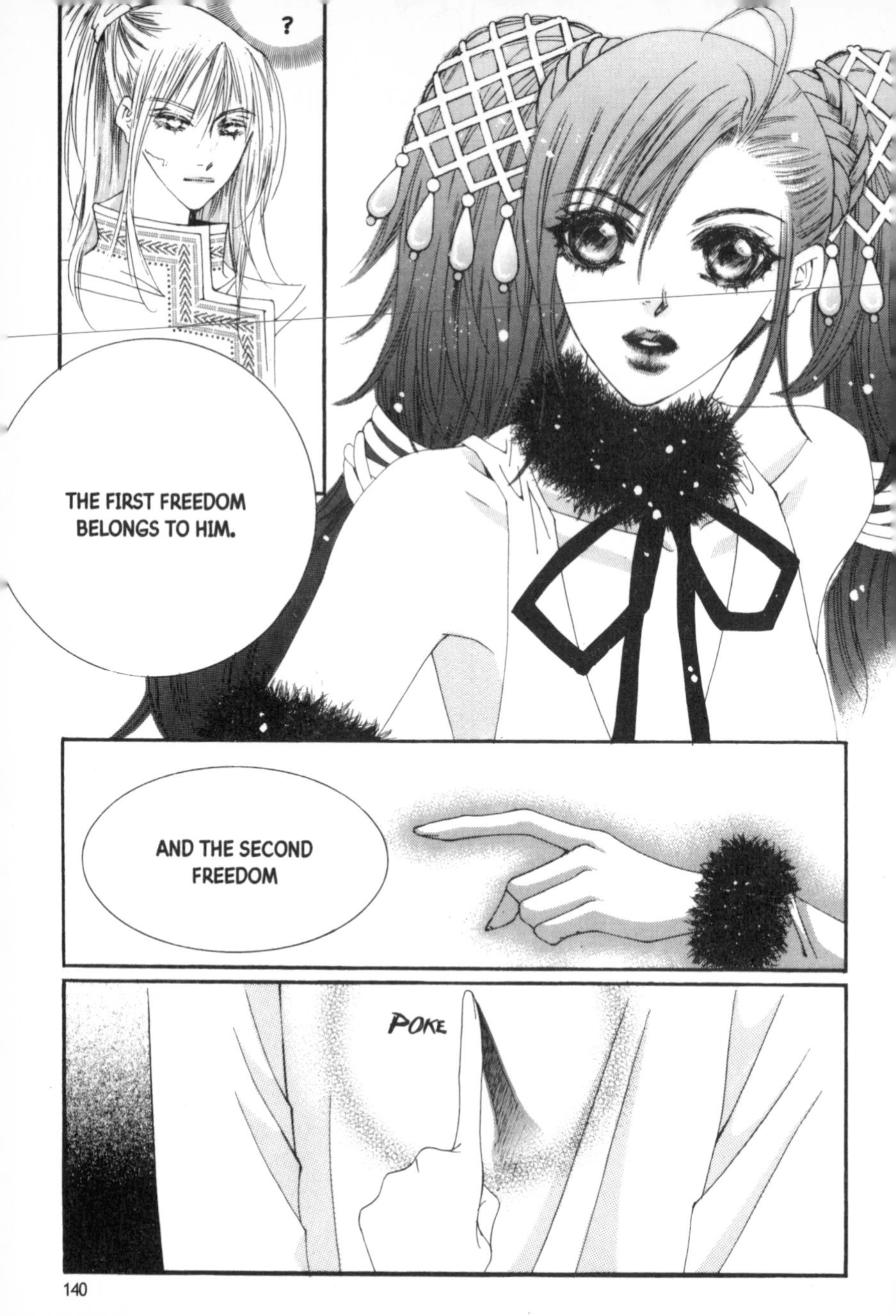
?
THE FIRST FREEDOM BELONGS TO HIM.
AND THE SECOND FREEDOM
POKE

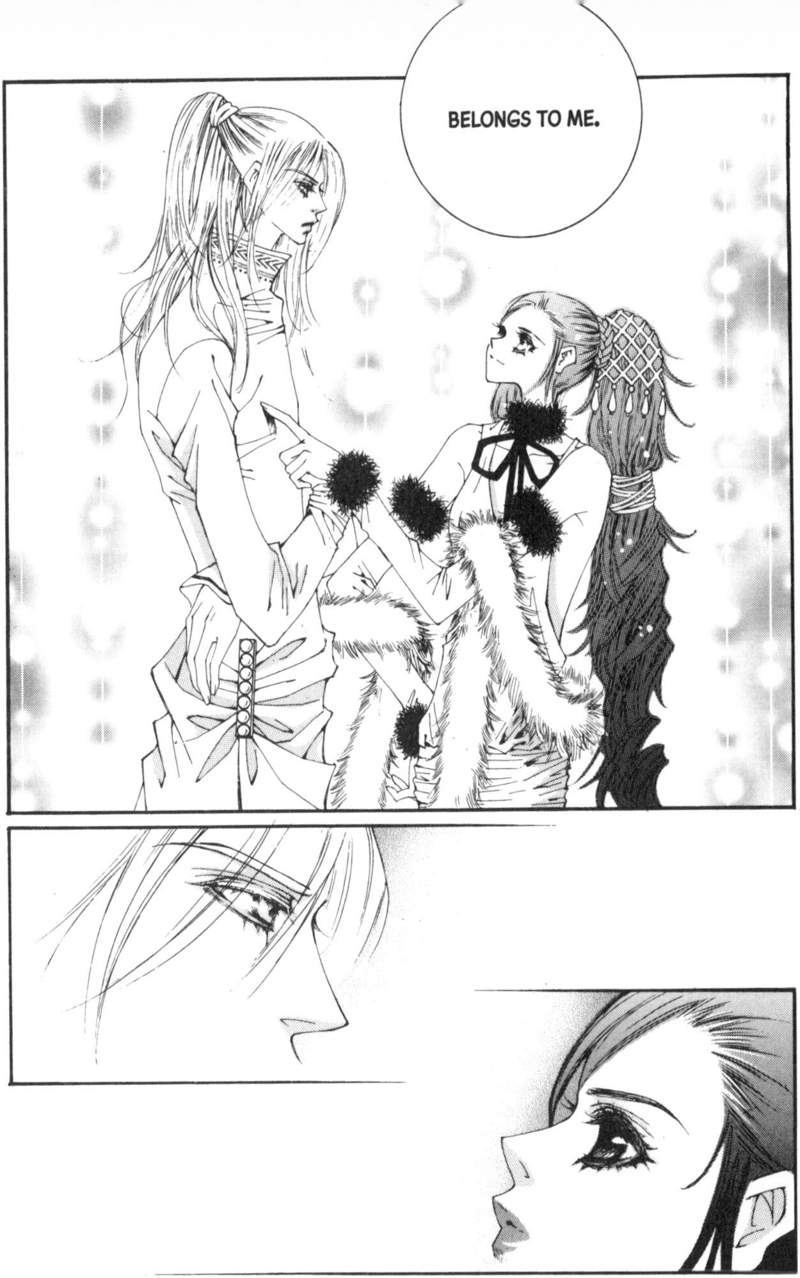
BELONGS TO ME.

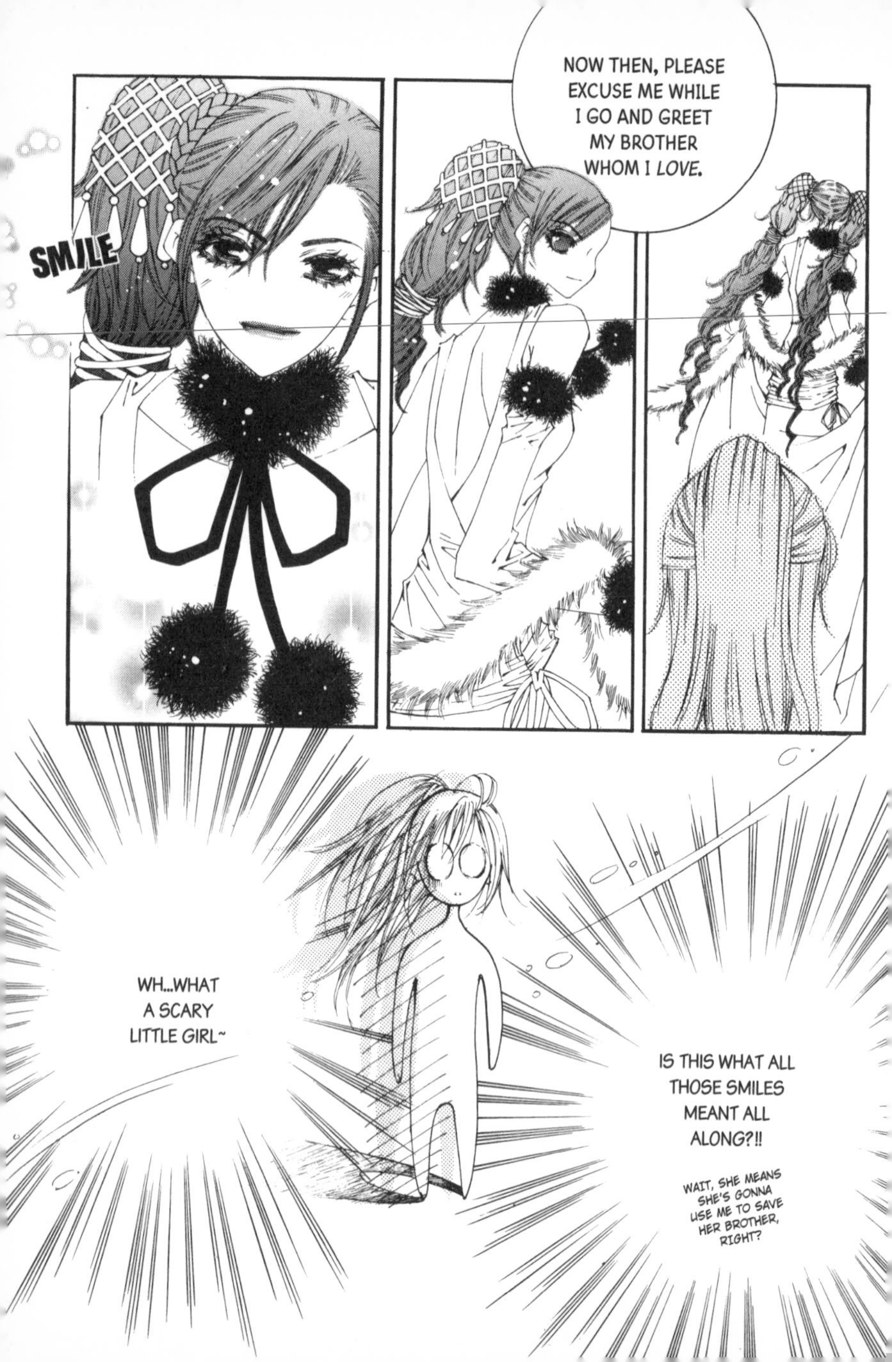
NOW THEN, PLEASE EXCUSE ME WHILE I GO AND GREET MY BROTHER WHOM I *LOVE*.
SMILE
IS THIS WHAT ALL THOSE SMILES MEANT ALL ALONG?!!
WAIT, SHE MEANS SHE'S GONNA USE ME TO SAVE HER BROTHER, RIGHT?
WH...WHAT A SCARY LITTLE GIRL~

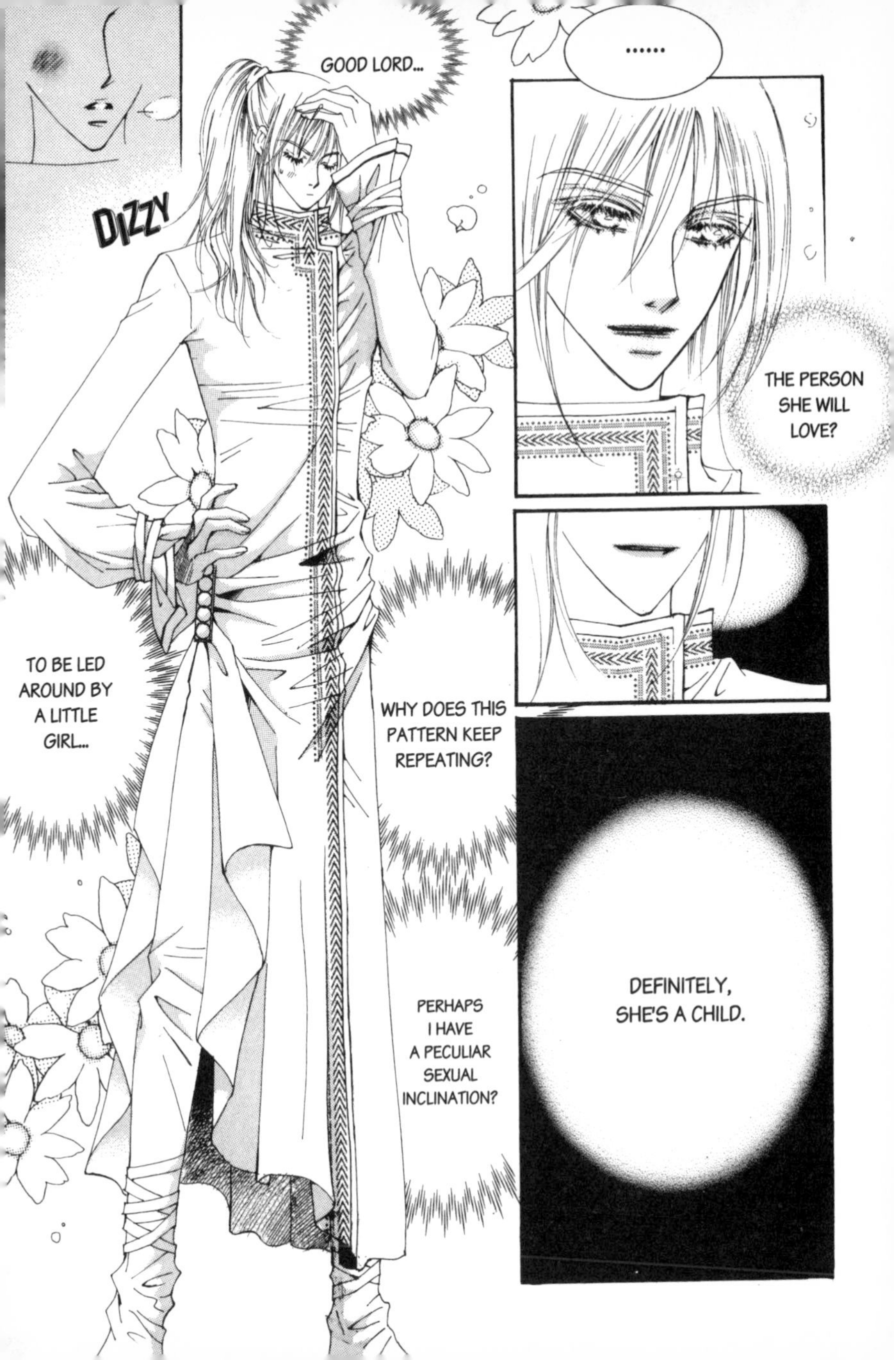
DIZZY
GOOD LORD...
TO BE LED AROUND BY A LITTLE GIRL...
WHY DOES THIS PATTERN KEEP REPEATING?
PERHAPS I HAVE A PECULIAR SEXUAL INCLINATION?
......
THE PERSON SHE WILL LOVE?
DEFINITELY, SHE'S A CHILD.

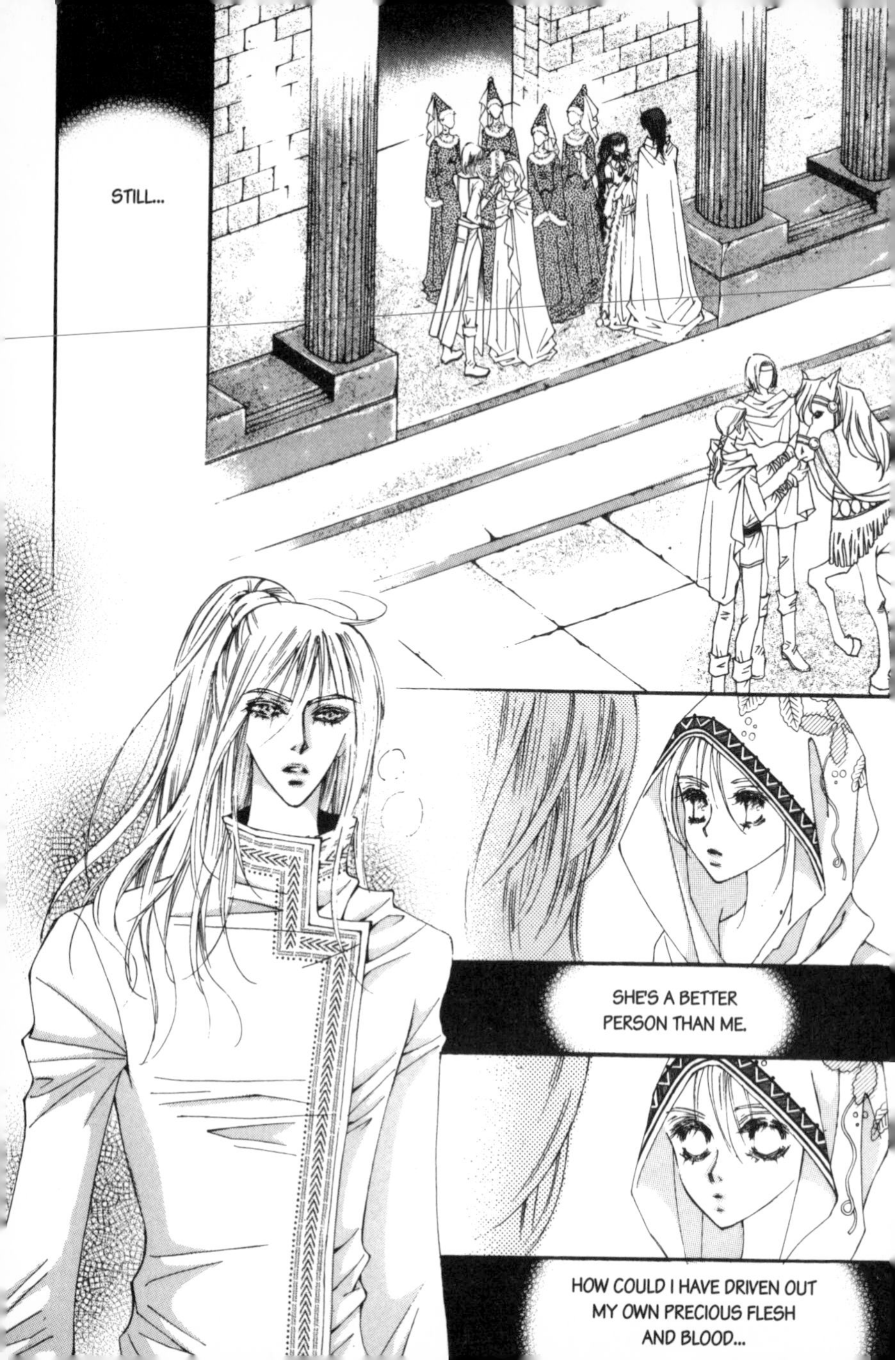
STILL...
SHE'S A BETTER PERSON THAN ME.
HOW COULD I HAVE DRIVEN OUT MY OWN PRECIOUS FLESH AND BLOOD...

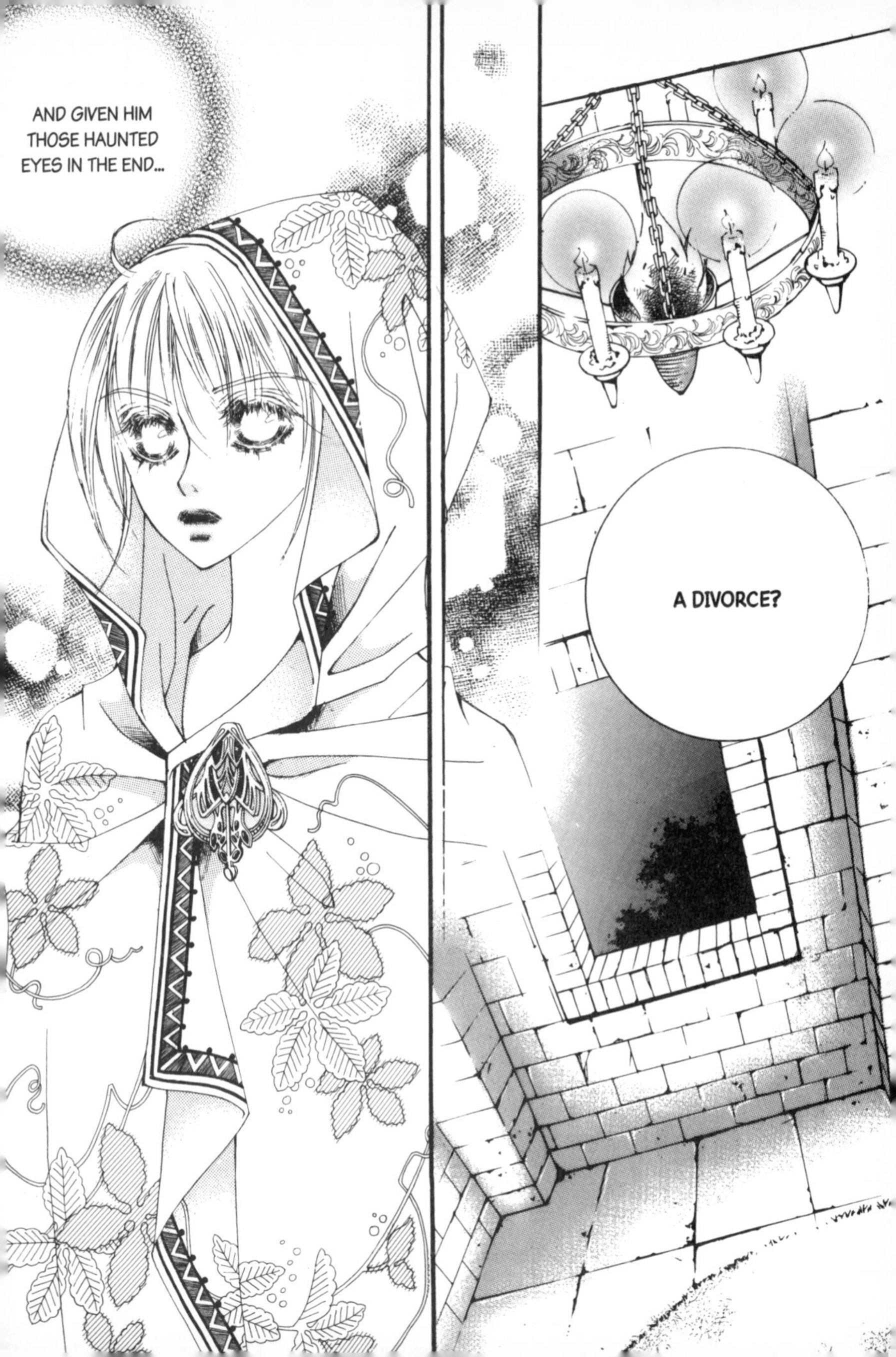
AND GIVEN HIM THOSE HAUNTED EYES IN THE END...
A DIVORCE?

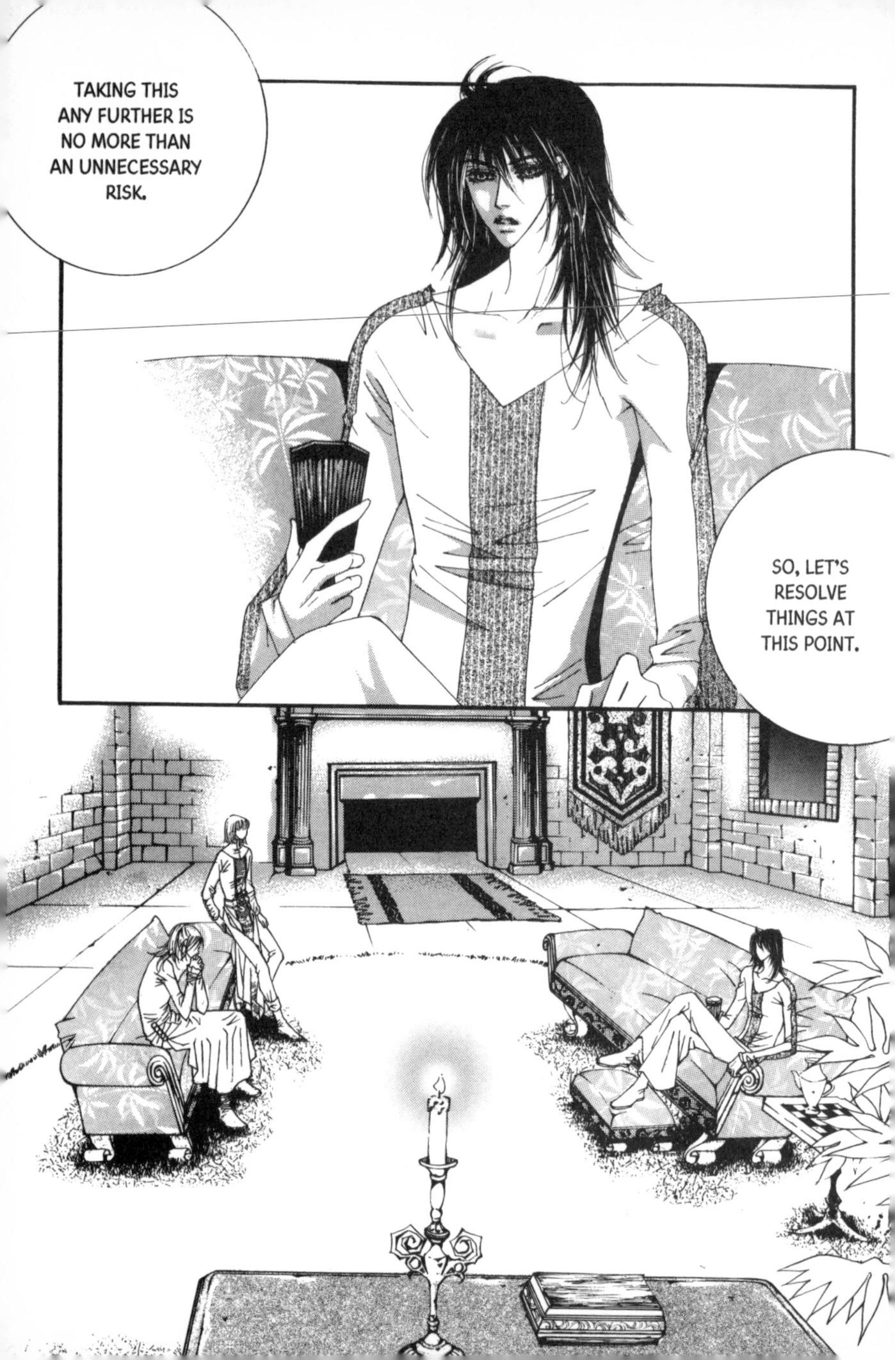
TAKING THIS ANY FURTHER IS NO MORE THAN AN UNNECESSARY RISK.
SO, LET'S RESOLVE THINGS AT THIS POINT.

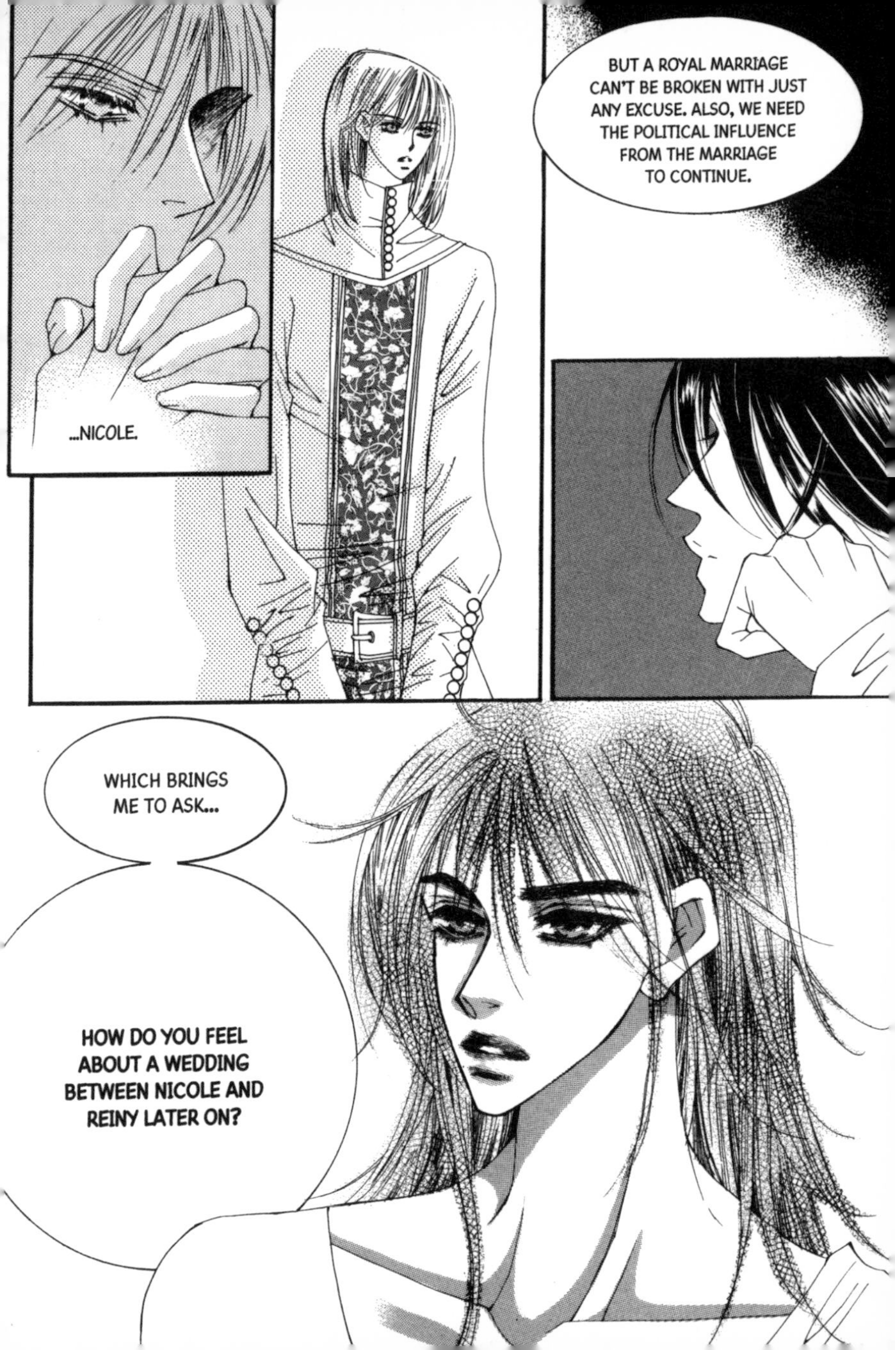
...NICOLE.
BUT A ROYAL MARRIAGE CAN'T BE BROKEN WITH JUST ANY EXCUSE. ALSO, WE NEED THE POLITICAL INFLUENCE FROM THE MARRIAGE TO CONTINUE.
WHICH BRINGS ME TO ASK...
HOW DO YOU FEEL ABOUT A WEDDING BETWEEN NICOLE AND REINY LATER ON?

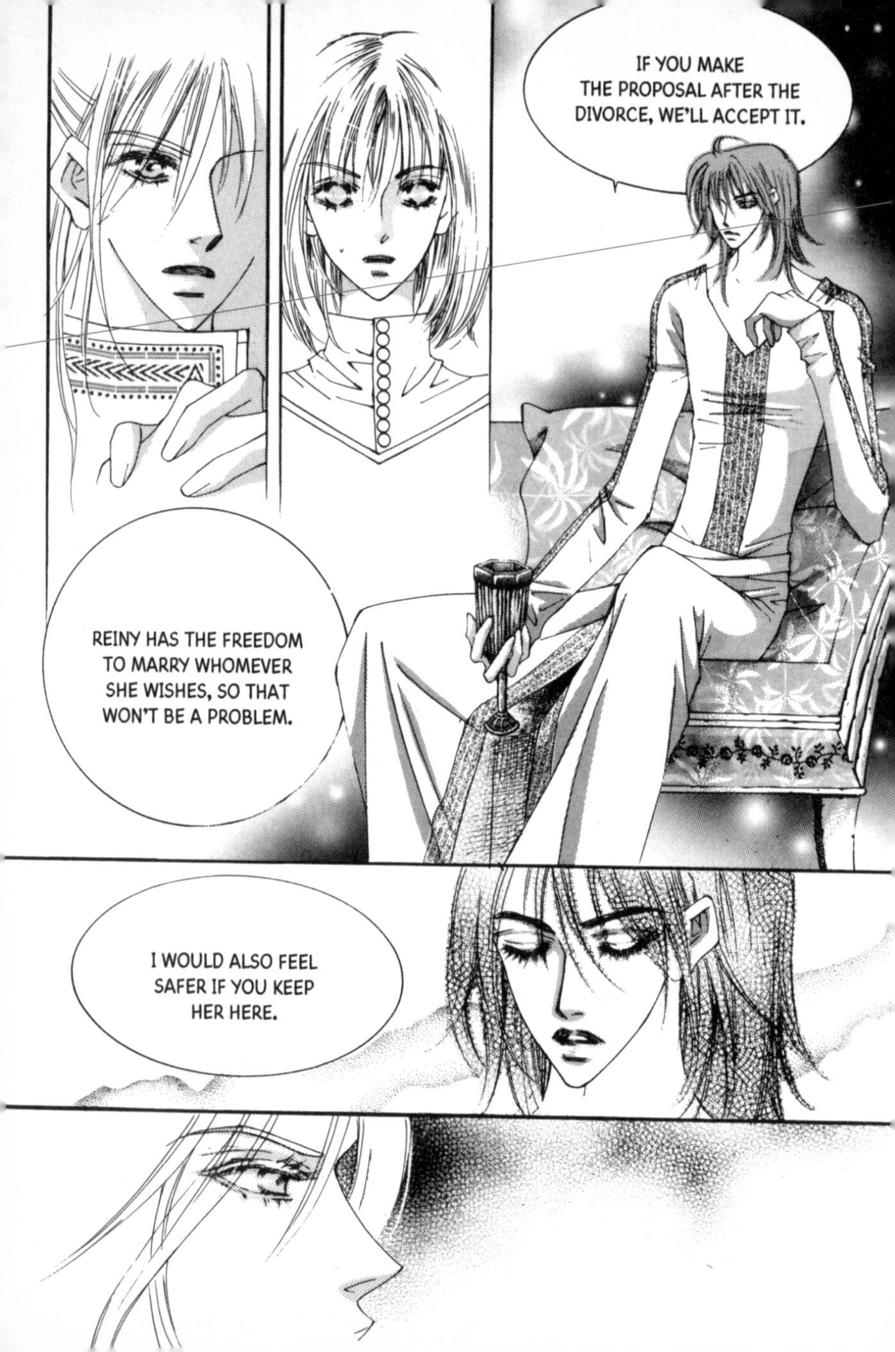
IF YOU MAKE THE PROPOSAL AFTER THE DIVORCE, WE'LL ACCEPT IT.
REINY HAS THE FREEDOM TO MARRY WHOMEVER SHE WISHES, SO THAT WON'T BE A PROBLEM.
I WOULD ALSO FEEL SAFER IF YOU KEEP HER HERE.

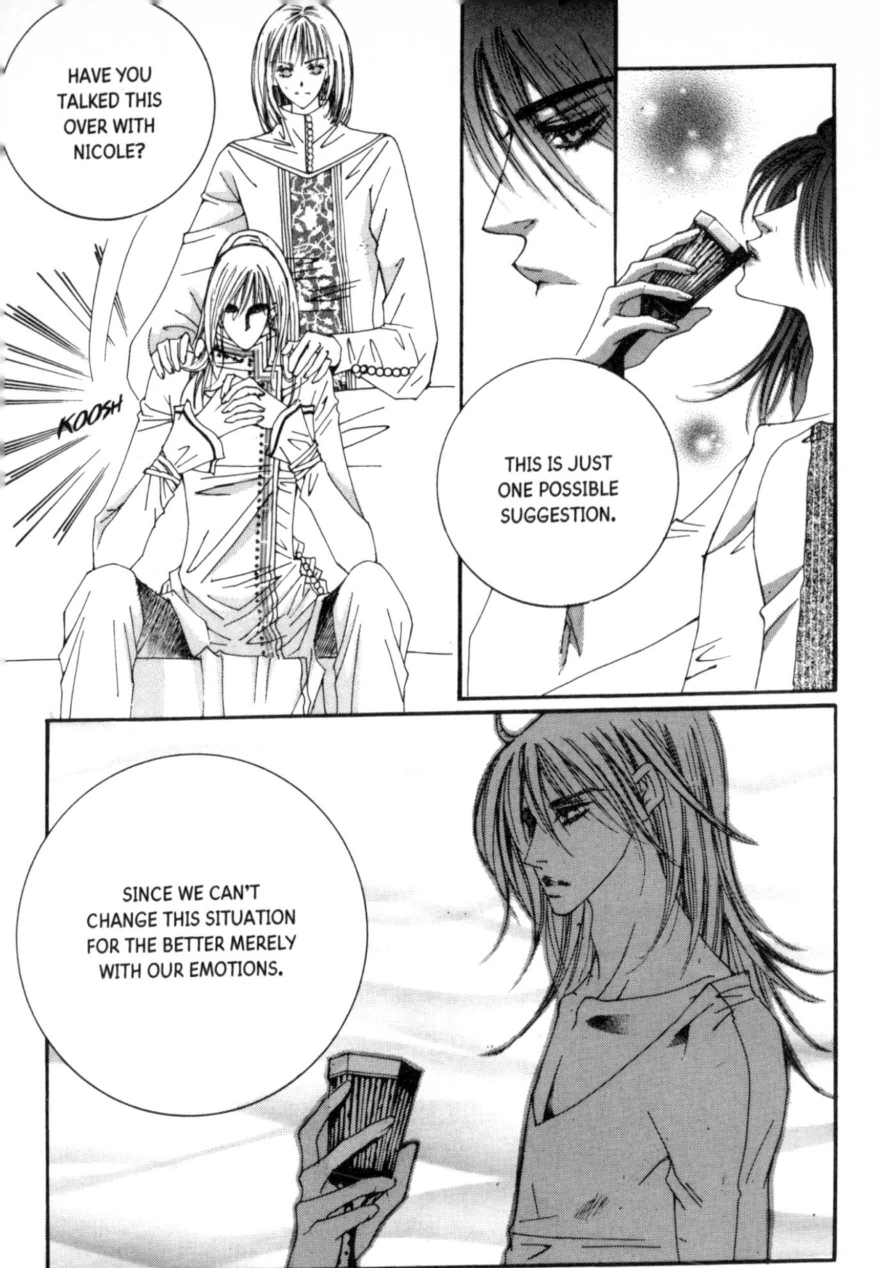
HAVE YOU TALKED THIS OVER WITH NICOLE?
KOOSH
THIS IS JUST ONE POSSIBLE SUGGESTION.
SINCE WE CAN'T CHANGE THIS SITUATION FOR THE BETTER MERELY WITH OUR EMOTIONS.

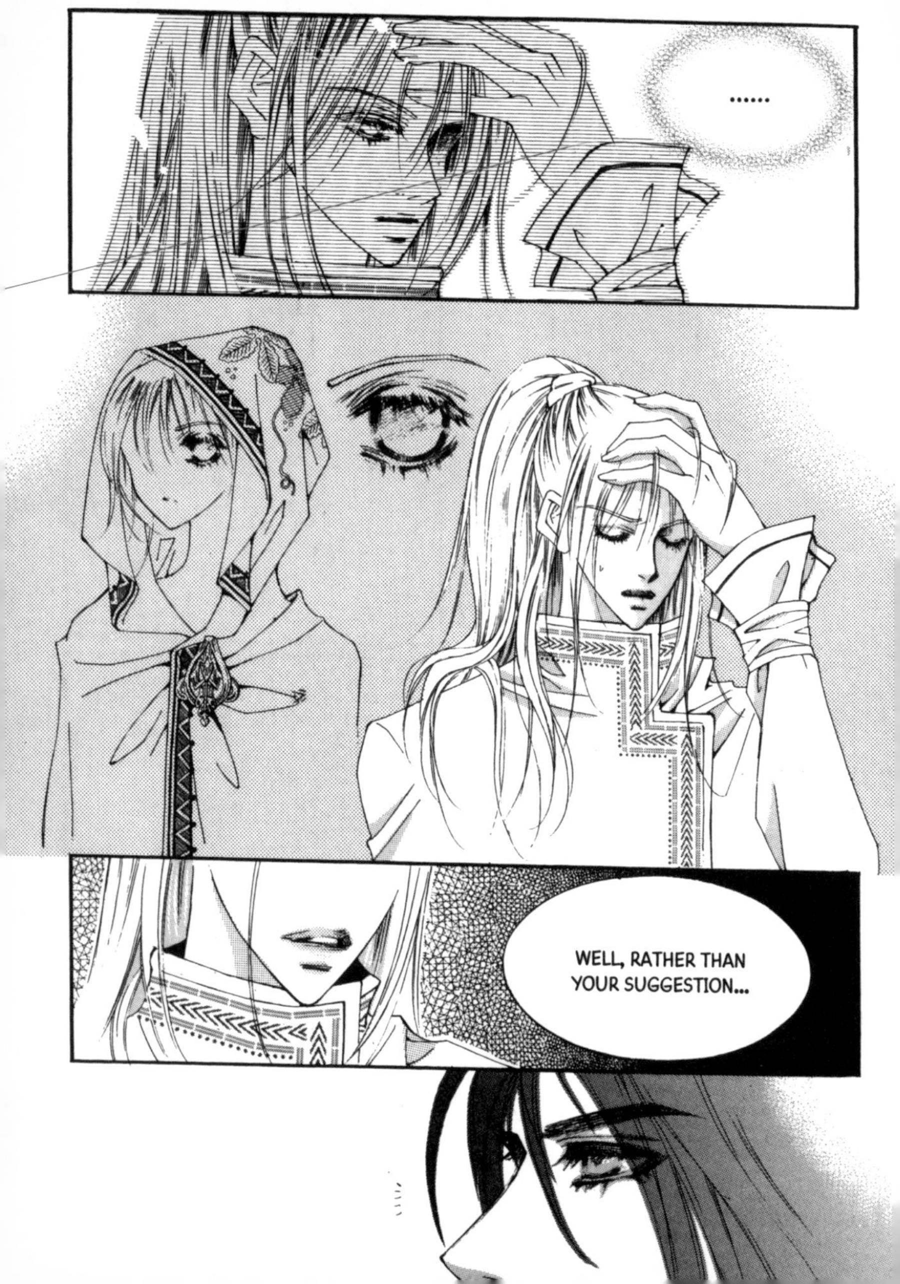
......
WELL, RATHER THAN YOUR SUGGESTION...

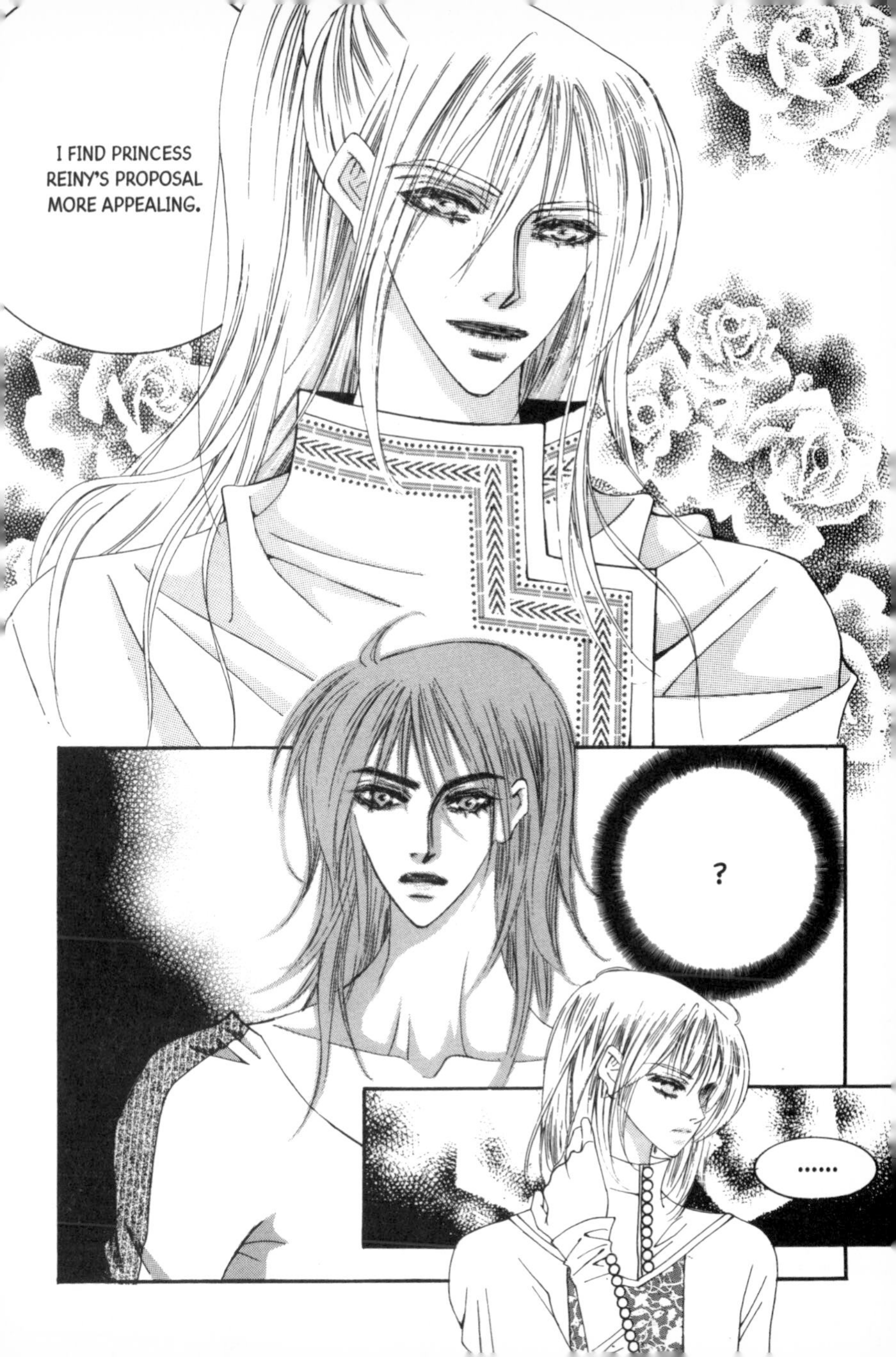
I FIND PRINCESS REINY'S PROPOSAL MORE APPEALING.
?
......

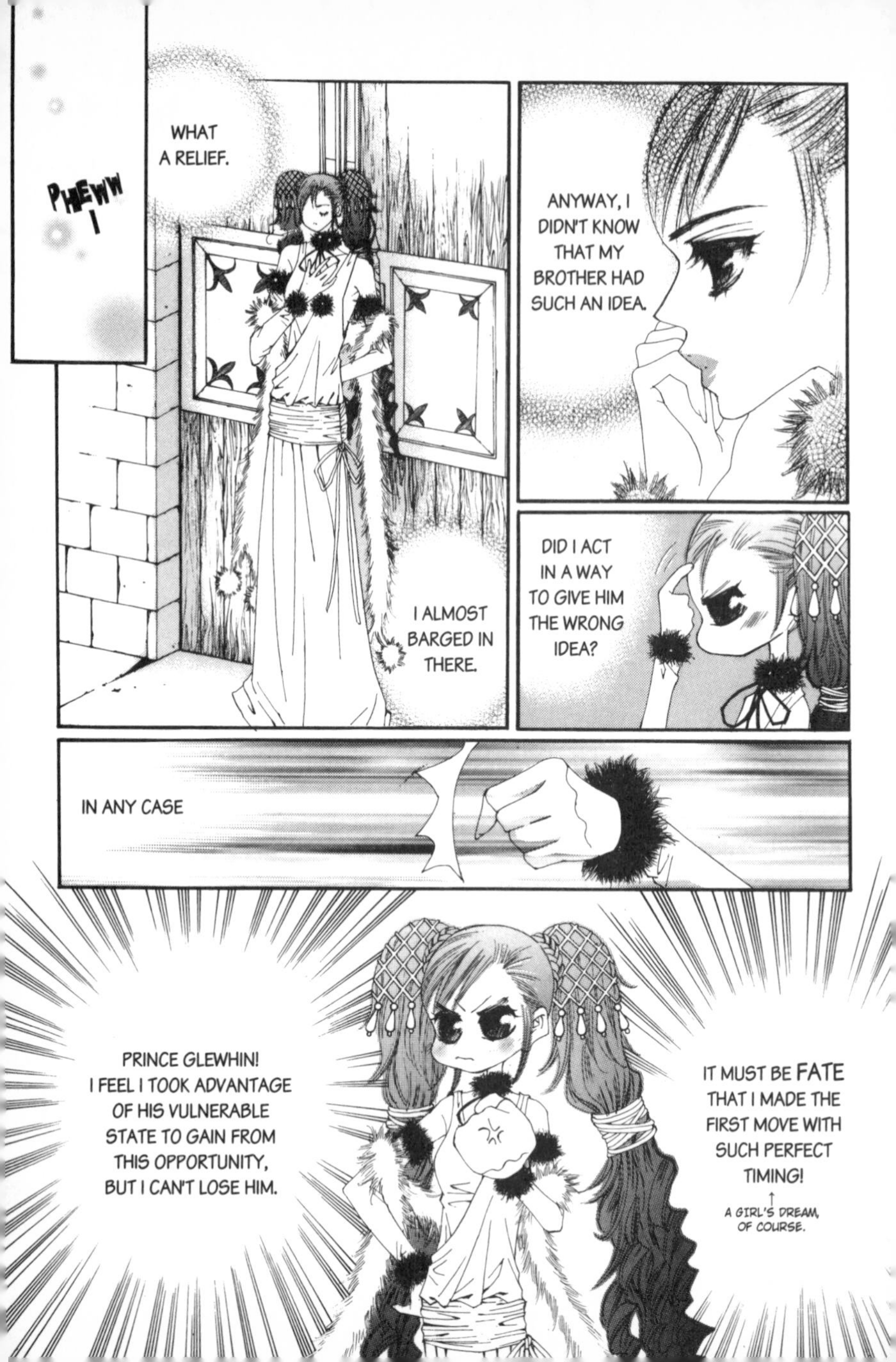
PHEWW!
WHAT A RELIEF.
I ALMOST BARGED IN THERE.
ANYWAY, I DIDN'T KNOW THAT MY BROTHER HAD SUCH AN IDEA.
DID I ACT IN A WAY TO GIVE HIM THE WRONG IDEA?
IN ANY CASE
PRINCE GLEWHIN! I FEEL I TOOK ADVANTAGE OF HIS VULNERABLE STATE TO GAIN FROM THIS OPPORTUNITY, BUT I CAN'T LOSE HIM.
IT MUST BE FATE THAT I MADE THE FIRST MOVE WITH SUCH PERFECT TIMING!
A GIRL'S DREAM, OF COURSE.

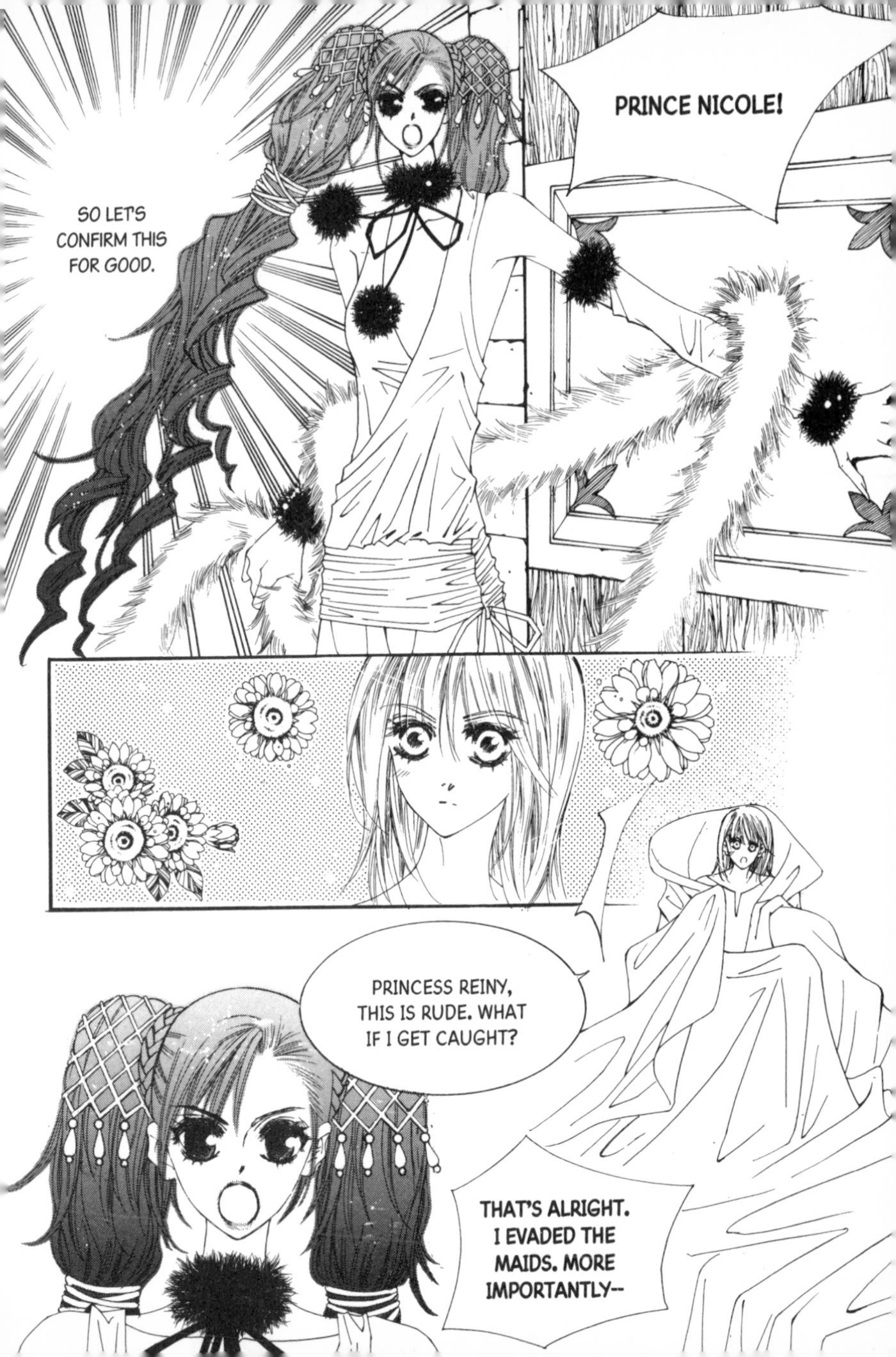
SO LET'S CONFIRM THIS FOR GOOD.
PRINCE NICOLE!
PRINCESS REINY, THIS IS RUDE. WHAT IF I GET CAUGHT?
THAT'S ALRIGHT. I EVADED THE MAIDS. MORE IMPORTANTLY--

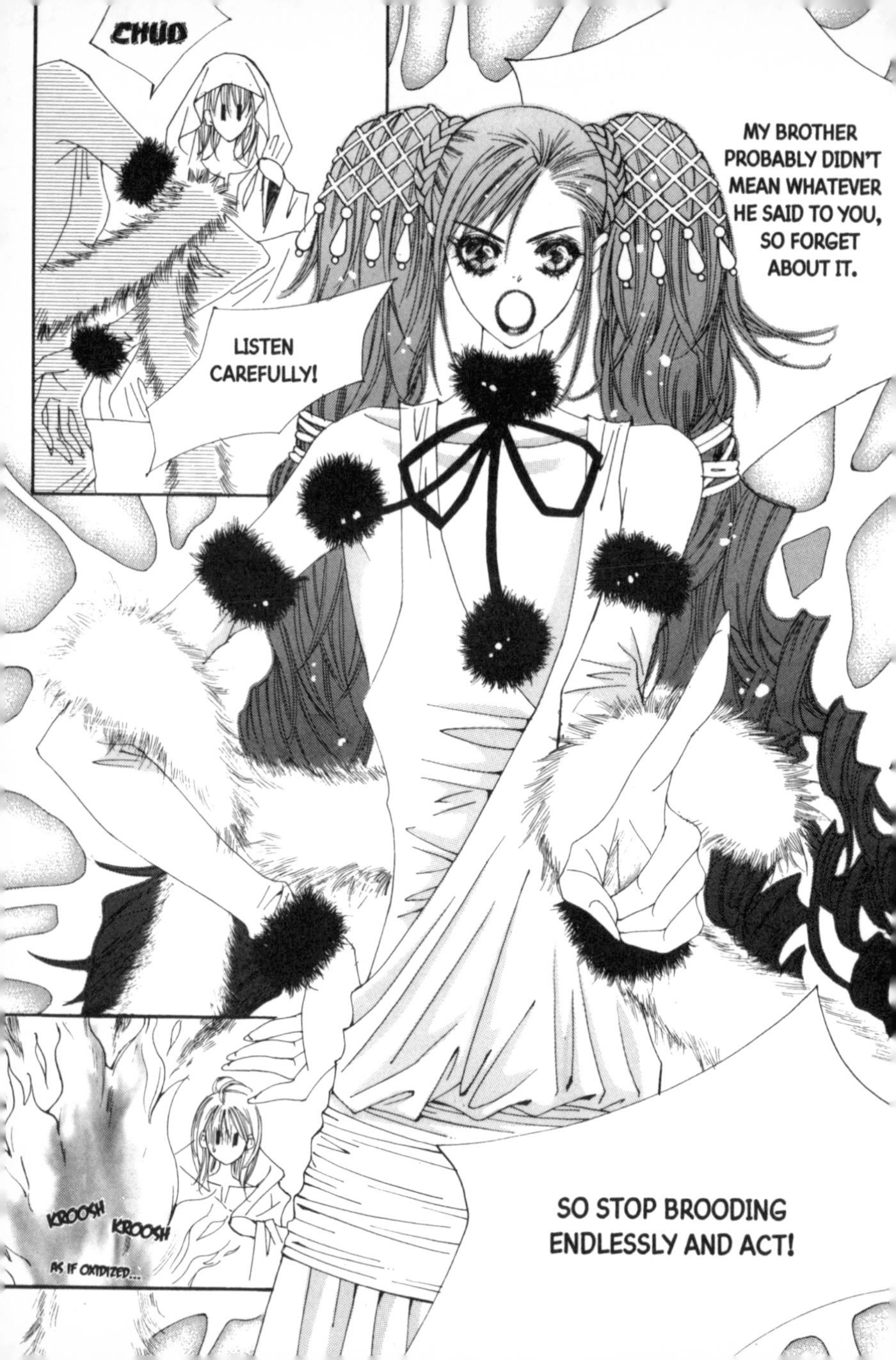
CHUD
LISTEN CAREFULLY!
MY BROTHER PROBABLY DIDN'T MEAN WHATEVER HE SAID TO YOU, SO FORGET ABOUT IT.
KROOSH
KROOSH
AS IF OXIDIZED...
SO STOP BROODING ENDLESSLY AND ACT!

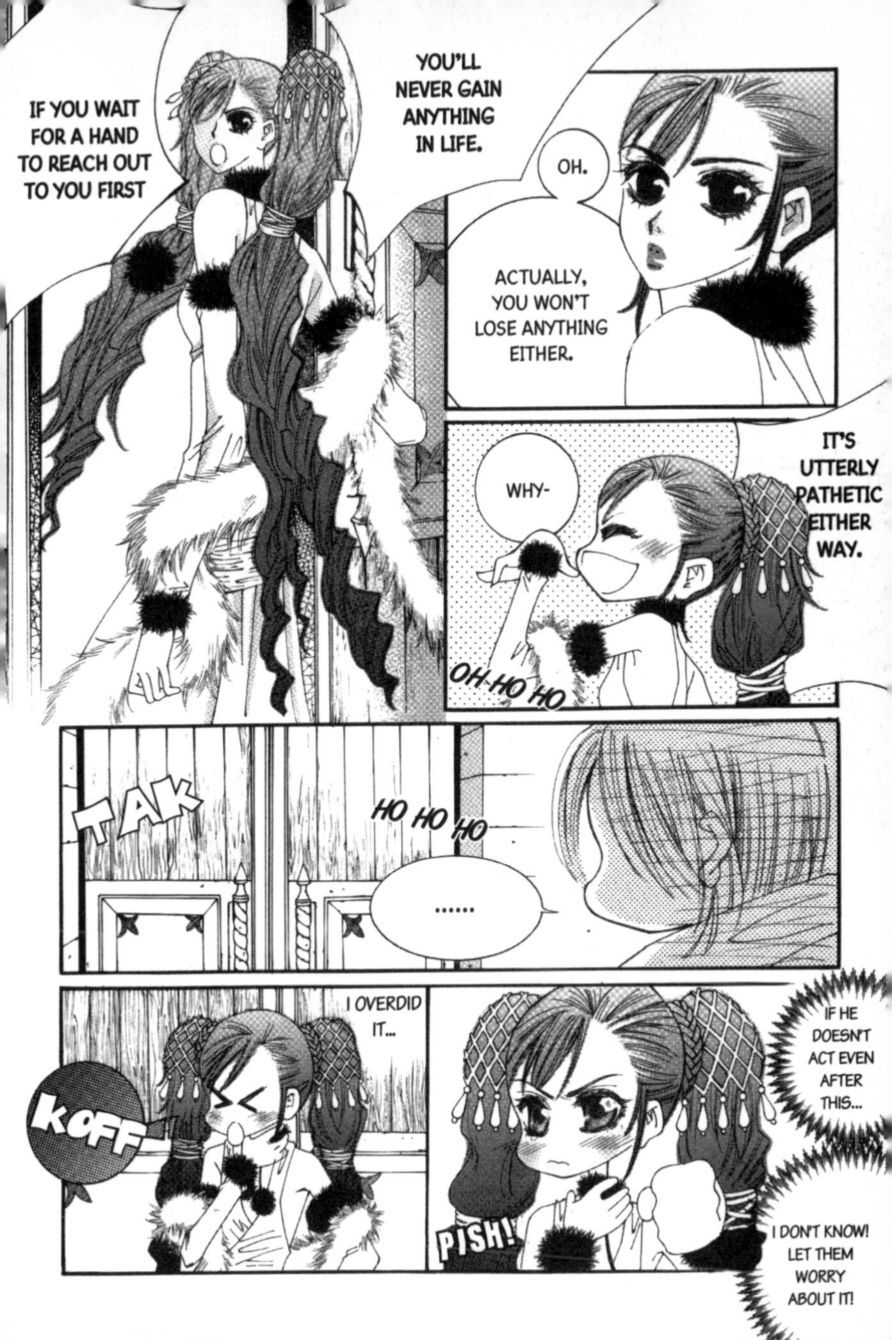
IF YOU WAIT FOR A HAND TO REACH OUT TO YOU FIRST
YOU'LL NEVER GAIN ANYTHING IN LIFE.
OH.
ACTUALLY, YOU WON'T LOSE ANYTHING EITHER.
WHY-
IT'S UTTERLY PATHETIC EITHER WAY.
OH-HO HO
TAK
HO HO HO
......
I OVERDID IT...
KOFF
IF HE DOESN'T ACT EVEN AFTER THIS...
PISH!
I DON'T KNOW! LET THEM WORRY ABOUT IT!

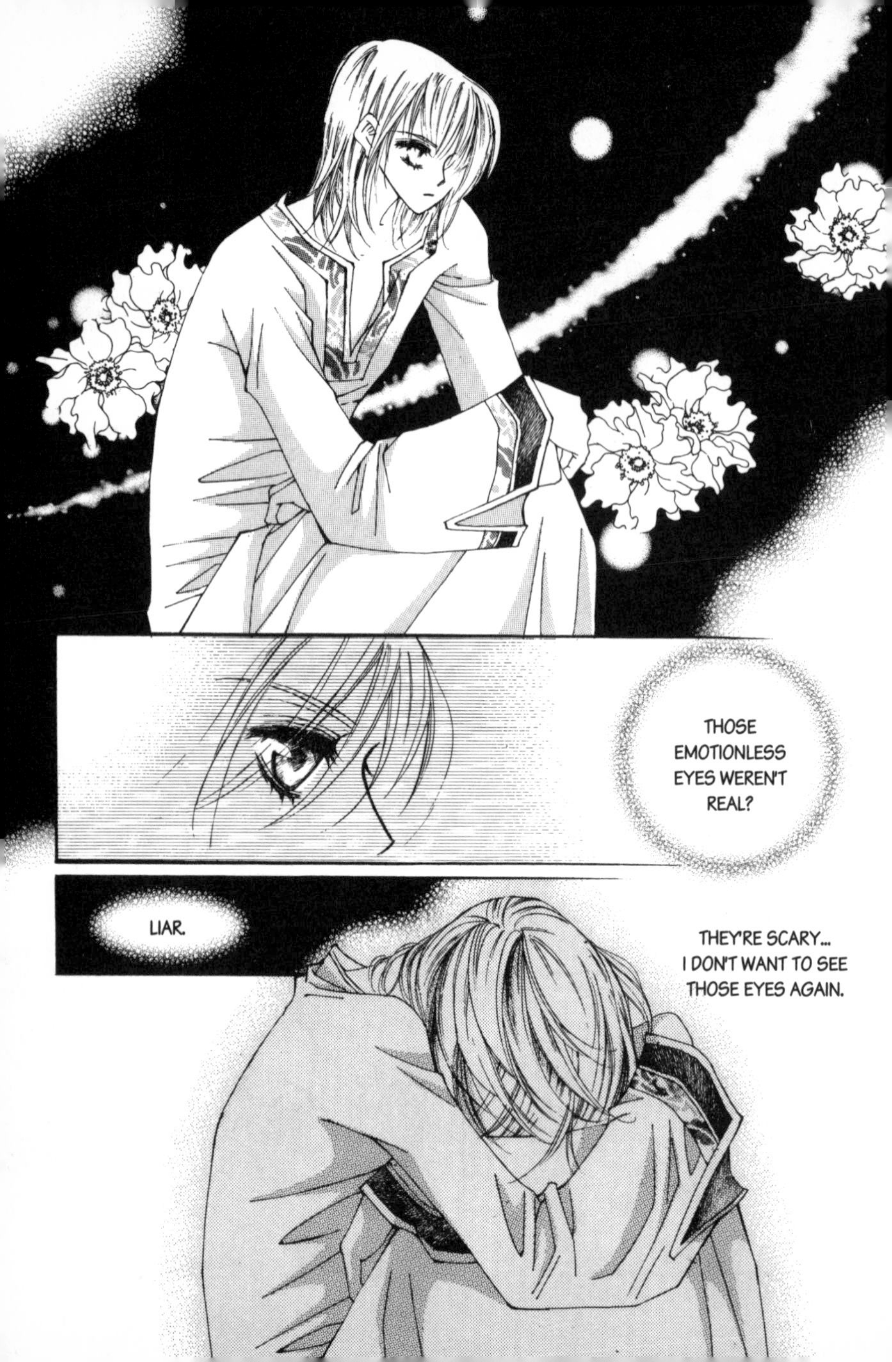
THOSE EMOTIONLESS EYES WEREN'T REAL?
LIAR.
THEY'RE SCARY... I DON'T WANT TO SEE THOSE EYES AGAIN.

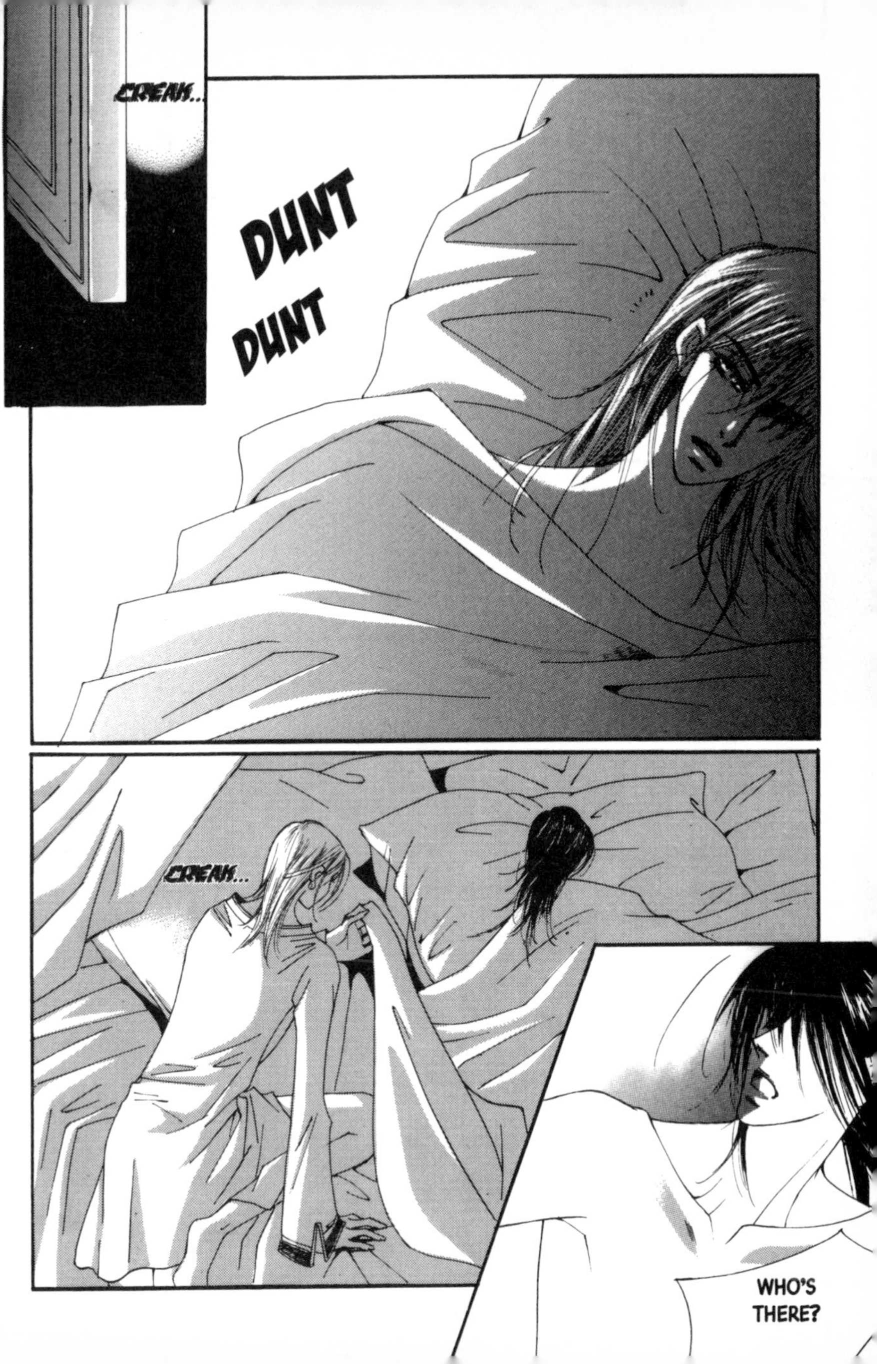
CREAK...
DUNT
DUNT
CREAK...
WHO'S
THERE?

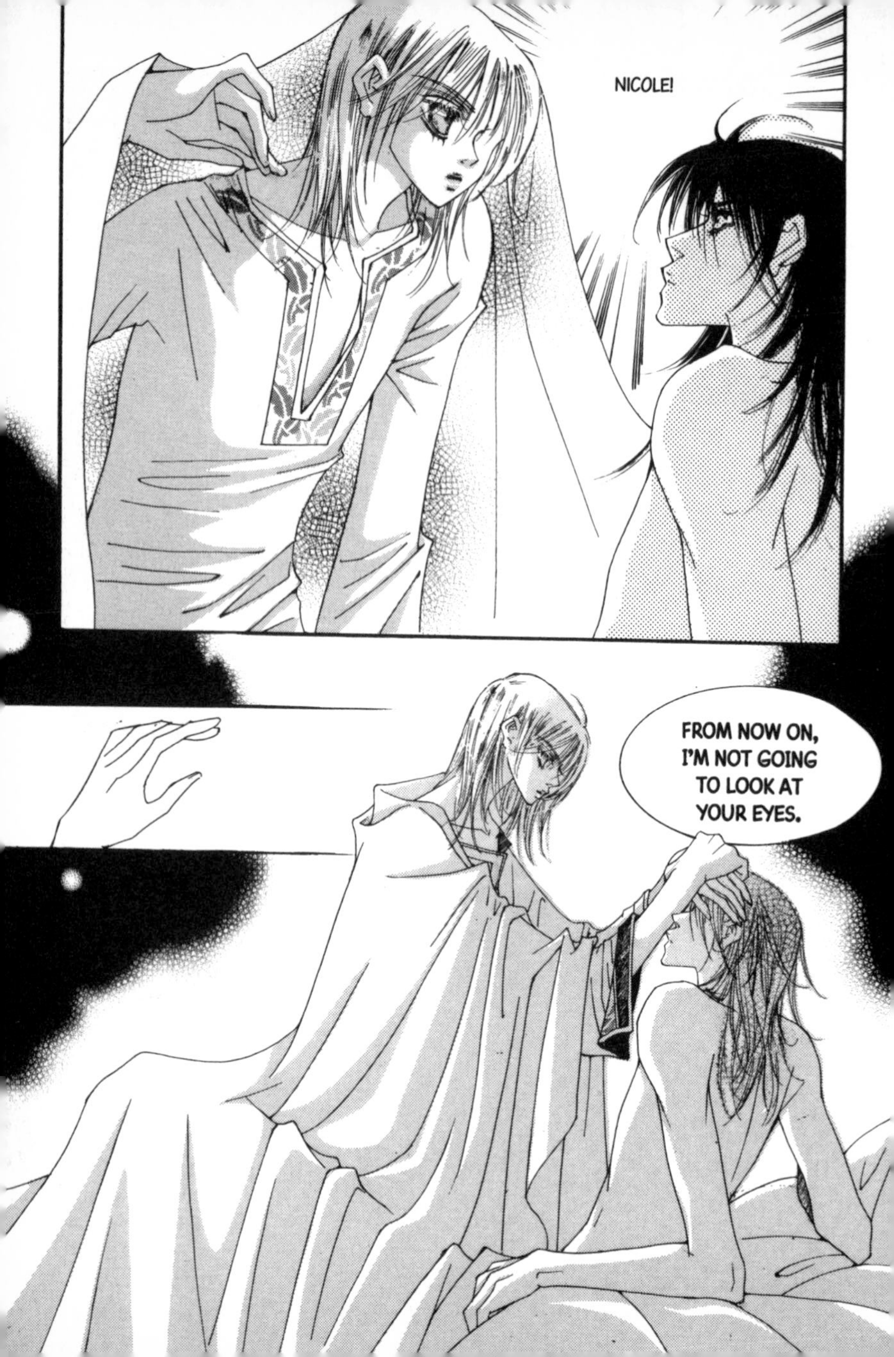
NICOLE!
FROM NOW ON, I'M NOT GOING TO LOOK AT YOUR EYES.

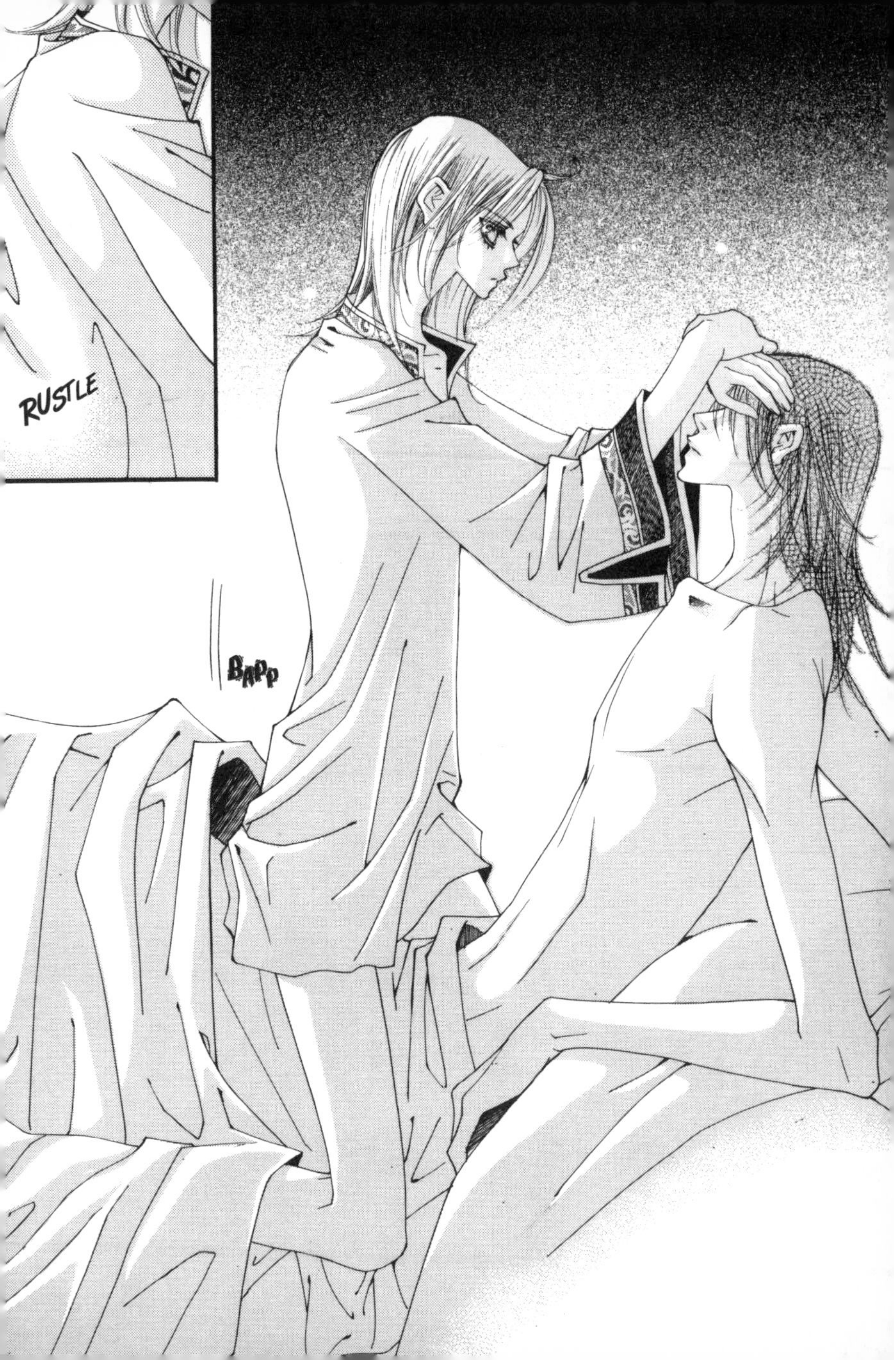
RUSTLE
BAPP

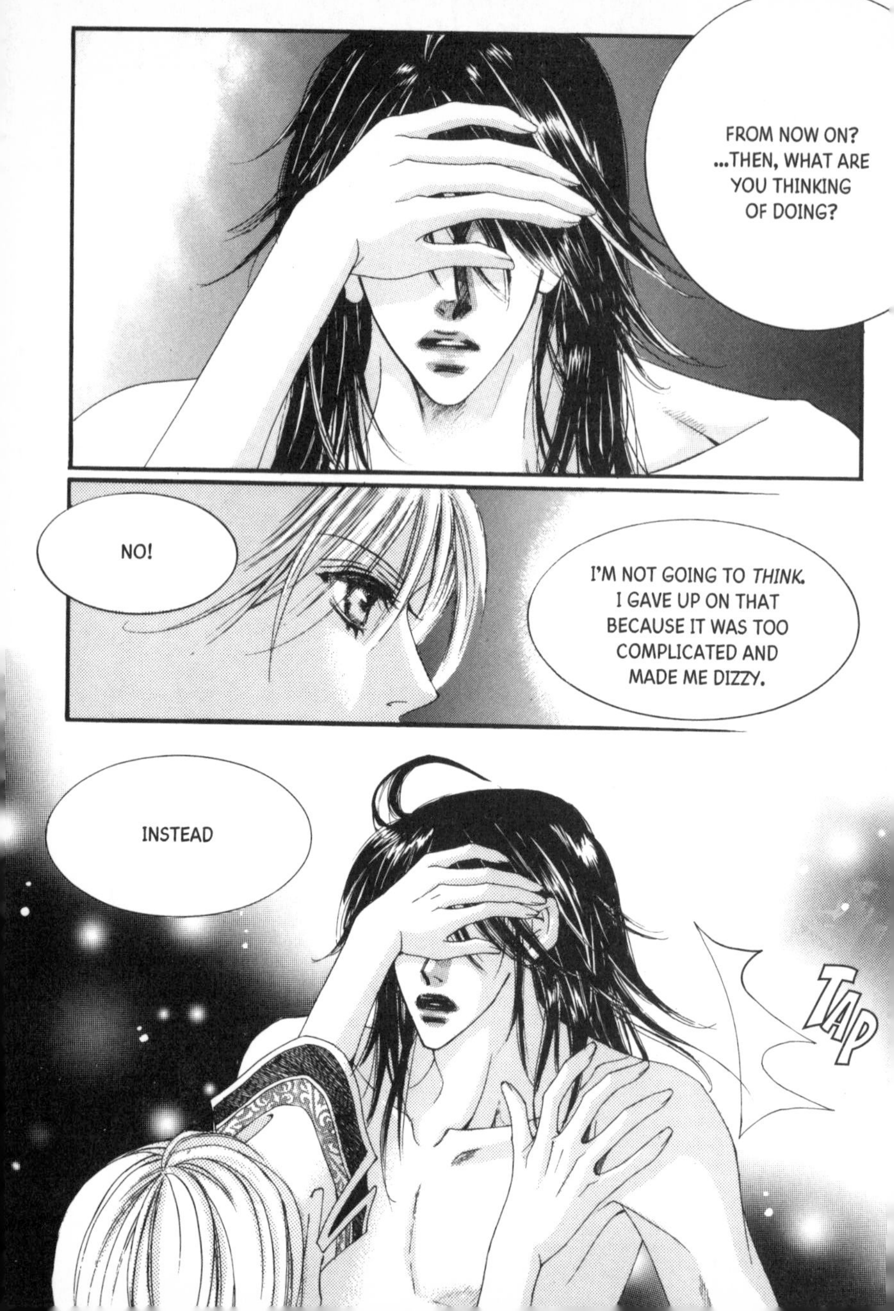
FROM NOW ON? ...THEN, WHAT ARE YOU THINKING OF DOING?
NO!
I'M NOT GOING TO *THINK*. I GAVE UP ON THAT BECAUSE IT WAS TOO COMPLICATED AND MADE ME DIZZY.
INSTEAD
TAP

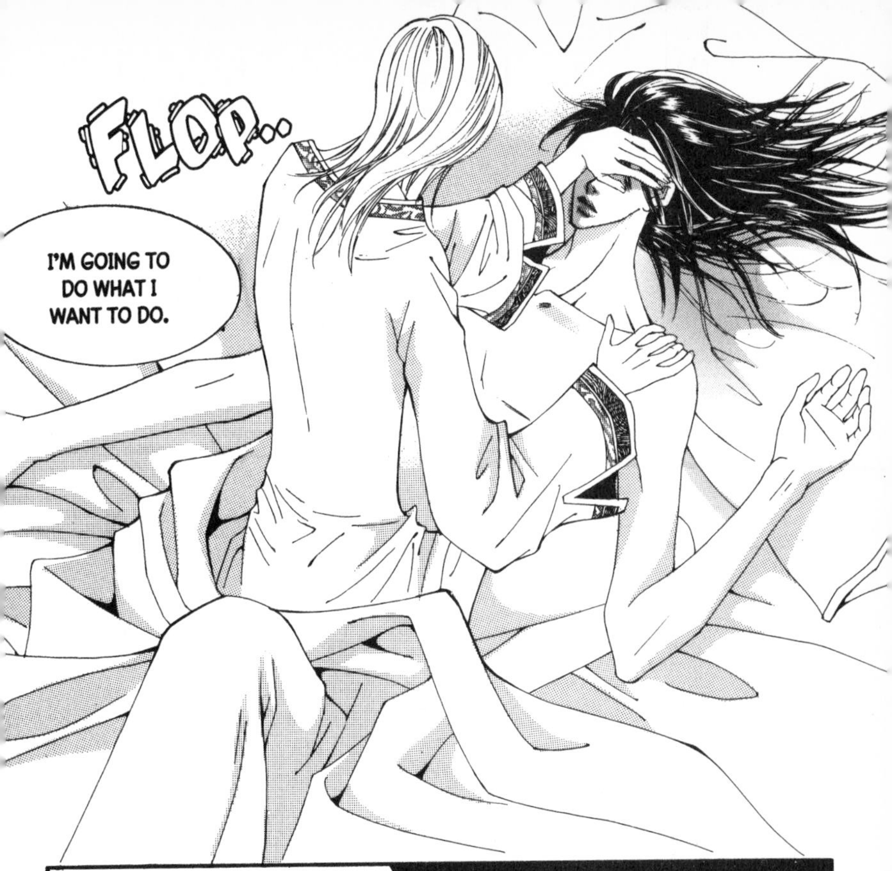
FLOP..
I'M GOING TO DO WHAT I WANT TO DO.
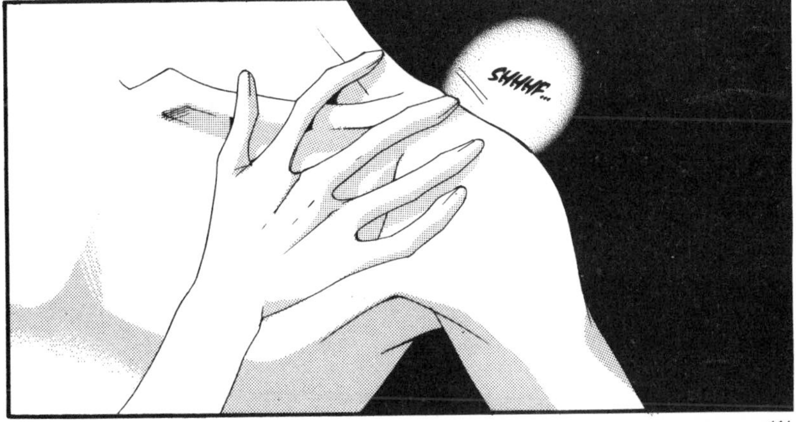
SHHHF...

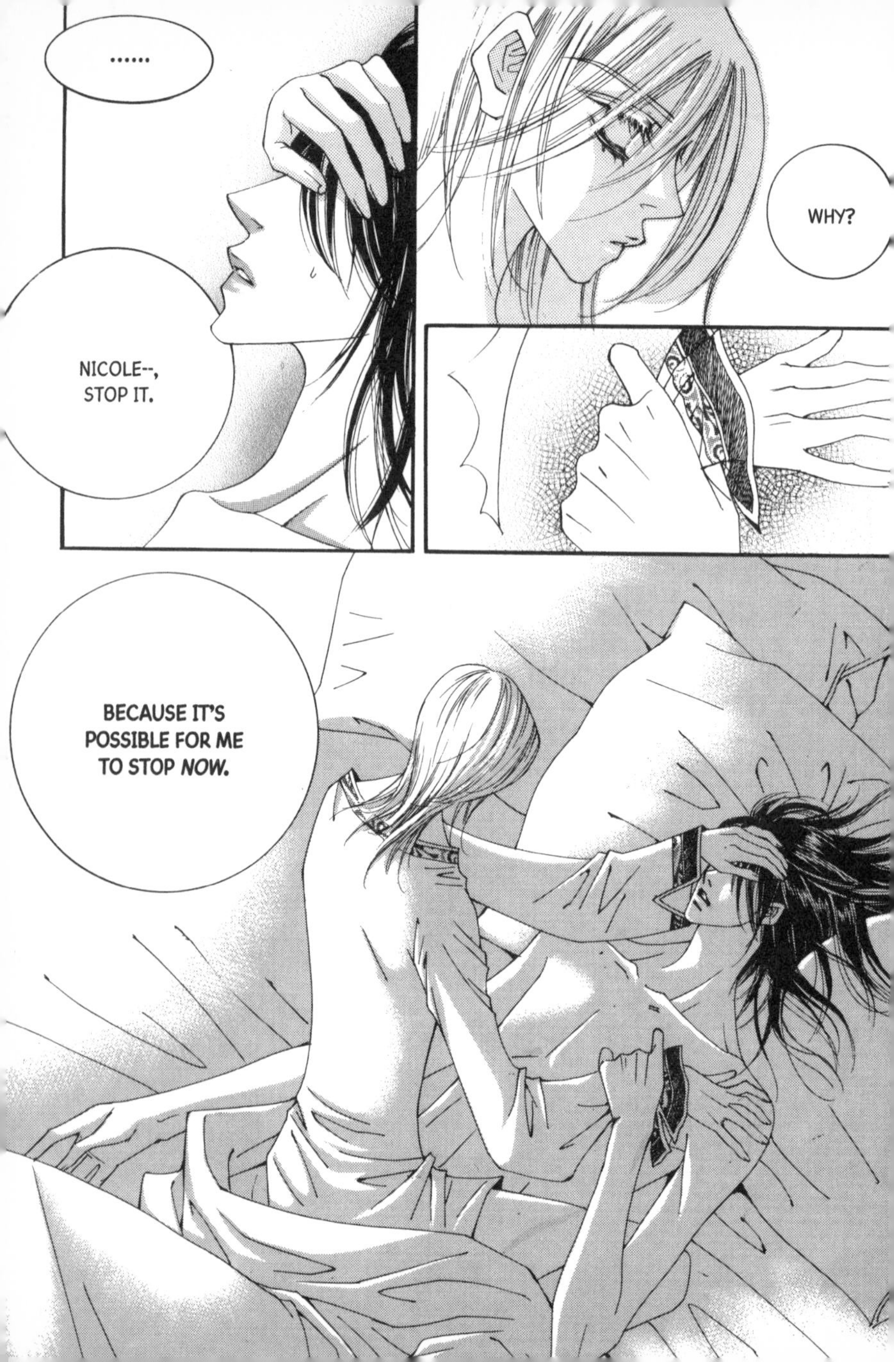
......
NICOLE--, STOP IT.
WHY?
BECAUSE IT'S POSSIBLE FOR ME TO STOP *NOW*.

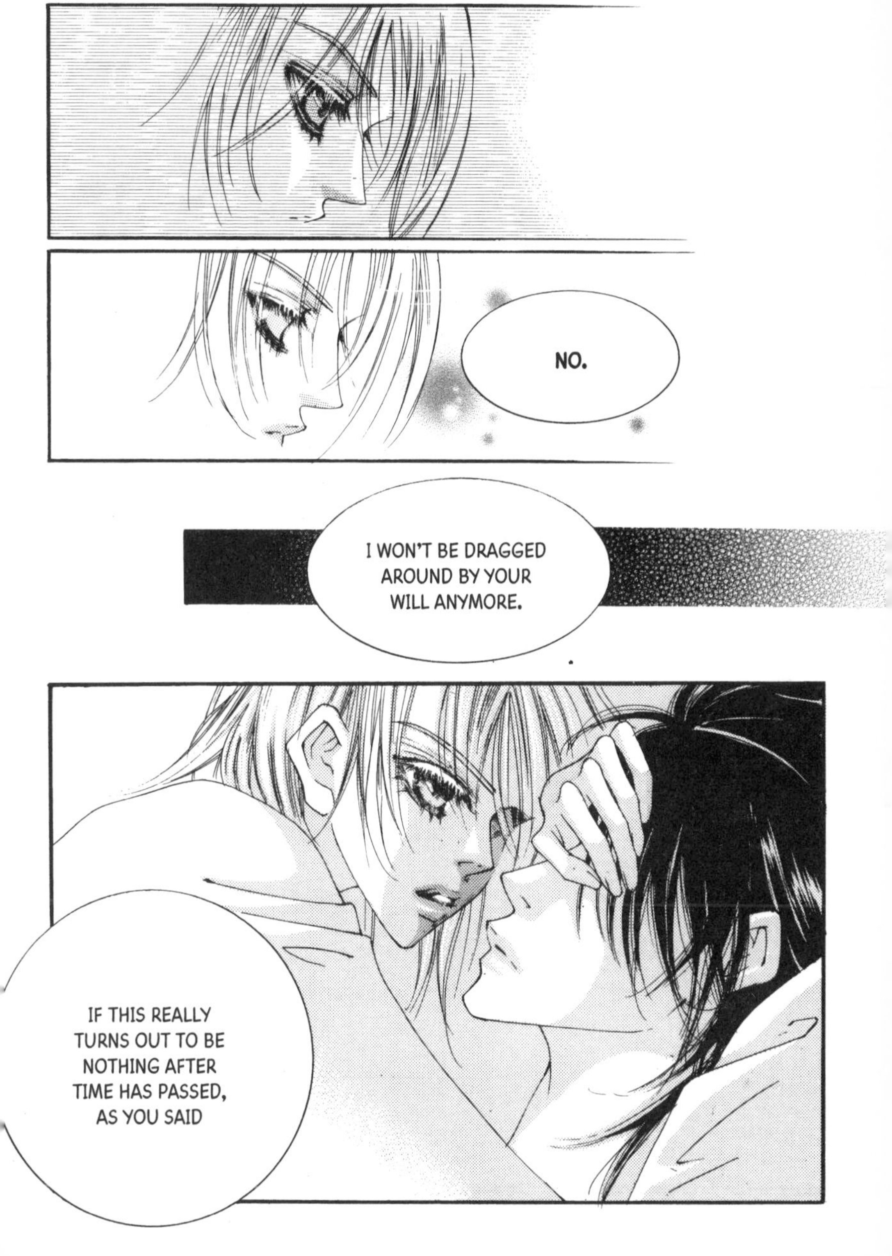
NO.
I WON'T BE DRAGGED AROUND BY YOUR WILL ANYMORE.
IF THIS REALLY TURNS OUT TO BE NOTHING AFTER TIME HAS PASSED, AS YOU SAID

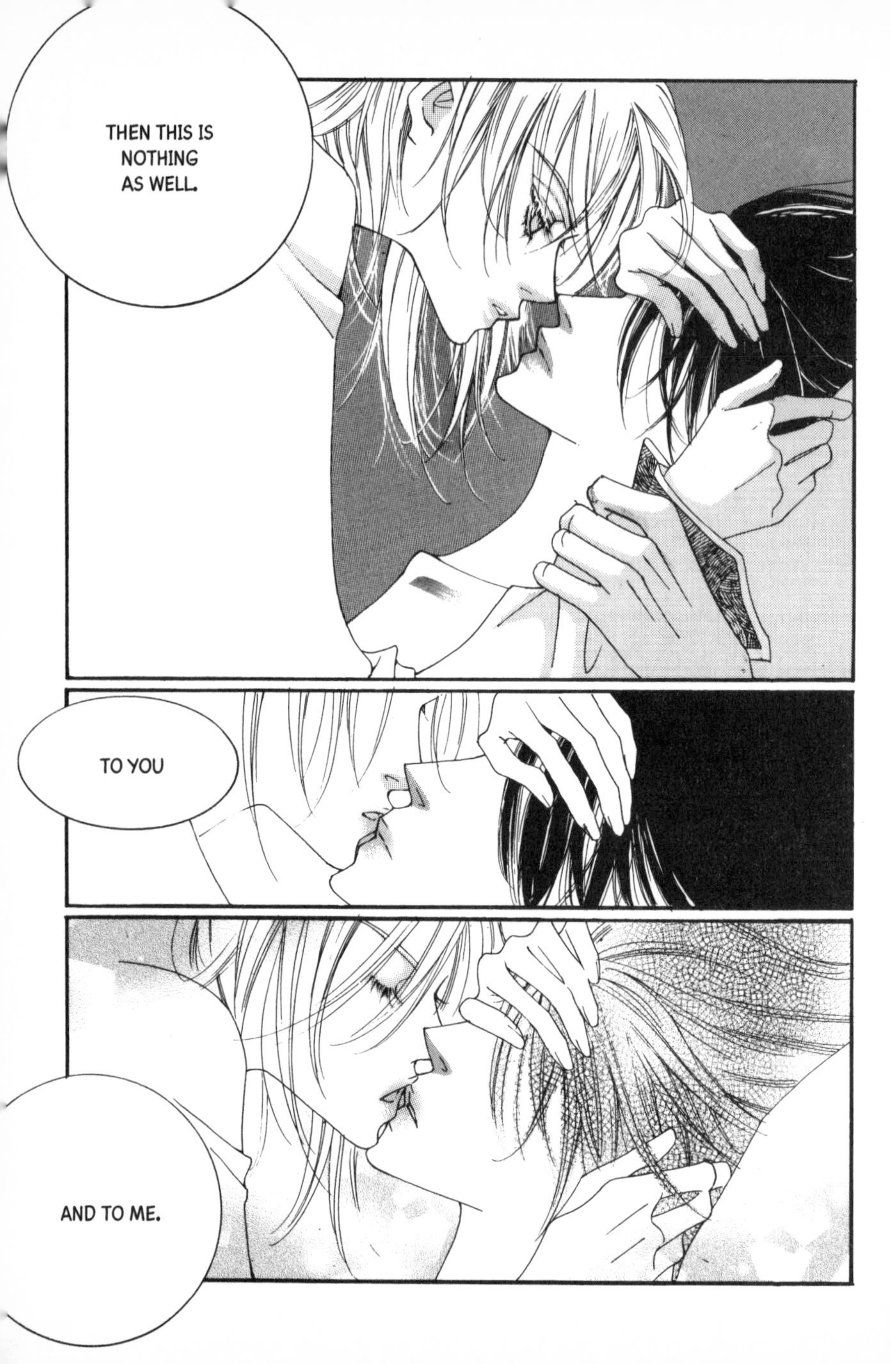
THEN THIS IS NOTHING AS WELL.
TO YOU
AND TO ME.

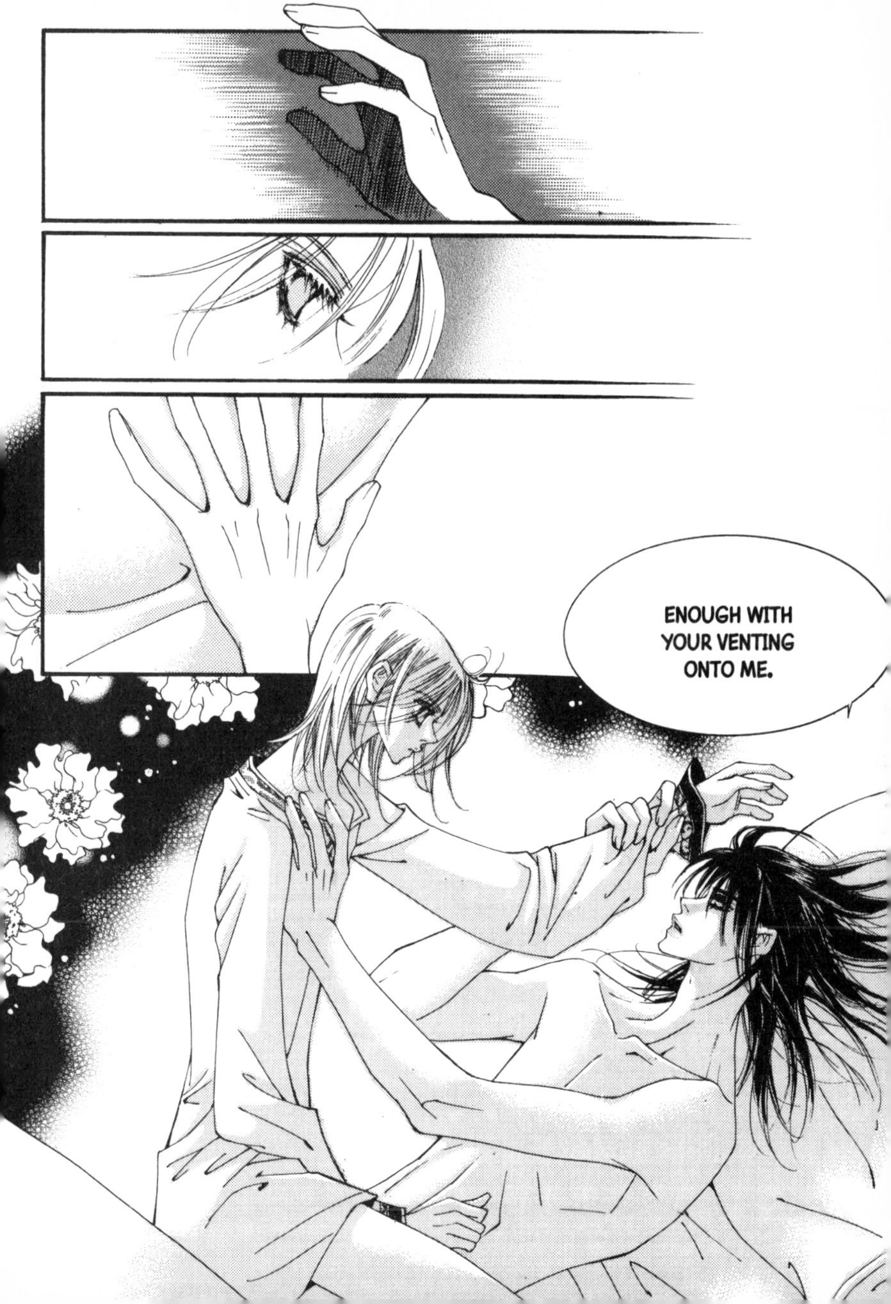
ENOUGH WITH YOUR VENTING ONTO ME.

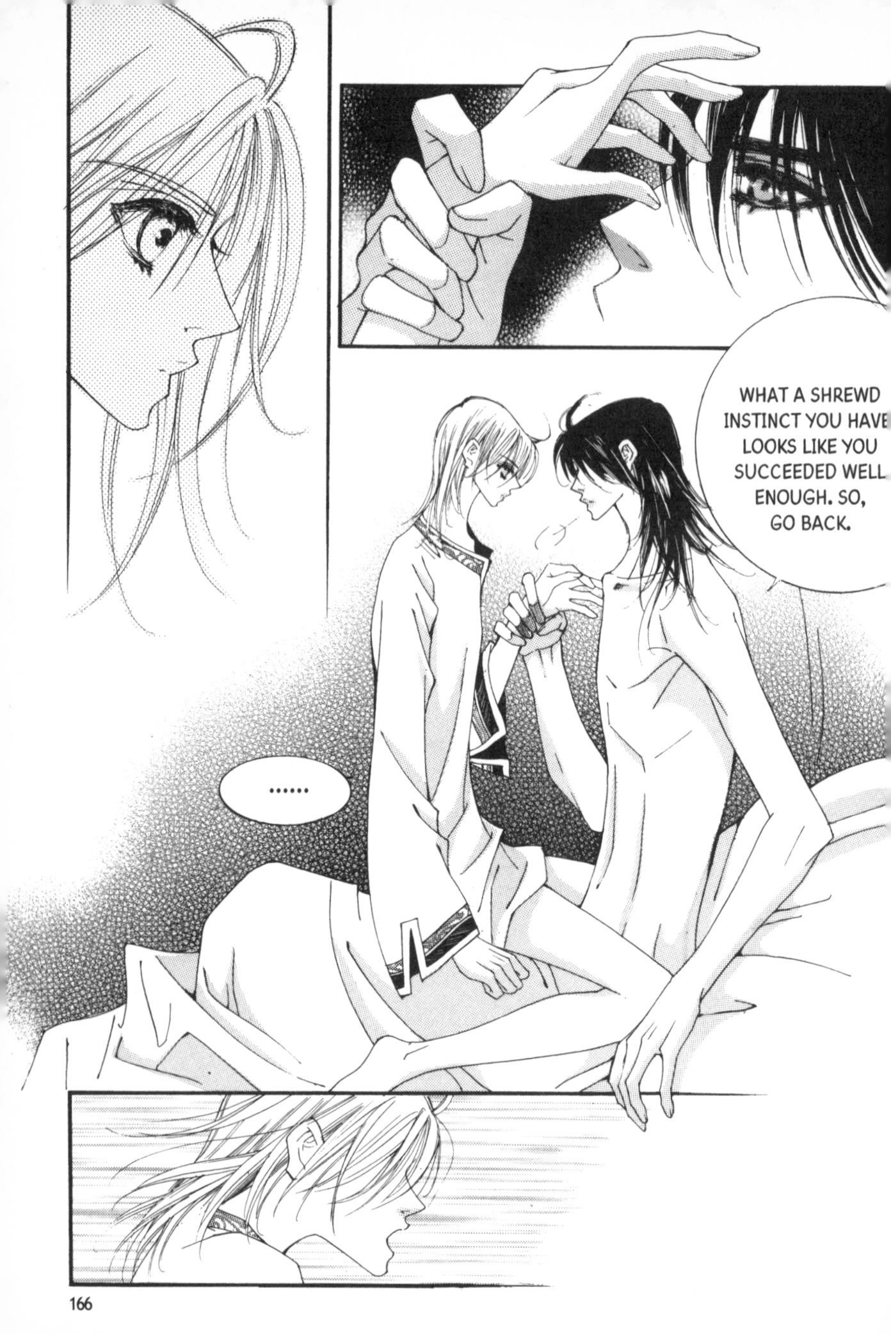
WHAT A SHREWD INSTINCT YOU HAVE LOOKS LIKE YOU SUCCEEDED WELL ENOUGH. SO, GO BACK.
......

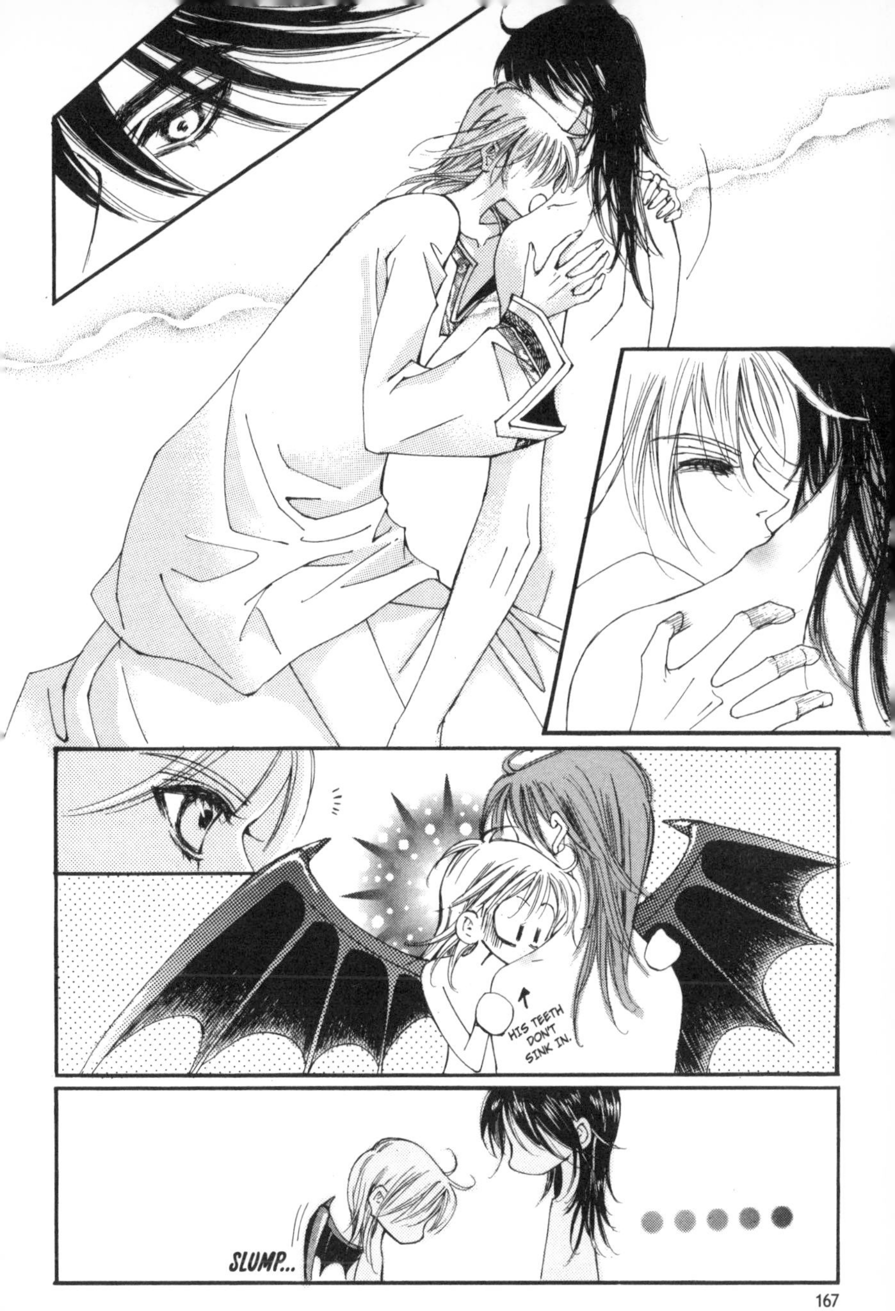
HIS TEETH DON'T SINK IN.
SLUMP...

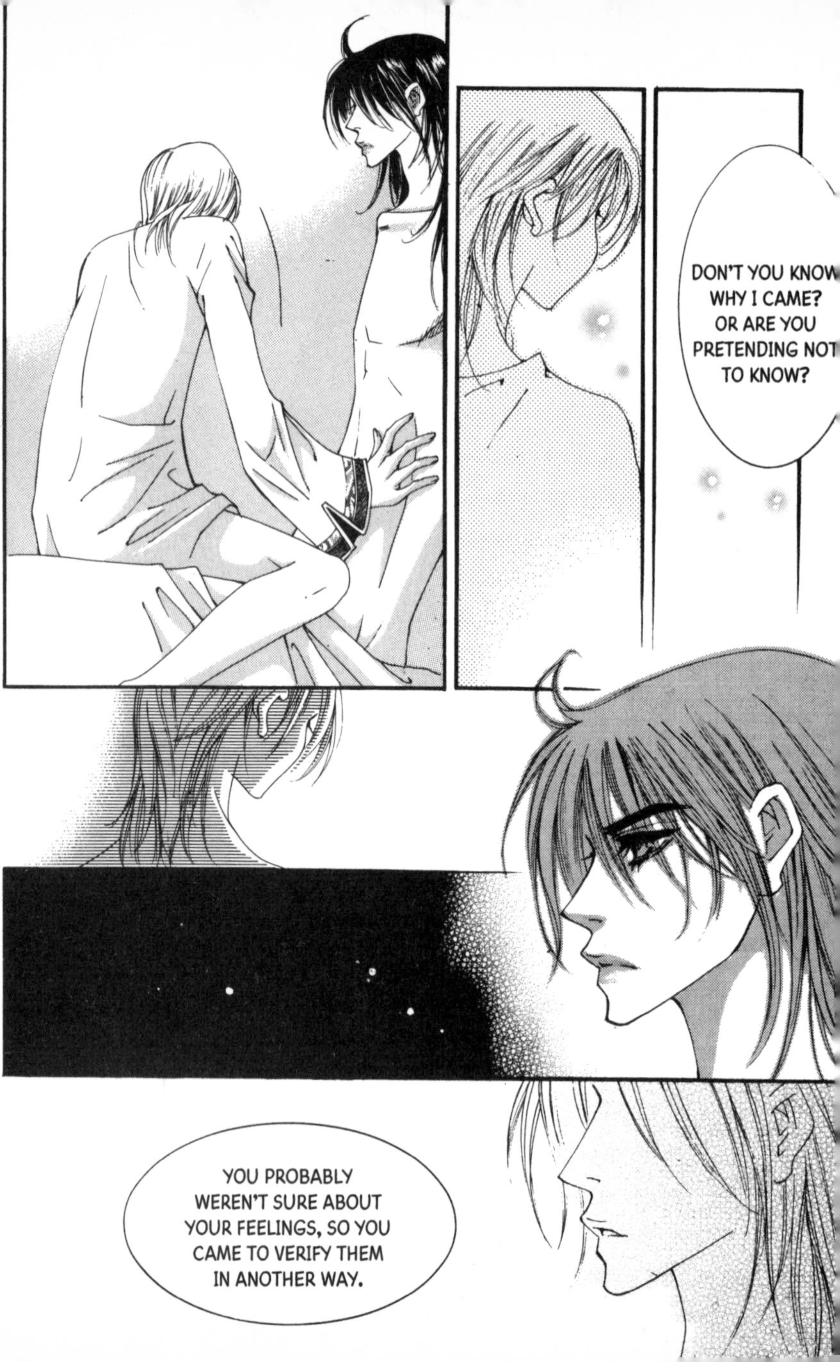
DON'T YOU KNOW WHY I CAME? OR ARE YOU PRETENDING NOT TO KNOW?
YOU PROBABLY WEREN'T SURE ABOUT YOUR FEELINGS, SO YOU CAME TO VERIFY THEM IN ANOTHER WAY.

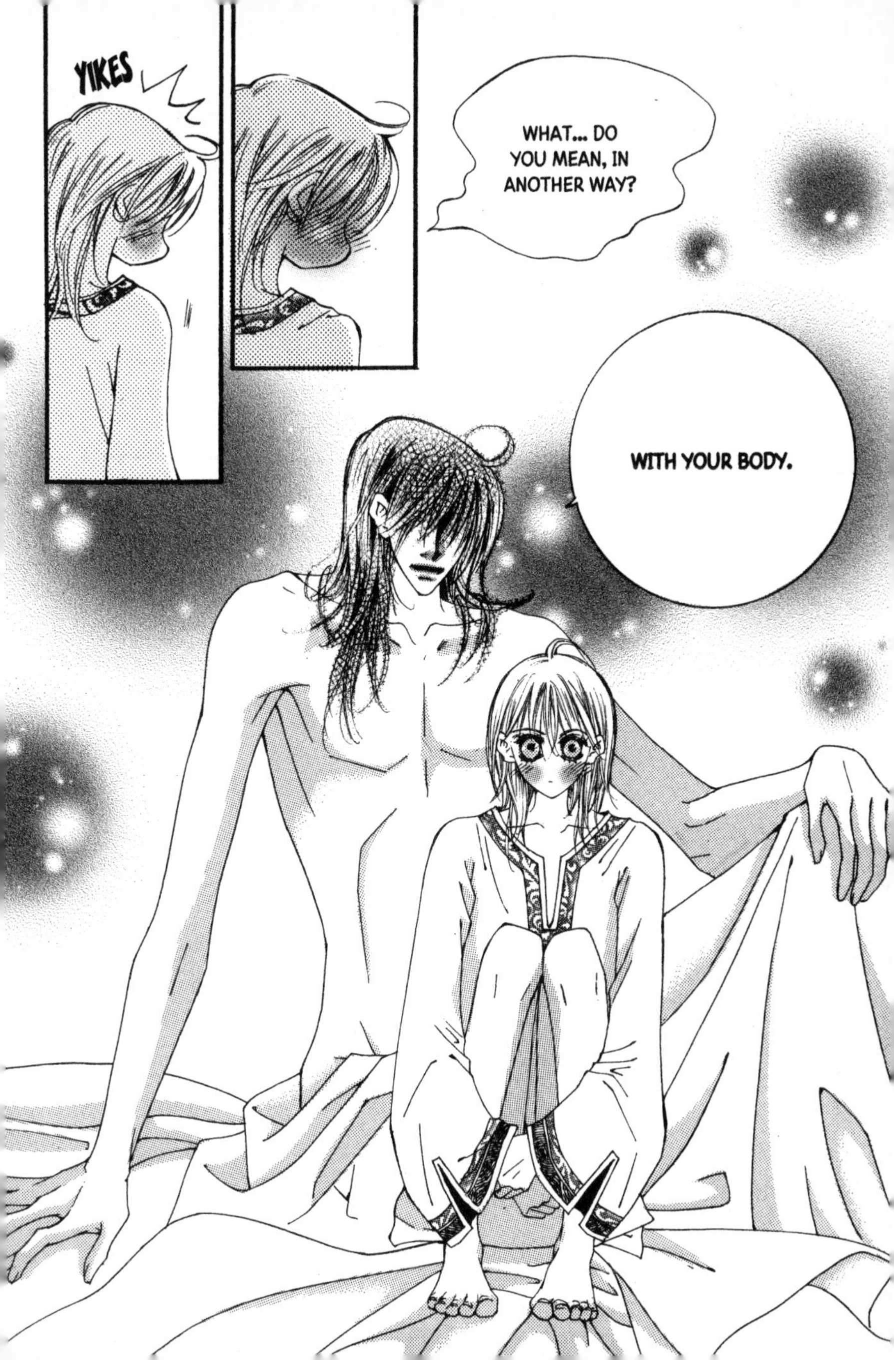
YIKES
WHAT... DO YOU MEAN, IN ANOTHER WAY?
WITH YOUR BODY.

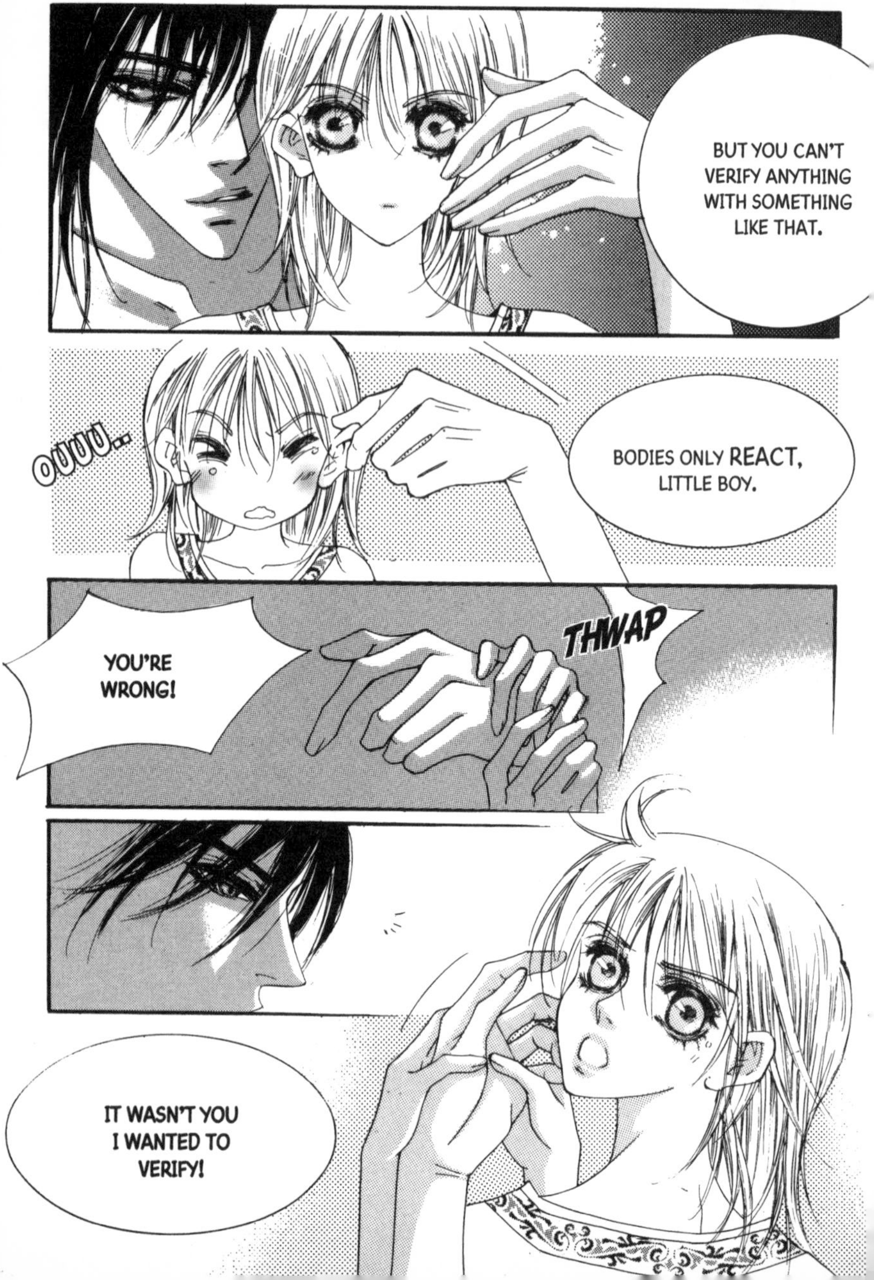
BUT YOU CAN'T VERIFY ANYTHING WITH SOMETHING LIKE THAT.
OUUU..
BODIES ONLY REACT, LITTLE BOY.
YOU'RE WRONG!
THWAP
IT WASN'T YOU I WANTED TO VERIFY!

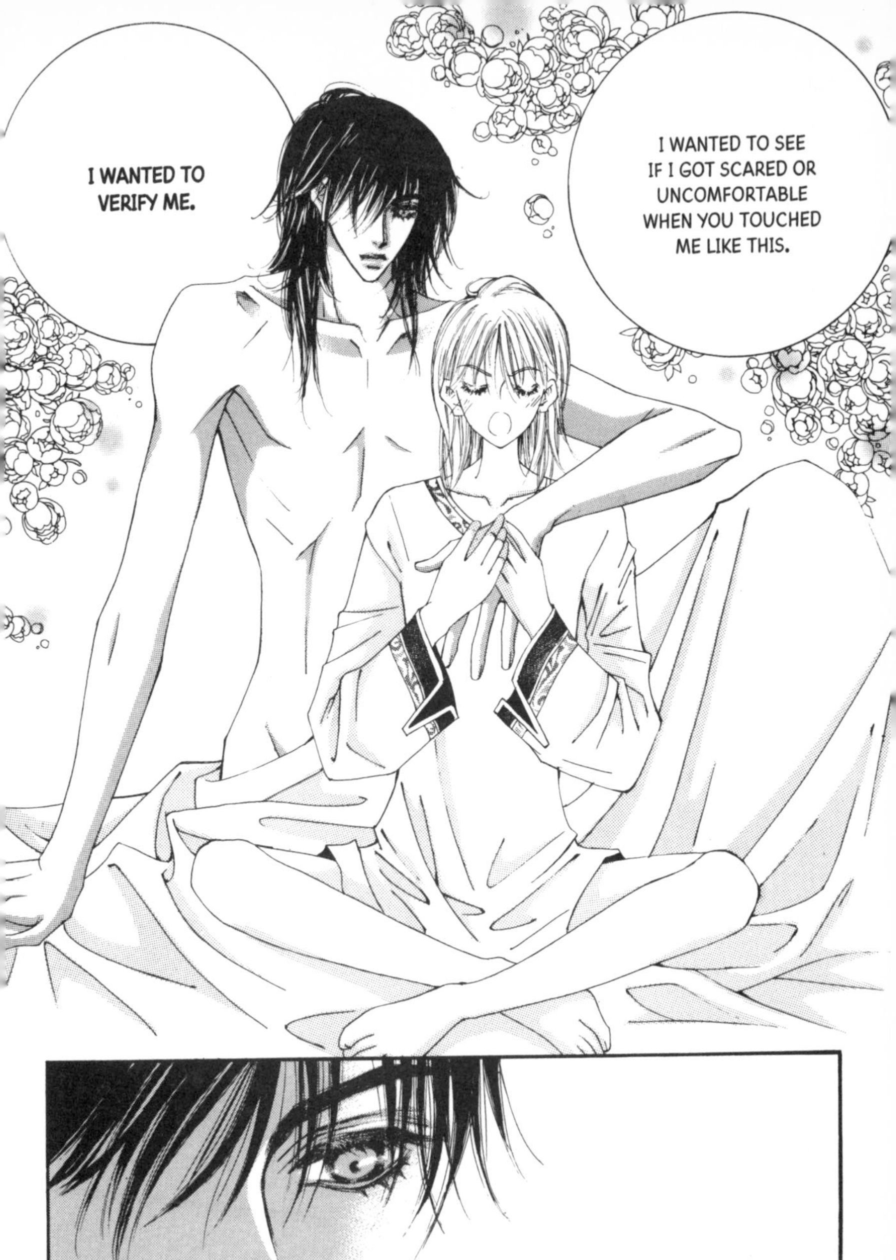
I WANTED TO VERIFY ME.
I WANTED TO SEE IF I GOT SCARED OR UNCOMFORTABLE WHEN YOU TOUCHED ME LIKE THIS.

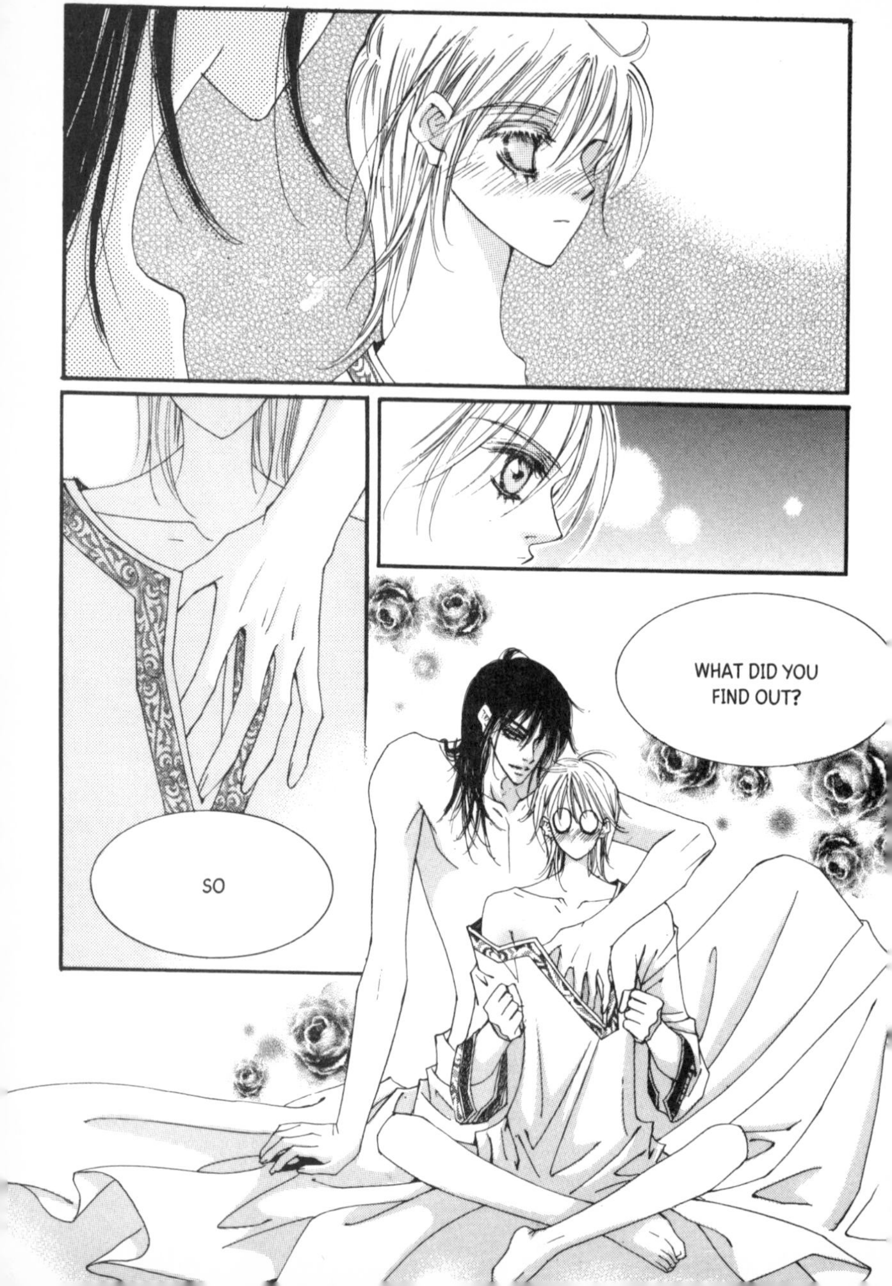
SO
WHAT DID YOU FIND OUT?

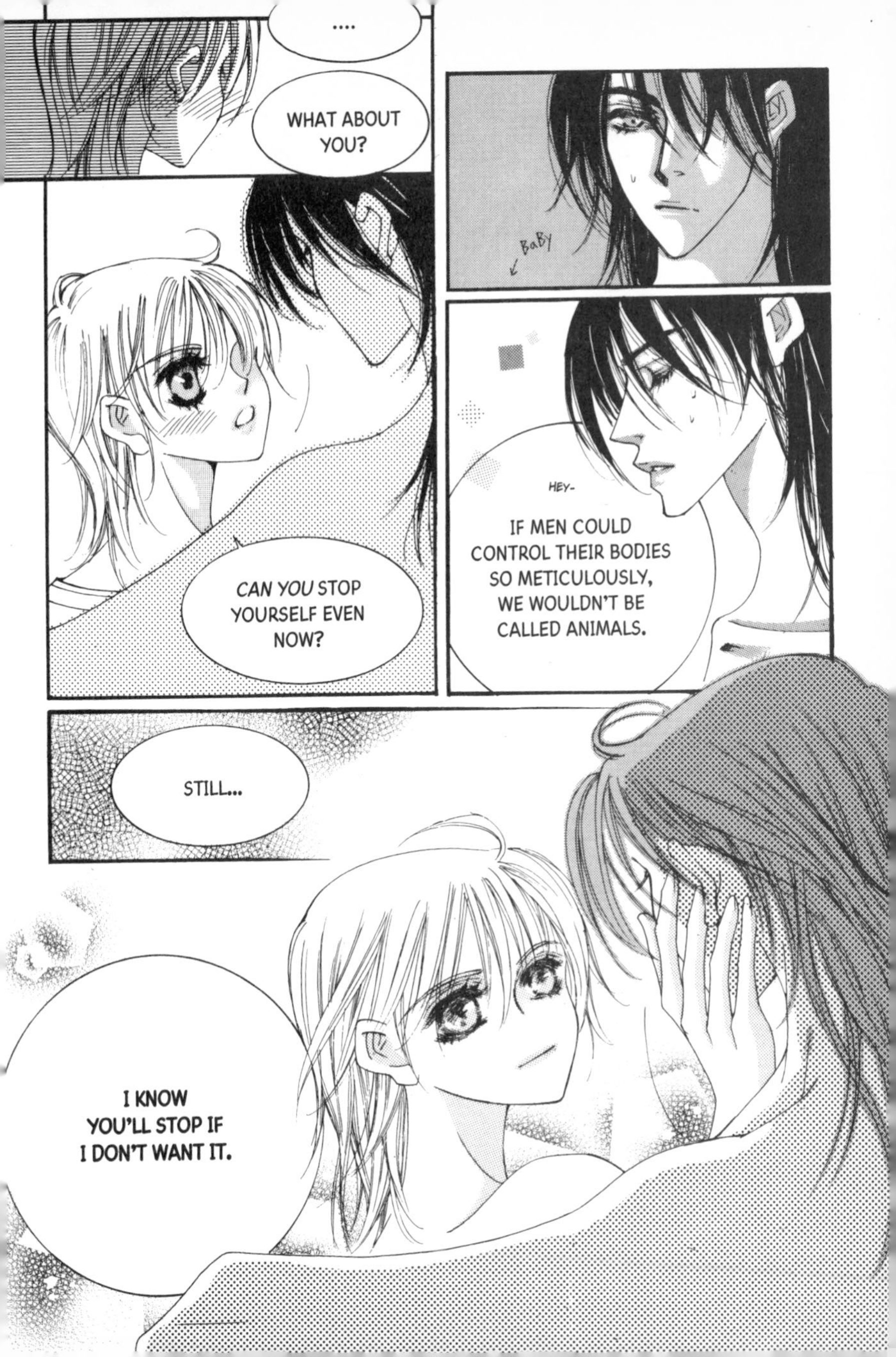
....
WHAT ABOUT YOU?
CAN YOU STOP YOURSELF EVEN NOW?
BaBy
HEY-
IF MEN COULD CONTROL THEIR BODIES SO METICULOUSLY, WE WOULDN'T BE CALLED ANIMALS.
STILL...
I KNOW YOU'LL STOP IF I DON'T WANT IT.

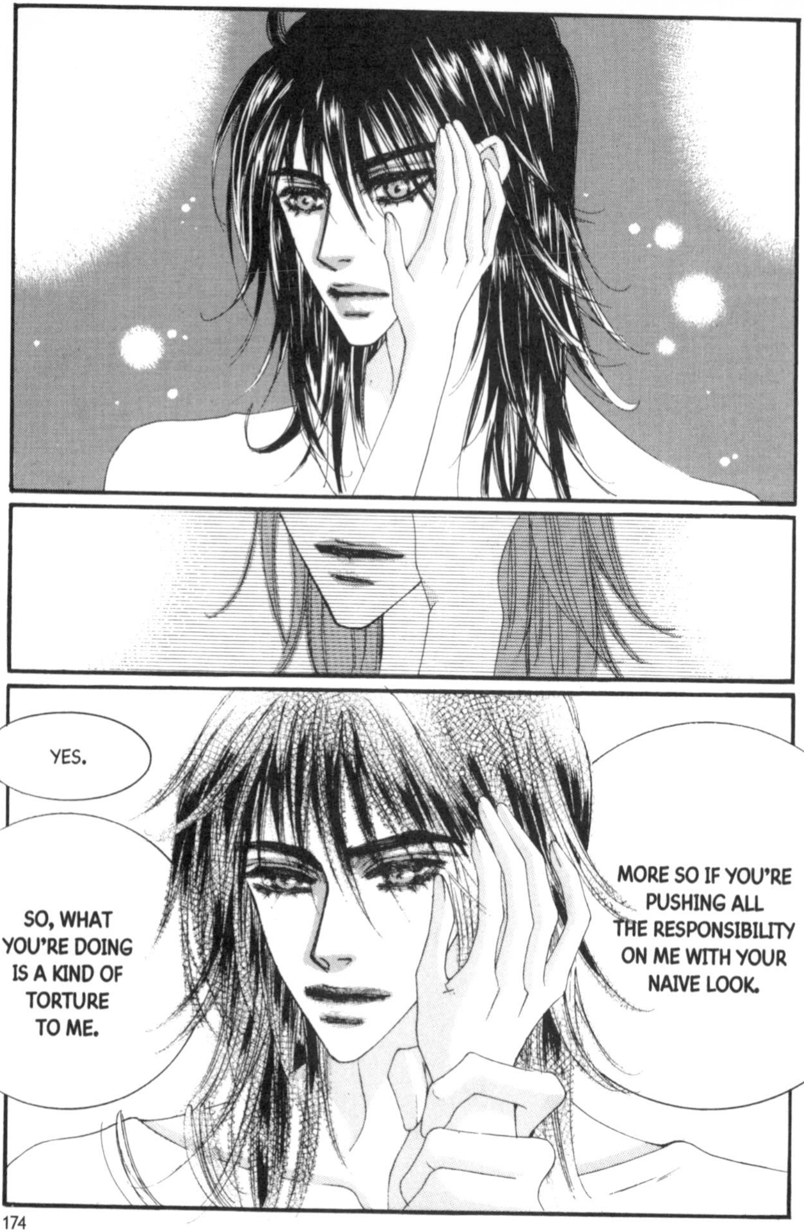
YES.
SO, WHAT YOU'RE DOING IS A KIND OF TORTURE TO ME.
MORE SO IF YOU'RE PUSHING ALL THE RESPONSIBILITY ON ME WITH YOUR NAIVE LOOK.

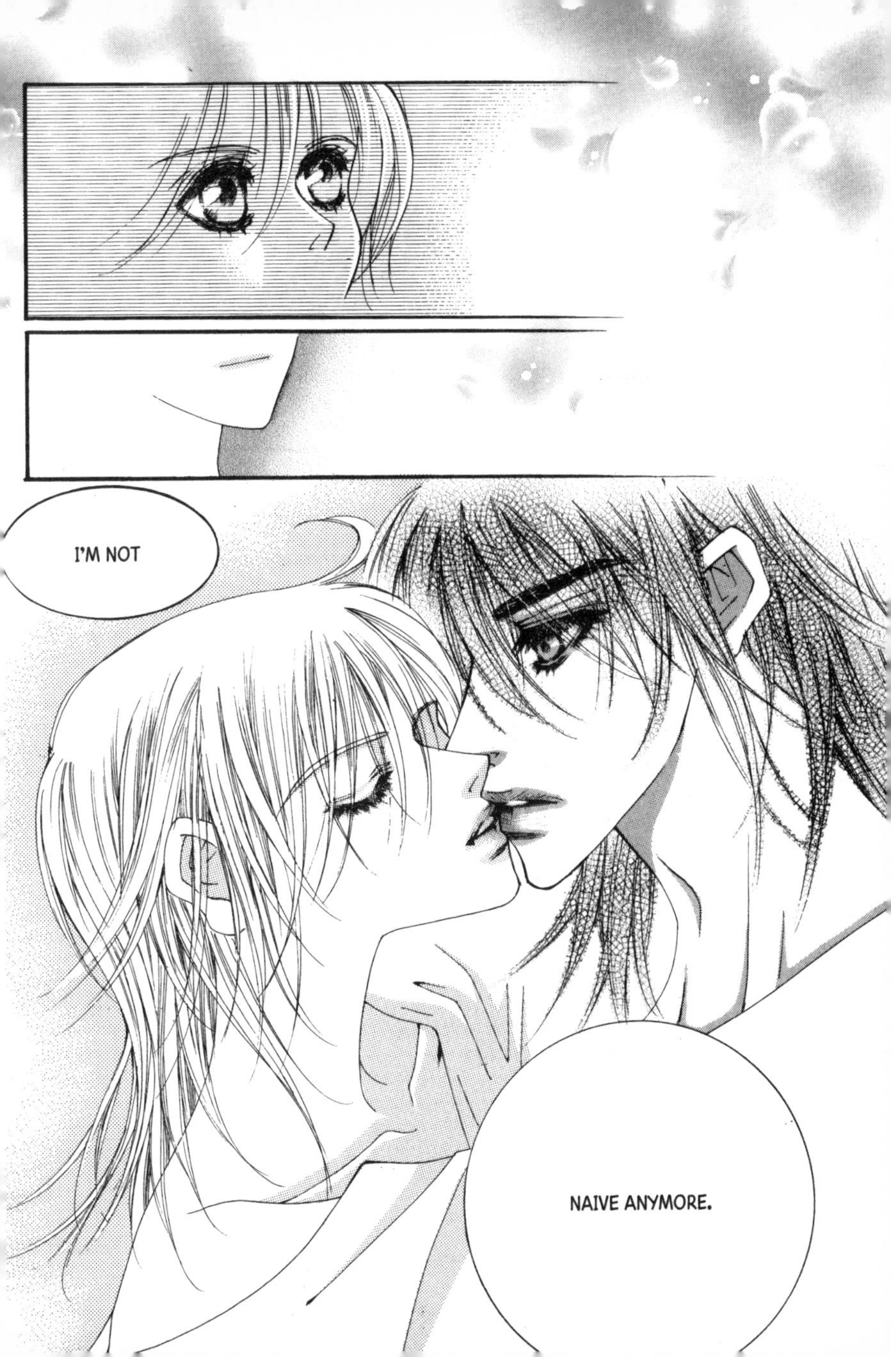
I'M NOT
NAIVE ANYMORE.

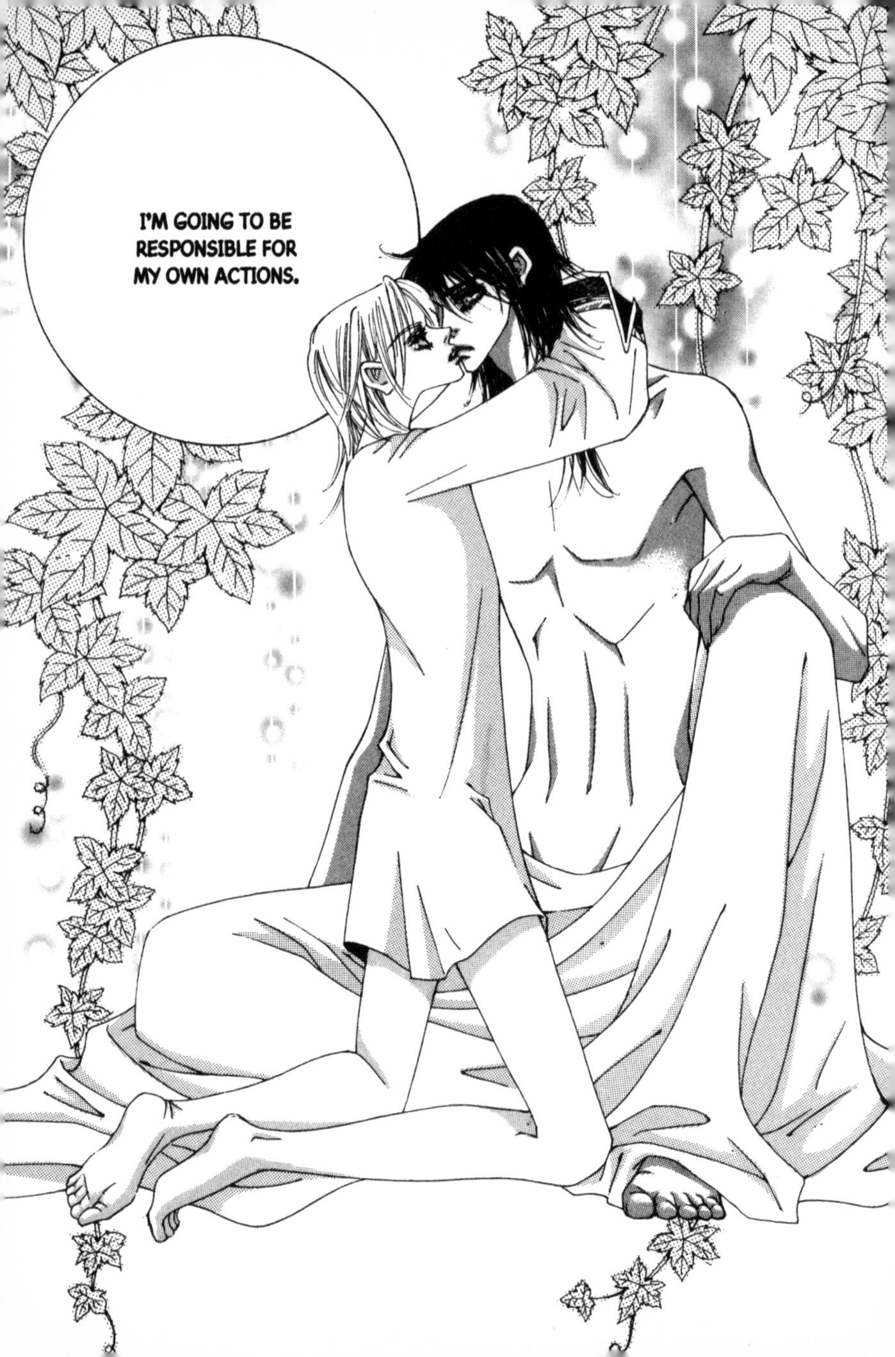
I'M GOING TO BE RESPONSIBLE FOR MY OWN ACTIONS.

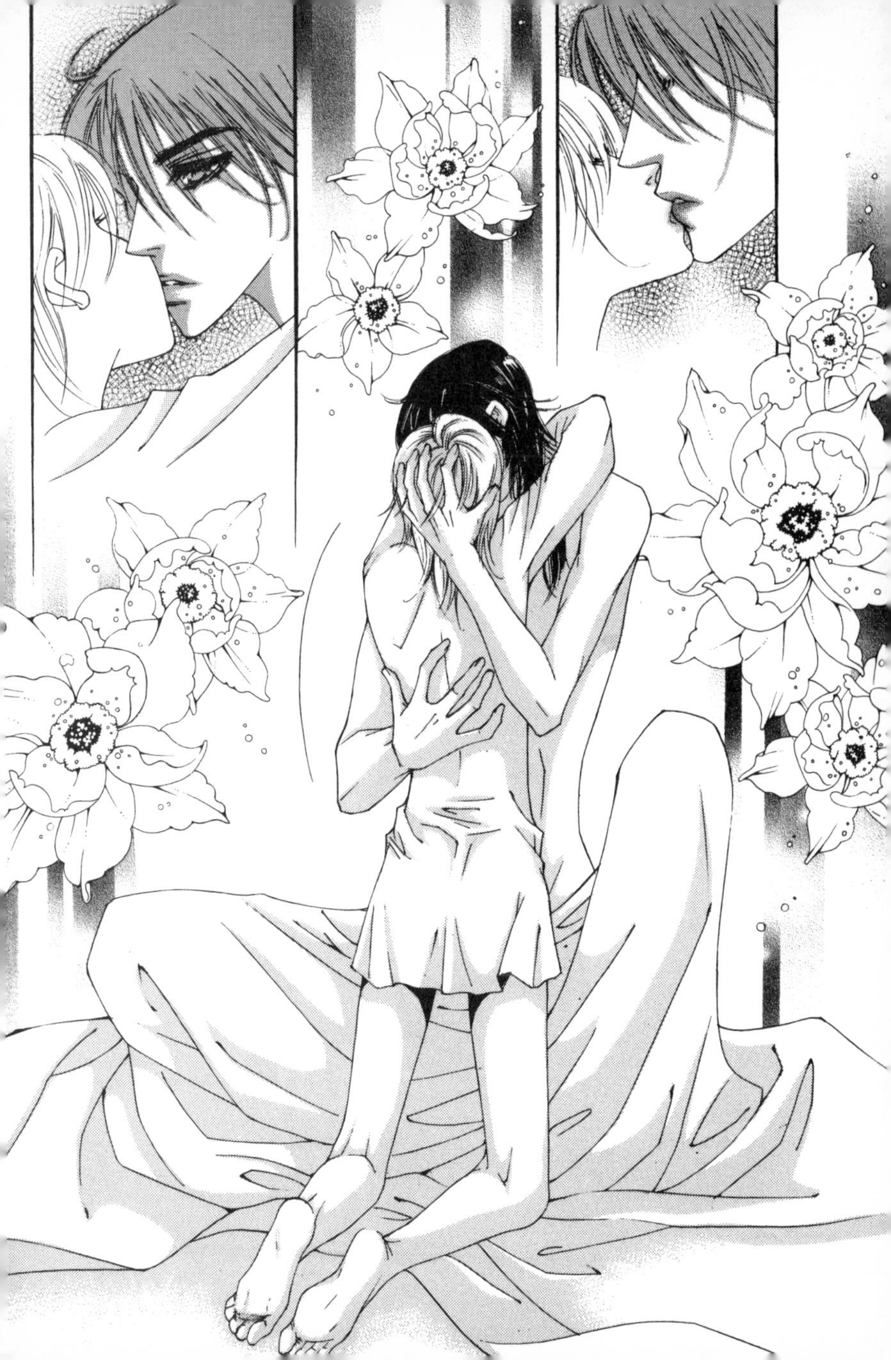

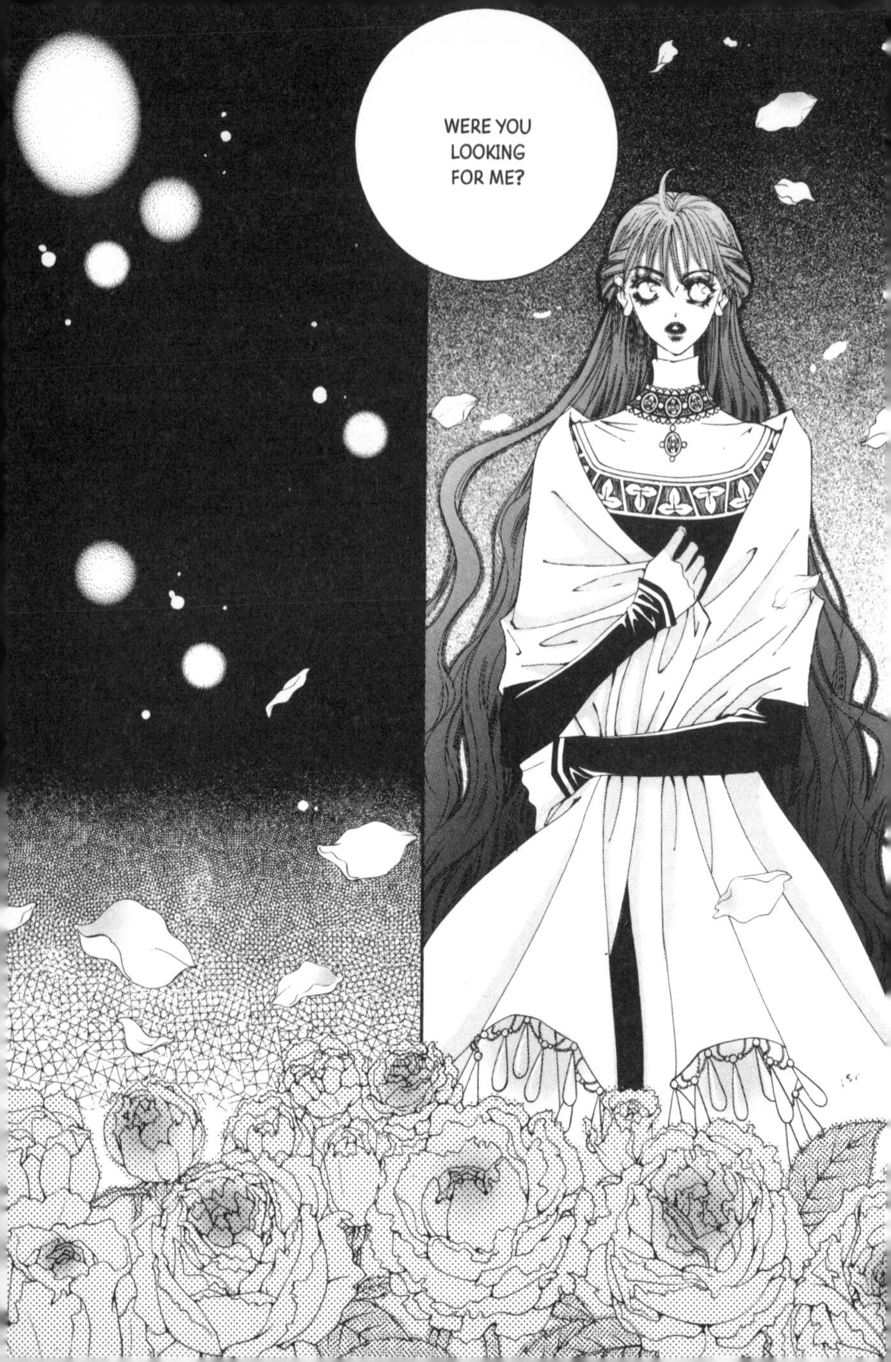
WERE YOU LOOKING FOR ME?

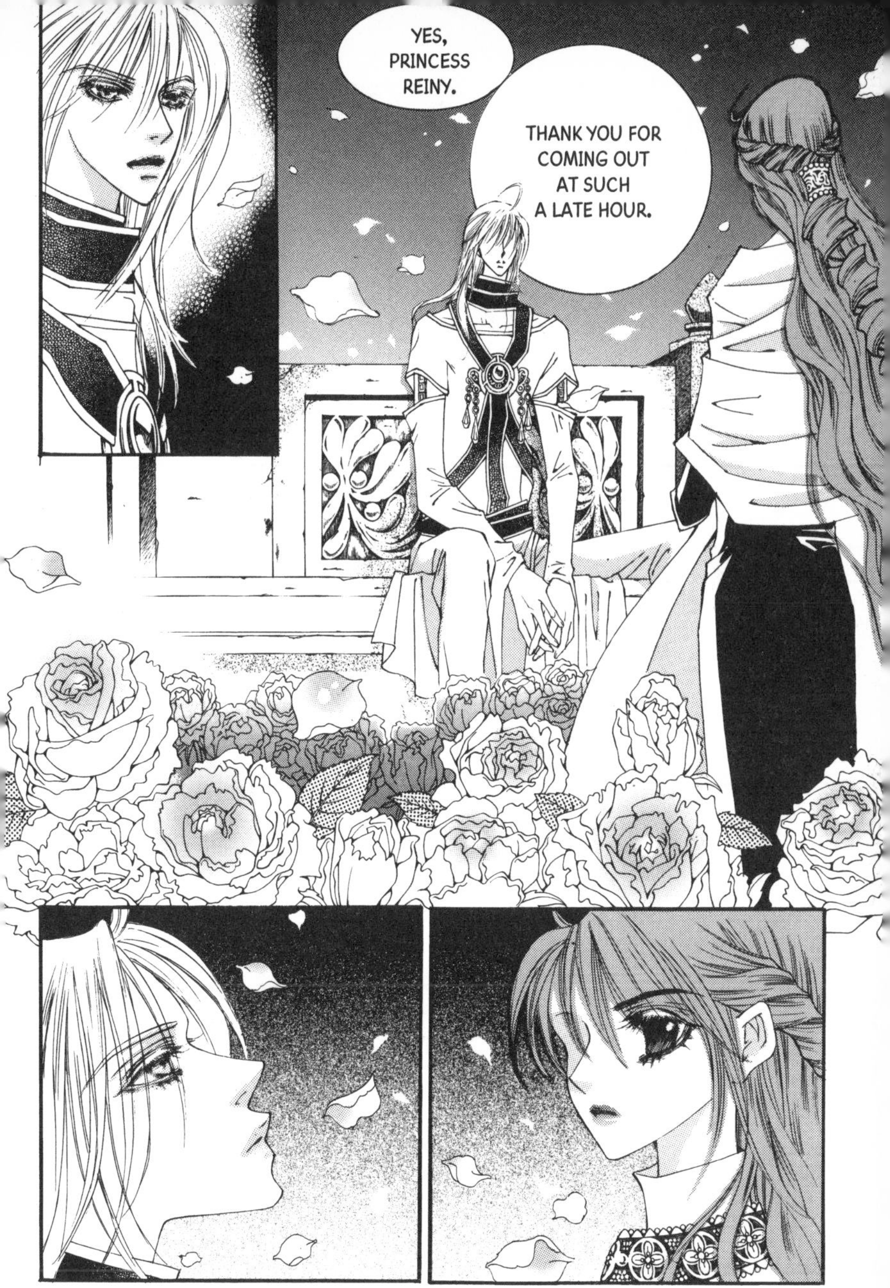
YES, PRINCESS REINY.
THANK YOU FOR COMING OUT AT SUCH A LATE HOUR.

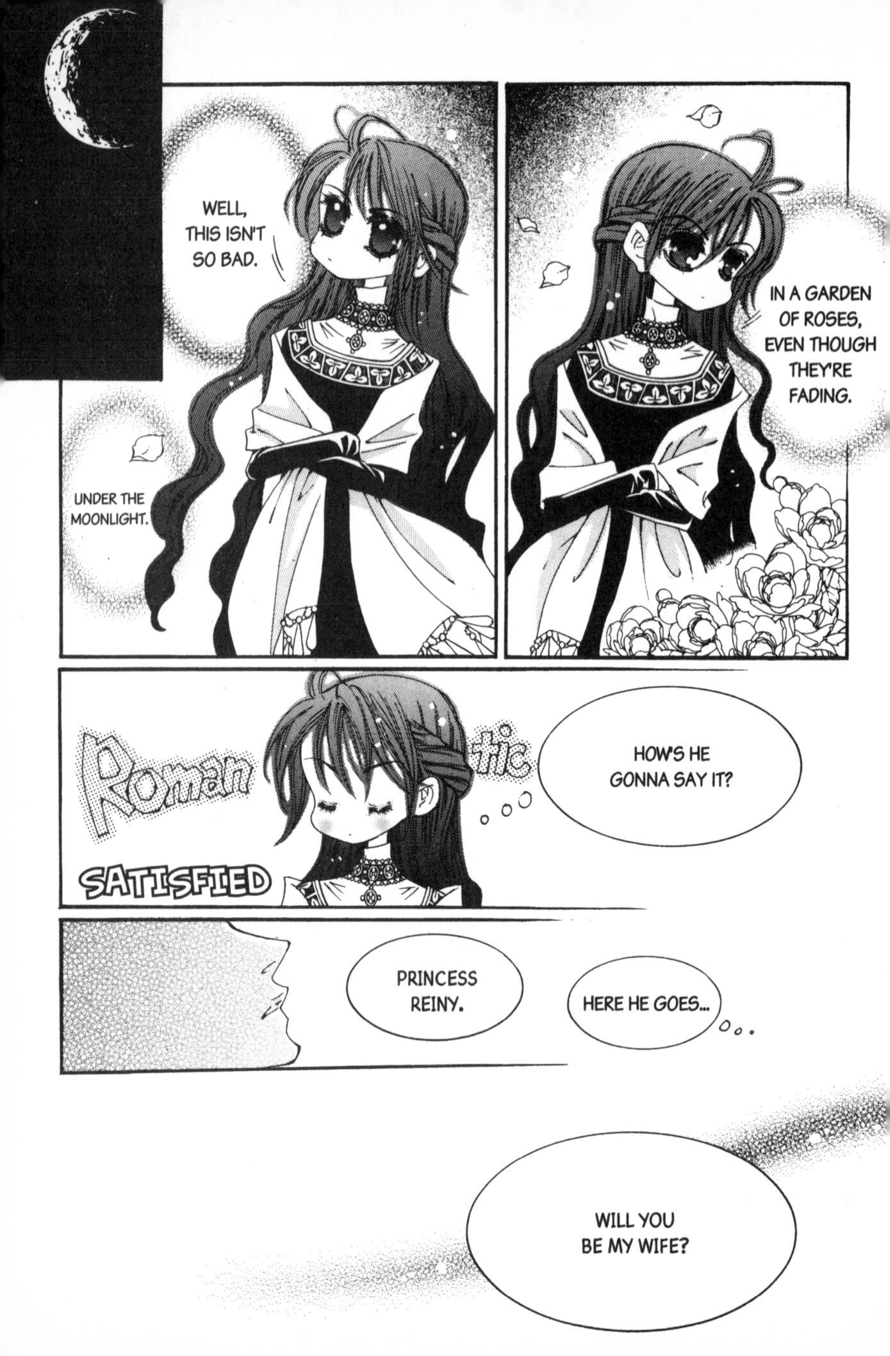
WELL, THIS ISN'T SO BAD.
UNDER THE MOONLIGHT.
IN A GARDEN OF ROSES, EVEN THOUGH THEY'RE FADING.
Romantic
SATISFIED
HOW'S HE GONNA SAY IT?
PRINCESS REINY.
HERE HE GOES...
WILL YOU BE MY WIFE?

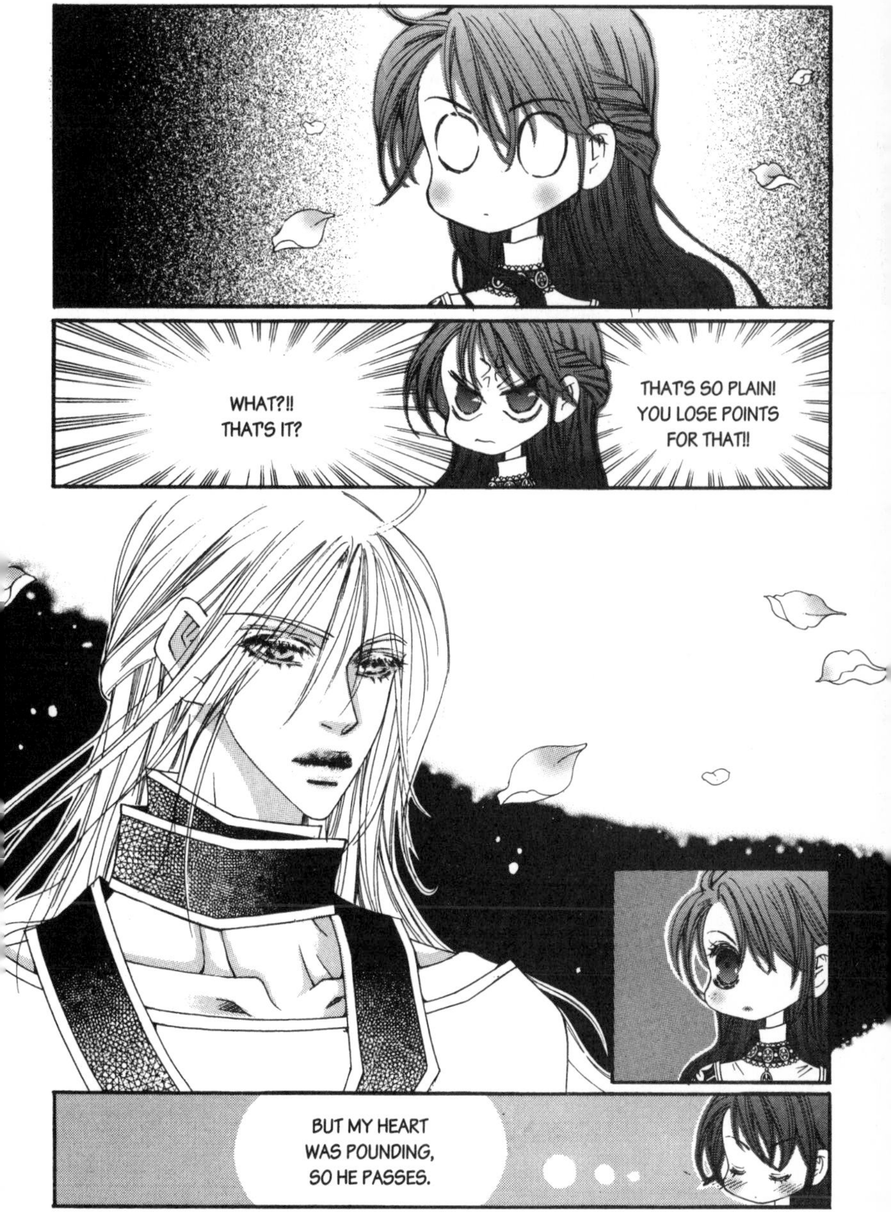
WHAT?!!
THAT'S IT?
THAT'S SO PLAIN! YOU LOSE POINTS FOR THAT!!
BUT MY HEART WAS POUNDING, SO HE PASSES.

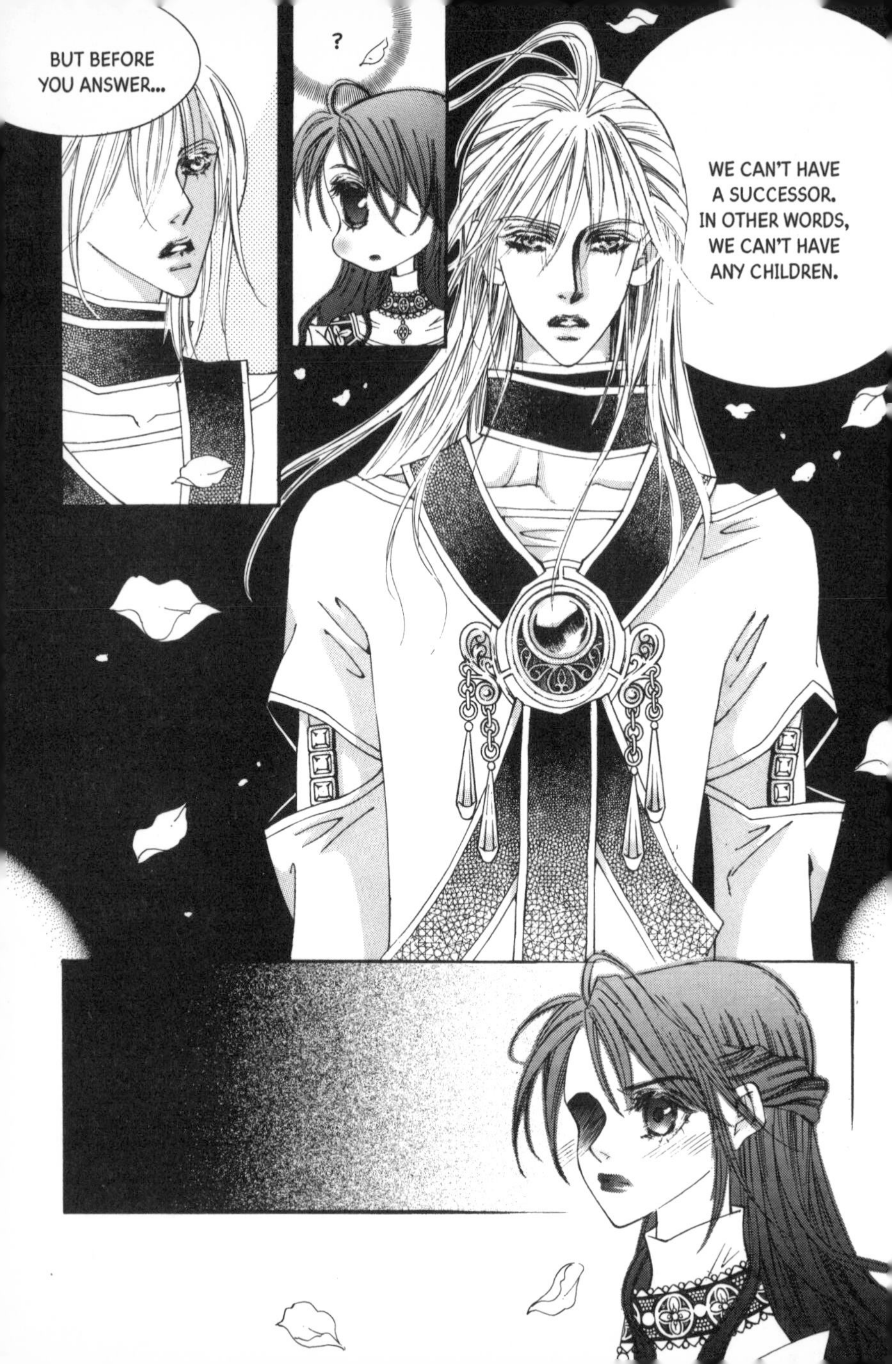
BUT BEFORE YOU ANSWER...
?
WE CAN'T HAVE A SUCCESSOR. IN OTHER WORDS, WE CAN'T HAVE ANY CHILDREN.

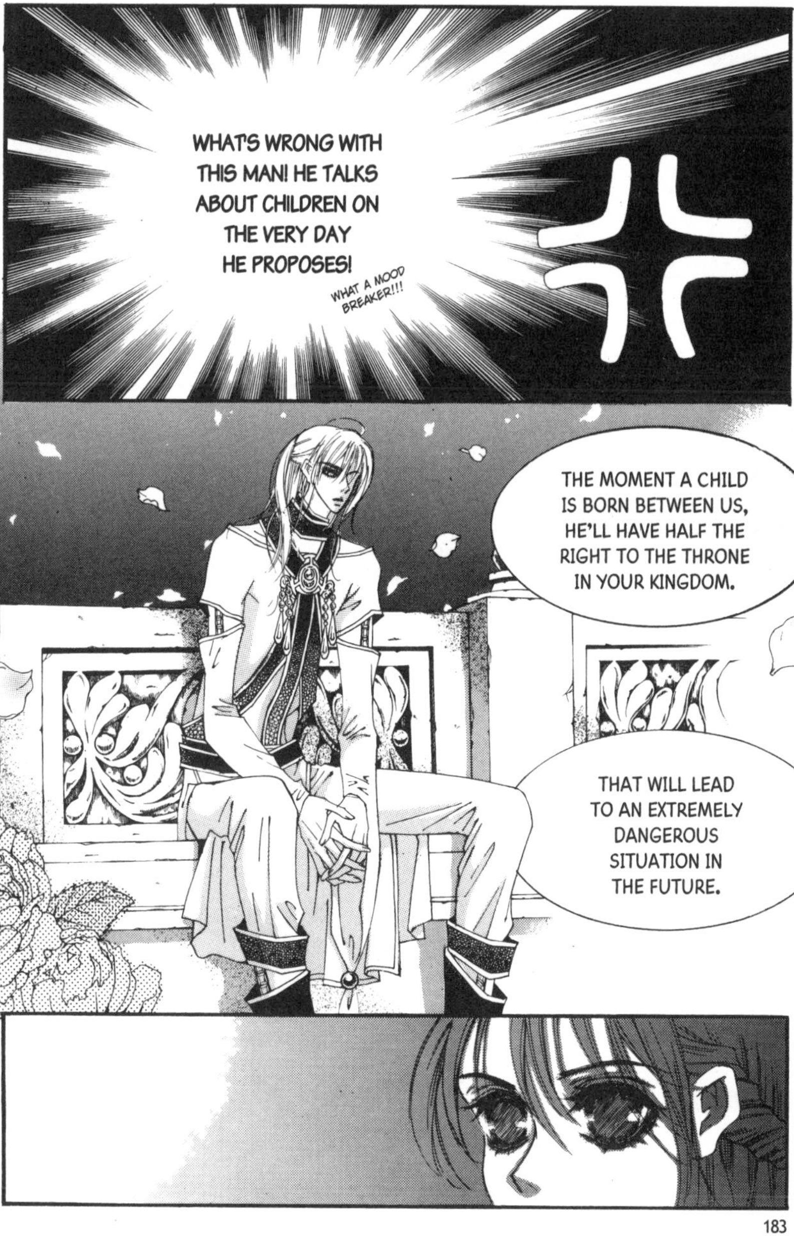
WHAT'S WRONG WITH THIS MAN! HE TALKS ABOUT CHILDREN ON THE VERY DAY HE PROPOSES!
WHAT A MOOD BREAKER!!!
THE MOMENT A CHILD IS BORN BETWEEN US, HE'LL HAVE HALF THE RIGHT TO THE THRONE IN YOUR KINGDOM.
THAT WILL LEAD TO AN EXTREMELY DANGEROUS SITUATION IN THE FUTURE.

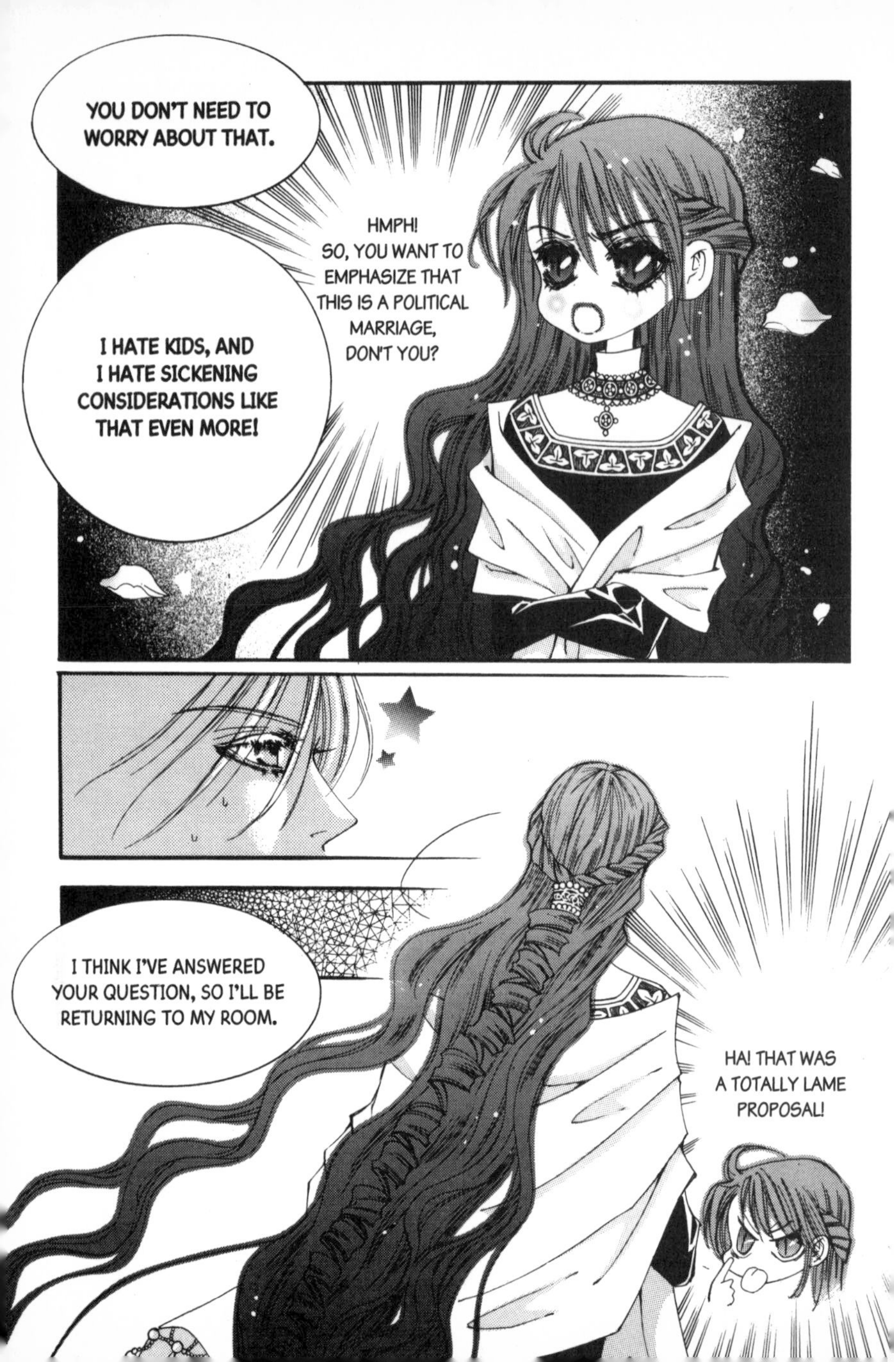
YOU DON'T NEED TO WORRY ABOUT THAT.
I HATE KIDS, AND I HATE SICKENING CONSIDERATIONS LIKE THAT EVEN MORE!
HMPH! SO, YOU WANT TO EMPHASIZE THAT THIS IS A POLITICAL MARRIAGE, DON'T YOU?
I THINK I'VE ANSWERED YOUR QUESTION, SO I'LL BE RETURNING TO MY ROOM.
HA! THAT WAS A TOTALLY LAME PROPOSAL!

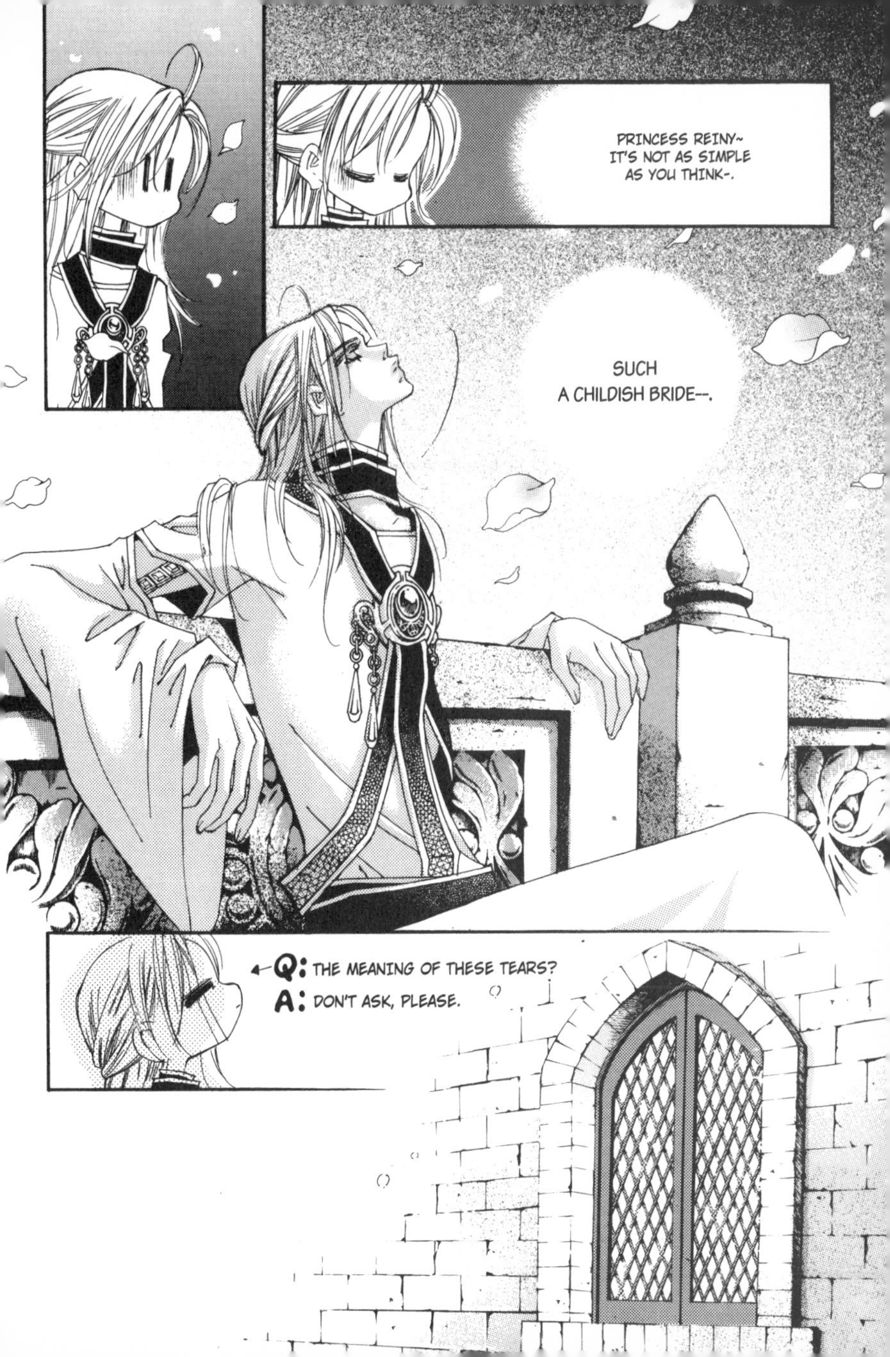
PRINCESS REINY~ IT'S NOT AS SIMPLE AS YOU THINK-.
SUCH A CHILDISH BRIDE--.
Q: THE MEANING OF THESE TEARS?
A: DON'T ASK, PLEASE.

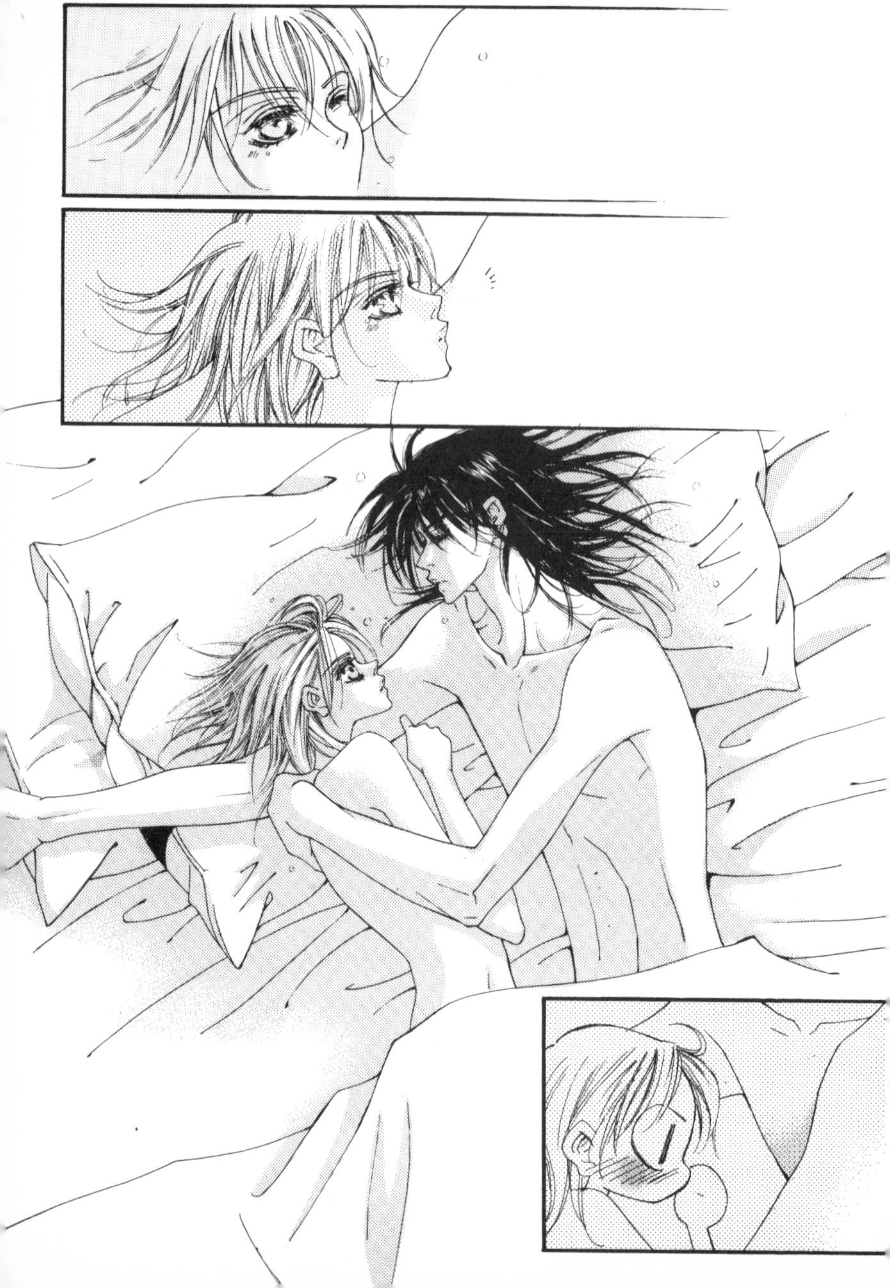

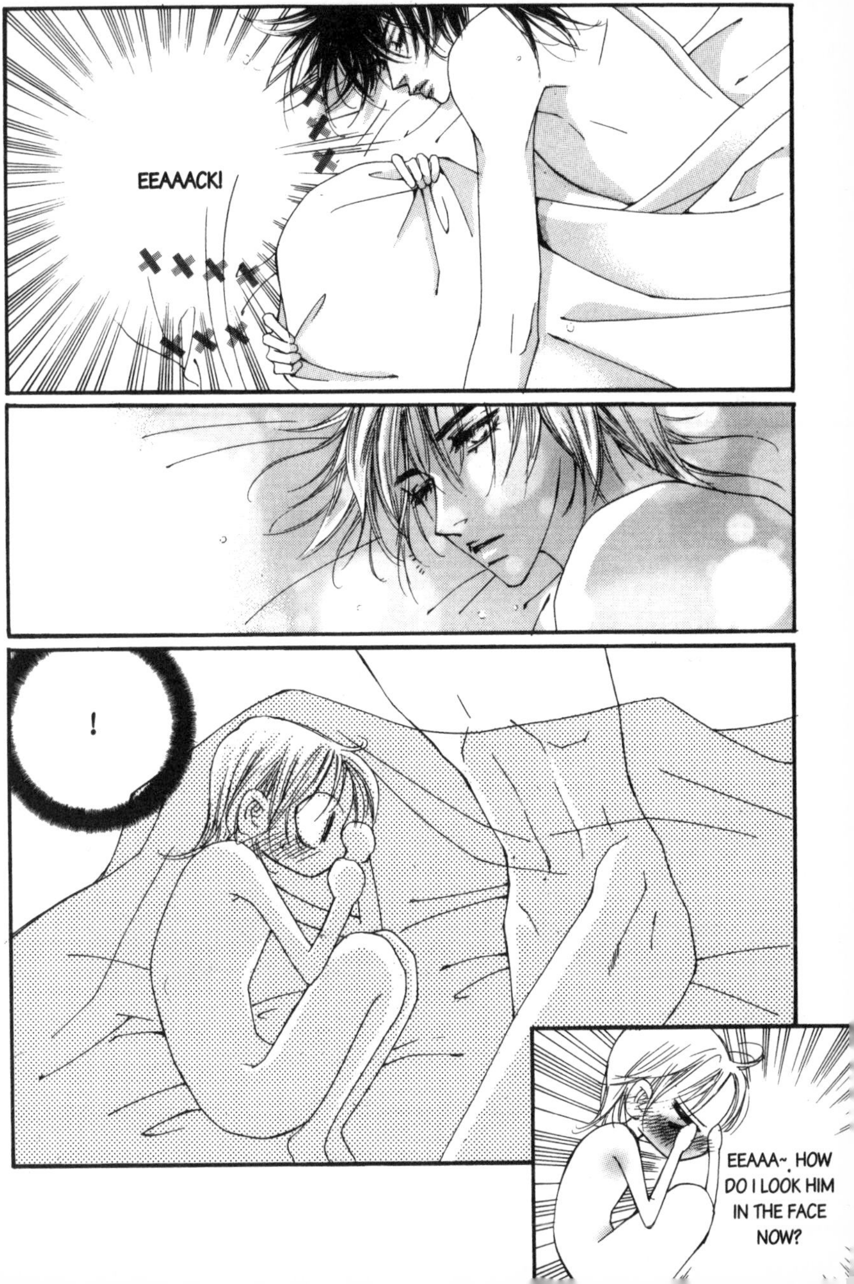
EEAAACK!
!
EEAAA~. HOW DO I LOOK HIM IN THE FACE NOW?

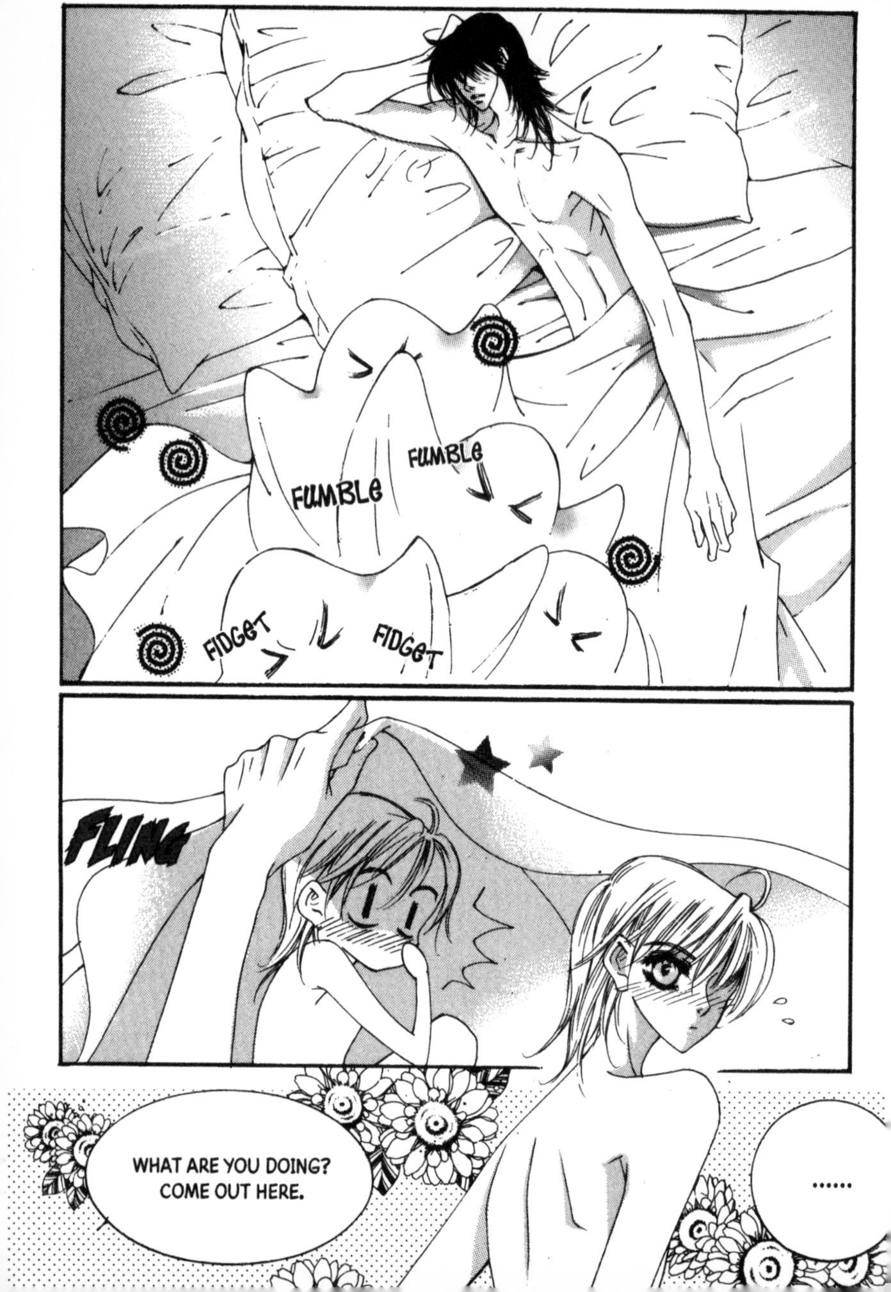
FUMBLE
FUMBLE
FIDGET
FIDGET
FLING
WHAT ARE YOU DOING? COME OUT HERE.
......

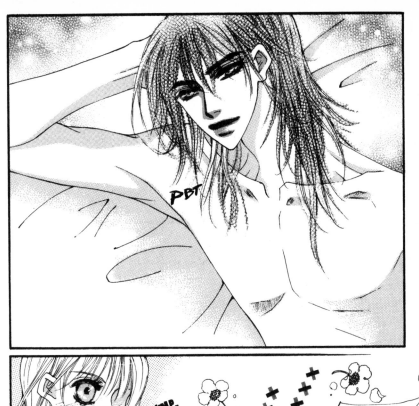

PBT

THUMP..

WHAT ARE YOU LAUGHING AT?!!

DON'T LOOK! DON'T YOU EVEN KNOW THE BASIC RULES OF ETIQUETTE?

NOW...

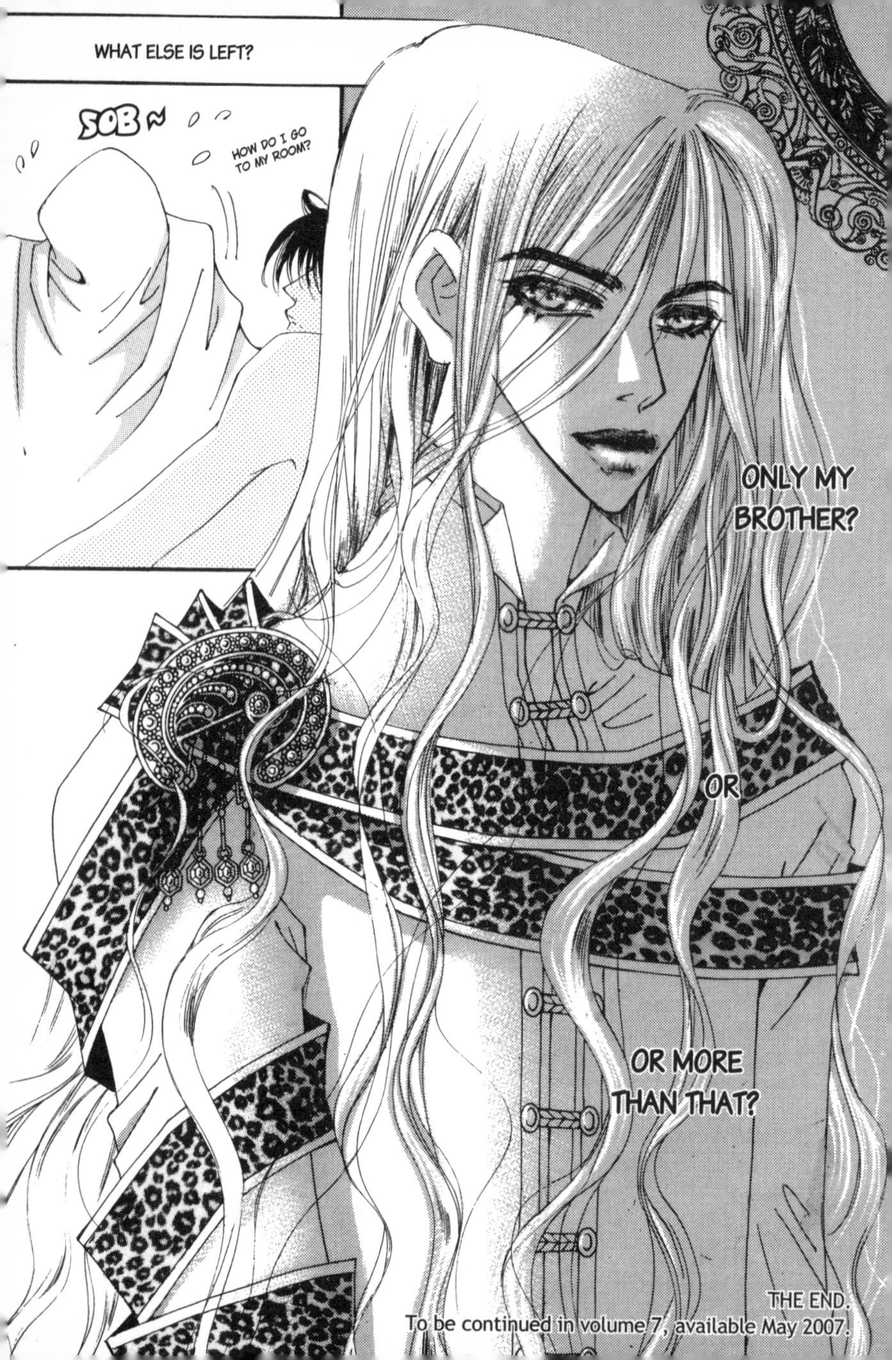
WHAT ELSE IS LEFT?
SOB ~
HOW DO I GO TO MY ROOM?
ONLY MY BROTHER?
OR
OR MORE THAN THAT?
THE END.
To be continued in volume 7, available May 2007.

Preview Vol. 7

Jed finally comes to terms with his love for Nicole, but at the terrible price of complete vulnerability to the political schemes of Prince Derek. Believing Nicole is pregnant, Derek and his mother conspire to poison the young "princess." However, Jed and the Apothecary's tribe secretly plan to thwart them. Little do they all know that the Apothecary Shahi has his own designs on their fate. Meanwhile, Prince Glewhin and Prince June travel to a meeting of their Alliance only to discover more political intrigue that threatens Glehwin's marriage to Princess Reiny, as well as the fragile peace that governs both their lands. Conspiracies abound, but only one faction may triumph. And treachery may be the determining factor.

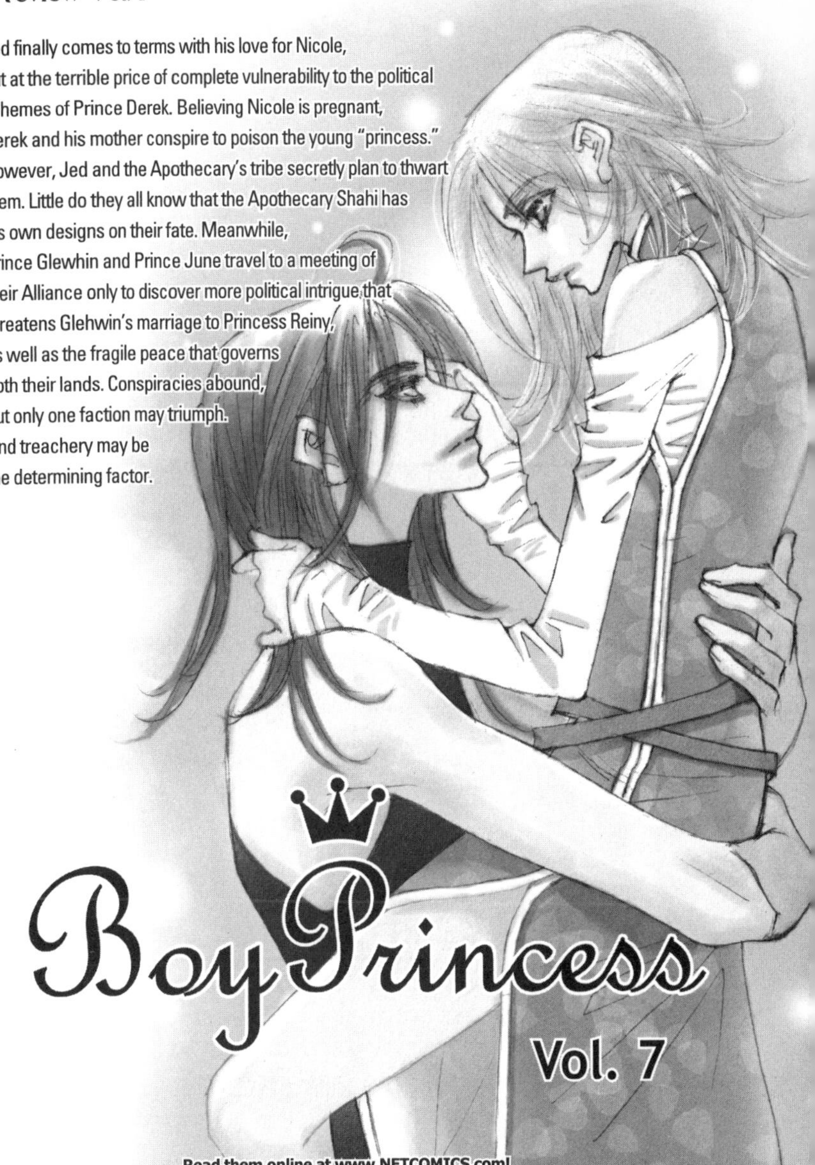
Boy Princess
Vol. 7

Click Vol. 1

"This story looks like it is going to be really fun. Nice art, cute characters, and gender-bending, which I always love.."

**– Rhonda Von Der Ahe,
NETCOMICS.com subscriber**

Land of Silver Rain Vol. 5

"Sometimes it is vague and ghostly, then very fine-lined realistic, and next is might be cartoony in an emotional situation... always engaging and entertaining."

– Comic Book Network Electronic Magazine

Let Dai Vol. 6

"For both the beautiful art and the characterization, *Let Dai* is a title that shouldn't be passed by."

– BoysonBoysonFilm.com

Can't Lose You Vol. 5

"A modern fairytale version of Cinderella... told in a complicated narrative interweaving comedy and action... with art and narrative that are superb."

– Manganews.net